# The Bible

## FAITH AND EVIDENCE

# The Bible

## FAITH AND EVIDENCE

*A critical enquiry into the nature of biblical history*

John R. Bartlett

British Museum Press

© 1990 John R Bartlett

First paperback edition 1994

Published by British Museum Press
A division of British Museum Publications Ltd
46 Bloomsbury Street, London WC1B 3QQ

British Library Cataloguing in Publication Data
A catalogue record for this book is available from the British Library

ISBN 0–7141–1754–4

Set in Garamond
Printed and bound in Great Britain by
Biddles Ltd, Guildford and King's Lynn


The author and publishers are
grateful for permission to include
biblical quotations from the
Revised Standard Version

# Contents

# Preface

THIS BOOK was originally conceived as yet one more book in the 'bible and archaeology' genre, but in the course of writing it became something quite different. There were several reasons for this, not least the publication of P.R.S. Moorey's masterly revision of Kathleen Kenyon's book, *The Bible and recent archaeology*, and of T.C. Mitchell's *The Bible in the British Museum*. With these two well-illustrated books available, there was clearly no need for another similar volume. What was needed was a book which might go beyond familiar attempts to illustrate biblical history from archaeology, and this book therefore aims to show how the biblical books – in particular the most historically oriented ones: not all biblical books are treated in detail – relate to their historical context and how they present the history of ancient Israel or the rise of Christianity. The biblical authors wrote from the standpoint of faith, but also from experience and knowledge of their world, and their writings may indeed be used for the reconstruction of the historical record. However, they must not be taken simply as presenting the definitive historical record. The authors of Genesis and Revelation were, in different ways, concerned with history, and the authors of the books of Kings and the Acts of the Apostles were historians of a high order, but in using them as historical sources we need to understand the nature of their work, and allow for their particular motives and limitations.

*The Bible: faith and evidence*, therefore, is neither a simple re-telling of the biblical tradition, nor yet one more general introduction to the books of the Bible and their background, but an attempt to take the biblical historians seriously as real people writing the truth as they saw it for the needs of their own times. Dr Moorey in his book has given us a reconstruction of the political and social history of the biblical period as evidenced by archaeological research; this present book seeks to complement his work by showing how the biblical authors presented and interpreted their historical traditions. Between the concern of the ancient biblical historian for God's dealing with the covenant people, and the concern of the modern archaeologist for the anthropology and sociology of ancient Israel and early Christianity there is a great gulf, but knowledge of both is important for our historical and theological understanding of the Bible.

Many friends and colleagues have contributed, knowingly or unknowingly, to this book, and have encouraged me to write it. Its genesis lay in a conversation with Dr T. Potter and its completion has been patiently encouraged by Celia Clear of B.M.P. Part was written at Emory University, Atlanta, and I am grateful for the stimulus given by Professor J.M. Miller and his graduate class and by Professor J.H. Hayes. Above all, I am grateful to the students of the Church of Ireland Theological College and the School of Hebrew, Biblical and Theological Studies in Trinity College, Dublin, who over almost twenty-five years have shared my exploration of the Bible. To all of them I dedicate this book.

DUBLIN, MAY 1990

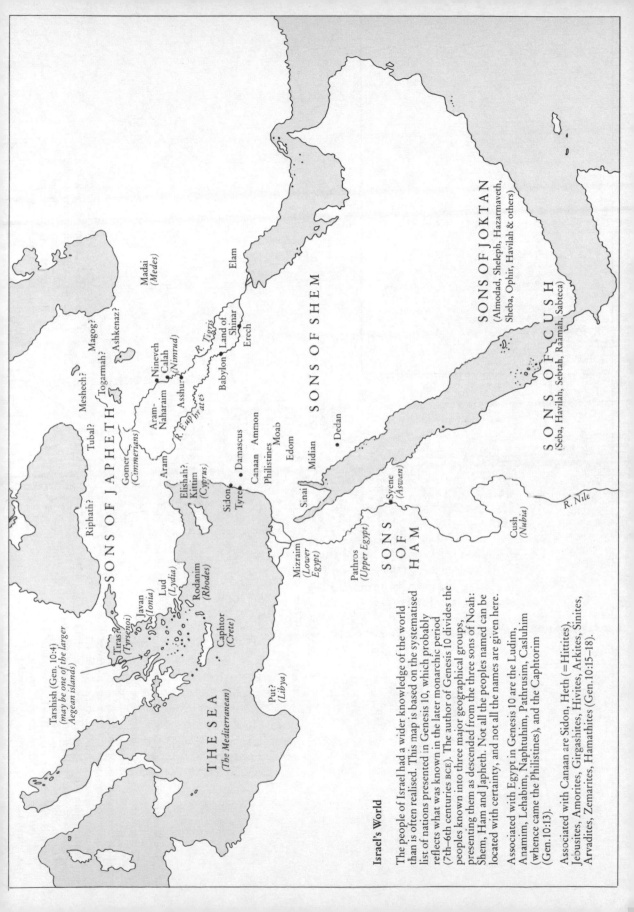

**Israel's World**

The people of Israel had a wider knowledge of the world than is often realised. This map is based on the systematised list of nations presented in Genesis 10, which probably reflects what was known in the later monarchic period (7th–6th centuries BCE). The author of Genesis 10 divides the peoples known into three major geographical groups, presenting them as descended from the three sons of Noah: Shem, Ham and Japheth. Not all the peoples named can be located with certainty, and not all the names are given here.

Associated with Egypt in Genesis 10 are the Ludim, Anamim, Lehabim, Naphtuhim, Pathrusim, Casluhim (whence came the Philistines), and the Caphtorim (Gen.10:13).

Associated with Canaan are Sidon, Heth (=Hittites); Jebusites, Amorites, Girgashites, Hivites, Arkites, Sinites, Arvadites, Zemarites, Hamathites (Gen.10:15–18).

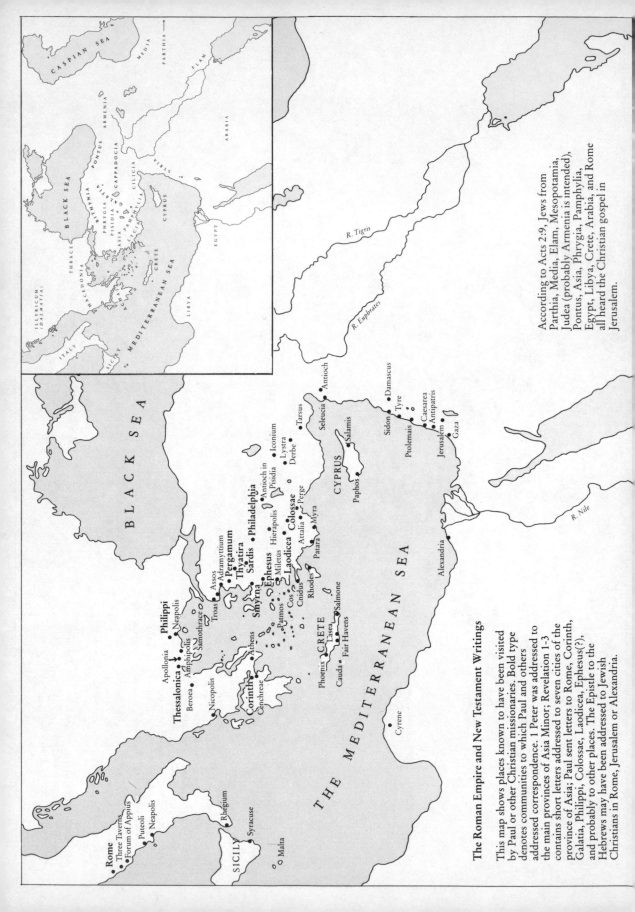

## The Roman Empire and New Testament Writings

This map shows places known to have been visited by Paul or other Christian missionaries. Bold type denotes communities to which Paul and others addressed correspondence. 1 Peter was addressed to the main provinces of Asia Minor; Revelation 1-3 contains short letters addressed to seven cities of the province of Asia; Paul sent letters to Rome, Corinth, Galatia, Philippi, Colossae, Laodicea, Ephesus(?), and probably to other places. The Epistle to the Hebrews may have been addressed to Jewish Christians in Rome, Jerusalem or Alexandria.

According to Acts 2:9, Jews from Parthia, Media, Elam, Mesopotamia, Judea (probably Armenia is intended), Pontus, Asia, Phrygia, Pamphylia, Egypt, Libya, Crete, Arabia, and Rome all heard the Christian gospel in Jerusalem.

# 1 Approaches to the Bible

The second half of the twentieth century has seen a dramatic expansion in the world of biblical scholarship. In America, Germany and the United Kingdom, to name the three most obvious places, the number of scholarly books and articles devoted to the biblical literature appears to increase annually. New publishers have appeared and prospered, new research journals have issued their first numbers and have stayed to reach double figures, new academic societies have been formed. Probably much of this activity is ultimately founded on the expansion since the 1950s of the universities and the enormous increase of student numbers. Not all these students have become engineers or computer programmers; many have continued to study the more traditional subjects of history and literature in the Arts faculties, and a growing number of them have chosen to enter the new departments of Theology, Biblical Studies, Semitic Studies, or the like, founded in the 1960s and 1970s. Such students have not necessarily been candidates for ordination in one of the churches; they have not necessarily been practising members of any Christian or Jewish congregation. They have not been limited to the young; many of them are 'mature students' with other training and experience behind them. In my own university, the opening of evening classes for a Diploma in Biblical and Theological Studies has met with an enthusiastic response, in spite of the high fees demanded. There is clearly a market for Biblical Studies and for text books and research publications in this field, and that market is not limited to people with strong church affiliations. The market is also indicated by the number of modern translations of the Bible currently available, even if many of the copies sold remain mostly unread. Interest in the Bible is revealed too by the success of recent programmes on both radio and television dealing with the archaeology and even with the literary history of the Bible.

This growing interest in biblical literature and history may be motivated as much by antiquarian as by religious concern, and similarly may be the result of improved general education in our society rather than of greater theological awareness fostered by the churches. But it arises at least partly from the fact that the last two hundred years have witnessed the steady growth of scholarly research into the biblical literature and the world from which it came. This research – into the languages used in the Bible, into the development of the canon of the biblical books, into the history of the textual tradition of the various books, into the dating of the different compositions which make up the Bible, into the sources

1

used by the biblical authors and editors, into the origins and development of the Israelite people and their religion, into the theological ideas of the people of Israel and the followers of Jesus, and into many similar questions – took place against the background of the opening up of the near east to travellers, explorers and scholars in the nineteenth century. The railway and the steamship replaced the coach and the sailing vessel, and the electric telegraph replaced the letter as a means of communicating important news fast. The British and the Germans were interested in the near east as a link between the Mediterranean and India and the trade and wealth of the far east; Turkey was 'the sick man of Europe' and the Ottoman empire was visibly dying. From the Napoleonic wars to the Great War, the near east was of interest and importance to the politicians and businessmen of the west, and throughout the nineteenth century an endless stream of travellers explored hitherto inaccessible regions in Syria, Palestine, Transjordan, Arabia, and Mesopotamia. Their records make fascinating reading, and cannot be catalogued here; but their work and publications caused an important shift of perspective for students of the Bible. Previously, the countries of the near east had been known to the west very largely through the pages of the Bible. The Old Testament had provided virtually all the available information about the empires of the Assyrians and the Babylonians, for example (just as Herodotus had provided most of the available information about the Egyptians and the Persians). But the work of men like Champollion, who deciphered the Egyptian hieroglyphics, Austin Henry Layard, who excavated Nineveh, and Henry Rawlinson, who deciphered the old Persian cuneiform texts, enabled scholars to assess the achievements of Egypt, Assyria, Babylon and Persia from first-hand evidence, with the further important result that the people of ancient Israel began to be seen no longer as the focus of the near east but as a small state which existed for a short period of time as part of a much wider cultural and political scene. Overnight, the archaeology of the ancient near east became of vital importance to the work of the biblical scholar; it not only threw new light on the subject but also increased the public interest in it. In Britain, the foundation of the Palestine Exploration Fund in 1865 made an important contribution both to scholarly research and to public interest. The Fund was formed 'for the purpose of investigating the Archaeology, Geography, Geology, and Natural History of Palestine'; the work was carried out on scientific principles, and the Society as a body was to abstain from controversy and was not to be started or conducted as a religious society.

The foundation of the Palestine Exploration Fund reflected the enquiring, scientific spirit of the nineteenth century, and the principles on which the Fund's work was to be based may have owed something to the fact that the previous year, 1864, had seen the synodical condemnation of the publication in 1860 of *Essays and Reviews*. This volume was the work of seven academics and churchmen who believed that theology was as open to free inquiry as any other subject. The essay that roused most ecclesiastical opposition was that by Benjamin Jowett, the Master of Balliol College, on 'The Interpretation of Scripture'. Jowett argued that the Bible should be interpreted by means of the same critical methods as were used on any other ancient literature. In spite of the resulting furore (some eleven thousand clergy signed a protest affirming their belief in the inspiration of the scriptures), the need for critical scholarship gained rapid acceptance in both academic and ecclesiastical quarters. The last victory of the older 'orthodox' was the dismissal of W. Robertson Smith in 1881 from his Chair of Old Testament by the Free Church of Scotland. The publication, however, of a new set of Anglican essays under the title *Lux Mundi* in 1889 showed that biblical criticism had been accepted by leading churchmen whose aim was 'to put the Catholic faith into its right relation to modern intellectual and moral problems'. The nettle of the problem of the historical reliability of the Old Testament was grasped by the editor Charles Gore, who wrote an important essay on 'The Holy Spirit and Inspiration'. The importance of biblical criticism had been established in Britain by scholars like S. R. Driver, A. B. Davidson, W. Robertson Smith and A. F. Kirkpatrick; Gore's essay was an admission from the church that biblical criticism could not be gainsaid, and had to be taken into account in the theological explication of belief.

In the hundred years from *Lux Mundi* to the present, the study of the biblical literature with the aid of every critical tool available has been the norm, whether in universities or in theological colleges. Indeed, the theological colleges have often relied on the nearest university for the instruction of their students in biblical literature, history and theology. Scholars and students, whether conservative, liberal, or radical, have seen the need to become proficient in the biblical languages, in literary analysis, in textual history, in the interpretation of archaeological evidence, and other problems of historical enquiry. For a century the universities and theological colleges have trained the clergy in the methods and results of biblical criticism. The somewhat perverse and paradoxical result seems to have been that the biblical literature – especially the Old Testament – is less read, less well known, less expounded from the pulpit, and less used as the basis for belief and behaviour, except among the more evangelical, fundamentalist, or conservative quarters of the church. That this is so, however, probably cannot be blamed simply on the growth of biblical criticism. While biblical criticism may have disturbed the faith of those who have not perceived the problems which biblical criticism has set out to answer, or brought intellectual relief to those who had perceived the problems, it has not helped those who find or believe the literature of ancient Israel totally irrelevant to their modern situation. Yet while the biblical literature, endlessly dissected by the century's scholarship, has become less real and less immediate to the clergy and their hearers, the wheel has come full circle and scholars are again concerned with the meaning and message of these writings in their final state and as a whole, and the university-educated professional classes will go to the theatre to hear the Bible read by professional actors, who have the skill to make the ancient texts live again.

One begins to wonder whether the effect of scholarly criticism has been to marginalise the Bible, by setting it too firmly in its ancient historical context. If the Bible is to be read as any other ancient literature, it will indeed become as forgotten as any other ancient literature, the preserve of scholars alone. This will not happen in the foreseeable future, however, because the biblical writings are treasured by both Jews and Christians as a theological heritage, an expression of tradition and faith, not to mention revelation. But this very view of the scriptures owes not a little to the work of scholarship, which has above all else shown that the Jewish Tanak or Christian Bible is a collection of writings written by believers for believers. The Jewish and Christian scriptures contain theological writings from different times and different places, reflecting different social backgrounds and different mental approaches. The Bible reflects a wide range of human experience of God drawn over many centuries, mostly from a Semitic, Jewish tradition and partly from a Hellenistic-Jewish and Christian tradition. It reflects a Jewish understanding of God, his people, and his world which was ultimately adopted and modified by the Christian understanding. The unfolding of this intellectual development has been one of the major concerns of biblical scholarship over the last century (it is sometimes referred to as 'biblical theology'); and while it may be true that scholarship has tended to intellectualise the biblical tradition, it cannot alone be blamed for marginalising it.

The theology expressed in the scriptures, however, is one thing, and the history of ancient Israel and early Christianity which can be written from the evidence of the scriptures is another. The Old Testament and the New Testament, together with the books of the Apocrypha (which are mainly Jewish writings from the last three centuries BC), are important as major source material for historians of ancient Israel and early Christianity. The historian has to learn how to use and interpret this literary evidence, and to relate it to the other evidence available – the evidence of archaeology, the evidence of ancient inscriptions and minor epigraphic material, and the evidence of other ancient literature. Much of this material may come from countries of the ancient world which had political or economic relationships with ancient Israel, or within which Jews or Christians lived and worked. The picture which the historian thus builds up is not necessarily the same as the picture drawn by the ordinary reader from the theologically motivated story-line of the Bible itself. For example, the professional historian's reconstruction from all the available evidence of the land of Canaan in the Middle Bronze Age and the Late Bronze Age (approximately 2000–1200 BC) is a far cry from the picture of Canaan in patriarchal times as presented by the book Genesis. The author or editor of the stories of Abraham, Isaac and Jacob in Genesis was not interested in writing a scholarly history of Canaan, even if he had the archival resources for such a history to hand, which seems unlikely. He was concerned rather to make the point to his contemporaries in the sixth century BC (when many Jews were in exile in Babylonia) that Israel's title to the land of Canaan had been guaranteed long ago by God's promises to the ancestors of Israel.

That the modern historian presents a picture which differs from that presented by the original biblical authors should not surprise or dismay us. Nor should we suppose that the work of the modern historian or biblical critic has undermined the 'truth' of the Bible. The meaning and importance of the divine promise to Abraham in Genesis 12 is not dependent upon an historian's demonstration that this particular Abraham can be identified and dated. And yet we cannot evade the historical challenge. While it is true that what matters for faith and theology is Israel's perception of what happened, her understanding of her history, it is also true that what matters for our peace of mind is that Israel's perception of her history was not too far removed from what actually happened. The link between what happened (so far as we can recover it) and what the Israelites or the early Christians believed to have happened must be intelligible and reasonably convincing. The biblical historian wants to know what happened at the Exodus and the beginnings of Israel, just as he or she wants to know what happened at the resurrection and the birth of the church. The biblical historian is concerned to find the roots of the theological tradition, to discover how that tradition began, how it developed, and how it became part of the believing community of Israel or of the Christian church. The historian's concern to delve behind the tradition is not intended to subvert the faith, but to understand it.

The biblical historian, however, will not succeed in the historical task without first coming to terms with the theological nature of the literary sources. Too many histories of Israel and biographies of Jesus have been written on the basis of an inadequate understanding of the nature of the Pentateuch (i.e. Genesis, Exodus, Leviticus, Numbers, Deuteronomy) or the Gospels. The modern historian in a sense has to *begin* the work of reconstruction by attempting to understand the faith and theological assumptions of the ancient literary sources. In the Bible, history and theology are inextricably intertwined, and the historian must be sensitive to this, remembering that in modern historiography also presentation and presuppositions are equally hard to disentangle. This present book is thus concerned with the nature of biblical history, and with the relationship between what the biblical writers made of it and what the biblical scholars now make of it. This book is concerned with biblical history and with the nature of the biblical writings, which are not simply what most people would call history books, but rather books which reflect history and life as seen by their authors. They are evidence for the historian to put alongside the evidence of archaeological strata or ancient inscriptions, and they need careful evaluation and interpretation.

In his book *The Bible and Recent Archaeology* P.R.S. Moorey with superb clarity presents the findings of recent archaeological research relevant to the history of ancient Canaan, Israel, and the world of the New Testament. He ends his book (p. 183) with the important qualification:

> Archaeological evidence, as this book has recurrently shown, can only throw light on the background to events and on the setting in which leading personalities flourished, not upon them themselves. For that written evidence is necessary and the skills of the historian not of the archaeologist.

That needs saying, and saying frequently. In this book I am concerned to show what the written evidence is good for. While biblical historians need to understand the limitations of archaeology for historical reconstruction, archaeologists need to understand the limitations of biblical (and other) ancient writings for historical reconstruction. In particular, we cannot demonstrate the 'truth' of the Bible simply by setting certain passages of it alongside particular archaeological discoveries. Such discoveries may, and often do, support the accuracy of the observation, memory, or record of the biblical writer; but the future discovery of (let us say) remains from Solomon's temple which demonstrate the accuracy of the description in 1 Kings 6 will not equally establish the existence of the God in whose name the temple was dedicated. Some archaeological discoveries – for example, the limited Late Bronze Age remains at Jericho – force the biblical historian to look again more critically at the story of the collapse of the walls of Jericho in the time of Joshua (Joshua 6), and force upon us the realisation that some biblical accounts are more theological than historical – but none the less 'true' for that. Truth is not to be found only in the identification of archaeological artefacts. History is not limited to the interpretation of archaeological strata, and theology is not bound by the historical activities of men and women. But in the reconstruction of the history of ancient Israel and of the early church, we have to take account of both the archaeology and the history. History, to borrow Oscar Wilde's phrase, is rarely pure and never simple.

## Bibliography

R. Alter and F. Kermode (eds.), *The literary guide to the Bible* (London: Fontana Press, 1989)

J. Barton, *Reading the Old Testament: method in biblical study* (London: Darton Longman and Todd, 1984)

Y. ben Arish, *The rediscovery of the Holy Land in the nineteenth century* (Jerusalem: Magnes Press/The Hebrew University; Detroit: Wayne State University Press, 1979)

J.H. Charlesworth and W.P. Weaver, *What has archaeology to do with faith?* (Philadelphia: Trinity Press International, 1992)

R. Davidson and A.R.C. Leaney, *The Pelican guide to modern theology, 3: Biblical criticism* (Harmondsworth: Penguin, 1970)

C.H. Gordon, *Forgotten scripts: the story of their decipherment* (London: Thames and Hudson, 1968)

C. Gore (ed.), *Lux Mundi: a series of studies in the religion of the Incarnation* (London: J. Murray, 1889)

F.C. Grant, *Translating the Bible* (London: Nelson, 1961)

K.M. Kenyon, *The Bible and recent archaeology* (revised edition by P.R.S. Moorey) (London: British Museum Publications, 1987)

S. Lloyd, *Foundations in the dust: a story of Mesopotamian exploration* (London: Oxford University Press, 1947)

D. Lührmann, *An itinerary for New Testament study* (London: SCM Press; Trinity Press International, 1989)

P.R.S. Moorey, *A century of biblical archaeology* (Cambridge: Lutterworth Press, 1991)

S. Neill, *The interpretation of the New Testament 1861-1961* (London: Oxford University Press, 1964)

J. Rogerson, *Old Testament criticism in the nineteenth century: England and Germany* (London: SPCK, 1984)

J. Rogerson (ed.), *Beginning Old Testament study* (London: SPCK, 1983)

J. Rogerson, C. Rowland and B. Lindars, *The history of Christian theology, 2: The study and use of the Bible* (ed. P. Avis) (Basingstoke: Marshall Pickering; Grand Rapids: W. Eerdmans, 1988)

H.H. Rowley (ed.), *The Old Testament and modern study* (Oxford: Clarendon Press, 1951)

N.A. Silbermann, *Digging for God and country: exploration, archaeology and the secret struggle for the Holy Land 1799-1917* (New York: A.E. Knopf, 1982)

C.M. Watson, *Palestine Exploration Fund: Fifty years' work in the Holy Land. A record and a summary, 1865-1915* (London: Palestine Exploration Fund, 1915)

H.B. Wilson (ed.), *Essays and reviews* (London: Longman, Green, Longman and Roberts, 1860)

# 2     The Nature and Scope of the Bible

The Bible may be pure, but it is certainly not simple. It is well known that the Bible is a collection of a large number of individual books, but it is not always appreciated that the word 'Bible' means different things to different people. For a Jew, the Bible is limited to the Hebrew scriptures of what Christians know as the Old Testament, and the Hebrew scriptures are named the *Tanak*, a name derived acronymically from the initial letters of the three major collections comprising the Tanak: the *Torah* (i.e., the Teaching, or Law, of Genesis – Deuteronomy), the *Nebi'im* (i.e. the Prophets, including the Former Prophets (Joshua, Judges, Samuel, Kings) and the Latter Prophets (Isaiah, Jeremiah, Ezekiel, and the Book of the Twelve Prophets)), and the *Kethubim* (i.e. the Writings, including the Psalms, Proverbs, Job, the five scrolls (Song of Songs, Ruth, Lamentations, Ecclesiastes, Esther), Daniel, Ezra-Nehemiah, Chronicles). These books derive from the ancient kingdoms of Israel and Judah, from the exiled people of Judah, and from the post-exilic state of Judah. They range in date from the work of the eighth-century BC prophets (Amos, Hosea, Isaiah, Micah) to the second-century BC book of Daniel. These books (apart from Daniel) seem to have formed a recognisable collection by the time of Jesus ben Sira, *c.* 180 BC who had devoted himself especially 'to the reading of the law and of the prophets and the other books of our fathers' (Ecclus., Prologue).

For Christians, the Bible includes the 'Old Testament' and the 'New Testament'. The word 'testament' derives from the Latin *testamentum*, which translates the Greek and Hebrew words for 'covenant', and the description of the Bible as comprising an old and a new covenant derives from Jeremiah 31:31–32. The New Testament itself is a collection of twenty-seven books, originating from the early Christian communities of the Mediterranean world. It contains four accounts (gospels) of the life and death of Jesus, a number of letters from early Christian leaders such as Paul, and a work of Christian apocalyptic (Revelation). These writings date from the second half of the first century AD, though some perhaps come from early in the second century. It was the Christian tradition which applied the Jeremianic concept of the 'new covenant' to the gospel brought by Jesus, and which subsequently came to describe the Jewish scriptures as the 'old covenant' or 'old testament', and it became Christian practice to bind the two collections within one volume which, in medieval times, became known as the 'Bible'. (The word derives from the Greek *biblia*, 'books', which is used in 1 Maccabees 1:56 and 12:9 of 'the books of the Law' and 'the holy books';

elsewhere, however, the scriptures were known as 'the writings' or 'the holy writings'.)

However, while there has been general agreement among Christians since the third century on the content of the New Testament, there remains some difference of opinion concerning the content of the Old Testament. This difference ultimately derives from the fact that much of the early Christian church used the Greek translation of the Hebrew scriptures known as the Septuagint (i.e., 'the Seventy', so named after the number of translators credited with the task). The Septuagint included a number of Hellenistic Jewish writings, mainly from the last three centuries BC and the first century AD, not found in the Hebrew Bible – for example, the Wisdom of Solomon, Ecclesiasticus, Judith, Tobit, Baruch, and 1 and 2 Maccabees. In the fourth century AD, Jerome, in producing a Latin translation of the scriptures now known as the Vulgate, drew a distinction between those books known from the Hebrew tradition (*'libri canonici'*) and those not (*'libri ecclesiastici'*, or 'Apocrypha', i.e., 'Hidden'). Jerome wished to exclude the latter from the rank of scripture, but on the whole they continued to be accepted. At the Reformation, however, the tendency to restrict the Old Testament scriptures to those known from the Hebrew tradition was revived by Protestant theologians, and most of the apocryphal books were relegated by them to the status of an appendix, though Luther granted that such books were 'useful and good to read', and the Thirty Nine Articles of the Church of England declared that 'the other Books (as *Hierome* saith) the Church doth read for example of life and instruction of manners; but yet doth it not apply them to establish any doctrine'. The Council of Trent in 1548 reaffirmed for the Roman Catholic church the canonical authority of all the disputed books except III and IV Esdras (i.e., 1 and 2 Esdras in the Protestant Apocrypha) and the Prayer of Manasseh; in 1672 the eastern Orthodox churches in Synod at Jerusalem took a mediating position and accepted Tobit, Judith, Ecclesiasticus and Wisdom of Solomon into the canon of scripture.

This history explains why it is possible today to find the English Bible in at least three different versions, represented by the Revised Standard Version (with or without Apocrypha), the Revised Standard Version Catholic Edition (in which the Old Testament includes all those books accepted as canonical by the Roman Catholic church), and the Revised Standard Version Common Edition (which prints the Old Testament in the standard Protestant form, followed by the Apocrypha *minus* 1 Esdras, 2 Esdras and the Prayer of Manasseh, which appear in a separate section as 'Deutero-canonical Books').

The problem of what should be included in the Bible is not limited to the problem of which books should be included. What should be done with passages which are considered on good evidence to be later additions to the text, or inauthentic? For example, it is generally agreed that the final verses of St Mark's Gospel (Mk.16: 9–20) are not from the hand of the author of the second gospel, and that the story of the woman taken in adultery (John 7: 53 – 8: 11) did not originally belong to the fourth gospel. Most modern editions of the Bible are content to leave them in their place, with an explanatory footnote or with a change of typeface; but there are many passages throughout the Bible which are clearly additional – the Bible itself might be said to be a body of literature which has come together by a long history of accretion – and it is hard to know where to draw the line between 'authentic' text and 'inauthentic' addition, particularly as in no case do we possess the author's original manuscript. The New English Bible, for example, omits the titles printed by other translations at the head of each psalm. These titles are thought by many scholars to be the work of Jewish exegetes, or expositors, of the fourth century BC. Clearly they are additional to the original text of the psalms, but are they therefore 'non-biblical'? The Revised English Bible (1989) (a revision of the New English Bible) restores these headings to the text.

At this point we become involved with the problems of text-criticism: how far is it possible to reconstruct the original text of a biblical book as the author wrote it, given that since the time of composition the biblical books have been copied and recopied many times, rarely with complete accuracy, and in some cases do not exist in their original language but only in translation? In most cases, the quest for the original text is virtually impossible; we can at best discover in what form a particular book was being read in the third or second century BC. This in itself is extremely important for our understanding of the history of the development and of the interpretation of the Bible, but to follow this trail here would be to divert from the purpose of this chapter.

To speak of the Bible or of Holy Scriptures is usually to refer to those ancient writings of the Jews or early Christians which have been selected, preserved and hallowed by religious tradition and formal recognition as vital to the continuing belief of the religious community, whether Jewish or Christian. For these purposes the original selection of certain books as valuable and their formal canonisation as authoritative are all-important. But the historian of ancient Judaism and early Christianity remembers that the biblical books are but a selection from a wider literature, and, for the purposes of history, is equally concerned with writings that were not included in the Jewish or Christian canons, such as those preserved in the Dead Sea Scrolls from the region of Qumran and other non-canonical writings in modern times generally collected and published under the heading of 'Apocrypha and Pseudepigrapha'. The historian is concerned with other material as well, whether from Israel and the early church or from non-Israelite, non-Christian sources outside, relevant to the history of Judaism and Christianity. Records from Egypt, from Syria, from Assyria and Babylon, from Persia, from the Greek world of the Ptolemies and the Seleucids, from the Roman world of the late Republic and early Empire, are all grist to the historian's mill, together with the findings of the geographers, the archaeologists, the anthropologists, the social scientists and others.

Thus there are many relevant sources for the history of Israel and the early church, but still the single most important source of evidence is the Bible. And faced with any such corpus of material, the historian begins by asking what sort of material this is, where it comes from, when it was written, by whom and for whom, and from what context. The historian goes on to ask what this material tells us about the community from which it was written, to assess its value as evidence for any historical past it might describe, to relate its evidence to that obtained from other sources, and ultimately from this evidence to present an interpretation of that aspect of the subject under review. One important point to note is that, in whatever sense we might consider the biblical writers to be inspired, these writers were human beings, drawing upon human intellect and experience, human records and archives, and human interpretations of history and society conditioned by their time and place; and how could it be otherwise? The Bible did not drop fully formed from heaven, but came to us through the mediation of men and women enlightened by faith and inspiration but limited by their human condition and context. They wrote about the divine from their experience of it as human beings, and that is what makes their writings valuable both to religious believer and to secular historian today. In order therefore to interpret the writings of these biblical writers accurately, we need to know something about their background, about the geographical environment which affected their life-styles, about the historical events which dominated their lives, and about the social relationships of their world. The 'biblical world', as it is often called, has been much studied, and there exist many general introductory works designed to help the student see the biblical writings in their ancient near eastern context. Much of our knowledge of that context derives from the writings and archaeological remains of ancient Israel's neighbours – Edom, Moab, Ammon, Egypt, Syria, Assyria, Babylon, Persia – and from archaeological evidence from within ancient Israel itself. However, part of the evidence for the context of the biblical writings is drawn from the biblical writings themselves, and the danger of circular argument is evident. The figure of Abraham may not be best understood from a picture of the world of Abraham reconstructed from the pages of Genesis, for the world they reflect may turn out to be that of the period of its author or compiler, perhaps a thousand years after the period of Israel's pre-Mosaic ancestors. The reconstruction of the context of the biblical world, however, has been immeasurably helped by the progress of archaeological research, and recently by the improved understanding of ancient societies, often based on the trial application of theoretical models drawn from other societies to those described in the ancient texts.

It is worth pausing at this point to outline that history, so that we can set the biblical books in their historical context, and so that we can see more clearly the way in which the biblical books present that history. The main difficulty in reconstructing Israel's history (especially her early history) is that we have little to go on except Israel's own later presentations for her folk memories or traditions. As preserved in the biblical books, they are mainly being used to explain Israel's beliefs or to justify her claims to territory in Canaan. In any case they are likely to be selective as well as partisan, and must therefore be used with considerable academic caution. This, of course, is equally true, *mutatis mutandis*, of traditions and records, where preserved, of Israel's contemporaries (a point which some historians, for all their scrupulous concern to be objective, forget). One can understand why some archaeologists prefer to ignore the biblical record, and reconstruct the history of Israel, so far as possible, from the stratified evidence of buildings, artefacts and inscriptions. At least this can offer some sort of independent check on the picture drawn from the biblical evidence and the records of Israel's neighbours. However, the historian of Israel cannot ignore the biblical record, any more than he or she can ignore the archaeological evidence or the archives of other ancient near eastern nations; each type of evidence must be properly sifted and its true value assessed.

The Jewish scriptures as they stand present the following picture of Israel's history. The Israelites were related to the peoples of Assyria and Syria as brother Semites ('the sons of Shem', son of Noah, Gen.10:21–31), and less closely to the Egyptians and Canaanites ('the sons of Ham', Gen.10:6–14). The Israelite ancestors had migrated from Ur of the Chaldees in southern Mesopotamia and Harran in northern Syria to settle in the land of Canaan, which the biblical writers present from the start as divinely promised to Israel. After three generations the growing family was forced to emigrate to Egypt, where they were oppressed (according to Gen.15:13, for four hundred years) and from which they were finally rescued by their leader Moses. After a forty-year period of wandering in the wilderness of Sinai, where God made a covenant with them and gave them a law to obey, they travelled through the regions east of the Dead Sea to enter the promised land via Jericho, which they captured and destroyed. They proceeded to divide up the promised land between the twelve tribes (the descendants of the twelve sons of Abraham's grandson Jacob); nine and a half tribes settled west of the Jordan, two and a half tribes east of it. For some three hundred years the Israelite tribes, under leaders called 'judges', established themselves on the land in the face of various enemies – Moabites, Canaanites, Midianites, Amalekites, Ammonites, Philistines and others – until a monarchy was established under Saul and his greater successor David. The climax of this monarchy was reached under David's son Solomon, who built the temple in Jerusalem; but his reign ended in disaster as his kingdom split into two.

The Books of Kings record the fortunes of the southern kingdom of Judah and the northern kingdom of Israel, parallel from about 930 BC until 722 BC when Israel became a subject-province of the Assyrian empire. In 587 BC the kingdom of Judah fell to Nebuchadnezzar and became part of the Babylonian empire. As in 722 BC the Israelites had been taken away to exile in Assyria and elsewhere, so now the people of Judah were exiled to Babylonia; to be more precise, the leading officials were killed, the king and 4,600 others were exiled (Jer.52:28–30) in three deportations, and the peasant population was left in place (2 Kings 25:12). The biblical account picks up the story some fifty years later and tells how Cyrus the Great of Persia provided for the repatriation of Jewish exiles and the rebuilding of the Jerusalem temple.

The next major events of importance to the biblical historian are the reading of the Law in Jerusalem by Ezra the Scribe, and the rebuilding of the walls of Jerusalem by Nehemiah the governor, who arrived in Jerusalem in 445/4 BC. From this point on, we are told virtually nothing of the history of Judah by any of the books preserved in the biblical canon, except for the book of Daniel, which records the political struggles of the Ptolemies of Egypt and the Seleucids of Syria as a prelude to the Maccabaean rebellion, and the books of 1 and 2 Maccabees, which in different ways record the course of the rebellion.

It is part of the aim of this book to demonstrate how, and with what emphases, the biblical writers presented the history of their people, but it will be clear even from this brief sketch that the biblical presentation of Israel's history is highly selective, and concerned above all with putting forward Israel as the people of God. A number of themes stand out as important. Israel has been promised, and given, a land of her own. She took it and held it in the face of enemies. The city of Jerusalem was of central importance as the seat of the Davidic monarchy and the site of the temple (which reveals that the historical tradition preserved in the Jewish scriptures derives in the end from sources favouring the southern kingdom of Judah, not the northern kingdom of Israel). The Law and the covenant with God made at Sinai were of foundational importance; it was Israel's failure to observe the demands of these which led to the destruction of the kingdoms of Israel and Judah. It was the attack on the institutions of the temple, and the Law, by Antiochus of Syria and his hellenising Jewish supporters that led to the Maccabaean rebellion. The book of Genesis epitomises the whole story of Israel in the figure of Abraham. Abraham is called by God to go to a new land, where God will make of him a great nation, and bless him. He goes to Canaan and establishes himself there, he is forced by famine to go down to Egypt; he runs into danger from Pharaoh, who is afflicted with plagues and sends Abraham away, richer than when he came. Abraham returns to Canaan, separates himself from Lot (the ancestor of the Ammonites and Moabites), pursues and defeats invading kings near Damascus, is promised the land 'from the river of Egypt to the great river, the river Euphrates' (the ideal extent of the Davidic empire) when the Lord makes a covenant with him, is called upon to be circumcised, is promised an heir and descendants as numerous as the stars, comes into conflict with the Philistines, is called upon to exercise faith and make the supreme sacrifice of his only son, and is rewarded for his obedience with God's blessing and renewed promise of posterity; and finally, he purchases land for his wife Sarah's burial place as a permanent possession. This has many features in common with the biblical presentation of the early history of Israel, and is almost a parable of what is required of and promised to the people called by God. The story of Abraham is the story of Israel.

The story of ancient Israel as told by a modern academic historian might look a little different. The modern historian is concerned more with human than divine motives, with political cause and effect, with economic and social geography, and with presenting the history of Israel in the wider context of the history of the ancient near east. Interlocking chronologies and cultural comparisons are likely to rank as highly as interpreting the ethical or theological concerns of an Amos or Isaiah. In particular, the modern historian is likely to present a rather different picture of Israel's origins. The question of Israel's origins, in fact, remains one of the most vexed in the whole field of Israel's history. The modern historian begins, not with Abraham, Isaac and Jacob, but with knowledge of Canaan and its environment in the second millennium BC drawn from the results of archaeological exploration and excavation, and from such Egyptian, Canaanite, and Mesopotamian records as are available and relevant. Until the nineteenth century, the stories of Genesis largely controlled the historian's presentation of ancient near eastern history in the second millennium BC. Nowadays, the material in Genesis, if it is relevant to the second millennium at all, which some scholars doubt, must be seen and interpreted in the light of what is known from other sources· about the Middle and Late Bronze Ages in Palestine.

For the historian today, then, the history of Israel begins at some indeterminate point at the end of the Late Bronze Age or the beginning of Iron Age I. The Middle Bronze Age (*c.* 2000–1550 BC) was the age when the great Canaanite cities such as Gezer, Lachish, Jericho, Shechem, Megiddo, Aphek, Dan, Hazor and many others flourished. The Late Bronze Age (*c.* 1550–1200 BC) saw a continuation of the same Canaanite culture, but also increasing Egyptian influence from the fifteenth century BC as the Egyptian rulers of the Eighteenth and Nineteenth Dynasties took over and controlled Palestine. The first external reference to the people of Israel appears on an Egyptian stele set up in the fifth year of the reign of Pharaoh Merneptah (*c.* 1224–1214 BC), celebrating the Pharaoh's triumphs in Canaan: 'Ashkelon is taken; Gezer is captured; Yanoam is made non-existent; Israel lies desolate; its seed is no more'. 'Israel' here is a people rather than a land, area, or city state like Gezer and Ashkelon, but little can be inferred from this document about the nature of Israel's presence in Canaan or her origins – except that by the late thirteenth century BC a group called 'Israel' could be named by an Egyptian Pharaoh alongside cities in southern Palestine. How this group 'Israel' came to be in Canaan, however, is uncertain.

Fifty years ago, the picture presented by the book Joshua, that the Israelites seized the land of Canaan by conquest, beginning with Jericho, was thought to be supported by archaeological evidence of the destruction of a number of Late Bronze Age cities such as Ai, Hazor, Lachish and Jericho; but further archaeological investigation has shown that Ai was unoccupied until the twelfth century BC, that Hazor was destroyed in the mid-thirteenth century, Lachish in the early twelfth century, and the small Late Bronze Age site of Jericho in the mid-fourteenth century. Not all destructions belonged to the same period, or could be credited to an invading people of Israel in the thirteenth century.

A subsequent theory proposed, on the basis of both biblical evidence and the study of Iron Age I settlement patterns in the hill regions of Galilee, Israel and Judah, that Israel's occupation of the land was largely a matter of peaceful infiltration and settlement by pastoralists and cereal farmers alongside the populations of the Canaanite Late Bronze Age cities. Local conflict might appear; Judges 9 perhaps evidences it at Shechem.

This view still presupposes that the Israelites entered the land from outside, but a third proposal suggests that the people of Israel emerged in the land by way of a social revolution of the under-privileged or dispossessed in the Late Bronze Age Canaanite cities. Certainly the view popularised by the author of Deuteronomy, that the incoming Israelites completely rooted out the Canaanites from the land, represents a theological ideal rather than historical fact. In reality, we must suppose that there was considerable continuity of population between the Late Bronze Age and Iron Age I, wherever the Israelites came from, and we must agree that social and economic factors played their part in the development of the people of Israel on Canaanite soil. What does seem clear from recent archaeological survey work is that the emergence of Israel in Canaan 'was primarily a rural phenomenon' (Moorey, 1987, 54). The Israelites seem to have gained control of the central hill country at roughly the same time as the Philistines, whose origin lay in the Aegean, took control of the towns of the coastal plain – Gaza, Ashdod, Ashkelon, Ekron and Gath – to the west. Between them, the Israelites and the Philistines brought about the end of Egyptian control of southern Palestine, and began a new, if relatively short-lived, era in Palestine.

Some historians argue that it is only with the beginning of the monarchic period in Israel – that is, with kings Saul, David and Solomon in the late eleventh and tenth centuries BC – that is becomes possible to write anything like a history of Israel. Certainly it is not until we reach this period that we see evidence of anything like archival sources appearing in the biblical books. At all events, from about 1000 BC, and more particularly from the end of Solomon's reign in *c.* 930 BC, it becomes possible to work out with reasonable accuracy – thanks to synchronisms with dates in Assyrian history and a firm date provided by astronomical data – a fairly close chronology for the kings of Israel and Judah down to 587 BC.

In the early tenth century BC King David unified the major tribal groupings of Judah and Israel, and focused the kingdom on his new capital city of Jerusalem, a former Canaanite city which lay conveniently between the territories of Judah and the tribes of Israel. This united kingdom, however, did not survive the political errors of Solomon, and fell apart into its two major constituencies. Both kingdoms survived to begin with because both Egypt and Syria were relatively weak. (There arose more or less contemporaneously and survived with them the smaller kingdoms of the Ammonites, Moabites and Edomites across the Jordan and the Dead Sea to the east and southeast.) But growing pressure came from Syria in the north, and then in the mid-ninth century irresistible pressure from Assyria to the northeast. After several tentative forays to the Mediterranean the Assyrians finally seized Syria in 733 BC and Israel in 722 BC. Judah joined a rebellion against Assyria and was attacked by Sennacherib in 701 BC, but by dint of heavy payments king Hezekiah survived to become Assyria's vassal.

It was in this period of the mid-eighth century, when the kingdoms of Judah and Israel were at the height of their prosperity and the empire of Assyria was poised for expansion, that some of the greatest of the biblical prophets were active – Amos and Hosea in the kingdom of Israel, Isaiah and Micah in Judah. Their appearance cannot be totally disconnected from the political pressure of their day, and it is hardly accidental that the next major group of prophets to appear – Nahum, Zephaniah and Habakkuk – belong precisely to the period when Assyria was about to fall before the growing power of Babylon, in the late seventh century BC. Nineveh fell in 612 BC, and by 605 BC Nebuchadnezzar had defeated Pharaoh Necho of Egypt and taken over Syria and Palestine. From now on, Judah was important to the Babylonians and their successors the Persians, and later to the Seleucid kings, because the route to Egypt, with all its potential wealth, lay through or beside Judah's territory.

We know remarkably little about what happened in Judah during the years of exile, between the fall of Jerusalem (for the second time) in 587 BC and the fall of Babylon to Cyrus the Persian in 539 BC. Presumably it was ruled by Babylonian governors as part of the Babylonian empire. Some Jews fled to Egypt, perhaps thus laying the foundations of the later large Jewish presence in Egypt. After 539 BC, Judah was ruled by Persian governors, who were – to begin with at least – from the old royal family of Judah. Persian rule lasted for just over two hundred years, from 539 to 331 BC. Only a few major events are recorded: the rebuilding of the temple (520–515 BC), some trouble at the beginning of Xerxes' reign (485 BC; Ezra 4:6), a frustrated attempt to rebuild the walls of Jerusalem in Artaxerxes' time (464–424 BC), followed by a successful rebuilding in the governorship of Nehemiah (445–432 BC), and the reading of the Law in Jerusalem by Ezra, possibly in 458 BC or in 398 BC.

What the books of Ezra and Nehemiah do not reveal (probably because it was not yet so very noticeable in Judah, a small enclave in the mountains set well back from the Palestinian coast) is that throughout the fifth and fourth centuries the Persians had their eyes firmly on the Mediterranean world to their west. Darius I, who allowed the Jews to rebuild their temple in Jerusalem, also began a canal to link the Nile and the Red Sea, campaigned north of the Danube towards Scythia, and led an expedition to punish Athens for its support of the revolt of the Ionian cities on the west coast of what is now Turkey. The history of the Persian empire is much concerned with Persia's attempts to control its Mediterranean seaboard, and to control Egypt, first captured for Persia by Cambyses in 525 BC. The Jewish leaders in Jerusalem must have been well aware of Persia's concerns in Egypt, and when the Persian empire fell to Alexander the Great in 331 BC, Judah was taken over within a dozen years by Alexander's general Ptolemy, ruling from Alexandria.

The Ptolemaic rule of Palestine lasted for just over a century, and combined traditional pharaonic autocracy with hellenistic technology and exploitative skill. The people of Judah mostly welcomed the Seleucid Antiochus III when he defeated Ptolemy IV in 200 BC at Paneion, and restored to the Jews the right to organise their society according to their traditional law. But when Antiochus took on the power of Rome, he incurred heavy fines by the Treaty of Apamea, in payment of which his successors were forced to raise money by the dubious methods of commandeering monies deposited in temples and selling political honours and favours. The Jews objected to Antiochus IV's replacement of their high priest and subsequent attempts to hellenise Jerusalem and its constitution, and the result was a bitter civil war, with the hellenising side heavily supported by the occupying Seleucid power.

The Maccabaean rebellion of 167 BC led eventually to the establishment of a monarchy once again in Jerusalem; the Hasmonaean dynasty ruled, first as ethnarch, general and high priest, and then as king and high priest, until rivalry for power between two brothers and their supporters (especially the supporters) brought the Roman general Pompey the Great in to adjudicate, and in 63 BC Judah became part of the Roman province of Syria. Judah remained under Roman control (though Herod the Great, as a client-king appointed by the Roman Senate, had some measure of independence) throughout the ensuing New Testament period, during which the major event was the rebellion in AD 66, put down by Titus in AD 70 with the destruction of Jerusalem and of the temple.

It is to this historical setting that the books of the Bible belong. They must be dated individually largely on grounds of internal evidence, and for the most part this is not particularly difficult. Complications arise with composite works put together from the work of more than one author, such as the book of Isaiah, or from varied and wide-ranging sources, such as the Pentateuch (i.e., Genesis, Exodus, Leviticus, Numbers, Deuteronomy), which incorporates material from many different sources, periods and contexts: folk-lore, law, liturgical codes, poetry, story-telling, archives, and so on. In their attempt to disentangle the historical development and growth of the Bible, biblical scholars over the last two centuries began by trying to date the individual books within the history of Israel and the early church. This led to a detailed study of the sources from which different works were composed, and then to a very lively attempt to explore the nature and background of the pre-literary, oral and liturgical traditions which were assumed often to underlie the literature. Following this exhaustive source- and tradition-criticism of the nineteenth and first half of the twentieth century, scholars have now turned to studying both the editorial activity that led to the present state of the biblical texts and the meaning of those texts for those who originally brought them together within the biblical canon and for those who now read them in that context. The Bible, after all, is a holy book, with meaning for those who belong to the Jewish and Christian traditions and whose faith is bound up with the biblical tradition. At this point, however, historical enquiry develops into systematic theology, and passes beyond our present concerns.

Our immediate concern is to set the literature contained in the Bible in its historical and geographical context, and to demonstrate that the different parts of the Bible were written and developed in different circumstances to meet a variety of needs. Any intelligent appreciation of the Bible must take account of those circumstances and needs. If we are concerned with historical enquiry, it is clearly important to relate the biblical writings to their proper historical context, or we shall misinterpret the evidence. If we are concerned with systematic theology, it is equally important that we interpret the biblical authors' words against the right background and historical context, in order to understand the authors' point or message, before we try to translate that message into the appropriate idiom of our own time or relate it to the contemporary world.

Behind the present text of parts of the Bible, especially in the Old Testament, may well lie a history of oral transmission of material. Stories, proverbs, poems, songs, laws, genealogies, and other types of material may have been transmitted orally over several or even many generations before being incorporated into some written composition. Prophetic oracles were uttered, and then perhaps long quoted (at least in some cases) from memory before being compiled in written form as a collection ascribed to one particular prophet. Liturgical responses may have been used for generations before anyone thought to record them. The Old Testament is full of material which had a pre-literary history which we can no longer trace for certain. It also contains material which had an earlier literary history; it incorporates letters, edicts, collections of laws, collections of oracles, collections of psalms, collections of proverbs, collections of stories, and archival material, all of which existed in written form before being incorporated by a biblical author or editor into his book. Both these points may be made also of the New Testament. The gospels, for example, contain material which derives from orally transmitted stories about Jesus or sayings of Jesus, and many scholars have held that we can reconstruct from the non-Marcan material common to Matthew and Luke a no-longer-extant document containing sayings of Jesus which (for want of a more accurate name) has been called 'Q' (for German *Quelle*, 'source').

Dating such early material, whether it derives from oral tradition or from an earlier literary context, can sometimes be almost impossible (how does one date a proverb like 'Pride goes before destruction'?) and sometimes relatively easy; if the biblical editor of Proverbs has got it right, Proverbs 25–29 are 'proverbs of Solomon which the men of Hezekiah king of Judah copied'. This at least indicates that the editor of Proverbs had reason to believe that there was literary activity at the court of king Hezekiah in the late eighth century BC. Dating some of the material now found in the Pentateuch is particularly difficult. Recently D.N. Freedman has argued that the poems in Genesis 49, Exodus 15, Numbers 23–24, Deuteronomy 33, and Judges 5 'are five of the poems that I regard as the oldest literature preserved in the Bible and hence the best available source of recovering a valid contemporary account of the religion of Israel in its earliest phases.' (Freedman, 1987, 315.) He dates Exodus 15 and Judges 5 to the twelfth century BC, and the others to the eleventh century, and he is prepared to refer the content of Genesis 49 to the pre-Mosaic, patriarchal age of the fourteenth-thirteenth century BC. He calls these poems 'literature', suggesting that he regards them as having been written down at these early dates. Not every scholar would agree that these poems were composed or written down as early as Freedman proposes, and certainly in their present form they reflect the conditions of the monarchy. Other early written material preserved in the Pentateuch includes the Decalogue (the Ten Commandments), to be found in slightly varying form in Exodus 20 and Deuteronomy 5, and the 'Book of the Covenant' (Exod.24:7–8), to be found in Exodus 21:1 – 23:22. Precisely how old these two quite different codes are is not clear, but both reflect a settled, organised agricultural society rather than city life, and in origin they may belong to the century before the establishment of the monarchy. In each case, however, the editor who incorporated them into the Pentateuch knew them as written documents; one is called a 'book', and the other, by tradition, was inscribed upon tablets. All this material indicates that Israel's literature began early in her history. Israel's tradition later ascribed the composition of music and psalms to king David, and the utterance, at least, of proverbs and songs to Solomon (cf. Amos 6:5; 1 Kings 4:32–33).

However, what we have in the Pentateuch is not as it stands simply a compilation of oral tradition and previously existing documents but a literary version of material, some of which may have been transmitted orally for a time, and some of which was edited or adapted from already existent written material. The completion of the Pentateuch as a body of material marks a certain stage in the development and interpretation of Israel's traditions, a stage which must be dated at least some time after the composition of Deuteronomy, which was incorporated as a block to make up the Pentateuch. The remaining material of the Pentateuch (i.e., Genesis, Exodus, Leviticus, Numbers, and a few verses at the end of Deuteronomy) is, in its present form, the product of editorial compilation and composition in the late seventh or early sixth centuries BC.

The earlier stages of the compilation of this huge mass of material are far from clear, and are currently being vigorously debated. Nineteenth-century scholarship argued, on the basis of source-criticism, for the development of a sequence of literary documents, J, E, and P, whose combination by an editor or editors with Deuteronomy produced the present Pentateuch. The earliest and most important of these hypothesised documents was J, so named because one of the major distinguishing features of material credited to this documentary strand of the Pentateuch was the use of the name Jehovah (Hebrew Yahweh or Jahweh) for God. The J document was thought to have originated in Judah, perhaps in the ninth or eighth century BC, though some have dated it as early as the tenth century and others as late as the sixth century BC. The siglum 'E' derived from the use of the Hebrew word Elohim for God in passages credited to the 'Elohistic' document, which was believed to come from the northern kingdom of Israel in the eighth century BC. There has always, however, been some doubt about the separate existence of this document, and while some scholars have preferred to speak of JE material, further analysis being too uncertain, others have wished to remove reference to E altogether. The siglum 'P' denoted the Priestly writer, whose contribution to the Pentateuch was isolated on grounds of its special vocabulary, its priestly interests (e.g., circumcision, sabbath, sacrifice, priesthood, tabernacle, and so on), and its formal characteristics. It was debated whether P represented an independent document, woven with J and E and then D (the nucleus of Deuteronomy) to make up the Pentateuch, or whether P represented the editor responsible for the final compilation of the Pentateuch from the other documents. P was dated generally to the exilic period and its author(s) located in Babylon among the exiles, though it has recently been argued that his work was known to Deuteronomy and Jeremiah, and that P should be dated earlier, to the time of Hezekiah in the late eighth century.

On this almost traditional scholarly source-critical view of the Pentateuch, much of the material of the Pentateuch took literary shape during the monarchic period, and was finally put together at the end of it or in the exilic period.

Certainly there are many small indications in the Pentateuch that the monarchy and circumstances of the monarchic period are known. For example, Genesis 36:31 appears to know that monarchy existed in Israel, and Genesis 27:40 that Edom had rebelled against Judah – an event which took place *c.* 845 BC. Exodus 12 describes the regulations for the Passover, but this feast is not evidenced in the historical books 1 and 2 Kings before the time of Josiah in the late seventh century BC. This may seem surprising, given that the Exodus is generally dated to the late thirteenth century BC, but the awkward absence of a clearly dated early reference to the feast must be taken seriously. These and many other indications make it clear that the development of Israel's traditions about its early, pre-monarchic history belongs, as indeed one might expect, precisely to the period when the independent kingdoms of Judah and Israel flourished, with their own royal courts and temples or sanctuaries where men of literary inclinations and abilities might flourish – for only at court or among the priesthood could such men find support for and interest in their activities.

It was also during the monarchic period that other types of Old Testament literature had their origins. We have already noted the heading to Proverbs 25, which says that a collection of Solomon's proverbs had been copied by employees of king Hezekiah. That the royal court might be the home for the preservation and use of educational literature is not surprising, for it was here that future counsellors and diplomats and heirs to the throne had to be trained for their duties. A number of psalms, especially those which focus on the king at his coronation, or his wedding, or as leading the nation in battle, or active in the cult, must also belong to the monarchic period; later tradition credited many of them in some sense to David, and even if the attributions were not always correct, at least this demonstrates that the psalms were connected in people's minds with the Davidic monarchy. Kings employed scribes, who wrote letters and kept records (cf. 2 Sam.8:16; 20:24, 25; 1 Kings 4:3), and it is certain that the late monarchic author of 1 and 2 Kings must have used such records in the compilation of his work.

It was in the monarchic period also that the oracles of some of the early prophets began to be collected; we are told that shortly before 733 BC the prophet Isaiah wrote a short, rather cryptic phrase on a tablet and had it witnessed (Isa.8:1); in Isaiah 8:16 the prophet himself appears to utter the instruction, 'Bind up the testimony, seal the teaching among my disciples. I will wait for the LORD who is hiding his face from the house of Jacob, and I will hope in him.' That is, the prophet Isaiah appears to instruct someone to preserve his teaching against the day when its accuracy will be clear. Amos, Isaiah, Hosea and Micah prophesied in the eighth century BC, and the process of preserving, collecting, and editing their oracles must at least have started in their lifetimes, though it seems clear from the brief introductions to the books in their names that these books were not completed until some later period. These prophetic books do not therefore spring directly from the pens of the prophets named in their titles, and that is probably also true of the late seventh-century prophets, Nahum, Habakkuk and Zephaniah.

The eighth-century prophets were responding to the social and political affairs of their day, and in particular to the advent of Assyria in the west, while the seventh-century prophets were responding to the rise of the Babylonian empire. But it was the arrival of Nebuchadnezzar of Babylon in the west, and the consequent destruction of the kingdom of Judah and the exile of its leading citizens, that was responsible for the creation of the major works of the Jewish scriptures and the Old Testament. The book of the prophet Ezekiel, who was deported from Jerusalem in 597 BC and carried on his prophetic ministry in exile until about 570 BC, is an immediate product of this crisis. Another is the book of Jeremiah, who was active in Jerusalem in the reign of Josiah and his successors up to the fall of Jerusalem in 587 BC, after which he was taken off to Egypt by Jewish refugees from the Babylonian administration. Jeremiah's writings were edited later in the sixth century by editors of the Deuteronomistic school of theology, who attributed the destruction of Jerusalem to the people's failure to keep the covenant made by God with their ancestors at Sinai (see for example Jer.11:1–13).

This same Deuteronomistic school had been responsible for the presentation of the history of the monarchies of Judah and Israel in 1 and 2 Kings somewhere about the turn of the seventh and sixth centuries, and for the second edition of that work later in the sixth century. The final version of the Pentateuch included the book Deuteronomy, but the overall story of the Pentateuch – which told how the Israelite ancestors had been promised land, had suffered hardship in Egypt, had emerged by God's grace and crossed the wilderness (where they were granted a covenant-relationship with God and given a law to keep) to arrive on the edge of the promised land, which they would enter if only they remained faithful to the covenant – must have been full of meaning for the exiles. It is no coincidence that the greatest of Israel's prophets, the so-called 'Second Isaiah' (whose real name is unknown, the name of Isaiah being borrowed because his work was added to that of the first Isaiah), fills his prophecies of encouragement and coming salvation for Israel with allusions to the old stories of God's dealings with Israel at the Red Sea and in the wilderness. These stories of God's past redemptive acts were deeply relevant to exiles suffering under a latter day Pharaoh in a strange land.

This vast amount of literature from the sixth century BC (to which must be added the short book of Lamentations, which mourns the fall of Jerusalem, and perhaps the book of the prophet Obadiah, who wrote invective against the Edomites) shows all too clearly the impression the fall of Jerusalem made on its people. Nothing else in Israel's history triggered such a spate of literature, and that in spite of the circumstances of destruction and exile. The fall of Jerusalem left its mark on all subsequent Jewish writing; Josephus, the first-century AD Jewish historian, saw Nebuchadnezzar's destruction as prefiguring the Roman destruction in AD 70. The sixth century BC witnessed the kingdom of Judah's final disaster, and the literary reaction to this produced a combination of historical and theological writing which formed the foundation for what ultimately emerged as Judaism.

The exilic period was followed by what used to be called the post-exilic period, but is now increasingly known as the Second Temple period. It began with the rebuilding of the ruined temple at Jerusalem, led by Zerubbabel the governor and Jeshua the high priest, urged on by the prophets Haggai and Zechariah (cf. Ezra 5:1–2). The books of Haggai, and Zechariah 1–8, record prophetic oracles focused on this event (520–515 BC). Also from this period, perhaps from the years after the temple rebuilding, comes the somewhat enigmatic collection of prophetic oracles comprised in 'Third Isaiah' (Isa.56–66), which reflects both a glowing hope in the coming new society and a disillusionment at some of the failings of the present. From the first half of the fifth century BC comes the prophetic book Malachi, which sharply castigates the failings of society, and especially those of the Jerusalem priests, who are not fulfilling their role of offering pure sacrifices and teaching the people the Torah. Also to the fifth century perhaps belong the books of Joel, whose background seems to lie in a famine caused by a locust plague, and of Jonah, which casts a somewhat satirical eye on Jewish attitudes to Gentiles, who are also capable of repentance before God.

Even less easy to date is the book of Job, a magnificent exploration of the theme of divine justice and human righteousness; it may belong anywhere between the sixth and fourth centuries BC. The book of Proverbs, like Job a book from the intellectual 'wisdom' tradition in Israel, contains material from earlier periods, but its final editing probably also belongs to this early post-exilic period. Wisdom is personified as a female figure, and perhaps even seen as an independent divine being closely related to God (Prov.8:22–31), an approach which must be compared with that in the second-century BC Wisdom of ben Sira (Ecclus. 24) and the first-century BC Wisdom of Solomon (ch.7). To the fourth century BC probably belongs the Chronicler's history (1 and 2 Chronicles), which re-presents the history of the kings of Judah in terms relevant to the Second Temple period, with emphasis on the kings' treatment of the temple, the priesthood and the law. The books of Ezra and Nehemiah come from the same school as the Chronicler, if not from the same hand, and give a somewhat confused and limited picture of what the author sees as the main events of Persian rule in Judah – the rebuilding of the temple, Ezra's reading of the law, and Nehemiah's rebuilding of the city of Jerusalem. The book of Esther is a novel set in the Persian empire, whose present purpose is to explain the background to the later Jewish feast of Purim.

It is clear from this list that, though the biblical sources record very little of the history of the Persian period, there was a considerable amount of intellectual and literary activity going on in Jerusalem. Clearly, the older works were being preserved, copied and read, as is demonstrated by the Chronicler's use of 1 and 2 Kings, and the editor's use in Proverbs of material from the monarchic period. The author of Jonah has also read 2 Kings, from which he takes the name of his anti-hero (2 Kings 14:25); the author of Joel knows his Isaiah or Micah (Joel 3:10; cf. Isa.2:4; Mic.4:3). There were probably other writings which have not survived, but those which have make an important contribution to the Jewish scriptures and to the development of Jewish theology. A note in an epistle perhaps datable to 164/3 BC, now prefacing 2 Maccabees, says that Nehemiah (mid-fifth century BC) 'founded a library and collected the books about the kings and prophets, and the writings of David, and letters of kings about votive offerings' (2 Macc.2:13). This may be put down to later enhancement of Nehemiah's reputation, but it is not an impossible or even unlikely thing for Nehemiah to have done.

With the arrival of the Hellenistic age, Jewish literature enters a new phase. There is a large amount of Jewish writing extant from the Hellenistic period, some deriving from the community in Jerusalem and Judah, but much from the Jews abroad in Babylonia or in Ptolemaic Egypt. Not much of this literature appears in the Bible, however, for it was not all acceptable to the rabbis of the period after the fall of Jerusalem in AD 70. Ecclesiastes, which was written in Jerusalem in the Ptolemaic period, in the third century BC, is a case in point. It was not overtly infected with Hellenism: indeed, it stood firmly in the Hebraic, biblical tradition, but it evidenced more obviously than previous wisdom literature an intellectual liberalism which was not entirely to the taste of less open minds. More traditionally pietistic is the story of Tobit, which probably came from the eastern diaspora in the third or second century BC, and more traditionally nationalistic was the heroic tale of Judith, who demonstrated how a woman might act to save her country in time of invasion (possibly the Maccabaean struggle was in the author's mind). Intellectually orthodox, but always revealing an interesting mind, is the early second-century BC Wisdom of ben Sira (Ecclesiasticus), which was written in Jerusalem by a learned scribe and teacher, but taken to Alexandria and translated into Greek there by the author's grandson in 128 BC. These works reveal well enough the major religious and theological concerns of third- to second-century BC Judaism, and so far they are not deeply affected by Hellenism. With the book of Daniel, however, which must be dated to about the time of Antiochus IV's death in 164 BC, things appear a little different. The Hellenistic Seleucid empire of Antiochus IV appears as a threat to the Jewish community both politically and religiously, and the book confidently asserts the belief that God will end Antiochus' rule and give final dominion to Israel instead. The book 1 Maccabees – which gives a history of the Maccabees from the standpoint of a supporter of the Hasmonaean rule in the time of John Hyrcanus (134–104 BC) – blames Jews who wished to make political alliances with the Gentiles and adopt their ways of life for the troubles which came upon the Jews in Antiochus' reign, while 2 Maccabees, perhaps written early in the first century BC, sees the struggle as one between Judaism and Hellenism; the author is, in fact, the first to use these terms in opposition to each other (2 Macc.2:21; 4:13). Yet in Alexandria, Judaism and Hellenism were not necessarily seen as being so opposed; the Hebrew scriptures were there translated into Greek, probably for the benefit of a Greek-speaking Jewish community, beginning in the third century BC. The non-biblical letter of Aristeas justifies the translation of the Jewish scriptures in Greek and presents a sympathetic picture of Ptolemy II Philadelphus and his court. A number of Jewish works written in Greek are known from Alexandria; the one that reached the Christian scriptures (the Roman canon and the Protestant Apocrypha) is the so-called Wisdom of Solomon, from the late first century BC. But that Greek versions could be made at

Jerusalem as well as at Alexandria is shown by the colophon to the Greek Esther, which says that this version had been translated by a Jerusalem resident and brought to Egypt, apparently in 77 BC.

This and other literature of the Hellenistic period will be discussed in greater detail later, but it is clear that there was no lack of Jewish writing in the Hellenistic period. Indeed, the early Christian scriptures were all written in Greek, for Christian communities in the Hellenistic-Roman world, and this literature might be seen as a branch of Jewish-Hellenistic literature. The earliest major Christian writer, Paul, was an Hellenistic Jew by origin, and his extant letters are addressed to Hellenistic cities such as Corinth, Philippi, Colossae, and Thessalonica. The letter to the Ephesians may not be from Paul's hand, but it makes the same point. The gospels were probably also destined for Christian communities in different cities, Mark perhaps for Rome and Matthew for Antioch, John for Ephesus, and Luke for Theophilus in some major Hellenistic city. The book of Revelation opens with a set of seven letters addressed to the churches in seven cities in Asia Minor. The letter or treatise to the Hebrews may have some connection with Alexandria. Much is uncertain, except that this early Christian literature belongs to the Mediterranean world of the second half of the first century AD; the most powerful theological statement in the collection is Paul's letter to the Romans, and the first gospel, that of Mark, may have been written from Rome. The thrust of early Christianity (so far as we can tell from the surviving evidence) was mainly westwards, towards the centre of the Roman empire and beyond; Paul voices the desire to go to Spain (Rom.15:28), though whether he ever got there is not known. The record of early Christian witness known as Acts of the Apostles, written by Luke the companion of Paul, ends with Paul preaching in Rome, where later he was put to death in Nero's reign.

Thus the writings which make up the Bible are drawn from over a thousand years of history, from the beginning of the first millennium BC to the early second century of the first millennium AD. There are contributions from Israel and Judah, from Jewish exiles in Babylon, from Jews in Alexandria, from Christians travelling the length and breadth of the Mediterranean. There are contributions from story-tellers, historians, poets, theologians, scribes, preachers, prophets, missionaries, visionaries and others. Copyists, translators, and editors have all left their mark. The successive combination of different writings on one scroll or within a larger collection has affected the interpretation and understanding of the material. The combination of the Christian writings with the Jewish scriptures within the covers of one Bible has greatly affected the way Christians have interpreted the Jewish scriptures; and the realisation among Christian theologians that the early Christian writings arose largely from a Jewish or Hellenistic-Jewish tradition has rightly affected the interpretation of the Christian scriptures. Interpretation of the Bible with any sensitivity to history is a demanding process, requiring many skills and much patience. In particular, it demands many hours' reading, for the Bible is a large volume.

## Bibliography

P.R. Ackroyd and C.F. Evans (eds.), *The Cambridge History of the Bible*, 1: *From the beginning to Jerome* (Cambridge: Cambridge University Press, 1970)

G.W. Anderson (ed.), *Tradition and interpretation* (Oxford: Clarendon Press, 1979)

R. Batey, *New Testament issues* (London: SCM Press, 1970)

R. Beckwith, *The Old Testament canon of the New Testament church* (London: SPCK, 1985)

S. Brown, *The origins of Christianity: a historical introduction to the New Testament* (The Oxford Bible Series. London: Oxford University Press, 1984)

B.S. Childs, *Introduction to the Old Testament as scripture* (London: SCM Press, 1979)

R.E. Clements, *A century of Old Testament study* (Guildford and London: Lutterworth Press, 1976)

R. Coggins, *Introducing the Old Testament* (Oxford: Oxford University Press, 1990)

F.M. Cross, *Canaanite myth and Hebrew epic: essays in the history of the religion of Israel* (Cambridge, Mass., and London: Harvard University Press, 1973)

R. Davidson, *The Old Testament* (London: Hodder and Stoughton, 1964)

M. Fishbane, *Biblical interpretation in ancient Israel* (Oxford: Clarendon Press, 1985)

D.M. Gunn and D.N. Fewell, *Narrative in the Hebrew Bible* (Oxford: Oxford University Press, 1993)

N.C. Habel, *Literary criticism of the Old Testament* (Philadelphia: Fortress Press, 1971)

J.H. Hayes (ed.), *Old Testament form-criticism* (San Antonio: Trinity University Press, 1974)

J.H. Hayes, *An introduction to Old Testament study* (Nashville: Abingdon Press, 1979; London: SCM Press, 1982)

P. Henry, *New directions in New Testament study* (Philadelphia: Westminster Press; London: SCM Press, 1979)

D.A. Knight (ed.), *Tradition and theology in the Old Testament* (London: SPCK, 1977)

D.A. Knight and G.M. Tucker (ed.), *The Hebrew Bible and its modern interpretation* (Philadelphia: Fortress Press; Chico, Cal.: Scholars Press, 1985)

H. Koester, *Introduction to the New Testament, 1: History, culture and religion of the Hellenistic age; 2: History and literature of early Christianity* (Berlin and New York: W. de Gruyter; Philadelphia: Fortress Press, 1982)

E. Krentz, *The historico-critical method* (Philadelphia: Fortress Press; London: SPCK, 1975)

W.J. Kümmel, *Introduction to the New Testament* (London: SCM Press, 1966)

J.M. Miller, *The Old Testament and the historian* (Philadelphia: Fortress Press; London: SPCK, 1976)

C.F.D. Moule, *The birth of the New Testament* (London: A. and C. Black, 1962)

A. Ohler, *Studying the Old Testament from tradition to canon* (Edinburgh: T. and T. Clark, 1985)

L.G. Perdue, L.E. Toombs, and G.L. Johnson, *Archaeology and biblical interpretation; essays in memory of D. Glenn Rose* (Atlanta: John Knox Press, 1987)

R. Rendtorff, *The Old Testament: an introduction* (London: SCM Press, 1985)

J. Soggin, *Introduction to the Old Testament* (Old Testament Library) (London: SCM Press, 1976)

G. von Rad, *Old Testament theology*, 1, 2 (Edinburgh: Oliver and Boyd, 1962, 1965)

W.E. Rast, *Tradition history and the Old Testament* (Philadelphia: Fortress Press, 1972)

G.M. Tucker, *Form criticism of the Old Testament* (Philadelphia: Fortress Press, 1973)

R.C. Walton (ed.), *A basic introduction to the Old Testament* (London: SCM Press, 1980)

R.R. Wilson, *Sociological approaches to the Old Testament* (Philadelphia: Fortress Press, 1984)

A.S. van der Woude (ed.), *The world of the Old Testament* (Bible Handbook, 2: Grand Rapids: W.B. Eerdmans, 1989)

# 3      Faith and Origins

All English Bibles begin with five books entitled respectively Genesis, Exodus, Leviticus, Numbers, and Deuteronomy. These names are transliterations of Greek names (apart from Numbers, which is a translation of the Greek *Arithmoi*), and derive from the Septuagint, the Greek translation of the Hebrew Bible, which dates from the third and second centuries BC. In the Hebrew tradition, the books are named by their opening words: *berešit*, 'in the beginning'; *šemot*, 'names'; *wayyiqra*, 'and he called'; *bemidbar*, 'in the wilderness'; and *debarim*, 'words'. These five books are generally known as the Pentateuch, a transliteration from the Greek adjective 'fivefold'; in the Hebrew tradition they comprise the 'Torah' (prologue to Ecclus., 2 Macc. 15:9), which basically means 'teaching', 'instruction'.

The translation of these books into Greek in the third century BC is the first certain evidence for their existence in their present form; they may be intended by the phrases 'the *tôrah* of Moses' or 'the book of the *tôrah* of Moses', but these phrases do not explicitly refer to five books. Before these references, we have no clear reference in the biblical literature to the Pentateuch as a whole (though we may have reference to the law of Deuteronomy in 2 Kings 22). The question arises, When did the Pentateuch, or the five books of the Torah, first appear as a literary work? Further questions follow. Who put it together in its final form? How was it composed? What were its sources? What purpose did the author(s) have in mind? What does the work reveal of the theological, philosophical or cultural background and presuppositions of the author(s)? What value has the work for the modern historian seeking to unravel the historical origins of Israel? The question of the origins of Israel and of her belief in Yahweh has for over a century been of major interest to scholars and theologians, and answers to it depend on answers to the prior literary questions. As R.E. Clements commented, there has been a basic assumption that 'a foundation of historical fact can be obtained by use of the appropriate methods of study, and that this historical foundation, when known, can shed light upon the true nature of biblical faith' (Clements, 1976, 3). It may be, however, that the appropriate methods of study may reveal less by way of historical foundation than has been expected.

At all events, the problem of the composition of the Pentateuch has always been a major one for students of ancient Israel, and at the risk of repeating yet once more an oft-told tale, it is worth sketching the outlines of the quest.

It is well to begin with a simple outline of the contents of the Pentateuch.

| Gen. | 1–11 | a prefatory account of the world and its peoples |
| | 12–36 | the story of Abraham, Isaac and Jacob |
| | 37–50 | the story of Joseph |
| Exod. | 1 – 15:21 | the deliverance of Israel from Egypt |
| | 15: 22 – 18: 27 | the journey from Egypt to Sinai |
| | 19–24 | the covenant at Sinai |
| | 25–31 | instructions for the making of a sanctuary |
| | 32–34 | Israel's apostasy and the renewal of the covenant |
| | 35–41 | the making of the sanctuary |
| Lev. | 1–7 | instructions for the sacrificial cult |
| | 8–10 | instructions concerning priesthood |
| | 11–15 | laws concerning cleanness and uncleanness |
| | 16 | the Day of Atonement |
| | 17–27 | the 'Holiness Code' (17–26) and other laws |
| Num. | 1–10 | a census of the people: the camp in the wilderness |
| | 10: 11 – 21: 13 | from Sinai to Kadesh |
| | 21: 14 – 36: 13 | from Kadesh to the borders of Canaan |
| Deut. | (presented as Moses' final speech) | |
| | 1: 1 – 4: 43 | review of events |
| | 5–11 | a sermon by Moses |
| | 12–26 | the code of laws |
| | 27–30 | blessings and curses on the obedient and disobedient |
| | 31–34 | Moses' final words, death, and burial. |

This outline suggests that the whole has a certain coherence and plan. It begins at the beginning, rapidly takes the reader via the nations of the world to the single figure of Abraham and the promise that he will be given land and descendants, and ends with those descendants on the borders of their promised inheritance. Internally, the story has direction: it moves from Babylon to Canaan, from Canaan to Egypt, from Egypt to Sinai, from Sinai to Kadesh, from Kadesh to the borders of Canaan. Here the story ends, with Moses' death; but the end is not yet, for the story points ahead to the work of Moses' successor Joshua, who leads Israel into the promised land. Clearly there is a sense in which Genesis-Deuteronomy are preparatory to the greater history of the people of Israel in their land, which follows in the books of Joshua, Judges, Samuel and Kings. To this further development and to the relationship between the Pentateuch and the following books we must return.

There can be no doubt that in its present state and context the Pentateuch forms a sophisticated literary unity, but for many centuries scholars have observed signs of literary composition and speculated on the sources used in the creation of the Pentateuch. The book Deuteronomy has stood out from earliest times as being different; the Greek translators described it as the 'second law', and the Christian scholars Athanasius and Jerome (and many successors) related it to the lawbook found in the Jerusalem Temple in the reign of Josiah (2 Kings 22), and the Jewish scholar Ibn Ezra (died AD 1167) concluded that Moses could not have been the author of the book. (In fact, in the Pentateuch as a whole Moses is credited with writing only 'all the words of the Lord' (i.e. the Ten Commandments, Exod.24:4, cf. Exod.34:27–28), the itinerary of Num.33 (Num.33:2), 'this law' (Deut.31:9,24; presumably the law-code of Deut.12–26), and 'this song' (Deut.31:22, referring to Deut.32); Moses is also told (Exod.17:14) to write an account of Amalek's attack on Israel in a book, but we are not told that he did. The phrase 'the *tôrāh* of Moses' or 'the book of the *tôrāh* of Moses' cannot be taken to imply Moses' personal authorship of the whole Pentateuch.) Over the centuries it has been pointed out that the Pentateuch incorporates such clearly separable passages as 'the book of the covenant' (Exod.21–23), the Decalogue (Exod.20, Deut.5), the Deuteronomic lawcode (Deut.12–26), and various poems and poetic fragments (e.g. Gen.49, Exod.15, Deut.33). It was observed that some stories appeared twice in similar versions (e.g. the stories of Hagar and Ishmael (Gen.16, 21), the story of God's covenant with Abraham (Gen.15, 17), the story of the commissioning of Moses (Exod.3, 6), and it was argued that some stories might have been composed by the interweaving of two parallel accounts (e.g. the story of the flood (Gen.6–9). It was noted that there were discrepancies between the provisions of different lawcodes, which did not, for example, list the same feasts or explain them in the same way (see Exod.23:14–17; Lev.23:1–44; Num.28–29; Deut.16), or give the same rule about the building of altars (Exod.20:24; Deut.12:1–4). And it was also noted that some passages suggested that the author was writing from the viewpoint of an Israelite from the monarchic period, who knew of the Philistines, the Aramaeans, the Edomites, the Moabites, and the Ammonites, who knew of places like Shechem, Beersheba and Bethel, important as cities and sanctuaries in the monarchic period, and who looked back to the time when the Canaanites were in the land (Gen.12:6). The Deuteronomist knew of the age of prophets, and could say (Deut.34:10). 'there has not arisen a prophet since in Israel like Moses'; indeed, the Deuteronomic law itself knows of prophets and kings (Deut.17:18–20, 18:15–22). And lastly, it was observed that the Pentateuch showed evidence of composition by authors apparently differing in style and vocabulary; most obviously, two names were used for Israel's God (Elohim, Yahweh), for the holy mountain (Horeb, Sinai), and for the predecessors of Israel in the land (Amorites, Canaanites).

Such observations and questions led scholars from the seventeenth century onwards to explore the possibility that the present Pentateuch had been compiled from a number of earlier written sources. An early suggestion (based on the observation that two different divine names were used in Genesis) was that Moses had used two primary sources, but it was soon realised that much, at least, of the Pentateuchal material could not be dated earlier than the monarchic period. Some scholars argued that the Pentateuch was compiled from a large number of originally independent stories, poems, laws and other material (the 'fragmentary hypothesis'), and others argued that one basic source (using 'Elohim' for God) had been supplemented by additional material (e.g. the Decalogue, the Book of the Covenant, and those narrative sections using 'Yahweh' for God); this became known as the 'supplementary hypothesis'. In the mid-nineteenth century Ewald presented the view that the Pentateuch, with Joshua, was the work of a series of narrators, each developing the work of his predecessor, the final stage being the incorporation of Deuteronomy. After the work of de Wette, the original independence of the Deuteronomic lawcode became the keystone of all attempts to explain the composition of the Pentateuch, and in particular of the 'documentary hypothesis', which in its classical form developed from the work of scholars like E. Reuss, H.G.A. Ewald, K.H. Graf and Julius Wellhausen.

This documentary hypothesis is particularly associated with Graf and Wellhausen, and is based on the division of the Pentateuch into four underlying documentary sources: Deuteronomy, two sources using 'Elohim' for God (the first, $E^1$, later known as P, visible in Exod.6, and the second $E^2$, later known as E, visible in Exod.3) and one using Yahweh for God ('J'). At first it was thought that the Yahwist was the latest writer, and that the Elohistic material had formed the basic source; but Graf argued in 1865 (following E. Reuss in 1834) that one of the two Elohistic sources, with its priestly legislation, was later than Deuteronomy, and was post-exilic in origin. This was taken up by Wellhausen, whose study of 1 and 2 Samuel (published 1871) had led him to realise that these books do not presuppose the existence and practice of the priestly legislation of $E^1$ (P): the Israelite monarchy had not been (on the evidence of the historical books) the sort of priestly theocracy presented in the legislation of Exodus-Leviticus-Numbers. Wellhausen therefore argued that the Pentateuch was composed of four major literary sources: he dated these by relating what each of them said or presupposed about cultic practice to what Wellhausen had reconstructed of the history of the cult in Israel from the other biblical sources. Deuteronomy, with its demand that the cult be centralised and that sacrifice be offered only at 'the place which the LORD your God will choose out of all your tribes to put his name and make his habitation there' (Deut.12:5), was related to the period of king Josiah in the late seventh century BC, and this dating became determinative for that of the other sources. J and E (which Wellhausen thought had been combined early by a redactor) assumed a variety of altars and sanctuaries, barely distinguished between laity and priests, and linked the cult with daily life and peasant farming. J and E were therefore seen as earlier than Deuteronomy, which confined the cult to Jerusalem, limited sacrificing to priests who were Levites, and combined the feast of Passover with that of Unleavened Bread (Deut.16:1–8; compare Exod.23:15). The fourth documentary source, P, which Wellhausen called 'Q' (from the Latin *Quatuor*, 'four', because according to Wellhausen the document told of four covenants, those made by God with Adam, Noah, Abraham and Moses), was seen as later than Deuteronomy because it presupposed that only one place of worship was in use, saw the Levites as a lower order of priests, and presented a considerably developed cultic calendar (Lev.23). In sum, J and E reflected the practice of the monarchic period, Deuteronomy the seventh century BC, and P the post-exilic period.

Wellhausen began publishing his views in 1876, and over a century later they remain influential. Most scholars accepted the documentary hypothesis in its Wellhausenian form; though there was dismay in some conservative quarters that a Mosaic Pentateuch should have been reduced to a mosaic Pentateuch. The search for documentary sources was not limited to the Pentateuch, but extended to other biblical writings; thus Isaiah, Zechariah, Proverbs and other books were also seen to be composite. The analysis of the Pentateuch did not stop with Wellhausen. Some scholars tried to find the continuation of Wellhausen's four documents in Joshua, Judges, and 1 and 2 Samuel; others subdivided J, E, D, and P into further strands or editions. In particular, there were several attempts to uncover an older source or sources used by and incorporated into J and E; thus Eissfeldt argued for a tenth- ninth-century BC source of nomadic background which he named L ('Lay'), and Fohrer argued for a similar source N ('Nomadic') from the late ninth century BC. Pfeiffer less convincingly proposed a documentary source from Seir or Edom (S), to which he attributed passages from Genesis relating to Edom and the south. These efforts have failed, but they reveal a concern which was manifested by the attempts of other scholars to trace the development of Israelite traditions prior to their appearance in the four documents. The documentary hypothesis had achieved a major breakthrough in the task of reconstructing the history of Israel; it had provided a rational dating for the literary sources for that history. But in dating these sources to the monarchic, exilic and post-exilic periods, it had raised two major questions: first, what evidence could now be found for the early history of Israel, for the time of the patriarchs, the settlement in the land, and the early monarchy; and secondly, what were the sources used by the creators of J, E, D, and P? Were they authors, writing with original creativity? Were they editors, collecting and ordering pre-exilic narratives, laws, poems, and other material? What part did unwritten, oral material play in the creation of the Pentateuch?

The key to the next stage of pentateuchal criticism lay in the close examination of the individual units identified as making up the documentary sources. The question was asked of each unit, 'What type (Fr. *genre*, German *Gattung*) of material is this?' We are accustomed to distinguishing in our own lives between such widely differing literary types as songs, letters, legal judgments, sale documents, political speeches, sermons, prayers, administrative records, genealogies, short stories, and so on; each of these is conventionally cast in different forms and is usually recognisable as much by literary form as by content. Each of these different types of material derives from a different context – entertainment, personal communication, law, politics, worship, and so on. Analysis of the forms or types of literature in question can therefore help us to knowledge of the context or *Sitz im Leben* ('life situation') to which each piece originally belonged (and also to the further recognition that a creative author such as a prophet can use traditional forms in new and original ways).

This approach to the pentateuchal material was adopted by Hermann Gunkel (though before him R.G. Moulton in America had approached the material along these lines), and presented in the preface to Gunkel's commentary on Genesis (1st ed., 1901). Under the name 'Form-criticism' (*Gattungsgeschichte*) this approach controlled the direction of research in biblical literature for the next half-century. Clearly, it is important to ask of the pentateuchal material what kind of literature it is. To recognise that one passage is legend and another of liturgical origin may be to save the historian from treating it as a piece of academic historiography and drawing a host of wrong conclusions from it. This point is of particular importance in connection with the patriarchal stories. Gunkel and others used the categories of legends, sagas, tales and myths. Legends were edifying but unhistorical stories about folk heroes such as Elijah and Elisha; while tales (German *Märchen*) were timeless stories, almost akin to fairy-tales, drawing on such stock themes as rival brothers, or the humble man raised to great honour. Sagas (German *Sagen*) were perhaps a step nearer the historical: they were popular stories about places and people, especially families, with a certain ill-defined basis in historical events. According to Gunkel, sagas 'set out to delight, to elevate, and to touch the heart'. Most of the patriarchal stories might fall into this category. Further comparisons were made with the Norse Sagas, which were literary epics about the Scandinavian colonisation of Iceland. Myth was defined in terms of stories about divine rather than human beings; the example usually quoted is Genesis 6:1–4, in which the sons of God come to earth to marry the daughters of men. Other categories of material relevant to the patriarchal narratives are itineraries and genealogies.

Once one starts classifying material in this way, it is hard to know where to stop, and other forms have been postulated, for example, oracles announcing a birth, tribal sayings, or aetiologies explaining place or personal names. When we move from Genesis into the following books, other forms appear, especially in the legal and cultic material. Since the work of A. Alt ('Origins of Israelite law', 1935; English translation by R.A. Wilson in *Essays on Old Testament History and Religion*, Oxford: Blackwell 1966), most scholars have distinguished between 'casuistic' and 'apodictic' laws. The former appear to be concerned with the affairs of community life in town, village and country, and are cast in the form 'if. . . , then. . . ' (cf. Exod.22:7); the latter are absolute prohibitions, cast in several forms: 'cursed be those who. . . ', cf. Deuteronomy 27:15–21; 'whoever does *x* shall surely die', Exodus 21:15; 'thou shalt not. . . ', Exodus 22:28. The *Sitz im Leben* of the former was perhaps the city gate where the elders met to hold court. The original context of the latter is more difficult to decide. The apodictic laws were perhaps used in ancient times as now in a cultic situation (cf. Deut.27, and also the use of the Ten Commandments in the Christian liturgy), but they may have arisen in a didactic context, for the purpose of instructing the young.

The approach of form-criticism has been applied to all the biblical literature, including the gospels and epistles of the New Testament, and as a result we now have a much clearer idea of the nature of the biblical literature, and to some extent of the society and writers which produced it. Gunkel and others, however, applied these techniques to the Pentateuch in order to probe behind the documentary sources J, E, D, and P. In the case of the patriarchal stories, Gunkel argued that these were originally independent *Sagen*, which had been transmitted orally at first and then collected into cycles of stories which the compilers of the documents took over and linked up, providing an overall framework. Gunkel's identification of the patriarchal stories as *Sagen*, orally transmitted folk-narratives, was derived from Axel Olrik, who had argued that such folk-narratives throughout the world had many characteristics in common and followed certain 'epic laws' – for example, that orally transmitted narratives have a clear structure, a unified plot, a continuous story-line avoiding irrelevant side issues, two main characters, and a final peaceful resolution of the tension of the plot. Other scholars followed A. Jolles in likening the patriarchal stories to the medieval Norse Icelandic sagas, which told in particular of the bloodthirsty conflicts and feuds relating to marriage, possessions, and inheritances within the family. These stories are assumed to have had a history of oral transmission before being committed to writing in the thirteenth century.

There are some difficulties in accepting these parallels; for example, it is not certain that the Icelandic sagas had an oral prehistory, or, if they did, what form this took. Further, it is not clear that Olrik's laws of epic story-telling could not apply equally to written compositions. It was an assumption of Gunkel's that the orally told story was likely to be brief in form and that expansion came when the story was committed to writing, but the opposite can be argued: the writer polishes and compresses, while the oral story teller expands and develops a theme at will, unrestricted by pen and page. However, the assumption that behind the documents J, E, D, and P lay a long history of oral transmission, stretching back vaguely into the pre-monarchic period of Israel, provided an escape from the strait-jacket posed by the documentary hypothesis for those who wished to write the history of early Israel on the basis of the biblical narratives. For the next two or three generations, scholars turned to studying the development of the pre-literary traditions, the transmission history (*Überlieferungsgeschichte*) of the different stories and traditions. Particularly important here was the work of G. von Rad and M. Noth, who in their respective works *Das formgeschichtliche Problem des Hexateuchs* (1938) and *Überlieferungsgeschichte des Pentateuchs* (1948) set out to explain the total historical development of the traditions of ancient Israel up to the point of the present form of the Pentateuch (Noth) or the Hexateuch (von Rad).

G. von Rad was particularly concerned to show how the individual units of tradition postulated by the work of Gunkel and others and the documentary sources postulated by Wellhausen and others had come together into the major literary unity of the Hexateuch. Von Rad argued for the prime importance of the Yahwist, hitherto seen merely as the compiler of the document J. Von Rad saw him as responsible for bringing together in a creative manner two collections or streams of tradition. One collection was the Sinai narrative, which since Wellhausen had been seen as a literary intrusion (Exod.19 – Num.11) into the narratives of the Israelites' wanderings in the wilderness. Von Rad believed that the Sinai tradition, with its covenant theme, was originally celebrated at Shechem (also associated with covenant-making, cf. Josh.24) at the autumn Feast of Booths. The other collection was the material devoted to the themes of the promises to the patriarchs, the exodus from Egypt, and the settlement in Palestine, which von Rad believed had become unified at an early stage. He found his evidence for this in what he defined as early credal statements preserved in

Deuteronomy 26:5–9, 6:20–24, and Joshua 24:2–13. The fact that these statements lacked any reference to the Sinai event suggested that in the tradition they represented, the Sinai event was not commemorated. These statements summarised for von Rad the traditions preserved by the southern tribes and celebrated annually at the Feast of Weeks at the sanctuary of Gilgal near Jericho. It was the Yahwist who combined these two complexes of tradition, placing the Sinai material between the exodus and wilderness themes, adding a number of patriarchal stories, and prefacing the whole with the primeval history of Genesis 1–11.

Von Rad dated the Yahwist's work to the reign of Solomon, arguing that the author saw God's promises to the patriarchs fulfilled in the successes of David's reign. The Yahwist is therefore using earlier material which had been preserved in Israel's worship at the cultic centres of Shechem and Gilgal. In this emphasis on the cult as the institution through which Israel's early traditions were preserved and transmitted, von Rad was dependent on the work of Albrecht Alt, who had argued for the early association of the original Israelite settlers and their religious cult of the gods of their ancestors with the second-millennium BC Canaanite sanctuaries of the land. That is, from almost the beginning of Israelite presence in Canaan the sanctuaries and their cult had provided a home for the transmission of Israelite tradition, and these sanctuaries remained important into the monarchic period.

Noth followed Alt and von Rad in assuming that the pentateuchal traditions were rooted in confessions of faith recited in the cult, and argued that these traditions, as individual units, were gathered into major complexes, focused around five main themes. The most important of these themes was that of Yahweh's guidance of Israel out of Egypt. The other four were the guidance of Israel into the arable land (different tribal groups each had their own particular memories), the promise to the patriarchs (the material deriving from the cultic sanctuaries of the early tribal groups), guidance in the wilderness (these traditions derived from southern tribes living on the edge of the wilderness), and the revelation at Sinai (the last material to be added). Different groups handed down their own traditions, which took some time to become the heritage of all Israel; this happened only as the different groups settled together on the land and developed a common identity as the people Israel. Noth believed that these five themes first came together in a now lost composition he called G ('*Grundlage*'), which he saw as the basis of the documentary sources J and E and dated to the late pre-monarchic period. Noth saw this material as moving out of its original cultic context into the lay context of popular story-telling and so, in the early monarchic period, into the hands of the individual authors of the documents.

The work of Gunkel, Alt, von Rad and Noth brought about a new understanding of the early traditions of Israel. Whereas Wellhausen's era had established that the traditions of Israel's patriarchs, exodus, wilderness wanderings, and settlement belonged as literature to the eighth and following centuries BC, Gunkel and his successors drew a picture of a history of oral traditions deriving ultimately from small local tribal or clan groups, combining and developing into major complexes of tradition, and finally being put into written form. All this took place over a period of centuries. When the process began depended upon where one dated the patriarchal period (it was variously dated between the beginnings of the Middle Bronze Age to the end of the Late Bronze Age, i.e., *c.* 2200–1200 BC). There was an assumption that the patriarchal age saw the arrival in Canaan of semi-nomadic Semitic groups, perhaps related to the Amorites of Syria, of whom the biblical Israelites were seen as descendants (cf. Ezek.16:3, though it is hardly certain that one should take this piece of prophetic invective as containing pure history). Subsequent research, however, both archaeological and literary, has made scholars less happy either to identify the patriarchs and their families too readily with any supposed semi-nomadic Semitic incomers of the second millennium BC, or to see the patriarchal stories as embodying a centuries-old, unchanging oral tradition. Even while most scholars still accepted the last presupposition, von Rad's supposed early, independent credal statements came under attack and were reinterpreted as Deuteronomic summaries of the story (summaries which *assumed* the existence of the Sinai covenant) rather than as a pre-existent framework for it. Similarly, the separation of the Exodus and Sinai traditions by von Rad and Noth seemed increasingly unconvincing to many scholars. Both traditions were inescapably attached to the figure of Moses and the activity of Yahweh, as indeed were some of the traditions of Israel in the wilderness. The thematic groupings of material under the headings of promise to the patriarchs, the guidance of Israel out of Egypt, the revelation at Sinai, the guidance in the wilderness, and the guidance into the promised land may not have been the result of the accumulation of material around originally distinct kernels of tradition so much as the editorial arrangement by which varied incidents and traditions were grouped. The assumption that material was transmitted through Canaanite cultic centres taken over by Israelite groups to develop into credal confessions and thence to historiography, though in some ways plausible, remains as assumption. We know far too little for certain about the cultic activities of sanctuaries such as Gilgal, Dan, Bethel, and Beersheba in the eleventh-tenth centuries BC in the first place, and there is increasing doubt about the necessary antiquity of the traditions credited by von Rad and Noth to these cultic, oral lines of transmission. Indeed, with reference to the possibility of oral sources lying behind the written narratives of the Pentateuch, R.N. Whybray has recently stated firmly that

> firstly, there is no assured way of distinguishing written from orally based literature; and secondly, even if it were possible to identify oral traditions in the Pentateuchal narratives, none of the techniques which has been devised is capable of demonstrating the *antiquity* of such traditions in relation to the date of the final completion of the Pentateuch.
>
> (*The making of the Pentateuch*, 236)

Whybray notes that 'since the techniques enumerated by Olrik's epic laws could be, and probably were, used by writers as well as by oral narrators, the "laws" cannot be used to prove the oral origin of any particular text' (ibid., 216); that study of the techniques of modern oral narrators has shown that they use considerable freedom in the telling and retelling of their stories, which are unlikely to retain a fixed form for very long, if at all (ibid., 217–18); that 'there is no evidence in the Old Testament for the existence of a class of professional story-tellers in ancient Israel' (ibid., 218); and that we cannot argue (as some Scandinavian scholars have done) that 'a large part of the Pentateuchal narratives were formed, transmitted and developed orally from very ancient times because writing was not used for such purposes in the ancient Near Eastern world until a later period (in the case of Israel, until the sixth century BC)' (ibid., 215), for this makes the gratuitous assumption that the pentateuchal narratives are early, and a further assumption that oral recitation could not coexist with a written text.

In short, the various attempts to discover ancient, pre-literary traditions underlying the written text of the pentateuchal narratives has recently come under serious attack. Whybray is prepared to concede that the author of the Pentateuch (he thinks of a single author) used oral traditions and folk-tales, but finds no reason to suppose that this material was necessarily very ancient (ibid., 239): 'the only tradition which can safely be regarded as ancient is that of the Exodus' (p.241), but even this 'has been buried in an enormously complex body of narrative: the deliverance from Egypt and the crossing of the Red Sea are themes or motifs rather than ancient narratives' (p.242).

If the possibility of the existence in Genesis-Numbers of ancient oral narratives, preserving traditions unchanged from the times of the patriarchs, the exodus, the wilderness wanderings and the entry to the promised land, is ruled out, we are forced back to studying the literary document that is the Pentateuch and asking once again when it was written, what were its sources, and what is its value to the historian of ancient Israel. Renewed attention to the Pentateuch has been focused on the theological aims of its editors or editor, and probably has its origins in von Rad's emphasis on the theological aims of the Yahwist, which he saw as playing a vital role in the construction of the Hexateuch.

Von Rad was important here because he was one of the first to insist that the Yahwist was not just a compiler or editor, but a theologian with a positive programme. Von Rad saw the Yahwist as turning the old cultic traditions of Israel into literature, and giving 'to the entire Hexateuch its form and compass' (Genesis 16–17). It was the Yahwist who saw God's providence as active in history rather than in cultic institutions, and who presented the events of David's reign as Yahweh's fulfilment of his promises to Israel's ancestors the patriarchs. This understanding of the Yahwist as a theologian was influential and prepared the way for many subsequent studies (e.g. P. Ellis, H. W. Wolff); but von Rad's dating of the Yahwist to the mid-tenth century BC was earlier than generally conceded. The Yahwist was more usually held to date from the ninth or eighth century BC and to reflect the religious and cultic attitudes of the monarchic period before the influence of the eighth-century BC prophetic movement.

A strong attack on this early monarchic dating of the Yahwist came from John van Seters (1975), who, studying the Abraham tradition in Genesis, argued that it developed in three stages. He saw its base in folk-tale material visible behind the three episodes of Genesis 12:10–20; 16; and 21. (The alternative versions of Gen.12:10–20 found in Gen.20 and 26, however, do not indicate to van Seters variant oral traditions, but reveal literary development by successive editors.) This material passed through two 'pre-J' editorial stages before it was taken over in the exilic period by the Yahwist, who was responsible for the bulk of the Abrahamic material. Although the Abrahamic tradition is earlier in origin than the exilic period (van Seters does not make clear how much earlier), nevertheless it was in his view precisely the circumstances of the exilic period that made the themes of Yahweh's promises to Abraham and covenant with him, Abraham's journey from Ur of the Chaldees (Babylonians) to the promised land, relevant to the Yahwist and his audience. Van Seters pointed to the fact that while the pre-exilic literature on the whole ignores the patriarchs, it is in the work of the exilic Second Isaiah that Israel's election is linked with reference to Israel's patriarchal ancestors, Abraham and Jacob. In a further book (1983), van Seters went on to compare the historical work of the Yahwist in the sixth century BC with the historiography of the early Greek historian Herodotus in the mid-fifth century BC and his contemporaries and predecessors. Both Herodotus and the Yahwist might be said to be providing histories aimed at encouraging their respective people's national pride at a time of threat from large empires (Babylon in Judah's case, Persia in the case of the Greeks), and both, it is argued, used similar literary compositional techniques.

Van Seters' work raised once again the importance of examining the literary composition of the Pentateuch (though it remained basically tied to the old structures of a pre-literary oral tradition and a form of the documentary hypothesis). It focused on the fact that it was in the exilic period that the pentateuchal themes had particular relevance for the people of Israel. Wellhausen and his followers had argued that the last of the four major documentary sources of the Pentateuch, P, reflected the concerns of the late exilic or post-exilic period; the Priestly strand (some saw it as a separate document, others as an editorial overlay) was seen as the most easily separable layer of the Pentateuch, distinguishable by vocabulary, style and its carefully ordered contents. It presented the early history of Israel as a series of important stages: the creation, the flood, the covenant with Abraham, the first Passover, the preparation of the Tabernacle in the wilderness, and perhaps (in Joshua) the entry to the land. These stages were connected by genealogies and marked by certain demands made by God of his people: the keeping of the sabbath (Gen.1:1 – 2:4; creation), the prohibition of blood (Gen.9:1–7; the flood), circumcision (Gen.17; the covenant with Abraham), the Passover ritual (Exod.12–13), the building of a sanctuary (Exod.25–31, 34–40) and the consecration of a priesthood (Lev.8–9), and the various demands of cultic cleanliness. In P, God is a transcendent God who reveals his glory to Moses alone (Exod.34:29), visits the sanctuary with his glory, and contacts his people through the cult and cult personnel. Israel must respond by walking blamelessly like Abraham and keeping the cultic laws: failures are atoned for by the sacrificial system. This picture of Israel as a sacred community, run by priests, not kings, was of relevance to post-exilic rather than pre-exilic

Israel. F.M. Cross argued that P was 'a program written in preparation for and in hope of the restoration of Israel' (1973, 325); W. Brueggeman emphasised the importance of the theme of blessing in P (Gen.1:28; 8:17; 9:1,7; 17:2; 28:1–4), arguing that P looked forward to Israel's regaining the land of Canaan and re-experiencing the first conquest. The Priestly editor or author was thus reinterpreting Israel's older traditions preserved in the JE documents to give a legal and spiritual foundation for the coming post-exilic period.

It cannot be denied that this material, whether ascribed to a separate document P or (as is more likely) to an overall editing of the pentateuchal material, makes a large contribution to the contents of the Pentateuch, and that its theology exerts a controlling influence. In recent years, given that the concerns of both the Yahwist and of the Priestly author have been seen to relate to the exilic period, there has been a growing tendency to look at the themes visible in the Pentateuch as it stands and to see the Pentateuch as a complete, unified literary work, and then to ask further questions about how this literary work was composed. The theological unity and the literary unity of the Pentateuch go hand in hand. It is not denied that the Pentateuch had sources, perhaps oral as well as literary, and a history of composition; but recent research into both has suggested that the composition of the Pentateuch did not necessarily take place through a long history of oral tradition followed by a sequence of literary documents produced over several centuries. The attack on the Wellhausenian documentary hypothesis was based on the unsatisfactory nature of the supposedly consistent theologies attributed to such 'documents' as J and P. In particular, it was not clear that a consistent theology could be shown to run throughout the material attributed to the Yahwist, and Rendtorff (1977) argued that such documents as J, E, P never existed, and that the Pentateuch was put together by the combination of several separate units or blocks of material. Each of these units was in itself a complex of traditions focused on a distinct theological theme (here one is reminded strongly of Noth's five themes); for example, the stories of Abraham, Isaac and Jacob formed a large unit, arising and developing quite independently of the following unit of the sojourn in Egypt and the exodus. The patriarchal stories do not look forward to or presuppose the coming events of the stay in Egypt, the plagues and the exodus (apart from certain later linking cross-references), and these stories in turn do not reveal knowledge of the earlier promises of land and people which run like a thread through the patriarchal stories. Indeed, Rendtorff makes the strong point that this theme of promise so prominent in Genesis is limited to the patriarchal stories, and cannot be seen as a theme running through a 'Yahwistic' source and providing a unifying thread. Further research has suggested that Genesis 1–11 was another independent grouping of material, and a strong case could be made out (as has been clear since Wellhausen's work) for the Sinai unit, as also for the wilderness and conquest narratives. However, some links between these units – for example, the figure of Moses in the exodus, Sinai and wilderness stories, or the hint of the exodus story in Genesis 12:10–20 – cannot be denied, and the relationship between the proposed units remains far from clear. This thesis also raises the question of how the separate units acquired their framework or developed the story-line that now joins them into a connected narrative. If this was the work of the Deuteronomic redactor in the exilic or early post-exilic period (the Deuteronomic hand is seen in such passages as Gen.15:13–16; 50:24; Exod.1:6;8; 32:13; 33:1; Num.14:23; 20:14–16; 32:11), was he using the sort of outlines presented in Deuteronomy 26:5–11 and Joshua 24:2–13 (von Rad's credal summaries)?

Recent scholarship therefore has tended to focus on the stage at which the Pentateuch was brought together into one literary unit. This stage used to be attributed to the Priestly editor. Rendtorff suggested that the separate units had an overall unity imposed on them by a Deuteronomic editorial stratum, Schmid by a late 'Yahwist' editor. That the process was late and belongs to the late seventh or early sixth century BC is generally agreed on the grounds (long-observed) that there is little or no sign of the patriarchal narratives or of the achievements of Moses in the pre-exilic prophets or other pre-exilic literature (apart from references to Jacob and the wilderness tradition in Hosea); it is not until the work of Ezekiel (597–571 BC or Second Isaiah (*c.* 550–540 BC) that the patriarchal, exodus and wilderness traditions are used. There are a number of indications that the Pentateuch draws on prophetic and Deuteronomic language and theology (rather than vice versa), as for example in the presentation of various covenants, the idea of the covenant being (it is argued) primarily Deuteronomic and dating from the seventh-sixth centuries BC. Indeed, this argument has been taken further, and the suggestion made that Genesis-Numbers was conceived as an introduction or prologue to the Deuteronomistic History (which would explain its position in the canon, its Deuteronomic editing, and the fact that its story appears to be unfinished, leaving Israel on the edge of the promised land at the end of Numbers and Deuteronomy). Overall, it is generally agreed that the Pentateuch as a whole, with its themes of promise of land, redemption from bondage, covenant relationship between Yahweh and Israel, the establishment of a sanctuary and a priesthood, and the provision of rules for a cultic community about to enter its homeland, meets very well the needs of the exiled Jewish community of the sixth century BC (cf. D. Clines, quoted below).

Professor R.N. Whybray has recently argued that once one takes the view that 'the Pentateuch is basically a single literary work – whether its author is called 'late J' or Deuteronomist, and whether or not its composition was preceded by a long period of gradual development of the material' (loc.cit. p.232), there is 'no reason why (allowing for the possibility of a few additions) the *first* edition of the Pentateuch as a comprehensive work should not also have been the *final* edition, a work composed by a single historian' (pp.232f.). Whybray sees the author both using folk-material and creating his own material when he wished, happily 'joining units of narrative loosely together without attempting to produce smooth continuous narrative' (p.240), following the canons of ancient rather than modern historians. Where Wellhausen and Noth and others analysed sources and documents from the monarchic age, and the history of independent pre-literary oral traditions from the settlement period, Whybray and T. Thompson demonstrate the connecting links and compositional skills of the author from the exilic period, and claim no great antiquity or historical value for the material.

However, this discussion, as must be apparent, has focused almost entirely on the narrative parts of the Pentateuch, and has ignored the large amount of legal and cultic material and the occasional poems incorporated into the narrative. There can be no doubt that the editors or author of the Pentateuch incorporated important material other than folk-tales or fiction. There are a number of poems and poetic fragments of uncertain origin and date, including the Testament of Jacob (Gen.49), the Song of Miriam (Exod.15), the oracles of Balaam (Num.23–24), the Song of Moses (Deut.32), the Testament of Moses (Deut.33), oracles about Jacob and Esau (Gen.27:27–29, 39f.), the Song of the Well (Num.21:17f.), the Song of Heshbon (Num.21:27–30), and the denunciation of Amalek (Exod.17:16). These poems must inevitably be compared with similar poetic material outside the Pentateuch (e.g., the Song of Deborah, Jud.5; the prayer of Habakkuk, Hab.3; and the Psalms), and individual pieces dated on internal evidence. D.N. Freedman, following the lead of W.F. Albright, has dated the Song of Miriam (along with Ps.29 and Jud.5) to the twelfth century BC, the Testament of Jacob (Gen.49), the oracles of Balaam (Num.23–24), and the Testament of Moses (Deut.33), to the eleventh century BC, and Deuteronomy 32 and certain other poetic material from the books of Samuel and the Psalms to the tenth century BC, largely on the basis of the distribution in these poems of divine names and titles. From this evidence Freedman then reconstructs the development of Israel's early religion from the patriarchal worship of El (Shaddai) (cf. Gen.49) to Mosaic Yahwism and the belief in the incomparable Yahweh of Sinai who rescued his people at the Red Sea (Exod.15), and thence to the synthesis of patriarchal and Mosaic traditions seen in the oracles of Balaam and the Testament of Moses (Num.23–24, Deut.33). The problem is that Freedman's early dating of these poems is far from secure, his historical conclusions from them are speculative, and his argument is circular (e.g. the Song of Moses dates to the twelfth century BC because it uses 'Yahweh' exclusively and predominantly, and therefore reflects the late thirteenth- to twelfth-century BC Yahwism of the age of Moses). If, however, these poems are independent pieces incorporated by the author or editor of the Pentateuch, their evidence needs careful scrutiny. Internal evidence suggests that each of these poems might equally belong to the monarchic as to the pre-monarchic era, even if they contain some archaic material.

The law codes of ancient Israel are on any showing important evidence for the nature of Israelite society, and the author or editor of the Pentateuch has incorporated a large amount of matter witnessing to civil law and cultic practice in Israel (Exod.20:21–23; 25:1 – 31:17; 35–40; Lev.1–27; Num.1:1 – 10:10; 15; 17–19; 28–36; Deut.12–26). Since Moses was regarded in later Israelite tradition as a lawgiver (see especially the books of Joshua, 1 and 2 Kings, 1 and 2 Chronicles, Ezra, Nehemiah, Dan.9:11, Mal.4:4), it is not surprising that the legal material preserved from ancient Israel should be attached in this way to the stories about Moses. Much of this material, however, at least in its present form, derives from a time long after Moses, reflecting affairs of daily life and law and liturgy from the period of the monarchy or even later. Thus, for example, the provisions of Exodus 21–23 relate to an established agricultural society; the Egyptian experience is long past and commemorated in festivals whose concerns are agricultural; and first-fruit offerings are directed to be taken to the house of the Lord, by which is probably meant the Jerusalem temple. The Deuteronomic code (Deut.12–26) has often been associated with the reforming activities of King Josiah of Judah (640–608 BC), and even if the Deuteronomic description of how a king should behave is somewhat idealistic (Deut.17:14–20), it reveals knowledge of Israelite tradition about the development of monarchy in Israel (cf. 1 Sam.8:5) and about the behaviour of Solomon (cf. 1 Kings 10:28, 11:1) and of Josiah (2 Kings 23:1–3). The cultic laws in Exodus 25–31, 35–40, Leviticus 1–27, and the book of Numbers presuppose a highly developed and regulated cult and priesthood, probably reflecting late monarchic practice at the Jerusalem temple or envisaging the restoration of the cult in the post-exilic period.

It must be clear from this sketch of the contents and composition of the Pentateuch that it is no longer possible, if it ever was, to use the pentateuchal narratives as direct evidence for the early history of Israel. Wellhausen and others demonstrated that they were put together in the monarchic and exilic ages and reflected the concerns of those ages; Gunkel and his successors tried to show that pre-literary oral tradition of great antiquity containing nuggets of information about Israel's settlement period had been incorporated into the literary, documentary tradition, but more recent research has thrown doubt on the antiquity of the folk-lore used by the Pentateuch and has emphasised that the Pentateuch in its final and perhaps even its first form derives from the exilic period and reflects the theological concerns of the seventh-sixth centuries BC. For knowledge of earlier periods we are dependent on what we can glean from the study of whatever may have been preserved by way of laws and poetry, and from the study of the other historical and prophetic works of the Old Testament, as well as from external sources such as Assyrian and Babylonian records, and from the evidence provided by archaeological surveys and excavations. Indeed, for the period of settlement in the Late Bronze and Early Iron Ages, archaeological research provides the primary and sometimes the only evidence. The Pentateuch in short can tell us little or nothing about Palestine in the second millennium BC; it is not that sort of book.

What the Pentateuch does give us is a picture of how Israelites of the exilic period understood themselves. In general, they saw themselves as the descendants of people related to the Aramaeans of Syria and Iraq, and as the descendants of slaves who had escaped from Egypt, and who knew their deity, Yahweh, as one who could be met at Mount Sinai. The narratives as they stand present this as the historical experience of all Israel, and in so doing reflect the concern of Israel for her political and religious unity and identity, especially in the exilic period. Thus David Clines (*The Theme of the Pentateuch, JSOT* Supplement Series 10 (Sheffield 1978)) finds the Pentateuch as a whole the product of the Babylonian exile, and the purpose of the work related to that origin:

> Wherever exilic Jewry opens the Pentateuch, it finds itself. Gen.1–11. . . are heard in exile as a story of God and Israel. The dispersion of the nations (Gen.11) is Israel's

own diaspora, the flood is the uncreation of Israel's life at the time of the destruction of Jerusalem, and the judgments of God upon primeval disobedience, murder, lust and hubris are his righteous judgments upon sinful Israel... In the patriarchal narratives, exilic Israel reads not only the lives of its ancestors but also its own life story... The bondage in Egypt is their own bondage in Babylon, and the exodus past becomes the exodus that is yet to be. Above all, in the books of Exodus and Leviticus, exilic Israel, in whatever measure it is listening to its Torah, hears anew the divine commands from Sinai and responds with an 'All that Yahweh has spoken we will do'... Numbers and Deuteronomy function among exilic Jewry, not primarily as the story of its past life, but as a dream for its future... The march across the desert, without ark of the covenant, fire or cloud, but nonetheless with devoted objects for the temple (cf. Ezr.1:5–11; 8:24–34), will be, as at the first, a divinely led procession... Nevertheless, even though Deuteronomy ends with the still potent blessing of Moses upon the tribes, and even though it is taken for granted throughout the book that Israel *will* enter the land, Moses' last speeches have emphasised that even on the brink of fulfilment of this third promise Israel is still open to the possibility of curse as well as blessing (Deut.27:11–28:68; 29:1 EVV.29:2–30:19; 31:26–29).

The Pentateuchal theme, in its several forms, functioned among the exiles as an interpretation of their history, a summons to obedience in their present, and a hope that led to action. Literature arising out of a vast array of historical situations had been welded into a new unity with a definite and effective function.

(pp.98–100)

All this is not to say that Genesis-Numbers is not 'history'; after all, what is history? History is the representation of the past as it is understood in the present and in the light of the concerns of the present. The author or authors of the Pentateuch were representing the outlines of Israel's beginnings, so far as they were known to them, to meet the concerns of their own age. They were concerned above all with the life and preservation of a community after the destruction of the kingdoms of Israel and Judah in 721 BC and 587 BC, and the themes of the Pentateuch – the relationship of the people with their God Yahweh, the promise of land and descendants, the covenant offered by God and the response required to it, the trials of the wilderness, the preparation for the future settlement in Israel – are what create the Pentateuch and the shape of the Pentateuchal history.

## Bibliography

H. Gunkel, *The legends of Genesis: the biblical saga and history* (New York: Schocken Books, 1964)

S.H. Hooke, *Middle eastern mythology from the Assyrians to the Hebrews* (Harmondsworth: Penguin, 1963)

E.W. Nicholson, *Exodus and Sinai in history and tradition* (Oxford: Blackwell, 1973)

M. Noth, *The laws in the Pentateuch and other studies* (Edinburgh and London: Oliver and Boyd, 1966)

G. von Rad, *The problem of the Hexateuch and other essays* (Edinburgh and London: Oliver and Boyd, 1966)

R. Rendtorff, *The problem of the process of transmission in the Pentateuch* (Sheffield: JSOT Press, 1990)

J. van Seters, *Abraham in history and tradition* (New Haven and London: Yale University Press, 1975)

T.L. Thompson, *The historicity of the Patriarchal narratives: the quest for the historical Abraham* (Berlin and New York: W. de Gruyter, 1974)

T.L. Thompson, *The origin tradition of ancient Israel*, 1: *The literary formation of Genesis and Exodus 1–23* (Sheffield: JSOT Supplement Series 55, 1987)

T.L. Thompson, *Early history of the Israelite people from the written and archaeological sources* (Leiden: E.J. Brill, 1992)

C. Westermann, *Genesis 1–11: a commentary; Genesis 12–36: a commentary; Genesis 37–50: a commentary* (London: SPCK, 1984, 1986, 1987)

C. Westermann, *The promises to the fathers: studies on the patriarchal narratives* (Philadelphia: Fortress Press, 1976)

R.N. Whybray, *The making of the Pentateuch: a methodological study* (Sheffield: JSOT Supplement Series 53, 1987)

# 4   The Importance
# of the Land

In Jewish tradition, the land of Israel has always been especially important. The Jewish people identified itself in biblical times as the people of their god, Yahweh:

> '. . .if you will obey my voice and keep my covenant, you shall be my own possession among all peoples; for all the earth is mine, and you shall be to me a kingdom of priests and a holy nation.' (Exod.19:5–6)

But the Israelites believed that, as part of the process of making them a holy nation, God had promised them possession of a land of their own. In Genesis, the story of Israel is presented in terms of the story of Abraham, and this begins with the Lord saying to Abraham:

> 'Go from your country and your kindred and your father's house to the land that I will show you. And I will make of you a great nation.' (Gen.12:1)

This promise of land is repeated to Abraham (15:18), Isaac (26:2–5), Jacob (28:13–15), Moses (Exod.3:7–8), and Joshua (Josh.1:3–5), and the land is described in glowing terms in Deuteronomy 8:7–10:

> 'For the LORD your God is bringing you into a good land, a land of brooks of water, of fountains and springs, flowing forth in valleys and hills, a land of wheat and barley, of vines and fig trees and pomegranates, a land of olive trees and honey, a land in which you will eat bread without scarcity, in which you will lack nothing, a land whose stones are iron, and out of whose hills you can dig copper.'

This theme recurs in the Psalms, and was celebrated in the worship of Israel, as is clear from the beautiful words of Psalm 65:9–13, and the references to God's gift of a land 'flowing with milk and honey' in the description of how Israelites celebrated the festival of First Fruits (Deut.26:1–11). God's settlement of Israel in the land is hymned in Psalm 78:54–55, as part of the celebration of the 'glorious deeds' of God on Israel's behalf:

> And he brought them to his holy land,
> to the mountain which his right hand had won.
> He drove out nations before them;
> he apportioned them for a possession
> and settled the tribes of Israel in their tents.

Compare Psalm 105:43–44:

> So he led forth his people with joy,
> his chosen ones with singing.
> And he gave them the lands of the nations;
> and they took possession of the fruit of the peoples' toil,
> to the end that they should keep his statutes,
> and observe his laws.

The Israelite tradition that God had brought his people into the land, evicting other peoples to make room for them, is presented briefly in Psalms 80:8 and 105:44, and at length in the books of Joshua and Judges. After the death of Moses at the end of the book Deuteronomy, the Bible continues in the book Joshua with an account of how the Israelites, under the leadership of Moses' successor Joshua, conquered the land west of the Jordan and distributed it among ten (or nine and a half) of the twelve tribes (the remaining two and a half tribes were given land east of the Jordan). In the first major section of the book (chapters 1–12), we read of the spies' visit to Jericho, from which they report that 'Truly the LORD has given all the land into our hands' (2:24). The Israelites cross the Jordan (which, like the Red Sea earlier, conveniently dries up for the crossing) (3:1 – 5:1); they circumcise the new generation of males born in the wilderness (5:2–7) and eat the Passover (5:8–12); the commander of the Lord's army appears to Joshua, presumably as a sign of divine support (5:13–15); the Israelites destroy Jericho (ch.6), but fail to capture Ai, because one man has taken plunder for himself at Jericho instead of destroying it as a thing devoted to God (ch.7; see 7:13, 15 and 6:18–19). The Israelites capture Ai on the second attempt (having duly executed the offender) (8:1–29). An altar is built on Mount Ebal in the centre of the land, and the law of Moses is written down, and read out (8:30–35). The people of the town of Gibeon, frightened by the success of Joshua at Jericho and Ai, trick the Israelites into making a pact (a 'covenant') with them (ch.9), but are forced to become 'hewers of wood and drawers of water' to Israel, i.e., second-class citizens. Joshua defeats a coalition of kings in the south (ch.10), and another coalition in the north (ch.11). The conclusion of the matter is given in 11:16–20:

> So Joshua took all that land, the hill country and all the Negeb and all the land of Goshen and the lowland and the Arabah and the hill country of Israel and its lowland from Mount Halak, that rises towards Seir, as far as Baalgad in the valley of Lebanon below Mount Hermon. And he took all their kings, and smote them, and put them to death. Joshua made war a long time with all those kings. There was not a city that made peace with the people of Israel, except the Hivites, the inhabitants of Gibeon; they took all in battle. For it was the LORD's doing to harden their hearts that they should come against Israel in battle, in order that they should be utterly destroyed, and should receive. no mercy but be exterminated, as the LORD commanded Moses.

In these chapters, the author presents the Israelites as entering the land and seizing it by military conquest, beginning in the centre and then turning to the south and north, and making a thorough job of destroying the previous inhabitants, with a few exceptions (the family of Rahab the harlot, who had helped the Israelites at Jericho, and the people of Gibeon). The land is thus thoroughly cleansed of all God's opponents. The conquest is described as sanctioned and commanded by God, and is accompanied by religious and ritual acts. For example, the Ark of the Covenant (a piece of portable cultic furniture, later believed to contain the two tablets on which were written the Ten Commandments) is carried in procession at the crossing of the River Jordan; the flow of the water is stopped as long as the priests carrying the Ark stand in the river, and stones are set up at Gilgal (in monarchic times an Israelite sanctuary) to commemorate the event. The entry to the promised land is marked by the circumcision of the uncircumcised males, and by the celebration of the Passover. The conquest proper is prefaced by the appearance of the commander of the Lord's army, an angelic figure. The ritual aspect is particularly prominent at Jericho in ch.6; for seven days the army circle the city, while the priests process with the Ark and blow their trumpets. On the seventh day they repeat this procedure seven times, and 'the wall fell down flat'. The people fail to capture Ai because one of their number has failed to observe the law of holy war imposed by the Lord, that all booty shall be 'devoted', i.e., consecrated to God by destruction.

In short, the conquest is presented as a religious event, accompanied by various rituals, completely successful and in accord with the commands of God. The author is particularly concerned to note the continuing importance of these events for his own time; thus he observes that the stones at Gilgal 'are there to this day' (4:9); 'the name of that place is called Gilgal to this day' (5:9); Rahab (or her family) 'dwelt in Israel to this day' (6:25); the place where Achan was punished is called the Valley of Achor 'to this day' (7:26); Joshua made Ai a heap of ruins 'as it is to this day' (8:28); and the Gibeonites became hewers of wood and drawers of water 'to continue to this day' (9:27).

The conquest is followed by the distribution of the captured land among the tribes to whom it has been allotted (Josh.13:6). The tribes of Reuben, Gad, and half the tribe of Manasseh receive land east of the Jordan (13:14–33). Land is apportioned to Caleb and Judah (14:6 – 15:63), to the people of Joseph (the tribes of Ephraim and Manasseh) (16:1–11), first to Ephraim (16:5–10) and then to the second half of Manasseh (17:1–17), Benjamin (18:11–28), Simeon 'in the midst of the inheritance of the tribe of Judah' (19:1–9), Zebulun (19:10–16), Issachar (19:17–23), Asher (19:24–31), Naphtali (19:32–39), Dan (19:40–48), and a particular inheritance to Joshua (19:49–50). This is followed by the establishment of 'cities of refuge' (ch.20), to which those guilty of manslaughter may flee, and of an inheritance for the otherwise landless Levites, the priestly tribe (ch.21). The Reubenites, Gadites, and the half-tribe of Manasseh are settled onto their allotted land in Transjordan (ch.22); by the river Jordan they erect an altar, which causes some diplomatic embarrassment. (In the Deuteronomic theological tradition, to which the author or editor of the book of Joshua belonged, only one altar was permitted to which offerings could be brought, and this was to be 'at the place which the LORD will choose in one of your tribes' (Deut.12:14); this altar was to be the one at the Jerusalem temple. The Transjordanian tribes are told, 'do not rebel against the LORD, or make us rebels by building yourselves an altar other than the altar of the LORD our God' (Josh.22:19), and the Transjordanian tribes tactfully explain that this new altar is not for sacrifice but as a witness that the builders are, like their brethren in the tribes settled west of the Jordan, faithful to the Lord.) In ch.23, Joshua makes a farewell speech (as Moses did in Deut.31), and in ch.24 presides over the making of a covenant between the Israelites and God at Shechem. The book ends with two short notes recounting the transfer of Joseph's bones from Egypt to Shechem, and the death of Aaron's son Eleazar the priest.

These chapters present a picture of the land as allotted to Israel and divided among the tribes as their inheritance from God (13:6-7). The concept of allotment suggests the drawing of lots for the different tribal areas, and this Joshua does at Shiloh (18:1-10), at least for the tribes of Benjamin, Simeon, Zebulun, Issachar, Asher, Naphtali and Dan. The idea is that the allocation of the land was in the hands of God (cf. Prov.16:33). The concept of inheritance was also important, and can be illustrated from the famous story of Naboth's vineyard; when king Ahab coveted it and offered a price for it, Naboth told the king, 'The LORD forbid that I should give you the inheritance of one of my fathers.' (1 Kings 21:3). An inheritance of land was (in theory) inalienable; it was God's land, given in trust to a clan or family or tribe. The author of Joshua is emphasising that the land of the people of Israel, the people of Yahweh, is ultimately God's land. A further point is made at the beginning of the section in 13:1-7, where the Lord says to Joshua that 'there remains yet very much land to be possessed', including the regions held by the Philistines, some of the Canaanites, and the Sidonians, whom God will in due course drive out. The author clearly has in mind an Israel whose proper extent is wider than that covered by the tribal territories known to him. For an even wider ideal land of Israel, we may compare the reference of Genesis 15:18 to 'this land, from the river of Egypt to the great river, the river Euphrates'.

The opening chapter of the following book of Judges also declares that the Israelite tribes did not succeed in taking over the whole land. It has often been suggested that this chapter gives a picture of the Israelite conquest which contradicts that given by the book Joshua, because Joshua tells of Israel's successful conquest of the land, while Judges 1 emphasises Israel's failures. In fact, however, Judges 1 is not inconsistent with Joshua and presupposes it. Judges 1 begins by telling how Judah, with Simeon (cf. Josh.19:1-9) went up to the territory allotted to it, in particular to the Negeb and the Shephelah, and the cities of Hebron and Debir (cf. Josh.15:13-19), and how they failed at Jerusalem (cf. Josh.15:63). (Difficulties are caused in this chapter by references to Judah's capture of Jerusalem in verse 8, and of the Philistine cities Gaza, Ashkelon and Ekron in verse 18.) The chapter continues with the activities of the house of Joseph (cf. Josh.16:1-17:18), which took Bethel, and then describes how Manasseh, Ephraim, Zebulun, Asher, and Naphtali failed to drive out the

Canaanites from certain cities, and how the tribe of Dan was forced to move back under pressure from the Amorites into the hill country in the north. The chapter, as John van Seters has pointed out, relates closely to the second half of the book of Joshua and presents the tribes in the same order, beginning with Judah and then the house of Joseph and the northern tribes (though there is no reference to Issachar). However, the chapter as a whole makes the point that the Israelite conquest was a struggle against the Canaanites, successful in some places (particularly the hill country) but not in others (Judah 'could not drive out the inhabitants of the plain, because they had chariots of iron', 1:19); the northern tribes of Manasseh, Ephraim, Asher and Naphtali could not capture the main cities but lived side by side with the Canaanites, in some cases (cf. Josh.16:10; 17:12) eventually subjecting them to forced labour; and the Danites were actually forced to retreat.

The subsequent chapters of Judges as they stand describe how, after the death of Joshua, Israel deserted Yahweh to serve other gods, so provoking Yahweh to punish her at the hands of the surrounding nations. When the Israelites appealed for relief from their enemies, God relented and sent a succession of 'judges' to rescue them; all would go well until the judge died, after which 'they turned back and behaved worse than their fathers, going after other gods' (Jud.2:19). God in response decided to leave the other nations (the Philistines, the Canaanites, the Sidonians and the Hivites, 3:3) in place, as a permanent test of Israel's loyalty and also 'that he might teach war to such at least as had not known it before' (3:2). The book goes on to describe a sequence of encounters between the Israelites and their enemies, in each of which Israel is saved by the leadership of a judge. In 3:7–11, Othniel of Judah saves Israel from Cushan-rishathaim ('Cushan of double wickedness'), king of Mesopotamia (it is possible that originally the text referred to Edom, not Mesopotamia, Mesopotamia being too far away to make good sense in the context). Chapter 3:12–30 tells how the Benjaminite Ehud saved Israel from subjection to the king of Moab. Chapters 4 and 5 tell in prose and then in poetry how Deborah, with Barak of Naphtali, preserved Israel from Sisera, the general of the Canaanite king of Hazor. Chapters 6–8 relate how Gideon, of a small family of the tribe of Manasseh, saved Israel from an incursion of Midianite raiders from the east and was invited to become king (but declined, on the grounds that the Lord was their ruler; cf. 1 Sam.8:7, 12:12). Chapter 9 describes how Gideon's son Abimelech took power in Shechem after killing his brothers, and ruled disastrously before being killed himself in the rebellion against him. Chapters 10–12 tell of Jephthah, a nobody from Gilead, who rescued Israel from the Ammonites in Transjordan, and led the Gileadites in a tribal dispute against the people of Ephraim. Chapters 13–16 describe the exploits of the Danite hero Samson against the Philistines; these stories seem to be a little nearer legend than the previous ones. Chapters 19–21 are an appendix describing how the tribes of Israel collectively punished the tribe of Benjamin for its outrageously inhospitable behaviour against a travelling Levite.

As it stands, the book of Judges is a collection of stories edited to present a picture of Israel in the period between the initial conquest and the beginnings of the monarchy (the book ends with the comment that 'in those days there was no kings in Israel; every man did what was right in his own eyes'). It shows an Israel more or less unified (though there are some unfortunate lapses) under the leadership of a series of judges, fighting against Edomites (?), Moabites, Canaanites, Midianites (with Amalekites and the people of the east), Ammonites, and Philistines, all well-known enemies of the later kingdoms of Judah and Israel. Closer analysis suggests that this book, like the preceding book of Joshua with which it is so closely connected, and the following books of Samuel, with which it is similarly closely connected, has a long and complex history of composition, and that the original individual constituent stories referred to minor local skirmishes rather than to unified national campaigns. Thus ch.3:12–30 concerns the Benjaminites and Moabites in the Jericho region, chs. 4 and 5 the tribes of Zebulun and Naphtali and Issachar in the region of Mount Tabor and the Jezreel valley (with the help, apparently, of Ephraim and Benjamin, but not of Reuben, Gilead, Dan, and Asher, whose absence is noted, or of Judah, who is not even mentioned). Chapters 6–8 concern the defence of part of Manasseh against a Midianite raid; Gideon chases the Midianites east into northern Transjordan. Chapter 9 is focused on Shechem and the surrounding area; chs. 10–12 on Gilead and the land of the Ammonites in Transjordan; chs. 13–16 on the original territory of Dan between Judah and Philistia. This assessment of the contents of Judges has helped scholars to reconstruct a little more realistically the pre-monarchic situation of Israel, in which local groups fought alone or with their nearer neighbours minor battles to defend their occupation and possession of the land.

However, the history of the settlement of the people of Israel in Canaan turns out to be far more complicated than the books of Joshua and Judges might at first sight suggest. In the first place, analysis of the books of Joshua and Judges has shown that they do not contain a smooth, contemporary or even nearly contemporary account of events in the land of Canaan in the period before the appearance of the kingdoms of Judah and Israel, but rather that in their present form they derive from the late seventh or early sixth centuries BC, some half a millennium later than the events they purport to describe, and that the authors or editors of these works are writing from motives more theological than academic. (Rather than writing the sort of account that would appeal to a modern secular historian, the authors are more concerned firstly to explain to the Israelite people, who had suffered the loss of their country, their king, and their temple, that nevertheless the land and the temple and to some extent the monarchy were God's gifts to Israel, secondly to explain why Israel failed to take all the land that had been promised, thirdly to show that the monarchy which Israel had demanded was a less than perfect solution to the problem of government, and, finally, to underline Israel's need to obey God's commandments and the consequences of failure to do so.)

In the second place, the development of the discipline of archaeology and the continuing archaeological research into the state of affairs in Palestine in the Late Bronze Age and Iron Age I – from *c.* 1500–1000 BC – has greatly affected our picture of Palestine in that period. Whereas fifty years ago, archaeological excavation was largely seen as a means of providing evidence to illustrate and support the biblical story, now archaeologists argue that the evidence they produce should be interpreted independently of the biblical account, for to begin by interpreting it in the light of the biblical story is to prejudice our understanding from the start. And indeed, it is proper and necessary to ask what the archaeological evidence, when professionally interpreted, supports, independently of the framework derived from a simplistic reading of the biblical narrative. It is equally proper and necessary to ask what the biblical account, as analysed in the light of the best available scholarship, supports, independently of the archaeological evidence. Only when the work has been done thus independently on both biblical and archaeological evidence is it proper to compare results and see how they may (or may not) fit. This is particularly the case with the current debate over the origins and settlement of ancient Israel.

On the biblical side, scholars began with the picture of the conquest drawn by the book Joshua. They accepted the general outline of the story, and tried to fix the date of the exodus from Egypt. Many of them dated this to the period of Rameses II (c. 1290–1224 BC), largely on the evidence of Exodus 1:11 that the Israelites helped build the store cities of Pithom and Ramses in the delta region of the Nile, and also on the evidence of the Merneptah stele, which records that Pharaoh Merneptah, towards the end of the thirteenth century BC, defeated the people Israel in Palestine, the people Israel being listed at the end of the sequence of place-names Ashkelon, Gaza, and Yanoam, which might suggest that the people Israel were located in the northern hill country, roughly where the kingdom of Israel was later established. This dating, however, did not entirely square with the biblical dating of 1 Kings 6:1, which dated the exodus 480 years before the building of Solomon's temple. As this must be dated c. 960 BC, the exodus would thus have been c. 1440 BC. Many scholars have indeed wished to date it here, because it allows not only the patriarchs of Genesis – Abraham, Isaac, Jacob and their families – to be identified with the presumed Amorite settlement of Syria and Palestine at the turn of the third-second millennium BC, but also the descent of Joseph and his family into Egypt to be identified with the ruling presence of the Hyksos in northern Egypt in the eighteenth–sixteenth centuries BC. Furthermore, this dating would allow the Hebrews of the Bible to be identified with the people called *habiru*, known to us from fourteenth-century BC Egyptian documents as refugees at the bottom of the social scale in Palestine in the early fourteenth century.

Superficially this is an attractive solution to the problem of the dating of the exodus, but it involves too many wide assumptions and dubious equations, and there is the further suspicion that the 480 years of 1 Kings 6:1 is an artificial figure, seen as a midpoint of Israel's history between the exodus from Egypt and a new exodus from Babylon at the end of the exile. It should be added that in recent years scholars have become much less willing to accept that the exodus was the large-scale affair the Bible implies, and would limit it to the experience of a small group of tribes or clans, including perhaps the Levites, and some of the northern tribes (e.g., the sons of Joseph, Ephraim and Manasseh), whose traditions gradually became accepted and shared by other tribal groups as they joined together to become the people of Israel.

Scholars then turned to the question of Israel's settlement in the land. Following the story of Joshua, and the evidence that was beginning to emerge from the excavation of Palestinian tells like Jericho (excavated by Sellin and Watzinger in 1907–8 and Garstang in 1930–6), Tell Beit Mirsim (Albright, 1926–32), and Gezer (Macalister, 1902–9), Albright and others concluded that the Late Bronze Age destructions of those cities were to be attributed to Israelite conquest under Joshua. Albright maintained that in archaeological strata above the destruction levels a new material culture appeared which he attributed to the Israelites. Subsequent excavation at Lachish and Hazor (reported as destroyed by Joshua in Josh.10:31–32; 11:11) was taken to support Albright's case. However, the Albrightian attempt to harmonise the findings of biblical scholarship and archaeology has not stood the test of further research. Of the cities whose destruction is attributed by the Bible to Joshua and the Israelites, Jericho, Ai, Heshbon, Arad, Gibeon, Jarmuth and Hormah can be discounted because they do not seem to have existed as walled cities in the thirteenth century BC. There is evidence that Hebron (Jud.1:8) and Debir (Jud.1:13; = Tell Rabud?) were destroyed in the thirteenth century BC, and that Lachish, Tell Beit Mirsim, and Gezer were destroyed about 1200 BC, but their destruction was not necessarily by Israelites. Gezer was rebuilt, probably by the Philistines. Thus Albright's reconstruction failed archaeologically for lack of LBA evidence at sites central to the biblical narrative, and also for lack of evidence of specifically Israelite settlement above the Canaanite cities such as Lachish and Gezer, though it remained true that the evidence from Hazor and perhaps Bethel might fit well enough.

As for the biblical evidence, since the work of Albrecht Alt and Martin Noth in the 1920s and 1930s, this had begun to be interpreted in a new way. Between them, these two scholars established the view that the Israelite occupation of Palestine was not a matter of unified military conquest so much as of peaceful infiltration by individual family groups or clans. This arose from two main considerations: first, the early Israelites should be seen as pastoral nomads, migrating annually between winter pastures in the steppes east of Palestine and summer pastures in the central hills of Palestine. In the course of time some began to settle permanently in Palestine, and as they prospered and increased in number they began to put pressure on the land of the Canaanite city-states in the valleys. Secondly, analysis of the traditions of Joshua and Judges showed that the picture of Israel as taking over Palestine in one unified act of military conquest was due to the later editing of separate traditions from individual clan groups or tribes. In particular, the bulk of the material in Joshua 2–12 focused on the tribal area of Benjamin and was originally associated with the sanctuary of Gilgal. The lists in Joshua 13–19 were evidence for the state of the pre-monarchic tribal holdings (Noth believed that the 'tribes' were not established from the smaller clan groups until after the entry to the land), but included a later list of the cities of Judah, from the time of king Josiah in the late seventh century BC.

Both these points had, and have, substance, and the general thesis remains influential. Its weak point is that it makes an assumption (based, it is true, on the general biblical picture) that the Israelites were in origin nomads entering Palestine from the desert to the east. Alt was right to consider carefully what a nomad might be, and to distinguish the pastoral nomad from the camel-riding son of the desert as romantically conceived in the nineteenth century. Subsequent debate, while largely accepting the results of Noth's biblical analysis, has focused on the sociological background of the early Israelites and their contemporaries in Canaan, and on the archaeological evidence (which Alt and Noth lacked) for settlement patterns in Palestine in the LBA and Iron Age I periods.

This assumption that the Israelites were intrusive nomads entering Palestine from the east (whether by infiltration or by conquest) has been attacked in recent years by two American scholars, G.E. Mendenhall and N.K. Gottwald. Mendenhall emphasised Alt's point of seasonal transhumance, underlining the fact that such 'nomads' were basically farmers – farmers whose primary concern was with rearing animals rather than with growing crops. Those who raised crops and those who tended animals, however, were mutually interdependent, and the real division lay, not between settled farmers and vagrant nomads, but between both and the urban population of the cities. The Hebrews originated not in nomadic groups from outside Palestine but in the reaction of the socially disadvantaged in Canaanite society to their oppressive feudal overlords in the cities (Mendenhall equates the 'Hebrews' of Exodus 1:22 and elsewhere with the well-known *habiru* mentioned in the Amarna letters of the fourteenth century BC and other Egyptian sources). These Hebrews in Canaan left the cities and settled in the hills as pastoral farmers, their identity reinforced by their acceptance of a new religion and its God, Yahweh – a religion totally opposed to the gods of Canaan.

A similar thesis is proposed by Gottwald, who likewise sees Israel as emerging as the result of evolution within Canaanite society (though the emerging Israelites are reacting not so much against the city as against the wealthy landowners). Those opting out of the Canaanite society became organised in tribal groups and were joined by a small group of refugees from Egypt, led by Moses, who introduced them to the worship of Yahweh. Their development of the hill country was made possible by new technologies such as the use of iron, improved water cisterns, and the building of terraces on the hillsides to prevent soil erosion and retain water.

These theories illustrate the new tendency to solve the historical problems of early Israel by applying models drawn from social, socio-religious and anthropological theory. These models are not limited to the view that cultural change must always be attributed to the arrival from outside of a new people bringing in new ways. (It is not surprising that the model of external conquest should be fashionable in the 1920s and 1930s, and that of internal social unrest and rebellion in the 1970s and 1980s; nor is it surprising, in the light of the present political situation of the renascent state of Israel, that the issue of Israel's historical possession of and title to the land should be of such moment.) The sociological model of recent years, however, faces two major problems: first, the biblical tradition (whatever historical value we may put upon it) presents the Israelites as entering Palestine from outside, not emerging from within, and, secondly, the material culture and settlement patterns of the LBA and Iron Age I settlements in the central hill country of Palestine do not appear to derive from the urban background of lowland Canaan (though there are certainly some points of contact). The biblical record knows of the distinction between the hills and the plain (Jud.1:19). Understanding of the Israelite settlement should surely start with the nature of the LBA and Iron Age I settlement in the central hill country, and this has been the focus of most recent discussion by archaeologists and anthropologists alike.

According to F. Frick, 'it is now an established fact, no matter what historical position we may subscribe to, whether of the "conquest", "the settlement", or the "revolt" tendency, that ancient Israel first became established as a recognisable socio-political entity in the hill country of Palestine'. I. Finkelstein, in his recent book *The archaeology of the Israelite settlement* (1988), admits that 'the starting point of a discussion about the characteristics of Israelite Settlement sites is the historical biblical text (the only source available), which specifies the location of the Israelite population at the end of the period of the Judges and at the beginning of the monarchy' (p.28). It is the biblical tradition, in fact, which has focused archaeological exploration and research on the central highlands area as the home of early Israel; indeed, one of the major problems for the archaeologist has been that of knowing by what criteria to distinguish Israelite sites from Canaanite sites. If Israelite sites cannot be distinguished on artefactual evidence, we are forced back to the biblical record for some clue.

Finkelstein explored the LBA and EIA sites of the central hill country, and concluded (on grounds of pottery analysis of the sites discovered and from excavation at Shiloh) that, while in MBA II in this area the Desert Fringe and North Central Range were well settled, in the LBA there was a dramatic fall in the number of sites occupied (these now being limited to the Central Range), and the early phases of the Iron Age showed the repopulation of the Desert Fringe and the North Range, beginning with the eastern side of the region and moving westwards as Iron Age I gave way to Iron Age II. This means that the initial settlement lay in the area of field crops and animal husbandry (Desert Fringe and North Central Range), and later in Iron Age II shifted to the regions of cereal and horticulture (Northwest slopes) and olive growing (Southwest slopes). This suggests to Finkelstein that the settlers came from a pastoral, not urban, background. He believes that the original MBA II population changed under social pressures in the early LBA period (taxation, war, insecurity, pressure on resources) from a sedentary to a pastoralist life and lived in tents (which leave fewer traces for the archaeologist) before resettling in the Iron Age. The region of Ephraim was resettled earlier than the regions of Beersheba in the south and Galilee in the north. Benjamin and Judah he sees as settled from Ephraim and Manasseh in the eleventh and tenth centuries BC. The important point to note is that Finkelstein does not attribute these Israelite settlements to people invading across the Jordan, or indeed to refugees from Canaanite towns, but to people who were there all along, though living with a different lifestyle.

This kind of reconstruction, based on field observation, is impressive, and should be compared with other studies of agriculture and society in the central highlands for this period. Thus R.B. Coote and K.W. Whitelam see the emergence of Israel in the highland settlements as a response to the collapse of trade in the Late Bronze Age; this forced the poorer folk of the Canaanite lowlands to move to the uplands and carve out a new way of life there for themselves. D.C. Hopkins discusses the way in which the various challenges to subsistence in the central hills shaped the life-style of the early settlers, who were forced to exploit the environmental diversity by raising varied crops and livestock, learning the art of storing grain in silos, developing techniques of water storage such as lined cisterns, and of erosion control by building terraces on the hillsides ('risk spreading strategies for coping'). 'It may be possible to understand the transformation of the settlement map of the Early Iron Age Highlands and the evolution of the large social body of Israel as a process propelled by the attempt of a growing population of settlers to meet the challenges of agricultural subsistence in the Highlands' (D.C. Hopkins, 1985, 271). 'Whatever the source of the population growth, it would be a mistake to conceive the transfiguration of the settlement map narrowly as the initial "settling down" of nomadic or migrant groups which had previously been socially distinct and unrelated to settled agriculturalists. Rather, it represents a movement along the pastoral-agricultural continuum in response to increasing demands for subsistence and social production' (ibid., 272). Similarly, Frick discusses the interaction of people and eco-systems.

Recent archaeological study of the Israelite settlement, therefore, has tended to argue that the re-emergence of settled communities at the beginning of Iron Age I *c.* 1200 BC is not to be attributed to the arrival of new settlers from the deserts to the east of the Jordan, but rather to the stimulus of the problems of the LBA society of Canaan. This poses once again the problem of how the Israelites are to be distinguished ethnically from the Canaanites, and, if so, by what criteria. The Merneptah stele in the late thirteenth century BC speaks of a 'people' Israel, but was Merneptah distinguishing them on ethnic or socio-political grounds? Perhaps it is historically safer to concentrate on seeking the origin of the historical political state of Israel, and admit that its antecedents remain obscure. The origins of the people of Israel have not yet been explained by archaeological research, where a major question remains that of continuity through the LBA and Iron Age I periods. It used to be argued that a break or change in material culture could be demonstrated between the LBA and the Iron Age I periods, but it is now becoming clearer that though there may be a decline in quality and a decline in foreign trade, nevertheless the Iron Age pottery forms develop from those of the Late Bronze Age without any dramatic change. How this is to be interpreted is another matter; it may suggest (as it does to V. Fritz) that the early, incoming Israelites lived alongside the Canaanites for a period and learned their ways and adopted their material culture.

At this point, we must return to the biblical tradition and try to assess it more accurately as evidence for what happened in Israel's early history. We need to know when the books of Joshua and Judges were composed, what sources they used, by whom they were written and for what purpose. We may begin by asking whether there is any sign of the traditions preserved in Joshua and Judges appearing elsewhere in the biblical tradition, and so discovering, perhaps, how early the conquest and settlement traditions were generally known in Israel. In fact, as N.P. Lemche has recently demonstrated, the evidence that these stories were in circulation before the exilic period is limited. The eighth-century BC Judaean prophets Isaiah and Micah refer between them only to the Gideon story (Isa.10:26, a passage suspected of being a post-exilic addition by many scholars). From the north, there is a brief and perhaps secondary reference to possessing the land of the Amorites in Amos 2:10, and a possible reference to the outrage at Gibeah in Hosea 9:9 (cf. Jud.19–21). If we turn to the Psalms to discover whether the conquest and settlement were celebrated in the cult, the results are surprisingly meagre. According to Psalm 80:8f.,

> Thou didst bring a vine out of Egypt;
> thou didst drive out the nations and plant it.
> Thou didst clear the ground for it;
> it took deep root and filled the land,

but there is here only a general reference to driving out the nations and settling Israel in the land (cf. Ps.105:44). Psalm 114 refers to the stopping of the flow of the Jordan (cf. Josh.3–4, and perhaps Ps.66:6). Psalms 78:54–66, and perhaps 81:11f. add reference to the disobedience of Israel portrayed in Judges 2 (cf. also Ps.106:40–46), and may be dependent on it. Possibly Psalm 68:7–14 refers to the battles of the Judges period, hinting at Judges 5:16,30. There is little in this cultic material which is certainly pre-exilic and independent of Joshua and Judges, and we must conclude that the conquest and settlement traditions were not much spoken of before the exilic period, when they become rather more prominent in the books of Jeremiah and Ezekiel. In Jeremiah, however, the reference is mainly to the land which God gave to Israel's ancestors (Jer.7:7) as a possession (32:22) or inheritance (3:18; 17:4), a land flowing with milk and honey (11:5; 32:22f., cf. Deut.6:3), a plentiful land which Israel defiled (2:7), and in which they did not obey God's law (32:23). Ezekiel similarly refers to God's promises to bring Israel into a land flowing with milk and honey (20:6, 15; cf. 33:24), but there is no specific reference to the conquest tradition of Joshua and Judges. There are no clear allusions to the conquest and settlement traditions in Second Isaiah (Isa.40–55) or in the post-exilic prophets. In short, it is quite remarkable, given the apparent importance of these traditions, how rarely they feature in biblical literature. They seem to belong in particular to the Deuteronomist and the literature influenced by him.

This brings us back to the question of the date of the composition of the books Joshua and Judges. The book Joshua used to be seen by some scholars as the final book of the Hexateuch (i.e., the unit of six books beginning with Genesis and ending with Joshua). This meant further that scholars sought in Joshua for evidence of the pentateuchal sources J, E, P, and D, and found JE in the stories of Joshua 1–12, and P in 13–19. The main reasons for this search and for belief in the Hexateuch as a unit were the correct observation that Joshua owed much to the preceding book Deuteronomy, to which it was clearly linked by its introduction and conclusion, and the undemonstrated supposition that the source documents J, E, and P must have contained a narrative of the conquest of Canaan. However, in his commentary on Joshua in 1937 (2nd ed., 1952), Martin Noth demonstrated to general satisfaction that Joshua was the second section of a long work which included Deuteronomy (Deut.1–11 being the introduction to the work), Joshua, Judges, Samuel and Kings. Noth called this work the Deuteronomistic History, because the narrative was presented in terms of the theological principles of Deuteronomy (see below).

Noth argued that the nucleus of Joshua 1–12 was a series of originally independent aetiological or explanatory tales, first collected together at the sanctuary of Gilgal near Jericho. (The cultic concern of these stories, and their geographical focus on the territory of Benjamin, and their interest in Jericho, Gilgal, Bethel and Ai is clear to any reader.) To this collection was added the figure of the Israelite leader Joshua (whose home was in Ephraim just across the border from Benjamin), and the stories of the defeat of the kings of the south (Joshua 10) and of the north (Joshua 11), and thus was developed an overall account of the conquest of Palestine. The whole is carefully ordered; Joshua leads Israel in the conquest of the central hill country, and then turns to south and north, Judah and Galilee, in turn.

Chapters 13–21 also show signs of a complex history of compilation. They are concerned with the distribution of the land of Canaan among the tribes, and were formerly credited to the P strand of the Pentateuch or Hexateuch. Noth argued that these chapters were basically composed of early, pre-monarchic boundary lists (15:1–12, Judah incorporating Simeon; 16:5–10, Ephraim; 17:1–12, Manasseh; 18:11–20, Benjamin), and a list of the cities of Judah (15:13–63) from the time of Josiah in the late seventh century BC (subsequently variously dated by other scholars to the tenth–ninth centuries BC (Cross and Wright, 1956, 202–26), Uzziah's reign in the mid-eighth century (Kellai, 1958, 134–60) or Hezekiah's reign in the late eighth century (Aharoni, 1959, 225–46)). To these were added a list for the Galilaean tribes (19:10–31), a list of cities to which those accused of manslaughter might flee (ch.20), and a list of cities apportioned to the otherwise landless Levites (ch.21).

The two major collections of material in Joshua 2–12 and 13–21 were put together and edited by a Deuteronomistic writer and incorporated into the larger Deuteronomistic History. The hand of the Deuteronomistic editor is clear throughout, but particularly clear in Joshua 1; 8:30–35; 12; 13:1–7; 23 and 24. The editor is anxious to underline that the land was Israel's by virtue of God's promises to the patriarch Abraham (Deut.30:2), to Moses, and to Moses' successor (Josh.1:3), and that, as was demonstrated by the actual possession of the land by the different tribes, 'not one of all the good promises which the LORD had made to the house of Israel had failed; all came to pass' (Josh.21:45). Secondly, the editor wished to emphasise that Israel had taken the land and would hold the land only by virtue of her obedience to the law of Moses. At the beginning of the book, Joshua is warned,

'Be strong and very courageous, being careful to do according to all the law which Moses my servant commanded you; turn not from it to the right hand or to the left, that you may have good success wherever you go.' (Josh.1:7)

In 8:30–35, Joshua follows the command of the law, builds an altar to the Lord, writes a copy of the law, and reads it out to the people. 'There was not a word of all that Moses commanded which Joshua did not read before all the assembly of Israel'. In his final speech (23:6f.), Joshua commands the Israelites

'to keep and do all that is written in the book of the law of Moses, turning aside from it neither to the right hand nor to the left, that you may not be mixed with these nations left here among you, or make mention of the names of their gods, or swear by them, or serve them, or bow down yourselves to them, but cleave to the LORD your God as you have done to this day'.

In the book of Joshua, the Israelites are (with one exception in ch.7) obedient to the law, and the result is that 'Joshua took the whole land, according to all that the LORD has spoken to Moses' (11:23). However, the Philistine region, some of the Canaanite territory, and the land belonging to the Sidonians in the north yet remained to be possessed (Josh.13:2–6; cf. Jud.3:4–6), and the success of Israel in taking this extra territory was to depend on her continued obedience after Joshua's death (Josh.23:1–16); in fact after Joshua's death Israel failed to remain obedient (Jud.2:11 – 3:6), and so these lands were left unconquered and Israel's enemies remained in place (the Deuteronomistic editors of Judges 2:20–23 and 3:1–2 explain that the nations were left to test Israel's loyalty to Yahweh, and to teach the art of war to such Israelites as had no experience of it).

This theme of obedience and disobedience incurring blessing and curse respectively, is Deuteronomic; its appearance in Joshua 8:30–35 is clearly dependent on Deuteronomy 27 and 28. The Deuteronomic demands upon the people are finally emphasised by the story of Joshua 24, in which Joshua forces the people to choose between the Lord and foreign gods (24:19f.). This is reminiscent of the instruction of Moses to the people in Deut.30:15–20:

'See, I have set before you this day life and good, death and evil. If you obey the commandments of the LORD your God which I command you this day, by loving the LORD your God, by walking in his ways, and by keeping his commandments and his statutes and his ordinances, then you shall live and multiply, and the LORD your God will bless you in the land which you are entering to take possession of it. But if your heart turns away, and you will not hear, but are drawn away to worship other gods and serve them, I declare to you this day, that you shall perish; you shall not live long in the land which you are going over the Jordan to enter and possess. I call heaven and earth to witness against you this day, that I have set before you life and

> death, blessing and curse; therefore choose life, that you and your descendants may live, loving the LORD your God, obeying his voice, and cleaving to him; for that means life to you and length of days, that you may dwell in the land which the LORD swore to your fathers, to Abraham, to Isaac, and to Jacob, to give them.'

Israel's continued dwelling in the land depends upon obedience, and in particular on not being drawn away to serve other gods. This is the Deuteronomic theme. The people opt for the Lord, and Joshua

> made a covenant with [better, 'for'] the people that day, and made statutes and ordinances for them at Shechem. And Joshua wrote these words in the book of the law of God; and he took a great stone, and set it up there under the oak in the sanctuary of the LORD. And Joshua said to all the people, 'Behold, this stone shall be a witness against us. . .' (Josh.24:25–27)

Covenant and law, again, are important Deuteronomic themes; they reappear in the famous passage about the new covenant which God is to make with his people in Jeremiah 31:31–34.

These Deuteronomic themes reappear also in the book of Judges, which, like Joshua, had a complex development. Basically, the Deuteronomistic Historian created a period of disobedience to follow the period of obedience under Joshua, and filled it by turning a set of stories about early heroes of Israel into a succession of ruling 'judges' in order to cover the gap between the entry to the land and the beginning of the Israelite monarchy. The chronology he adopts for the period is of a piece with the overall chronology of the books of Samuel and Kings, the mid-point of which is the foundation of the temple in Solomon's reign, 480 years after the exodus from Egypt (1 Kings 6:1). (The building of the second temple follows 480 years later, 430 years of which cover the reigns of the kings of Judah between the building of the temple and the fall of Jerusalem to Babylon; the editors probably supposed the exile to cover the remaining 50 years.)

The most recent analysis of the book of Judges suggests that the book was put together in the following manner. Sometime in the monarchic period, the stories of Ehud of Benjamin, Deborah and Barak of Issachar, Gideon of Manasseh, and Abimelech of Shechem were collected in prophetic circles in the northern kingdom as an account of God's deliverance of Israel. To this collection was later added a theological framework, which set the stories into a sequence with a repeated pattern: Israel did what was evil in the sight of the Lord; the Lord gave Israel into the hands of an enemy; Israel cried out of her distress to the Lord, who raised up a deliverer; the enemy was subdued, and the land had rest for a period, before the cycle of events was repeated. The stereotyped story of Othniel (3:7–11) was added as a prefatory example (perhaps also to provide a story for the tribe of Judah, who otherwise does not appear). This stage of the composition perhaps took place in Judah after the fall of the northern kingdom in 722 BC; in this period, it might have had some point as a comment on the way Israel's repeated wickedness incurred punishment.

The next stage added the stories of Jephthah and Samson (with their own preface in 10:6–9, referring to the Ammonites and Philistines, the enemies of

Jephthah and Samson respectively), together with the short lists of 'minor judges' which appear in 10:1–5 and 12:7–15. The story of Jephthah shows him as one who delivered Israel from the Ammonites, but he appears also as one of the minor judges on the list. This combination of the pre-exilic collection of stories of deliverance with the Jephthah and Samson stories and the list of minor judges was the work of the Deuteronomistic Historian, and this created the core of the book of Judges as we have it. The historian gave it a new preface in Judges 2:11 – 3:6, making clear that the judges succeeded one another as saviours sent by God. A second Deuteronomistic editor added further to the prefatory material in Judges 2:11 – 3:6 and 10:6–9 in order to explain that Israel's failure to hold the land was due to her violation of the covenant relationship (Jud.2:20-23; 10:10-16). A final stage was the addition of 1:1 – 2:5 and the stories of chs.17–18, 19–21, which intrude into the otherwise continuous story-line; the end of Joshua is continued in Judges 2:6, and the stories of Samson and the Philistines have their natural continuation in the stories of 1 Samuel, which also speak of the Philistines as Israel's major enemy. The prologue and epilogue of Judges are seen as pro-monarchic propaganda (cf. Jud.21:25, 'In those days there was no king in Israel; every man did what was right in his own eyes'), later than the Deuteronomic editor.

The book of Judges may have come together by some such sequence of composition, but as it stands it presents an overall picture of Israel's early history between the death of Joshua (1:1) and the beginning of the Israelite monarchy (21:25). In between, it sees a period of repeated failure, beginning with Israel's failure to take all the land available (ch.1) and ending with two stories illustrating the lawlessness of pre-monarchic society. The book underlines repeatedly the dangers of religious apostasy and the snare of foreign religions, and hints at the dangers of monarchy in the story of Gideon, who declines to accept it, Abimelech, who abuses it and is killed, and Jephthah, who makes a tragic error of judgement. These references show the influence of Judah and Israel's experience of monarchy, and share in the Deuteronomistic view of it; we might compare, for example, the Deuteronomistic view of the reign of Manasseh, whose failings are described in 2 Kings 21:1–16: he did evil 'according to all the abominable practices of the nations whom the LORD drove out before the people of Israel' (2 Kings 21:2; cf. Joshua's final sermon, Josh.23:2–16, and the Deuteronomistic introduction to Judges, Jud.2:11–13). The book also affirms, however, that with the help of the Lord and the deliverers he raises up, Israel can overcome her enemies, the Moabites, Canaanites, Midianites, Ammonites and Philistines, and the land can gain rest and will remain at rest as long as Israel remains faithful to the covenant. There is no clear reference in all this material to the fall of Israel in 721 BC or to the fall of Judah in 587 BC, though such reference might have been seen to be appropriate. It may therefore be that the stories of Judges had been collected and edited at least before the exile of Judah and were incorporated as a block into the larger Deuteronomic work. In any case, the historian did not need to underline the message of the exile at this point; that could wait for his presentation of the events of the monarchic period in the books of Samuel and Kings to which we now turn.

## Bibliography

Y. Aharoni, *The land of the Bible: a historical geography* (revised by A.F. Rainey) (London: Burns and Oates, 1980)

Y. Aharoni, *The archaeology of the land of Israel* (London: SCM Press, 1982)

A. Alt, 'The settlement of the Israelites in Palestine', *Essays on Old Testament history and religion* (Oxford: Blackwell, 1966; Garden City: Doubleday, 1967)

A.G. Auld, *Joshua, Moses and the land* (Edinburgh: T. and T. Clark, 1980)

D. Baly, *The geography of the Bible*, 2nd ed. (Guildford and London: Lutterworth Press: New York: Harper and Row, 1979)

R.D. Barnett, *Illustrations of Old Testament history*, 2nd revised edition (London: British Museum Publications, for the Trustees of the British Museum, 1977)

J.R. Bartlett, *Jericho* (Cities of the Biblical World) (Guildford: Lutterworth, 1982)

J. Bright, *A history of Israel*, 3rd ed. (London: SCM Press; Philadelphia: Westminster Press, 1981)

W. Brueggemann, *The land* (London: SPCK, 1978; Philadelphia: Fortress Press, 1977)

R.B. Coote and K.W. Whitelam, *The emergence of Israel in historical perspective* (Sheffield: Almond Press, 1986)

I. Finkelstein, *The archaeology of the Israelite settlement* (Jerusalem: Israel Exploration Society, 1988)

D.N. Freedman and D.F. Graf (ed), *Palestine in transition: the emergence of ancient Israel* (Sheffield: Almond Press, 1983)

F.S. Frick, *The formation of the state in ancient Israel* (Decatur, Ga.: Almond Press, 1985)

N.K. Gottwald, *The tribes of Yahweh: a sociology of the religion of liberated Israel, 1250–1000 BC.* (Maryknoll, N.Y.: Orbis Books, 1979; London: SCM Press, 1980)

J.H. Hayes and J.M. Miller, *Israelite and Judean history* (Philadelphia: Westminster Press; London: SCM Press, 1977)

D.C. Hopkins, *The highlands of Canaan: agricultural life in the Early Iron Age* (Decatur, Ga.: Almond Press, 1985)

K.M. Kenyon, *The Bible and recent archaeology*, revised by P.R.S. Moorey (London: British Museum Publications; Atlanta: John Knox Press, 1978)

H. Darrell Lance, *The Old Testament and the archaeologist* (Philadelphia: Fortress Press, 1981)

N.P. Lemche, *Early Israel: anthropological and historical studies on the Israelite society before the monarchy* (Vetus Testamentum Supplement 37; Leiden: Brill, 1985)

N.P. Lemche, *Ancient Israel: a new history of Israelite society* (Sheffield, JSOT Press, 1988)

A.D.H. Mayes, *Israel in the period of the Judges* (London: SCM Press, 1974)

A.D.H. Mayes, *The story of Israel between settlement and exile: a redactional study of the Deuteronomistic history* (London: SCM Press, 1983)

A.D.H. Mayes, *Judges* (Old Testament Guides) (Sheffield: JSOT Press for Society for Old Testament Study, 1985)

T.C. Mitchell, *The Bible in the British Museum: interpreting the evidence* (London: British Museum Publications, 1988)

M. Noth, *The history of Israel*, 2nd ed. (London: A and C. Black; New York, Harper and Row, 1960)

D.W. Thomas (ed.), *Archaeology and Old Testament study* (London: Oxford University Press, 1967)

R. de Vaux, *The early history of Israel* (London: Darton, Longman and Todd; Philadelphia: Westminster Press, 1978)

M. Weippert, *The settlement of the Israelite tribes in Palestine* (London: SCM Press, 1971)

# 5    Politics and History

## I.  *1 and 2 Samuel*

The first five books of the Old Testament present a theological interpretation of Israel's origins and vocation as the people of Yahweh. The books Joshua and Judges explain how Israel, at first, obediently following the leadership of Joshua, conquered her land, and then, repeatedly disobeying the judges found herself under continual pressure from the nations left in the land. The book of Judges hints on several occasions (e.g., Jud.8:22f.; 9:1-6; 18:1; 19:1; 21:25) at the coming of monarchy. The story is continued in the books of Samuel, which describe the beginnings of monarchy in Israel in the persons of Saul and David, and in the books of Kings, which describe the accession and reign of David's son Solomon (1 Kings 1-11), and the history of the two kingdoms of Israel and Judah from their creation after the death of Solomon to their destruction at the hands of the Assyrians (722 BC) and the Babylonians (587 BC) respectively.

The narrative of the books of Samuel, on inspection, seems to be made up of a number of fairly well-defined blocks of material.

(1)  1 Sam.1:11 – 4:1 prepare for the coming monarchy by telling of the birth of Samuel and his call to prophetic service at the sanctuary of Shiloh, and prepare for the future Jerusalem temple by indicating the disaster coming upon Shiloh and its priesthood, headed by Eli and his sons.

(2)  1 Sam.4:2 – 7:2 continue the theme by telling of the capture of the Ark by the Philistines and the death of Eli's sons in battle and the death of Eli himself from shock. 'The glory has departed from Israel for the ark of God has been captured' (1 Sam.4:22). But possession of the Ark brings trouble on the Philistines, and they send it back to the Israelites at Kiriath-jearim. This section, together with the story of the transfer of the Ark to Jerusalem in 2 Sam.6, has often been seen as deriving from a separate 'Ark Narrative' used as a primary source by the historian of 1 and 2 Samuel. This section says nothing of Samuel, but has clear links with the Shiloh narrative of chs. 1-3. The story appears to be rounded off by 7:3-14, in which God, without human agency, puts an end to Philistine oppression 'all the days of Samuel'.

(3)  1 Sam.7:15 – 12:25 is a complex section probably composed from a number of sources. It links the rise of the monarchy with the end of the period of the judges, Samuel being presented as the last effective judge, his sons being corrupt (7:15 – 8:3). The narrative goes on to describe how Samuel, the prophet,

gives way to the popular request for a king, though warning the people of the dangers (ch.8). He privately anoints Saul as a prince (*nagid*) (10:1), publicly presides over the election by lot of Saul as king at Mizpah (10:17–27) and over his coronation at Gilgal (11:15), and preaches a sermon warning Israel that, though they have done wickedly in seeking a king, God will support them as long as they and their king fear the Lord and keep his commandments (12:1–25). Clearly, the general tenor of the narrative is less than enthusiastic about the monarchy, and reflects the approach of the Deuteronomic editors of Samuel and Kings. Samuel, like the prophets later in the Deuteronomistic History, is critical of kingship; he writes down 'the rights and duties of the kingship' in a book (1 Sam.11:25), which is reminiscent of the provision of the Deuteronomic law (Deut.17:18) that the king shall have and use a copy of the Deuteronomic law; indeed, the whole incident reflects the expectation of Deuteronomy 17:14–17 that when the Israelites enter their land, they will want to establish a monarchy, like the nations round them, and though this will be allowed, it is only under certain conditions.

Within this somewhat overwhelming Deuteronomic editorial framework are incorporated two older narratives, one (1 Sam.9:1 – 10:16) explaining how Saul met Samuel (Saul, seeking his father's lost asses, goes to the seer for help), and the other (1 Sam.11:1–11) demonstrating that Saul was a worthy successor to the former judges and saviours of Israel such as Gideon and Jephthah on whom the spirit of the Lord had come (1 Sam.11:6; cf. Jud.6:34; 11:29). This second narrative is often taken to provide the real reason for Saul's rise to power.

(4) 1 Sam.13:1 – 15:35. Most of Saul's reign appears to have been spent fighting the Philistines (1 Sam.13–14; 17; 24:1; 28; 29; 31), and the death of Saul in battle against the Philistines is not reported until 1 Sam.31; but from the start, the narrative of Saul's reign indicates that Saul is a failure and that the future lies with David. Perhaps by some textual corruption, we no longer know how long Saul reigned (1 Sam.13:1). Almost immediately Saul disobeys Samuel's instructions (1 Sam.10:8; 13:8–15), in spite of Samuel's warning (12:14f.), and Samuel tells Saul that his kingdom will not continue, for the Lord has already (!) appointed another *nagid* (1 Sam.13:14). The subsequent narrative of battle against the Philistines shows Saul making a rash oath which brings his son Jonathan into danger (just as the judge Jephthah had endangered his daughter, Jud.11:30–40), and the episode ends with a summary of Saul's reign and a genealogy, as if concluding his life-story (1 Sam.14:47–51). Chapter 15 tells how Saul failed to destroy the Amalekites and their possessions completely, as commanded by God, and this seals Saul's fate: 'the LORD repented that he had made Saul king over Israel' (1 Sam.15:35).

(5) 1 Sam.16 – 2 Sam.8. This section begins with the anointing of David, son of Jesse, by Samuel (as Saul had been anointed), and ends with Nathan's oracle promising David a 'house' or dynastic succession (2 Sam.7), followed by a summary of David's achievements (2 Sam.8). It has been called the story of the rise of David, and it contains some of the best-known story-telling in the Bible. There is debate as to where this section ends and the next begins, for the

following section, the so-called 'Succession Narrative' or 'Court History' (2 Sam.9–20) is seen by some to have its roots in 2 Samuel 6:20–23; on the other hand, the story of the rise of David is taken by some to end with 2 Samuel 10. This debate in fact reveals the literary craft of the historian, and for practical purposes we shall draw the dividing line for the moment after 2 Samuel 8. The narrative sequence is then as follows. David, the youngest son of Jesse, is anointed by Samuel to replace Saul as *nagid*. (The rejection of the oldest son, a tall man (2 Sam.16:7), may subtly allude to the rejection of Saul, 'taller than any of the people from his shoulders up' (1 Sam.10:23).) The Spirit of the Lord is with David that day, and departs from Saul (1 Sam.16:13, 14). David enters Saul's service according to 1 Samuel 16:14–23 as a musician (the tradition that David was a musician appears in the eighth-century BC prophet Amos (Amos 6:5), and in the titles of many psalms), and according to 1 Samuel 17 as a warrior previously unknown to Saul. The Goliath story (1 Sam.17) is a piece of folk-lore; in true folk-lore style, the hero wins royal recognition, the hand of the king's daughter, and great riches. The real giant-killer, however, appears to have been Elhanan of Bethlehem (2 Sam.21:19), the story subsequently being credited to David (the reverse procedure is much less likely). David's successes arouse Saul's jealousy, and he makes various attempts to kill David. David flees to the wilderness, promising to keep faith with Saul's son Jonathan and his descendants, and collecting *en route* the sword of Goliath from the sanctuary at Nob (which brought Saul's vengeance on the priests there). Saul pursued David into the wilderness, where, entering a cave, he unwittingly gave David a chance to kill him, which David refused to take.

The centrepiece of this section is the story of David and Abigail in ch.25. When Abigail's husband Nabal ('churlish') refused to pay David's men protection money, Abigail with great diplomacy saved her husband from David's anger and saved David from the strategic error of incurring blood-guilt and alienating local support. This is followed by another story of how David spared Saul (ch.26). David now joins Saul's enemies, the Philistines, and deceives the Philistine king, Achish of Gath, into believing that David is raiding Judah when he is in fact raiding the enemies of Judah to the south. Then comes the climax of Saul's career and his final campaign against the Philistines. Samuel is dead (1 Sam.25:1), and Saul, in fear, consults Samuel through a medium, and hears once again the news that

> 'the LORD has torn the kingdom out of your hand, and given it to your neighbour, David. Because you did not obey the voice of the LORD, and did not carry out his fierce wrath against Amalek, therefore the LORD has done this thing to you this day. Moreover the LORD will give Israel also with you into the hand of the Philistines; and tomorrow you and your sons shall be with me; the LORD will give the army of Israel also into the hand of the Philistines' (1 Sam.28:17–19)

When battle is joined at Aphek, David is spared the embarrassment of having to fight on the Philistine side against Saul because the Philistine generals mistrust him and have him dismissed; instead, David attacks the Amalekites, sending the spoil to his supporters in Judah. (The narrator, however, finds the importance of the story in David's equal division of the spoils between those who campaigned and those who stayed behind to mind the baggage, and this equal division became 'a statute and an ordinance for Israel to this day' (1 Sam.30:25).) Saul, meanwhile, committed suicide on the battlefield. When an Amalekite came to David's camp to claim responsibility (hoping for a reward), David killed him, saying, 'Your blood be upon your head; for your own mouth has testified against you, saying, "I have slain the LORD's anointed"' (2 Sam.1:16). David follows this with his famous lament over Saul and Jonathan (2 Sam.1:19–20):

> 'Thy glory, O Israel, is slain upon thy high places!
>    How are the mighty fallen!
> Tell it not in Gath,
>    publish it not in the streets of Ashkelon;
> lest the daughters of the Philistines rejoice,
>    lest the daughters of the uncircumcised exult.'

This is clearly a turning point in the narrative, and David now actively pursues rule over the region of Judah and over the kingdom of Saul (2 Sam.2–5). He is anointed king over Judah in Hebron (2 Sam.2:1–4) and diplomatically praises the men of Jabesh-gilead who buried Saul (2:4–7). The forces of Saul's son, Ishbosheth, led by Abner, meet the forces of David, led by Joab, at Gibeon, with casualties on either side. Abner kills Joab's brother, Asahel. The plot now thickens; Abner, angered by the criticism of his royal master Ishbosheth, makes overtures to David, to bring over to him Saul's kingdom, but Joab murders Abner in revenge for the death of Asahel. Ishbosheth is killed by two army captains, who hope for David's commendation but are executed instead. Now leaderless, the tribes of Israel come to Hebron and make David king over Israel. David and Joab capture Jerusalem, a Canaanite city lying between Judah in the south and the tribes of Israel in the north, and make it the new capital city. David finally suppresses the Philistine opposition (2 Sam.5:17–23), and brings the Ark of the Lord from Kiriath-jearim to Jerusalem. David wished to replace its tent with a permanent house (i.e., a temple) (2 Sam.7:2), but in a remarkable oracle from Yahweh, the court prophet Nathan tells David that the Lord has not previously required anyone to build a house (i.e., a temple) for him, but that the Lord will make for David a house (i.e., a dynasty): 'Moreover the LORD declares to you that the LORD will make you a house... And your house and your kingdom shall be made sure for ever before me; your throne shall be established for ever.' (2 Sam.7:11,16). (This oracle seems to have been extended in verses 12–15 by reference to the birth of Solomon who would build a house, i.e., a temple, and would incur God's chastening but not God's rejection.) This promise of an everlasting dynasty is clearly the climax to the story of David's rise to kingship; and the account is rounded off by a summary of David's wars, conveying a picture of an empire extending from Syria in the north to Edom in the south, and a list of David's officials (2 Sam.8).

By any reckoning, this is a remarkable piece of narrative, effective because it is so direct, vivid, and personal. The story-teller's hero is David, who can do no wrong (in this he contrasts with the David of the next major section, 2 Samuel 9–20, who fails so lamentably). David is ruddy, has beautiful eyes, and is handsome (2 Sam.16:12); the Lord, however, does not look upon the outward appearance but the heart (2 Sam.16:7), and has chosen David and is with him (2 Sam.16:18). Indeed, Saul is afraid of David, because the Lord was with him but had departed from Saul (1 Sam.18:12), and Saul becomes David's permanent enemy (1 Sam.18:29). But all Israel and Judah love David (1 Sam.18:15), and Saul's son Jonathan also loves David (1 Sam.20:17). Increasingly, David is accepted as the future ruler of Israel. Saul realises that as long as David lives, Jonathan will not succeed to the throne (1 Sam.20:31); Jonathan himself says to David, 'You shall be king over Israel, and I shall be next to you; Saul my father also knows this' (1 Sam.23:17). Abigail looks forward to the time 'when the LORD has done to my lord according to all the good that he has spoken concerning you, and has appointed you prince over Israel' (1 Sam.25:30). Even David's enemies respect him, and Saul himself utters a blessing on David (1 Sam.26:25). Achish of Gath is ready to make David his bodyguard for life (1 Sam.28:2), and sees him as honest and blameless (1 Sam.29:6,9). Abner recognises that David has control of the land (2 Sam.3:12), and the tribes of Israel recall that 'when Saul was king over us, it was you that led out and brought in Israel; and the LORD said to you, "You shall be shepherd of my people Israel, and you shall be prince over Israel"' (2 Sam.5:2). David himself acts honourably at all times, refusing to take advantage of Saul as the Lord's anointed (1 Sam.24:1–22; 26:1–25), avoiding fighting on the Philistine side against Saul, killing the self-proclaimed regicide, lamenting the deaths of Saul and Jonathan, thanking those who buried Saul, publicly disavowing Abner's death, avenging the murder of Ishbosheth, and finally taking the Ark up to Jerusalem and seeking to provide a temple for it. Right at the end, however, David suddenly appears less than perfect; his wife Michal, Saul's daughter, sees him dancing in abandoned fashion before the ark, 'uncovering himself today before the eyes of his servants' maids, as one of the vulgar fellows shamelessly uncovers himself!' (2 Sam.6:20). David responds by taking her at her word, and the narrator makes clear the point: 'and Michal the daughter of Saul had no child to the day of her death' (2 Sam.6:23). This was a sign of trouble to come.

This narrative section strongly supports David's right to be *nagid*, the anointed prince, of Israel and Judah. Samuel anoints him, and Samuel is brought up from Sheol to tell Saul to his face that he has been rejected in favour of David. These chapters are clearly composed by a supporter of David's dynasty, though by one who is not without sympathy for Saul and Jonathan, whom David honours. P.K. McCarter in his recent commentary thinks that this composition goes back to the time of David himself; T.D. Mettinger dates it from the early years of the divided monarchy, when it defended Davidic claims to rule all Israel. J. van Seters, however, credits the composition to the Deuteronomic Historian in the seventh/sixth centuries BC, and firmly rules against its being a document contemporary or nearly contemporary with David and Solomon's time. It must be noted, however, that evidence of standard Deuteronomic phraseology is rare until we reach 2 Samuel 7, and virtually non-existent between 1 Samuel 16 and 2 Samuel 5, but also that the combination of support for the Davidic throne and respect for the prophet Samuel and the original royal house of Israel could fit the Deuteronomistic school very well.

(6) 2 Sam.9–20, 1 Kings 1–2 ('The Court History', or 'The Succession Narrative'). The story of the rise of David to the throne is balanced by the following narrative, which culminates in the succession of Solomon to the throne of David. Since the work of L. Rost in 1926, this has been seen as a unified narrative answering the question of 1 Kings 1:20,27, 'who will sit upon the throne of my lord the king after him?'. Many have seen it as an originally independent piece, one of the major sources for the Deuteronomistic History, but if so, it is not clear where this source began (for Nathan's prediction of a 'house' for David (2 Sam.7), Michal's childlessness (2 Sam.6), and perhaps also the story of Joab, Abner and Asahel (2 Sam.2:8 – 4:12) seem to be presupposed by the story) or where it ended (for 1 Kings 1–2 are divided from 2 Samuel 9–20 by 2 Samuel 21–24, intrusive though they may be, and 1 Kings 1–2 could equally well belong to the narrative of the reign of Solomon, whose right to the throne they defend). There are no clear literary or linguistic criteria marking out 2 Samuel 9–20 and 1 Kings 1–2 as an originally separate source, and the chapters are well integrated into the surrounding material, with links both backward and forward in Samuel and Kings. J. van Seters argues that the Succession Narrative is not a source for the Deuteronomistic Historian, but a later addition to the work; but it may be simpler and more profitable to see it as part of the historian's composition, balancing the previous chapters about the rise of David.

Certainly 2 Samuel 9 marks a new beginning after the summary of David's reign in 2 Samuel 8. We now return to the almost forgotten theme of David's covenant with Jonathan: 'Is there still anyone left of the house of Saul, that I may show him kindness for Jonathan's sake?' (2 Sam.9:1); and Jonathan's crippled son Mephibosheth is found. The Ammonite war is introduced, this in turn introducing the story of Bathsheba, the wife of David's soldier Uriah the Hittite. Nathan rebukes David in a famous parable and promises that David's wives will in turn be given to his neighbours (a prophecy fulfilled when David's son Absalom takes his father's concubines). David's first child by Bathsheba dies, and a second, Solomon, or Jedidiah, is born. Chapter 13 tell how Amnon, David's firstborn son by Ahinoam of Jezreel, raped his half-sister Tamar, and how her brother Absalom, David's son by Maacah, daughter of Talmai king of Geshur, revenged her by killing Amnon, and then had to flee to Geshur. David, however, longed for Absalom, and Joab engineered his pardon and return to Jerusalem. Absalom, however, was dissatisfied, gained a following, and raised the standard of revolt, having himself crowned at Hebron. David had to flee east across the river Jordan; Absalom pursued (though not immediately, as advised by Ahitophel, whose good advice was countered by David's agent at court, Hushai), and was killed by Joab. David sacked Joab, replacing him with his brother Amasa, pardoned a previous opponent, Shimei, punished Mephibosheth for not joining him in his flight from

Absalom, and rewarded a Transjordanian supporter, Barzillai, for his help. However, on his return to Jerusalem, a dispute arose between David's northern and southern supporters, resulting in the northerners' secession. David sent Amasa to deal with the revolt, but Joab killed him and resumed command. He besieged the northern rebel leader in Abel-beth-maacah, whose head the people of the city had thrown over the wall to Joab, in order to save themselves.

At this point there follows a list of David's officials (2 Sam.20:23–26), apparently reduplicating the earlier list at 2 Samuel 8:16–18, and this is followed by the story of a famine, which is blamed on the unavenged murder of some people of Gibeon (a non-Israelite village north of Jerusalem) by Saul. The Gibeonites ask that they be allowed to hang Saul's sons, and David grants this, but spares Mephibosheth for the sake of Jonathan, and has the bones of Saul and his sons buried in the land of Benjamin. This tidies up the history of Saul's family, and may very well have belonged originally between 2 Samuel 8 and 9, being moved and set alongside the parallel story of the pestilence sent against Israel on account of David's sin in numbering the people. As Saul's sin had to be paid for, so did David's, and David paid for it by the purchase of land which was to become the site of Solomon's temple. Each story ends with the remark that God 'heeded supplications for the land' (2 Sam.21:14; 24:25). However, the stories have been separated by the intrusion, first, of various archival materials relating to David's warriors (2 Sam.21:15–22; 23:8–39), and by the insertion of a psalm of David (2 Sam.22; cf. Ps.18), and 'the last words of David' (2 Sam.23:1–7). David, like other Old Testament heroes, must praise God before he dies. Thus the way is prepared for the succession of Solomon, which follows in 1 Kings 1–2.

If the story of the rise of David presents David at his best, the 'Court History' or 'Succession Narrative' presents a very different picture. David begins by showing kindness to Saul's family, it is true, but prejudices his own reputation and his own family by his affair with Bathsheba and his disposal of Uriah. His own firstborn son then rapes his half-sister and gets himself killed; Absalom, apparently the next in line of succession, rebels (making capital out of David's failure to do justice, 2 Sam.15:1–6), and when his rebellion fails is killed by Joab. David loses the support of the northern tribes, the men of Israel, and makes matters worse by alienating the support of his faithful general Joab. The census story of 2 Samuel 24:1–9 shows that David temporarily lost even the support of the Lord, as Saul had lost it before him. In short, it begins to look as if the material in 1 and 2 Samuel presents David in terms of his rise and fall, and is not primarily concerned with the story of the succession. The narrator does not reject David, however, and the sequel in 1 Kings 1–2 makes it clear that the continuation of the Davidic house is not in question.

More difficult questions arise when we ask about the date and historical value of this narrative. Many scholars have seen it as an authentic record, almost contemporaneous with the events it describes, mainly on the grounds of its candid and vivid characterisation of David and others. But such characterisation may reflect the skills of the novelist as much as those of the historian, and the story of the rise of David may be likened to an historical novel rather than to an academic study; who but a novelist could recount the many private conversations given in these chapters? It is not easy to assess accurately the genre of this historical writing. The author devotes almost exactly as much space to the period of Samuel, Saul and David (who perhaps span half a century or more) as he does to the period of the monarchy from Solomon to Zedekiah, the last king of Judah (which spans almost four centuries). 1 and 2 Samuel have less archival content and more story-telling than 1 and 2 Kings, which provide a framework composed of archival material for all the kings, filling it out with story-telling about the kings and the prophets who challenged them. The possible archival material in 1 and 2 Samuel seems limited to the introduction to Saul's reign (though the text here seems incomplete), details of Saul's achievements and family (1 Sam.14:47-51), of Ishbosheth (2 Sam.2:8-11), of David's family (2 Sam.3:2-5), reign (2 Sam.5:3-5, 13-16), achievements (2 Sam.8:1-14), his officers (2 Sam.8:15-18; cf. 20:23-26), and his warriors (2 Sam.21:15-22; 23:8-39). The sequence of the rest appears to be the author's construction, based on thematic rather than chronological considerations, and any reconstruction of the history of the reigns of Saul and David must bear this in mind.

Our knowledge of the sources used by the author of 1 and 2 Samuel remains tentative, being based largely on the hypotheses of the existence of originally independent narratives about the Ark, the rise of David, and the 'Succession Narrative', but these 'sources' are seen to be closely interwoven, and inter-dependent, and the more this is so, the less convincing is their alleged originally separate existence. The date of this literary work in its present form is probably the late seventh-early sixth centuries BC, for its picture of Samuel the prophet and of the institution of monarchy reflect Deuteronomistic ideals, and Samuel's word about the relative value of sacrifice and obedience (1 Sam.15:22) compares closely with attitudes seen in the books of the eighth-century BC prophets (cf. Amos 5:21-23; Mic.6:6-8; Hos.6:6). The author, however, must have drawn upon more than his inventiveness, and we must still ask what sources would have been available. The short answer must be that the author drew on much popular story-telling, upon which he exercised his own creative skills; such stories as underlie, for example:

| | |
|---|---|
| the call of the boy Samuel | 1 Sam.3:2-18 |
| the effect of the Ark on the Philistines | 1 Sam.5,6 |
| the lost asses | 1 Sam.9 |
| the explanation of Saul's prophesying | 1 Sam.10:9-13 (cf.19:20-24) |
| Saul's campaign against the Ammonites | 1 Sam.11:1-11 |
| the exploit of Jonathan at Michmash | 1 Sam.14 |
| the killing of Goliath | 1 Sam.17 |
| the price David paid for Michal | 1 Sam.18:20-29 |
| Saul's attempts to kill David | 1 Sam.19 |

| | |
|---|---|
| David's appearance at Nob | 1 Sam.21 |
| David's sparing of Saul in the wilderness | 1 Sam.24,26 |
| Nabal and Abigail | 1 Sam.25 |
| Saul's consultation with Samuel through a medium | 1 Sam.28 |
| David's attack on the Amalekites | 1 Sam.30 |
| Abner's killing of Asahel | 2 Sam.2 |
| the death of Ishbosheth | 2 Sam.4 |
| the capture of Jerusalem | 2 Sam.5:6–10 |
| the transfer of the Ark and the dancing of David | 2 Sam.6 |
| the shaving of the beards of David's envoys | 2 Sam.10:1–5 |
| the wooing of Bathsheba and the death of Uriah | 2 Sam.11 |
| the rape of Tamar | 2 Sam.13 |
| the death of Absalom | 2 Sam.18 |
| the murder of Amasa | 2 Sam.20 |
| the death of Sheba | 2 Sam.20 |
| the revenge of the Gibeonites | 2 Sam.21 |

Most of these are memorable stories about individuals, which have been collected and woven into the tapestry. Poetic material is incorporated at 1 Sam.2:1–10; 18:7 (cf.21:11; 29:5); 2 Sam.1:19–26; 3:33–34; 22:2–51 (cf.Ps.18); 23:1–7.

It has often been noted that the prose of the Deuteronomistic theologian is not much in evidence, but it makes an unmistakable appearance in several key passages. The Deuteronomistic editorial hand is visible in the incorporation of Eli (1 Sam.4:18) and Samuel (1 Sam.9:15) into the sequence and chronology of the 'judges' of Israel, and in the integration of the reigns of Saul, Ishbosheth and David into the chronology of the kings of Israel (1 Sam.13:1; 2 Sam.2:10f.; 5:4f.). Deuteronomistic theological concerns, however, are made clear in the programmatic speeches of the man of God to Eli (1 Sam.2:27–36), the speech of Samuel (1 Sam.7:3f.), the account of the people's request for a monarchy (1 Sam.8:4–22), and Samuel's farewell speech after making Saul king (1 Sam.12:1–25), Abigail's speech to David (1 Sam.25:24–31, especially v.30), and above all in Nathan's oracle to David and David's prayer (2 Sam.7:1–17, 18–29).

Thus, Samuel speaks of the need to return to the Lord and put away foreign gods (1 Sam.7:3f.; cf. Yahweh's words in 8:8), describes the dangers inherent in accepting the rule of kings (1 Sam.8:11–18), and then, when the elders of Israel have accepted monarchy, warns them in Deuteronomistic language that

> 'if you will fear the LORD and serve him and hearken to his voice and not rebel against the commandment of the LORD, and if both you and the king who reigns over you will follow the LORD your God, it will be well; but if you will not hearken to the voice of the LORD, but rebel against the commandment of the LORD, then the hand of the LORD will be against you and your king.' (1 Sam.12:14f.)

In 2 Samuel 7, Nathan's oracle, with its two themes of the Davidic dynasty and the building of the temple, announces the two major themes of the whole subsequent history and establishes the historian's programme. Nathan's oracle links these themes with the previous history of the judges; David's prayer refers back to the Deuteronomistic theology of God and his people (2 Sam.7:22f.):

> 'Thou art great, O LORD God; for there is none like thee, and there is no God besides thee... What other nation on earth is like thy people Israel, whom God went to redeem to be his people, making himself a name, and doing for them great and terrible things, by driving out before his people a nation and its gods? And thou didst establish for thyself thy people Israel to be thy people for ever; and thou, O LORD, didst become their God.'

The historian voices his main themes through the mouths of his leading actors, as previously through Joshua (Josh.1:2-9; 23:2-16), and it is noticeable that in Samuel there is no explicit reference to the need to obey the law of Moses, as in Joshua 1:7. This theme has been temporarily eclipsed by the emphasis on the Davidic dynasty; the two themes later come together (as in David's deathbed charge to Solomon, 1 Kings 2:1-4, and the account of Josiah's reformation, 2 Kings 22:2; 23:25). These passages give direction to the whole narrative; they show that the narrator is concerned with Israel's call to live on the land in obedience to the law of Moses and with Israel's fall from that grace. At first God ruled Israel; when the people sinned and fell into the hands of their enemies, God rescued them by means of judges. When they rejected God and demanded a king, to be like the nations round about, God – against better judgment – allowed the request, with the proviso that as long as the people and their king obeyed the commandments all would be well. Saul did not obey; David was in every way better and favoured by God, but even David lapsed, and this led under Solomon to the division of the kingdom and to the eventual disasters of Israel's destruction at the hands of the Assyrians and Judah's destruction at the hands of the Babylonians. But this brings us to the story of the books of the Kings.

## II. *1 and 2 Kings*

Chapters 1 and 2 of 1 Kings show clearly that they continue the story presented in the books of Samuel, and are believed by many scholars to be the continuation of the 'Succession Narrative'. Further, since the work of Martin Noth 1 and 2 Kings have been seen as the final part of the Deuteronomistic History. It was probably the Greek translation of the Hebrew scriptures, the Septuagint (LXX), which first divided the books of Samuel and Kings into four books (which it calls 1,2,3 and 4 Kingdoms); the Hebrew text did not divide Samuel and Kings into 1 and 2 Samuel, 1 and 2 Kings until the fifteenth century AD.

1 and 2 Kings fall more readily than 1 and 2 Samuel into obvious sections. 1 Kings 1-2 tells of Solomon's accession to the throne; 1 Kings 3-11 describes Solomon's reign; 1 Kings 12 – 2 Kings 17 narrates the history of Israel and Judah from their division into two kingdoms at the death of Solomon to the fall of Israel to Assryia in 722 BC. The final section, 2 Kings 18-25, tells the history of

Judah from that point to its destruction by Nebuchadnezzar of Babylon in 587 BC. The books of Kings cover the history of Judah and Israel from the tenth to the sixth centuries BC, and along with the evidence of the prophetic books Amos, Hosea, Isaiah, and Micah from the eighth century BC and of Nahum, Habakkuk and Zephaniah in the late seventh century and of Jeremiah and Ezekiel in the early sixth century provide our major sources for the history of the monarchic period. Like the books of Samuel, the books of Kings contain a number of stories (especially about prophetic figures) of limited value to the political historian, being legend rather than archival record; legends apart, however, these books contain a large amount of material apparently drawn from official archives or chronicles, held together by a carefully integrated chronological scheme. Most historians of ancient Israel feel confident that 1 and 2 Kings give us a reasonably reliable sequence of events for the monarchic period and follow it fairly closely.

The historian's general confidence is increased by the fact that a number of important people and events are corroborated by the records of other contemporary peoples – the Moabites to the east, the Syrians to the north, and the empires of Assyria and Babylonia to the east. The stele of king Mesha of Moab (cf. 2 Kings 3:1) refers to Israel's king Omri and his son, and the men of Gad. In Syria, the stele of king Zakir refers to the king Barhadad son of Hazael, probably to be identified with the Hazael of 2 Kings 8:7–16, and the Benhadad son of Hazael of 2 Kings 13:3. The Assyrian records tell of the tribute paid by Jehu of Israel in 841 BC, the fall of Samaria in 722 BC, Sennacherib's campaign against Lachish and Jerusalem in 701 BC, and the fall of Jerusalem under Jehoiachin in 597 BC.

The books of Kings contain an enormous amount of detail, and it would be impossible within one chapter to retell in full the history of the two kingdoms as given by 1 and 2 Kings, but it will be valuable to outline the story and note some of the problems it raises for the modern historian.

1 Kings 1–2 tells how in David's old age his second son Adonijah conspired with David's general Joab and the priest Abiathar to succeed to the throne, but a counterplot by Bathsheba, Nathan the prophet and Zadok the priest – with the help of Benaiah the commander of the mercenary troops – resulted in the succession of Bathsheba's son Solomon. Solomon promptly removed Abiathar from office, had Adonijah, Joab, and David's old enemy Shimei executed, and 'so the kingdom was established in the hand of Solomon' (1 Kings 2:46). This narrative, which belongs in style and content with the historical stories of 2 Samuel, clearly supports Solomon's accession and justifies his ruthlessness.

1 Kings 3–11 presents a carefully organised picture of Solomon's reign. He begins well, requesting and obtaining the gift of wisdom from the Lord. With the help of Hiram of Tyre, and the use of forced labour, Solomon undertakes the temple-building forbidden to David, completes it and dedicates it (chs.5–8). But 1 Kings 9 contains the Deuteronomistic warning that if Solomon turns aside from following Yahweh and serves other gods, Yahweh will cut off Israel from its land and the temple will become a heap of ruins (as indeed happened in 587 BC). The narrative goes on to hint that Solomon's relationship with Hiram (9:10–14), his use of forced labour and his marriage to Pharaoh's daughter all held potential for

disaster. Yet outwardly all was well; the Queen of Sheba praised what she saw and blessed Yahweh for it, and Solomon's kingdom prospered (1 Kings 10). But Solomon's love of foreign women angered Yahweh (11:1–10), who announced that he would make good his previous warning:

> 'Since this has been your mind and you have not kept my covenant and my statutes which I have commanded you, I will surely tear the kingdom from you and will give it to your servant. Yet for the sake of David your father I will not do it in your days, but I will tear it out of the hand of your son. However I will not tear away all the kingdom; but I will give one tribe to your son, for the sake of David my servant and for the sake of Jerusalem which I have chosen.' (1 Kings 11:11–13).

These words, with the prophecy of Ahijah to Jeroboam (11:29–39), set the stage for the following history of the two kingdoms, Israel and Judah. Before Solomon's reign is over, he is facing opposition from Hadad in Edom to the south and from Rezin in Damascus to the north, and finally from Jeroboam, formerly overseer of his own labour force, in central Israel.

These chapters on Solomon clearly emphasise the importance of the Jerusalem temple (1 Kings 5–8) and the peace and prosperity of a united Israel under a ruler whose wisdom came from Yahweh, before Solomon, like Saul and David before him, fell from grace. The fall resulted from Solomon's love of women and consequent apostasy (1 Kings 11:1–7), leading first to the creation of the northern kingdom, which in turn fell because of its apostasy (2 Kings 17), and ultimately to the fall of Jerusalem itself. The presentation of the reign of Solomon is an integral part of the explanation of the collapse of Judah and the exile of the historian's own day, a possibility spelt out in Solomon's prayer at the dedication of the temple (1 Kings 8:46–52). That the historian has used the reign of Solomon in this way, however, does not mean that all the details preserved here are without historical value, and modern historians have tended to base their picture of Solomon's kingdom on such items as the list of regional officers (1 Kings 4:1–19), the details of Solomon's buildings and his military preparations (1 Kings 7:1–12; 9:15–19; 10:26f.), and his trading ventures (9:26–28; 10:14–22, 28–29).

It is hard to know how to assess the historicity of these details, however, for we have no clear criteria for identifying and dating the historian's sources. The list of officials (1 Kings 4:7–21) is far from coherent and shows signs of revision. Some argue that the description of the temple (6:1–11) is an exilic attempt to preserve details of the now-destroyed temple. The description of Solomon's labour force (5:13–16), apparently raised 'from all Israel', appears to be contradicted by 11:20–22. The trade and wealth of Solomon's kingdom appears exaggerated. The reference to his marriage with a pharaoh's daughter cannot be supported from Egyptian sources and is suspect as part of the attempt to glorify Solomon. However, it seems that the references to Solomon's building activity at Hazor, Megiddo and Gezer (9:15–17) can be correlated with the archaeological evidence from these sites, whose four-chamber gateways and casemate walls, some have argued, were designed by the same architect. Unfortunately the site of 'Ezion-geber, which is near Eloth on the shore of the Red Sea' has not been identified with any certainty, and there is no firm evidence available at present for the precise position and outline of the temple at Jerusalem, though it almost certainly lay somewhere within the confines of the later Herodian temple platform, still visible today. The descriptions of the extent of Solomon's kingdom in 1 Kings 4:21 and 24 are not entirely consistent; the first appears to exclude and the second to include Philistia, but both appear to give the Euphrates as the northern border, which seems unlikely, especially in view of what we are told about the kings of Syria (Hadadezer of Zobah and Rezin of Damascus) in 1 Kings 11:23–25. The general picture of peace and prosperity in Israel in 1 Kings 4:25–28 seems overdrawn, especially in view of the internal dissension evidenced by the rebellion led by Jeroboam the Ephraimite (1 Kings 11:26–28; 12:1–33). In short, Solomon held together for a time the two halves (Judah and Israel) bequeathed to him by David, attempting to consolidate them by economic development and military control; by his death, however, his kingdom was under pressure from both outside and inside, and the historian's picture of the Solomonic era as one of power, peace and plenty must be somewhat exaggerated.

The central section of 1 and 2 Kings is found in 1 Kings 12 – 2 Kings 17, and presents the parallel histories of the two independent kingdoms of Israel and Judah, from their creation after the death of Solomon to the destruction of Israel by the Assyrians in 722 BC. The stage is set before the death of Solomon by the prophecy of Ahijah of Shiloh to Jeroboam. This prophecy, which represents the viewpoint of the Deuteronomistic Historian, is far from unsympathetic to the creation and existence of the independent northern kingdom of Israel, but warns Jeroboam (as Solomon was warned) that the kingdom's survival depends on obedience to God's commandments (in the Deuteronomic law):

> 'And if you will hearken to all that I command you, and will walk in my ways, and do what is right in my eyes by keeping my statutes and my commandments, as David my servant did, I will be with you, and will build you a sure house, as I built for David, and I will give Israel to you.' (1 Kings 11:38)

Israel, with ten tribes, seems to be more important than Judah with one tribe (Benjamin), and in the following history, the historian gives an account of the reign of Jeroboam of Israel before turning to that of Solomon's son Rehoboam in Judah. The historian tells the history reign by reign, alternating between Israel and Judah. After the reign of Jeroboam of Israel, he describes the reigns of Rehoboam, Abijam, and Asa of Judah, whose reigns began within the reign of Jeroboam of Israel. Then follow the reigns of those Israelite kings whose reigns begin in Asa's reign – Nadab, Baasha, Elah, Zimri, Tibni, Omri, and Ahab (1 Kings 15:25 – 16:34). Then comes a series of prophetic stories about Elijah and Micaiah ben Imlah, all related to the reign of Ahab, culminating in the death of Ahab (1 Kings 17:1 – 22:40), at which point we turn to Jehoshaphat of Judah, whose reign began in Ahab's reign (1 Kings 22:41–50); then to Ahaziah of Israel (1 Kings 21:51 – 2 Kings 1:18) and Jehoram of Israel (2 Kings 3:1 – 9:26), whose reigns began in Jehoshaphat's reign. Meanwhile, in the reign of Joram of Israel began those of Joram of Judah (2 Kings 8:16–24) and Ahaziah of Judah (2 Kings 8:25 – 9:29). Many scholars have suspected some reduplication here, thinking it unlikely that both kingdoms should have an Ahaziah and a Jehoram/Joram in close succession, almost contemporaneously, and many have suggested that Jehoram of Israel and Jehoram of Judah are the same person, Jehoram of Israel ruling both kingdoms for a time. Both Jehoram of Israel and Ahaziah of Judah were killed by Jehu of Israel, whose rule is described in 2 Kings 9:30 – 10:30. The historian now reverts to affairs in Judah with the reigns of Queen Athaliah and king Jehoash (2 Kings 11–12); then to Jehoahaz and Joash of Israel, who came to the throne during the reign of Jehoash of Judah (2 Kings 13; 14:15–16). In the reign of Jehoash of Israel, began the reign of Amaziah of Judah (2 Kings 14:1–22 (minus 14:15–16)); and in his reign began the reign of Jeroboam II of Israel (2 Kings 14:23–29). In Jeroboam's reign began the reign of Azariah of Judah (2 Kings 15:1–7), and in Azariah's reign began those of Zechariah, Shallum, Menahem, Pekahiah and Pekah in Israel (2 Kings 15:8–31). In Pekah's time Jotham and Ahaz came to the throne in Judah (2 Kings 15:32 – 16:20). In Ahaz's reign began that of Hoshea of Israel, which saw the end of the kingdom of Israel (2 Kings 17:1–6). In Hoshea's reign began that of Hezekiah of Judah (2 Kings 18:1 – 20:21), who was followed by the final kings of Judah: Manasseh, Amon, Josiah, Jehoahaz, Jehoiakim, Jehoiachin, Zedekiah (2 Kings 21–25).

In this alternating system, the historian dates the accession of each king of Judah by reference to the regnal year of his opposite number in Israel (and vice versa), and gives the number of years each king ruled. However, a number of chronological problems arise. For example, from the death of Solomon and the accession of Rehoboam and Jeroboam until the fall of Samaria in 722 BC, the kings of Israel reigned, according to the Deuteronomistic Historian, for a total of 241½ years (for the same period, the reigns of the kings of Judah total 262 years). If we calculate backwards from 722 BC on the Israelite figures, the divided kingdoms began in 962 BC, which is certainly too early for Shishak, Pharaoh of Egypt, to invade in Rehoboam's fifth year (1 Kings 14:25). For the Judahite monarchy, the historian gives a total of 393 years from the accession of Rehoboam to the death of Zedekiah and the fall of Jerusalem in 587 BC. This would date Rehoboam's accession to 979 BC, which is inconsistent with the figures for the kings of Israel, and appears to be far too early. As the reigns of Rehoboam and Jeroboam begin within months of each other, the historian's figures need some adjustment, or at least some explanation. The difficulties have been compounded by mistaken attribution to the reigns of Ahab and Jehoram of battles against Benhadad of Syria and stories about Elisha which properly belonged to the time of Jehu and his successors.

Attempts have been made to solve the major chronological problems by postulating the use of different ways of calculating reigns in Israel and Judah (depending on whether the period between the accession and the first autumn New Year festival of the reign, or the year following the first New Year festival in the reign, was counted as the king's first year), or by postulating co-regencies (e.g., between Jehoshaphat and Jehoram of Judah, or Uzziah and Jotham of

Judah), or, recently, by postulating that Asa, Jehoash, Amaziah and Azariah (Uzziah) in Judah, and Baasha in Israel, for various reasons abdicated their thrones. In the case of Judah, this suggestion would have the effect of reducing the total period given for the kings of Judah between Rehoboam and 722 BC by some sixty years, thus allowing a more reasonable space for the lengthy reigns of David and Solomon. Israel's overrun is met by slight reductions in the reigns of Omri (one year), Ahab (seven years), Jehu (ten years), and by supposing that for sixteen of the twenty years attributed to him, Pekah was a rival to his predecessors Menahem and Pekahiah, ruling officially for only four years. (See the chart on p.254.)

Certainty may be impossible, for the Hebrew writer was only the first of a long line of scholars attempting to make a coherent scheme out of what appeared to be contradictory information, but some fixed points can be established by reference to the contemporary Assyrian and Babylonian records. Shalmaneser III of Assyria records that he defeated a coalition of kings from Syria and Palestine, among whom was Ahab of Israel, at Qarqar in Syria in 853 BC; Shalmaneser's 'Black Obelisk' (now in the British Museum) shows Jehu ('Iaua, son of Omri', though in fact Jehu was not the son of Omri, but an usurper of unknown origins) kneeling before him, and describes the tribute he brought (841 BC). Adadnirari III (810–783 BC) says, on the stele found in 1967 at Rimah in Syria, that he received the tribute of Joash of Samaria; this was probably about 796 BC. Tiglath-pileser III (744–727 BC) mentions receiving tribute from Menahem of Israel (737 BC) (cf. 2 Kings 15:19–20), and putting Hoshea on the throne of Israel (732 BC) (cf. 2 Kings 15:29–30). (This fact makes it difficult to accept at face value the ascription in 2 Kings 15:27 of twenty years' reign to Pekah between Menahem and Hoshea.) Shalmaneser V (727–722) conquered Samaria in 722 BC (2 Kings 17:3–6), and shortly afterwards Sargon II (722–705 BC) rebuilt it, settling there new inhabitants. In 701 BC Sennacherib (705–681 BC) besieged Hezekiah and received his tribute (2 Kings 18:13–16; 18:17 – 19:36). The firmest correspondence of all between the chronological data of 1 and 2 Kings and the external records comes from comparison of 2 Kings 24:10–17 and the Babylonian Chronicles of Nebuchadnezzar, which report that he began a siege of Jerusalem in December of his seventh year, capturing it on the second day of the month Adar (15 or 16 March, 597 BC). This is a key date for the reconstruction of the chronology of the monarchic period.

Chronology is not, however, the primary concern of the central section of 1 and 2 Kings, although the author is concerned enough to set the kings of Israel and Judah as accurately as possible in historical relationship with one another, and to supply a number of historical details about each. Of the kings of Judah, the author records the king's name and date of accession, his age on accession, the length and place of his reign, the name of the queen mother, and an assessment of the king's piety (judged by comparison with David's). In the conclusion of his report on each king, he notes the source of further information, details of the king's death and burial, and names his successor. (In the case of the kings of Israel, the wickedness of each king is judged by comparison with that of Jeroboam, and there is no reference to the king's age on accession, or to any queen mother.) Between the formal introduction and conclusion to each reign, the historian narrates events of particular importance, and it is here that we see his particular interests: war, between Judah and Israel (1 Kings 12:21; cf. 14:30; 15:6,16–22; 2 Kings 4:8–14), between Israel, Judah and Syria (1 Kings 20,22; 2 Kings 6:24 – 7:20; 9:14–15; 10:32–33; 13:1–7; 15:28), between Judah and Edom and Moab (1 Kings 11:14–22; 2 Kings 3; 2 Kings 8:20–22; 14:7), and internal conspiracies (1 Kings 11:26–40; 15:27–28; 16:9–10; 2 Kings 9:11; 14:19; 15:10,15,25,30; 17:4).

He is also interested in the cult, both in Judah and Israel. The history of Israel begins with Jeroboam's sin in putting golden calves in Bethel and Dan, sacrificing to them, appointing a new priesthood and establishing a new autumn feast on the fifteenth day of the eighth month ('like the feast that was in Judah' on the fifteenth of the seventh month). (Jeroboam's sin is followed by Nadab, Baasha, Elah, Zimri (he reigned seven days!), Omri, Ahab, Ahaziah and Joram; not even that active campaigner Jehu turned from the sin of Jeroboam (2 Kings 10:31), nor did his successors Jehoahaz, Jeroboam II, Zechariah, Menahem, Pekehiah, and Pekah. The last king, Hoshea, like the rest, did what was evil in the sight of the Lord, 'yet not as the kings of Israel who were before him', and there is no reference to Jeroboam, surprisingly. In the final verdict (2 Kings 17:21–23), Israel as a whole is condemned for following Jeroboam's sin.) Moreover, Ahab married Jezebel from Sidon and built an altar and a temple for Baal in Samaria (1 Kings 16:32); in due course this was destroyed by Jehu, along with the worshippers of Baal, and turned into a latrine (2 Kings 10:18–27). In Judah, Asa (1 Kings 15:8–14) initiated cultic reforms, and Joash repaired the temple (1 Kings 12:4–16), though Ahaz let the side down by unlawful sacrifice and by importing to the Jerusalem temple a new altar made after the pattern of an Assyrian or Syrian altar at Damascus.

Above all, however, the historian is interested in the contribution of the prophets to the monarchy in both Israel and Judah, and much of the content of 1 King 12 – 2 Kings 17 is taken up with stories about the prophets. This interest has already appeared in the Deuteronomistic Historian, beginning with Deut.18:21–22, where the Deuteronomist explains how true and false prophets are to be distinguished:

> 'And if you say in your heart, "How may we know the word which the LORD has not spoken?" – when a prophet speaks in the name of the LORD, if the word does not come to pass or come true, that is a word which the LORD has not spoken; the prophet has spoken it presumptuously, you need not be afraid of him.'

Samuel the prophet anoints the first and second kings, and warns them and their subjects of the dangers and the consequences of disobeying God's commandments (1 Sam.8:10–18; 12:1–25). Nathan speaks the word of the Lord to David (2 Sam.7), and with Zadok the priest anoints Solomon king (1 Kings 1:34). Ahijah the prophet from Shiloh announces to Jeroboam that the Lord will tear the kingdom from the hand of Solomon and give Jeroboam ten tribes (1 Kings

11:31–39). In 1 Kings 13, a prophet at Bethel announces that Jeroboam's illegal altar will be torn down and desecrated, a prediction whose fulfilment is recorded in 2 Kings 23:15–18. Coupled with this is the story in which this prophet is himself punished for failing to return home directly, as God has commanded him. In 1 Kings 14, Ahijah prophesies to Jeroboam through his wife that because Jeroboam has made for himself other gods and molten images, the Lord

> 'will cut off from Jeroboam every male, both bond and free in Israel, and will utterly consume the house of Jeroboam, as a man burns up dung until it is all gone. Any one belonging to Jeroboam who dies in the city the dogs shall eat; and any one who dies in the open country the birds of the air shall eat; for the LORD has spoken it. . . Moreover the LORD will raise up for himself a king over Israel, who shall cut off the house of Jeroboam today.' (1 Kings 14:10–14)

The fulfilment is told in 1 Kings 15:29. Jehu the son of Hanani brings a similar prophetic word to Baasha (16:1–4), fulfilled in 16:12.

In 1 Kings 17, we have three prophetic legends about Elijah (he is fed by ravens, miraculously feeds a widow of Zarephath, and revives her child), and in 1 Kings 18 we read the story of the contest between Elijah, the sole remaining prophet of the Lord, and the four hundred prophets of Baal, the protégés of Ahab and Jezebel, on Mount Carmel. All the prophets of Baal are killed, and in fear of Jezebel's revenge (1 Kings 20) Elijah goes to Horeb, the mount of God (= Mount Sinai), where he experiences the presence of the Lord and is given a new commission, to anoint Hazael king over Syria, Jehu king over Israel, and Elisha as prophet in his own place (1 Kings 19:15–18). The story of Elijah continues in 1 Kings 21, where Elijah challenges Ahab's wickedness in acquiring Naboth's ancestral property, and threatens that Ahab's dynasty will go the way of the dynasties of Jeroboam and Baasha (1 Kings 21:21–24). In 2 Kings 1 Elijah conveys to king Ahaziah the word of the Lord that Ahaziah will not recover from his illness, because he looked for help from Baalzebub the god of Ekron rather than from Yahweh. When Ahaziah reacts by sending the military to arrest Elijah, Elijah has two platoons of soldiers consumed by fire before sparing the third. In 2 Kings 2, Elijah is taken up to heaven in a whirlwind, and Elisha inherits his mantle.

The activities of Elisha fill 2 Kings 2:1 – 8:15 and 9:1–3; for the most part they comprise a series of miracle legends, including the promise of water in the wilderness for the armies of Judah and Israel (2 Kings 3:13–20), the miraculous provision of oil for a widow (4:1–9), the promise of a son for the Shunammite woman, and when the boy died, his resuscitation (4:10–37), and the healing of Naaman the leper (5:1–27). According to 2 Kings 8:7–15, Elisha encourages Hazael's *coup d'état* against king Benhadad in Syria, and according to 2 Kings 9:1–10 sends a young prophet to anoint Jehu king in Israel, with the message,

> 'Thus says the LORD the God of Israel, I anoint you king over the people of the LORD, over Israel. And you shall strike down the house of Ahab your master, that I may avenge on Jezebel the blood of my servants the prophets, and the blood of all the servants of the LORD.'

The result is Jehu's revolution, in which Jehu kills the kings of Judah and Israel, and Jezebel the widow of Ahab, the seventy sons of the king of Israel, forty-two kinsmen of the king of Judah, and all those worshippers of Baal who accepted his invitation to attend a sacrifice to Baal in Samaria.

Together with this material about Elijah and Elisha go other prophetic stories all relating to Israel's wars against Syria in the second half of the ninth century BC: in 1 Kings 20 the king of Israel is condemned by a prophet for failing to kill the captured Syrian king Benhadad (as once Saul was condemned by Samuel for failing to slay Agag). In 1 Kings 22 (a story which reveals superbly how prophets functioned) Micaiah ben Imlah in a magnificent exit-line warns Jehoshaphat and Ahab as they prepare to campaign against Syria at Ramoth-gilead that 'if you [Ahab] return in peace, the LORD has not spoken by me'. 2 Kings 6:8 – 7:20 and 13:14–21 tell of Elisha's involvement in wars between Israel and Syria.

These stories of Elisha and of wars between Syria and Israel have been set in the reigns of Ahab and his successors of the Omride dynasty, ending with Jehu's revolution, but there are many indications that they really belong to the time of Jehu's dynasty; their connection with Ahab, Jehoshaphat, Jehoram and Ahaziah has caused considerable complications for the Deuteronomistic Historian's synchronisms. The main purpose of this editorial arrangement was to counter the wickedness of Israel's Omride dynasty (especially of Ahab and Jezebel, who supported Baal) with the prophetic opposition of both Elijah and Elisha, who supported Yahweh. Jehu is the prophetically supported leader who, full of zeal for the Lord like a judge of old (2 Kings 10:16), brings judgment on the house of Ahab (2 Kings 9:7–10). The prophetic activity does not stop here, however; there is a reference to a Jonah the son of Amittai from Gath-hepher (whose name was later taken for the hero, or anti-hero, of a prophetic book) in 2 Kings 14:25. More importantly, the Deuteronomistic Historian follows the account of the destruction of the kingdom of Israel (2 Kings 17:1–6) with an explanation: this happened because the people of Israel sinned by their pagan worship.

> Yet the LORD warned Israel and Judah by every prophet and every seer, saying, 'Turn from your evil ways and keep my commandments and my statutes, in accordance with all the law which I commanded your fathers, and which I sent to you by my servants the prophets.' But they would not listen, but were stubborn, as their fathers had been. . .

For the Deuteronomistic Historian, the prophets were an essential part of the monarchy; they provided Yahweh's corrective to the permanent tendency of the kings to apostatise.

The final section of 1 and 2 Kings is 2 Kings 18–25, which tells the story of the kingdom of Judah after the fall of the kingdom of Israel in 722 BC. After the cultic failings of Israel, and the cultic failings of Ahaz of Judah (2 Kings 16:10–20), we get the story of the cultic reform of Judah under Hezekiah, the cultic lapse under Manasseh and Amon, and the final cultic reform under Josiah (with whose reign some scholars believe the first edition of the Deuteronomistic History ended, 2 Kings 23:26 – 25:20 being an appendix from the exilic period to bring the work up to date in the second edition).

Hezekiah is highly praised for his cultic reforms (2 Kings 18:3–6); nevertheless, he suffered Assyrian invasion and capture of the cities of Judah, and paid a penalty (18:13–16). He is further threatened, apparently, with a siege of Jerusalem (18:19–37), but the prophet Isaiah prophesies that the Assyrian king Sennacherib will return to his own land and be killed (19:1–7) and will not besiege Jerusalem (19:32–34) – and so it turns out (19:35–37). These narratives about the Assyrian attack on Jerusalem are a complex collection, containing what are apparently two parallel accounts (18:17 – 19:8,36–37; 19:9–35), in each of which Hezekiah receives a threat from Assyria, goes to the temple, and receives an oracle offering hope for Israel. Some scholars believe that these two narratives refer to a later Assyrian attack on Jerusalem in 690 BC, but it is difficult to date Hezekiah's rule much beyond 700 BC, and there is no Assyrian evidence for a later campaign. Sennacherib's own inscription supports the picture given in 2 Kings 18:13–16:

> As to Hezekiah the Jew, he did not submit to my yoke. I laid siege to 46 of his strong cities, walled forts and to the countless small villages in their vicinity, and conquered them by means of well-stamped earth-ramps, and battering rams brought thus near to the wall combined with the attack by foot-soldiers, using mines, breaches as well as sapper work. I drove out of them 200,150 people, young and old, male and female, horses and mules, donkeys, camels, big and small cattle beyond counting, and considered them booty. Himself I made prisoner in Jerusalem, his royal residence, like a bird in a cage. I surrounded him with earthwork in order to molest those who were leaving his city's gate. His towns which I had plundered, I took away from his country and gave them over to Mitinti, king of Ashdod, Padi, king of Ekron, and Sillibel, king of Gaza. Thus I reduced his country, but I still increased the tribute... Hezekiah himself, whom the terror–inspiring splendour of my Lordship had overwhelmed and whose irregular and élite troops which he had brought into Jerusalem, his royal residence, in order to strengthen [it], had deserted him, did send me, later, to Nineveh, my lordly city, together with 30 talents of gold, 800 talents of silver...

Clearly, Sennacherib reduced Hezekiah to submission, but he left Hezekiah in place as a vassal king and did not destroy Jerusalem. The Deuteronomistic Historian presents this as a major act of miraculous salvation, and so in a sense it was, at least for Jerusalem, though the cities of Judah can hardly have seen it in that light. Chapter 20 gives two further stories about Hezekiah; in the first (20:1–11), he becomes ill, but prays and is promised a further fifteen years of life. In the second (20:12–19), Hezekiah cultivates new diplomatic relationships with Merodach-baladan of Babylon (a century later, Babylon would take over rule of the near east from Assyria), and meets rebuke from the prophet Isaiah. A final reference to how Hezekiah 'made the pool and the conduit and brought water into the city' may be illuminated by the Siloam tunnel inscription, which records how the tunnel was dug, and probably refers to Hezekiah's preparation for the expected siege of Jerusalem:

[? the completing of] the piercing through. And this is the story of the piercing through. While [the stone-cutters were swinging their] axes, each towards his fellow, and while there were yet three cubits to be pierced through, [there was heard] the voice of a man calling to his fellow, for there was a crevice [?] on the right ... And on the day of the piercing through, the stone-cutters struck through each to meet his fellow, axe against axe. Then ran the water from the Spring to the Pool for twelve hundred cubits, and a hundred cubits was the height of the rock above the head of the stone-cutters.

(DOTT, 210)

Manasseh, Hezekiah's successor, had a long reign of fifty-five years in Jerusalem, of which we can say nothing except that Manasseh brought back 'the abominable practices of the nations whom the LORD drove out before the people of Israel', and 'shed very much innocent blood'. The result is that we know very little indeed of the history of the seventh century BC; it is interesting that if Yahwism was at such a low ebb in Judah as the historian says, there seem to have been no contemporary prophets to complain at it whose works have survived in the biblical canon. The reference to prophets in 2 Kings 21:10–15 is merely an excuse for the historian to express his message that it was Manasseh's wickedness that brought disaster to Judah (a point repeated after the account of Josiah's reign in 2 Kings 23:26–27):

And the LORD said by his servants the prophets, 'Because Manasseh king of Judah has committed these abominations, and has done things more wicked than all that the Amorites did, who were before him, and has made Judah also to sin with his idols; therefore thus says the LORD, the God of Israel, Behold, I am bringing upon Jerusalem and Judah such evil that the ears of every one who hears of it will tingle. And I will stretch over Jerusalem the measuring line of Samaria, and the plummet of the house of Ahab; and I will wipe Jerusalem as one wipes a dish, wiping it and turning it upside down. And I will cast off the remnant of my heritage, and give them into the hand of their enemies, and they shall become a prey and a spoil to all their enemies, because they have done what is evil in my sight and have provoked me to anger, since the day their fathers came out of Egypt, even to this day.' (2 Kings 21:10–15)

The two-year reign of Amon merely repeats on a small scale the reign of Manasseh. The reign of his son and successor, Josiah, however, was different: 'he did what was right in the eyes of the LORD, and walked in all the way of David his father'. 2 Kings 22–23 focus on Josiah's reform of the cult. In Josiah's eighteenth year (621 BC), repairs are started on the temple (2 Kings 22:3–7). Hilkiah the high priest finds a law book, which is brought to the king and read to him. Josiah sends to enquire of the prophetess Huldah, who repeats the prophetic message that God will send evil on Jerusalem and its inhabitants ('all the words of the book which the king of Judah has read' – probably a reference to Deut.28:15–68) for their apostasy, but promises that Josiah 'will be gathered to [his] grave in peace'. (This prediction does not agree well with the note of Josiah's death in battle, 2 Kings 23:29–30, unless the words are a formula meaning only that the king received decent burial in his own tomb, cf. 23:30.) The king then gathered the elders of Jerusalem and Judah, and all the priests, prophets and the people, to the temple, and covenanted 'to walk after the LORD and to keep his commandments and his testimonies and his statutes, with all his heart and all his soul', and followed this with a drastic purge of improper cultic practices in the temple and at local shrines in Jerusalem and Judah, from Geba north of Jerusalem to Beersheba in the south. In particular, Josiah deposed the priests of the local shrines, and defiled the shrines themselves (23:8), especially the one at Bethel where Jeroboam had erected an altar (see 1 Kings 13:1–10, and p.78 above). The account ends with the celebration of a Passover such as had not been kept 'since the days of the judges who judged Israel, or during all the days of the kings of Israel or of the kings of Judah; but in the eighteenth year of King Josiah this passover was kept to the LORD in Jerusalem' (2 Kings 23:22–23). The final estimate of Josiah (2 Kings 23:25) notes that 'Before him there was no king like him, who turned to the LORD with all his heart and with all his soul and with all his might, according to all the law of Moses; nor did any like him arise after him.'

Josiah, who walked in all the way of David and according to all the law of Moses, is certainly presented by the Deuteronomist as an ideal king, who follows Hezekiah (2 Kings 18:3–6) in achieving the combination of Davidic and Mosaic virtues hoped for in Solomon (1 Kings 2:1–4). This account of Josiah's reformation has occasioned much discussion. The book of the law mentioned in 2 Kings 22:8 has since de Wette (1806–7) been assumed to be Deuteronomy, or an early version of it, mainly on the grounds that Deuteronomy 12 demands that sacrifice be limited to one sanctuary, and that Deuteronomy 18:6–7 allows for Levitical country priests to minister in the central sanctuary (cf. 2 Kings 23:9, where the historian comments that the priests – presumably Yahwistic, not idolatrous priests – ejected by Josiah from the local shrines did not come to Jerusalem). This whole account echoes themes and cultic details from earlier in 1 and 2 Kings: thus Josiah repairs the temple as Joash had done (2 Kings 12:4–16), and, together with the people, makes a covenant with the Lord as Jehoiada had done (2 Kings 12:17), and reforms various details of the cult, as Asa (1 Kings 15:9–15), Jehoshaphat (1 Kings 22:46), Jehoiada (2 Kings 11:18) and Hezekiah (2 Kings 18:4) had done. In particular, Josiah destroys the high places (which the historian notes that most kings of Judah failed to do), and above all, the altar at Bethel, thus fulfilling the prophecy of 1 Kings 13:1–10. Josiah, in short, purges both Israel and Judah. The Deuteronomistic Historian concentrates on the cultic aspects of Josiah's work, and makes Josiah fulfil all that previous kings of Judah could not or would not do. The historian says nothing about Josiah's political contribution, except that he was killed at Megiddo (609 BC), apparently opposing Pharaoh Necho who was marching north to help Assyria against Babylonian attack. Possibly Josiah was hoping that Assyria's collapse would give Judah a chance to regain independence. If so, Josiah's political judgment was poor.

After the death of Josiah, the end of the kingdom of Judah came quickly, and is summarily presented in 2 Kings 23:31 – 25:25; Jehoahaz II was removed by Pharaoh Necho, who put Jehoiakim on the throne. Nebuchadnezzar took over

Palestine in 605–604 BC, but in 601 BC Jehoiakim rebelled. In 598 BC Nebuchadnezzar set out to punish him, but when he took Jerusalem in March 597 BC, Jehoiakim had died, and his young son Jehoiachin was on the throne. Nebuchadnezzar removed him to exile, putting Jehoiachin's uncle Zedekiah in his place. He too rebelled, and Nebuchadnezzar reappeared before the walls of Jerusalem in 589 BC, capturing it and destroying its temple in summer 587 BC, and leaving the land under a governor, Gedaliah. 2 Kings ends with a note that Nebuchadnezzar's successor Evil-merodach, on coming to the throne in 561 BC, released Jehoiachin from gaol and gave him a place at court (though did not send him back to Judah). Some scholars have seen this as indicating that the Davidic dynasty was not dead, and perhaps as suggesting hope for the restoration of the dynasty. But the Deuteronomistic Historian is clear that the Assyrian and Babylonian exiles were fitting punishment for Israel and Judah respectively, and there is no sign here that the historian expected Jehoiachin or his successors to be restored. The prayer of Solomon (1 Kings 8) prays only for a return from exile:

> 'When thy people Israel are defeated before the enemy because they have sinned against thee, if they turn again to thee, and acknowledge thy name, and pray, and make supplication to thee in this house; then hear thou in heaven, and forgive the sin of thy people Israel, and bring them again to the land which thou gavest to their fathers.' (1 Kings 8:33–34)

The Deuteronomistic Historian is concerned with things that mattered to the people of Judah in the sixth century BC, whether at home in Judah or in exile abroad. He focuses on the Davidic monarchy and the temple (2 Sam.7) as the centre of the nation's identity. He recounts the succession of the kings of Israel and Judah and tells how each king related to the Jerusalem temple: the kings of Israel rejected it and the kings of Judah variously desecrated it, ignored it, repaired it, or reformed its cult. Both kingdoms fell, to the Assyrians and the Babylonians respectively, because their kings and people had failed to keep the commandments and statutes 'in accordance with all the law which I commanded your fathers, and which I sent to you by my servants the prophets' (2 Kings 17:13; cf. 21:10–15); in the case of Judah, Manasseh in particular is blamed (2 Kings 23:26–27). The prophets play an important role throughout, and the word of the Lord which each utters, whether for good or evil, is always fulfilled. Kings and people should have listened to the law, from Moses onwards, and to the prophets, from Samuel onwards, and remained faithful to the Davidic dynasty, from Rehoboam onwards. If they had, then the disasters of 722 and 587 BC would not have happened.

The modern historian, however, having allowed for the message of the Deuteronomistic Historian, must ask how far the historian's information can be trusted. To what extent is the Deuteronomistic History 'history'? This, of course, depends upon what is meant by 'history'. It seems churlish, if not even faintly ridiculous, to deny the author of Samuel and Kings the title of historian – particularly if we define an historian as someone who rewrites the story of the past in the light of the new insights and problems of his or her own day. To tell history 'as it actually happened' is impossible anyway; no one person can know in full 'how it actually happened' in the present, let alone in the past. In any one historical event, too many persons and motives may be involved. The Deuteronomistic Historian presents a personal view of stories and events known to him, against the context of the disaster which had overtaken his people. Obviously, that disaster affected the way he presented what he knew. He was commenting on known facts and explaining them in a theological context (to borrow some words of J. Soggin); but to do that is still to write history, for all history is an attempt at explanation. He was not writing an historical novel, such as Ruth or Esther (though some scholars indeed describe the 'Succession Narrative' in these terms); he was attempting to portray the story of the monarchy, selecting what he saw as important for his purpose.

We still, however, have to assess the value to the modern historian of what this ancient historian (or these ancient historians) tells us. We have to accept, first of all, that the historian selected from his sources, and that what was unimportant to him as he made his point – for example, 'the rest of the acts of Asa, all his might and all that he did, and the cities which he built' (1 Kings 15:23) – would be of great interest to the modern historian, and that some of the omitted material might, if we had it, change our view of the sequence of events, their comparative importance, and the social and economic history of the period and so on. But our evaluation of what we have depends very largely on our assessment of the different types of material and on the nature of the sources used in the Deuteronomistic History.

It is easy to isolate certain genres of material, and to distinguish the author's sources from his own composition. The author himself composed the running framework which introduces and concludes the account of each king, probably deriving the details of names and length of reign from two separate lists for Israel and Judah respectively; the synchronisms were worked out when the lists were brought together, probably by the historian himself. This means that the basic details given have to be treated seriously. The mind and interpretative work of the historian can be seen in the overall scheme of this framework, which joins the kings of Israel and Judah into the unified history of what is virtually one people, whose real focus is the Mosaic law, the Davidic kingship, and the Jewish temple and its cult, and whose chronological history is given an overall scheme which reckons 480 years between the exodus from Egypt and the building of the temple (1 Kings 6:1), and a further 480 years between the building of the first and the second temples. (The reigns of the kings of Judah from the temple-building in Solomon's fourth year to the fall of Jerusalem in the eleventh year of Zedekiah (2 Kings 25:2) total 430 years: this would allow a further 50 years between the destruction of 587 and the beginning of the second temple after the return from exile, i.e., between 587 BC and the opening years of the reign of Cyrus when, according to the opening chapters of the book of Ezra, at least, the rebuilding of the temple began.) The author's interpretation is clear, too, in the assessment made of each king, in the programmatic essays given in 1 Kings 11:9–13; 2 Kings 17:7–23, 24–41, and also in the speeches put into the mouths of major figures, for example, Samuel (1 Sam.8:10–18; 12:6–25), Nathan (2 Sam.7:4–17), David (2 Sam.7:18–29; 1 Kings 2:1–9, Solomon (1 Kings 8:15–21, 22–53, 54–61), the Lord (1 Kings 9:2–9), Ahijah the prophet (1 Kings 11:31–39; 14:7–16), Jehu the son of Hanani (1 Kings 16:2–4), Rabshakeh and Hezekiah (2 Kings 18:19–25; 28–35; 19:14–29) and Huldah (2 Kings 23:15–20).

As we have already seen, the Deuteronomistic Historian is particularly interested in the contribution of the prophets, and he incorporates a large amount of prophetic legends and miracle stories (e.g., 1 Kings 13:1–32; 17:12–24; 18:1–46; 2 Kings 1:1–16) and other stories about the prophets and their part in the Syrian wars (e.g., 1 Kings 20; 22; 2 Kings 3; 2 Kings 6;7). This material, often anti-monarchic in tone, came from popular, rather than official sources, and must be used with caution for historical reconstruction. Some scholars hold that separate collection of the Elijah and Elisha stories existed before the historian incorporated them into his work, but such unified pre-existing collections are hard to prove (especially for the Elisha material), and it is easier to believe that the historian himself gave form and style to a rich vein of varied and sometimes related popular stories from within Israel, along with similar prophetic stories from Bethel (1 Kings 13) or Shiloh (1 Kings 14), and some material about the prophet Isaiah (2 Kings 18:17 – 20:19, later used in the compilation of the book of Isaiah, cf. Isa.36–39).

Apart from the historian's own composition, and borrowed popular stories, the historian claims to be using 'the book of the acts of Solomon' (1 Kings 11:41), 'the book of the chronicles of the kings of Judah' and 'the book of the chronicles of the kings of Israel'. It is very hard to be sure exactly what these books were, except that the first is said to have contained 'the rest of the acts of Solomon, and all that he did, and his wisdom', which suggests that this work was in effect a larger version of 1 Kings 3–11, though without the Deuteronomistic overtones. The books of the chronicles of the kings of Israel and Judah would presumably have been similar; according to the regular formula they contained 'the rest of the acts of ... and all that he did', to which, in the case of the kings of Israel, is sometimes added 'and all his might'. Other additions are 'and all the cities that he built' (Asa, 1 Kings 15:23), 'the conspiracy which he made' (Zimri, 1 Kings 16:20), 'the ivory house that he built, and all the cities that he built' (Ahab, 1 Kings 22:39), 'and how he warred' (Jehoshaphat, 1 Kings 22:45), 'the might with which he fought against Amaziah, (Joash, 2 Kings 13:12), 'how he fought and how he recovered for Israel Damascus and Hamath, which had belonged to Judah' (Jeroboam II, 2 Kings 14:28), 'the conspiracy which he made' (Shallum, 2 Kings 15:15), 'and how he made the pool and conduit, and brought water into the city' (Hezekiah, 2 Kings 20:20), 'and the sin that he committed' (Manasseh, 2 Kings 21:17). On this evidence, these chronicles contained reports of the kings' various military and building activities not unlike those which are recorded in 1 and 2 Kings, and we may conclude that most of the extant reports of such activities were drawn from these sources.

But who compiled the book of the acts of Solomon, and when? And who compiled the chronicles of the kings of Judah and Israel, and when? The

Solomonic material (particularly if it contained the wisdom of Solomon) probably derives from a period when Solomon's wisdom was becoming legendary (cf. the story of Solomon and the two harlots in 1 Kings 3:16–28, or the story of the Queen of Sheba in 1 Kings 10:1–10); the interest of these chapters in trade with Tyre, Egypt, and Ophir, the political interest in Syria and Edom, and the references to Chemosh of Moab and Molech (Milcom) of the Ammonites all suggest (though they do not prove) the background of the later monarchic period after the wealthier days of Uzziah and Jeroboam II. The interest of Hezekiah's time in Solomon's wisdom is visible in Proverbs 25:1: 'These also are proverbs of Solomon which the men of Hezekiah king of Judah copied'.

The chronicles of Solomon's successors in Israel and Judah are mentioned up to the reigns of Pekah in Israel and Josiah in Judah, and were presumably compiled by addition over the centuries; if so, they must be taken seriously as evidence. This means that the third-person reports of royal activity, where there is no obvious reason for invention, may be accepted as recording the bare bones at least of an important event, though important matters such as its timing, motivation, purpose, and results may be omitted. Such events might include, for example, Shishak's campaign (1 Kings 14:25–28), Baasha's building of Ramah and what followed (1 Kings 15:16–22), Baasha's conspiracy (1 Kings 15:27–29: note how the historian has added his interpretation in verses 29–30), Jehoshaphat's attempt at the maritime trade from Ezion-geber (1 Kings 22:47–48), Edom's rebellion (2 Kings 8:20–22: note the comment, 'So Edom revolted from the rule of Judah to this day', and its implications), the conspiracy of Joash's servants (2 Kings 12:20–21), and so on. These episodes consist mainly of wars, conspiracies, and building activities. There is no evidence that these chronicles took the form of annals (i.e., listing the royal activities year by year), for these events are undated (though a case might be made for the reign of Hezekiah, major events being ascribed to his fourth, sixth and fourteenth years (2 Kings 18:9,10,13) ). These chronicles have been compared with similar works known from the Neo-Babylonian empire in the early sixth century BC.

The Deuteronomistic Historian used the lists of the kings of Israel and Judah, popular stories and legends, chronicles preserved at court or temple; for Solomon's reign he may also have used archival material such as the lists of officers and regional governors (1 Kings 4:1-6, 7–19), the record of Solomon's forced labour (1 Kings 5:13–18), and perhaps a list of Solomon's buildings (1 Kings 7:1–12), though it has recently been argued with some force that the description of the temple (1 Kings 6:2–10, 14–35) is not from Solomon's reign but 'a memory of things past, as if it had been written after their structures were destroyed' (J. van Seters, 1983, 301). What is surprising, perhaps, is that lists and archival records other than the chronicles mentioned are not obviously evidenced in the history of the divided monarchy. It is possible, however, that the historian drew on building inscriptions (e.g., the Siloam tunnel inscription; cf. 2 Kings 20:20), tombs and burial inscriptions (e.g., that of Shebna, the steward; cf. Isa.22:15), and other public memorials (such as the stele of Mesha, from Moab; similar steles probably existed in Jerusalem or Samaria, doubtless destroyed in 722 and 587 BC).

Wars and buildings are the very stuff of public inscriptions to this day.

In sum, the books of Samuel and Kings make up an impressive piece of historiography. Its author or authors used sources from public memorials, court and temple records, popular story-telling and written chronicles to present a picture of the rise of the monarchy and the history of the united kingdom of David and Solomon and of the divided kingdoms of their successors which would show the importance of loyalty to the Mosaic law (as interpreted by the Deuteronomist) and of loyalty to the Davidic dynasty, together with the need to listen to the word of God as spoken by the prophets. The latter are presented as supporting the monarchy, so long as it was faithful to the law (in particular to the demand for the limitation of sacrifice to one sanctuary, at Jerusalem) and as keeping the cult free of the worship of foreign deities. To modern eyes, the Deuteronomist has his limitations as an historian; he gives no analysis of social and domestic politics, economic problems or diplomatic relationships, and subordinates almost everything he preserves to the Deuteronomistic theology.

About the dating of the work there are two main schools of thought. The earlier school sees it as deriving from the time of the exile, whether in Babylon or in Judah, its aim being to explain to Israelites saddened by the fall of Samaria in 722 BC or the fall of Jerusalem in 587 BC the problem of why Yahweh had punished or deserted his people. The more recent tendency has been to argue for a complex history of composition, with at least two main editions. The first edition ended with the triumphant reign of Josiah, who purged the priesthood and temple cult and upheld both the Deuteronomic law and the ideal of the Davidic dynasty. The future of Israel lay with Jerusalem; the old kingdom of Israel had been punished and had disappeared, and Josiah had even destroyed the northern cult site of Bethel. The second edition added the gloomy record of Judah's history after Josiah, blaming Jerusalem's disaster on the sin of Manasseh, which was so bad as to negate the goodness of Josiah (2 Kings 21:10–15; 23:26–27). A more recent proposal sees three editions: a basic Deuteronomistic History, ending at 2 Kings 25:21, subsequently edited by successive editors, the first, sometime after 580 BC, emphasising the importance of prophecy (particularly in Samuel and Kings), and the second emphasising the importance of law (visible particularly in Joshua and Judges). Yet, while it is comparatively easy to see the editorial joins and harmonisation of chronologies, as the author compiled and coordinated his work, it is hard to excise material relating to the law and the prophets as separately added stages without making nonsense of the presumed original work. It is easier to argue that law and prophecy were the interests of the historian who compiled the whole, and accept some roughness as due to the juxtaposition of varied material and sometimes conflicting sources.

At all events, the books of Samuel and Kings are, in their present form, an attempt from the exilic period to show why things were as they were, and to point the people of God to the need to abide by the teaching of the law and the words of the prophets in a situation where the monarchy had fulfilled the worst fears of the prophets and had utterly failed to preserve the unity and welfare of the people of God.

## Bibliography

G.W. Ahlström, ed. D. Edelman, *The history of ancient Palestine from the palaeolithic period to Alexander's conquest* (Sheffield: JSOT Press, 1993)

G. Garbini, *History and ideology in ancient Israel* (London: SCM Press, 1988)

R.P. Gordon, *1 and 2 Samuel* (Old Testament Guides) (Sheffield: JSOT Press for the Society for Old Testament Study, 1984)

R.P. Gordon, *1 and 2 Samuel: a commentary* (Exeter: Paternoster Press, 1986)

B. Halpern, *The first historians: The Hebrew Bible and history* (San Francisco: Harper and Row, 1988)

J.H. Hayes and P.K. Hooker, *A new chronology for the kings of Israel and Judah and its implications for biblical history and literature* (Atlanta: John Knox Press, 1988)

B.O. Long, *1 Kings* (The forms of the Old Testament literature, 9) (Grand Rapids: Eerdmans, 1984)

A.D.H. Mayes, *The story of Israel between settlement and exile: a redactional study of the Deuteronomistic history* (London: SCM Press, 1983)

J.M. Miller and J.H. Hayes, *A history of ancient Israel and Judah* (Philadelphia: Westminster Press; London: SCM Press, 1986)

M. Noth, *The Deuteronomistic history* (Sheffield: JSOT Supplement Series, 1981)

J. van Seters, *In search of history: historiography in the ancient world and the origins of biblical history* (New Haven and London: Yale University Press, 1983)

J.A. Soggin, *A history of Israel from the beginning to the Bar Kochba revolt, AD 135* (London: SCM Press, 1984)

D.W. Thomas (ed.), *Documents from Old Testament times* (London: Nelson, 1958)

R.N. Whybray, *The Succession Narrative: a study of 2 Samuel 9–20 and 1 Kings 1–2* (Studies in Biblical Theology 2/9) (London: SCM Press, 1968)

# 6    Politics and Prophets

## The prophetic writings

In the Jewish tradition, the books Genesis – Deuteronomy are known as the Torah, and the books Joshua, Judges, 1 and 2 Samuel and 1 and 2 Kings are known as the Former Prophets. The title 'Latter Prophets' is reserved for the collection of prophetic writings which includes the books of Isaiah, Jeremiah, Ezekiel, and the twelve minor prophets Hosea, Joel, Amos, Obadiah, Jonah, Micah, Nahum, Habakkuk, Zephaniah, Haggai, Zechariah, and Malachi. The Latter Prophets are on the whole much easier to date than the Former Prophets of the Torah, for many of the prophecies they contain refer directly to known political events. Perhaps the earliest of these prophets was Amos, who prophesied, according to the editorial introduction to his book, 'in the days of Uzziah king of Judah and in the days of Jeroboam the son of Joash, king of Israel, two years before the earthquake'; most scholars date his activity c. 760 BC. Hosea also prophesied in the reigns of Uzziah (c. 787–736) and Jeroboam II (787–747), though his editor notes that his work extended into the reigns of Jotham, Ahaz and Hezekiah of Judah, in whose reigns Micah was also active (Mic. 1:1). Contemporary with Micah was Isaiah, who began his prophetic career towards the end of Uzziah's reign and was active through the reigns of Jotham, Ahaz and Hezekiah, at least until 701 BC. These four eighth-century prophets reflect the political struggles of their time, and in particular the continuing expansion east of the Assyrian empire, culminating in Sargon's conquest of Samaria in 722 BC and Sennacherib's conquest of Judah and Jerusalem in 701 BC. No prophetic literature is credited to the reign of Manasseh (696–642 BC) (later Jewish legend said that Isaiah was sawn in half in his reign), and the next extant prophetic writings are those of Nahum, Habakkuk, and Zephaniah, probably from the reign of Josiah (639–609 BC); they reflect the fall of Assyrian Nineveh to the Babylonians (the Chaldaeans, Hab. 1:6) and their allies.

The reign of Josiah saw the beginnings of the work of Jeremiah, whose prophesying continued through the reigns of Jehoiakim and Zedekiah until the fall of Jerusalem in 587 BC, when Jeremiah was taken into Egypt with other refugees. Meanwhile Ezekiel, exiled from Jerusalem in 597 BC by Nebuchadnezzer, was active in Babylon, and remained intermittently active (to judge from the dates given to a number of his oracles) until at least 571 BC. As the Babylonian empire began to give way before the energetic conquests of Cyrus the Persian, a new prophet appeared in Babylon whose oracles are preserved in Isaiah 40–55; his real name is unknown but because his oracles have been attached to those of the eighth-century Isaiah, he is known as Deutero-Isaiah or Second Isaiah, and he was active *c.* 550–540 BC. The next two prophets date their oracles precisely in the opening years of the reign of Darius I of Persia, Haggai to the second year of Darius in the sixth, seventh, and ninth months, and Zechariah to the second year of Darius in the eighth month, and the fourth year in the ninth month. The main concerns of Haggai and Zechariah were the restoration of the temple and its high priest, and of the political leadership in Jerusalem. Also from this post-exilic period, though much harder to date, are the oracles preserved in Isaiah 56–66 ('Third Isaiah'), the book of Malachi (perhaps to be dated *c.* 475 BC), the two collections headed 'An Oracle' (Heb. *massa*') in Zechariah 9–11, 12–14, the book of Jonah and the book of Joel (fourth century BC?).

Other prophets are mentioned in the Hebrew scriptures as well as in the Apocrypha and in the New Testament, but those listed above are the prophets under whose names oracles have been collected and preserved. It is immediately obvious, first of all, that the historical appearance of such major prophets was directly related to the various historical crises reflected in their work: the rise of Assyria, the fall of Assyria to Babylon, the destruction of Jerusalem, the circumstances of exile, the fall of Babylon to Persia, the rebuilding of the temple. Prophecy responded to the challenge of the moment with a memorable 'Thus saith the LORD'. Secondly it is noticeable that prophets in ancient Israel, from Samuel in the days of Saul to Jeremiah in the days of Zedekiah, address themselves to the king and to matters of political as well as social or religious concern. Their attitude to monarchy is often critical, but not hostile; at the end of the exile, Haggai and Zechariah appear to hope for its restoration. And thirdly, it is clear that, though most individual prophets can be dated with fair accuracy, the collections of writings ascribed to them went through a lengthy process of compilation and editing. Internal evidence suggests that this happened in the post-exilic period. The book of Isaiah itself is a composite book whose final chapters come from the period shortly after the end of the exile, perhaps *c.* 500 BC. The book of Jeremiah incorporates prose material which represents the reworking of Jeremiah's message at the hands of Deuteronomistic editors in the exile, and in its final form must derive from the exilic period or later. The book of Ezekiel cannot be earlier than *c.* 570 BC, but Ezekiel's original oracles have been greatly expanded by subsequent editors, and its appearance in its present form was probably much later. The book of the Twelve gathers together shorter prophetic writings from the eighth century down to the fifth if not the fourth century BC, and so presumably dates as a collection from the Persian period or the beginnings of the Hellenistic period.

It was not with the needs of the modern historian in mind that the prophetic books were written, and the constituent oracles were uttered, but as the oracles were uttered and the books compiled in response to particular historical situations and social contexts, they are all grist to the historian's mill. The ancient editors seem to have recognised the need to set the different prophets' oracles into their proper historical context, and all the prophetic books are prefaced by longer or shorter formulas of introductory explanation. Some books incorporate longer passages of historical narrative closely related to the Deuteronomistic History (e.g., Isa. 36–39, Jer. 52), and some incorporate biographical accounts of the prophet's activity in the third person: e.g., Isaiah 7:1–17; Jeremiah 20:1–6; 21:1–14; 32–45; Hosea 1:2–11; Amos 7:10–17; Haggai 1–2; Zechariah 7. The origin of such biographical writings is not clear; the usual suggestion is that they derive from one of the prophet's followers – Jeremiah's scribe Baruch, for example – or 'disciples' (Isa 8:16), or from a member of the prophetic 'school' which kept alive the prophet's memory (though there is little evidence that such schools existed). Such biographical material was probably the work of the editors who compiled the prophetic collections, but there is a surprising absence of information in the Old Testament about the work of such people. Putting a lengthy work together on parchment or papyrus was a major task, done presumably by a professional scribe. But when and where it was done, and by whom the scribe was paid, and by whom the completed work might be read, we do not know. It is clear from Ecclesiasticus 44–49 that in the early second century BC an educated man like Jesus ben Sirach had read 'the law and the prophets and the other books of our fathers', 'acquiring considerable proficiency in them' (Ecclus., Prologue), and his reading seems to have included the works of Isaiah, Jeremiah, Ezekiel and the twelve prophets. As he is a teacher, with a school (Ecclus. 51:23), it is possible that he taught the contents of the law and the prophets to his students, and that texts were copied as much for the use of the teaching profession as for use in worship. Texts were certainly copied at Qumran for the purpose of daily study by members of the Qumran community.

The particular contents and concerns of the prophets' oracles will be considered in later chapters. Here, however, it is worth noting that scholarly research on the prophetic literature over the last century has taken much the same course as that taken by pentateuchal research. The first generation of modern enquiry concentrated on isolating the literary units and attempting to distinguish between the authentic and inauthentic words of the individual prophets. In particular, Bernhard Duhm distinguished in a famous commentary between the first, second and third Isaiahs. But with this approach went an understanding of the prophets as individual, creative theologians preaching a sort of humanistic morality for the whole of mankind (not just for Israel). G. Hölscher saw Israel's prophets as part of a wider cultural phenomenon, noting their ecstatic habits of music and dancing (cf. 1 Sam. 10:5) for which he found parallels in Canaan, Syria, and Asia Minor. He emphasised the psychology of the prophets, explaining Ezekiel's visions, for example, as heightened ecstatic openness to the divine activity, and restricting the authentic Ezekiel utterances to the poetic oracles. The second generation of research, in the first half of the twentieth century, emphasised that the prophets uttered their oracles by word of mouth in public, and that their dissemination in written form came later; consequently, scholars examined the development of the tradition from the original utterances via the smaller complexes of material to the completion of the collection.

The development of form-criticism (which analysed the different types of speech and written literature) led to deeper consideration of the different social contexts influencing the prophetic speech. Thus Gunkel, following Hölscher and others, accepted the prophets as poets with abnormal spiritual and ecstatic experience, but he used the techniques of form-criticism to define the different ways in which the prophets received and uttered their oracles. They received their message by auditions and visions; they uttered them by threats, promises, proclamations of impending woe, funeral dirges, marriage songs and so on, and in particular by forms drawn from a liturgical background – notably laments and hymns. This recognition of the prophetic debt to the cult received extended treatment as the twentieth century progressed, and whereas it had once been supposed (on the basis of such texts as Amos 5:21–24, Mic. 6:6–8, Isa. 1:10–17) that the prophetic religion in Israel was in opposition to the priestly religion, now it was argued that prophetic connection with the temple was clear in the cases of Isaiah, Jeremiah, Ezekiel, Haggai, Zechariah and Malachi, and that perhaps the utterances of Obadiah, Nahum, Habakkak, Zephaniah and Joel (all rich in mythological themes and suggesting rituals for the control of nature or of Israel's enemies) might be located within the cult. The prophets may on occasion have criticised the cult, but much of their language and imagery was borrowed from it, and some of them may even have played a role in it.

In fact, of course, analysis of the language of the prophetic oracles shows what one might expect, that the prophets, in reaching out to their public, were able to draw upon the practice and experience of almost every aspect of life in ancient Israel – on agriculture, on the cult, on business, on war, on law, on social intercourse, on wisdom (whether the more popular or the intellectual variety), and so on. The prophets' precise place and role in society has been much studied, and we must return to it, noting merely at this point that to judge from the amount of prophetic material preserved in the Old Testament, the prophetic contribution to Israel's understanding of her own relationship with God and her role in the world was seen as deeply important in Israel's post-exilic religious tradition.

More recent research into the prophetic literature has focused on the way the exilic and post-exilic compilers and editors of the prophetic oracles used their materials to present a message for their own time and situation. This is exactly what the pentateuchal editors and the Deuteronomistic Historian did, and it should not surprise us. The books of Isaiah, of Jeremiah, of Ezekiel and the others are in fact to be seen (in their final form) as the embodiment of a lengthy tradition of reinterpretation, from the time of the utterance of the first oracle of each prophet to the time of his book's inclusion in the greater prophetic corpus of the prophets, and even beyond; for with each extension of the scriptural canon, the individual prophetic book is given a new context and perhaps a new interpretation. Each stage of this development is to be explored; but for the moment we may note, by way of example, the work of R. P. Carroll and R. E. Clements on the book of Jeremiah. Carroll argues that we can no longer conduct a quest for the historical Jeremiah in the way J. Skinner did in his famous book *Prophecy and religion*, by stripping off accretions to Jeremiah's original words.

Such an approach does insufficient justice to the book. The book of Jeremiah is the work of successive generations of people handing on and adapting the Jeremiah tradition to meet their own needs. R. E. Clements continues this sort of exploration of the book by arguing that Jeremiah's prophecies were handed down by Deuteronomistic interpreters working in Judah, and used to provide an explanation for the debacle of 587 BC. A similar approach can be applied to the book of Isaiah: Third Isaiah, for example, is patently using the oracles of Second Isaiah and reapplying them to the situation in Judah in his own day, a generation or two later.

## Early Israelite prophecy

The first prophet whose oracles survived in a collection, ultimately to become part of the Hebrew scriptures and Christian Old Testament, was Amos, who flourished in the mid-eighth century BC. For the words and works of his prophetic predecessors, we are dependent on the books of the Pentateuch and of the Deuteronomistic Historian. The Pentateuch has little to say about prophecy. In Genesis 20:7, God tells king Abimelech to restore to Abraham his wife, 'for he is a prophet, and he will pray for you, and you shall live'. The prophet here is seen as an intercessor (as is Moses in Num. 11 and Balaam the son of Beor in Num. 22-24; cf. Jer. 11:14; 14:11). In Exodus 7:1, God tells Moses that his brother Aaron will be his prophet, telling Pharaoh to let the people go; here the prophet delivers a message. In Exodus 15:20, Moses' sister Miriam is a prophetess, who dances and sings praise to the Lord. In Numbers 11:16-30, the spirit of prophecy with which Moses is endowed is passed on to seventy elders (and to two others who had not been selected for this honour). This story appears to validate spirit-filled prophecy by presenting Moses as the spiritual father of Israelite prophecy (cf. Deut.18:15; 34:10); in Numbers 12:6-7, however, Moses is distinguished from prophets in that while God makes himself known to prophets in visions and dreams, he speaks to Moses 'mouth to mouth, clearly, and not in dark speech' (cf. Deut.34:10, 'a prophet like Moses, whom the Lord knew face to face'). Deuteronomy 13:1-3 and 18:20-23 deal with the problem of distinguishing true prophets from false: the true prophet predicts correctly, but does not encourage the people to follow foreign gods. These references do not tell us anything specific about early, pre-monarchic prophecy, but they do reveal much about how prophets were understood – as spiritual descendants of Moses, as endowed with the spirit of Yahweh, as loyal to Yahweh, predicting what will happen, delivering messages from God, praising God, interceding with God, and as sometimes ambiguous persons.

Perhaps the most interesting portrait of a prophetic figure in the Pentateuch is that of Balaam in Numbers 22-24. The king of Moab tries to hire him with 'fees of divination' to curse the invading Israelites on behalf of Moab. This biblical tradition of a Transjordanian prophetic figure called Balaam son of Beor has been confirmed by the discovery at Tell Deir 'Allā in the Jordan valley of a seventh-century BC Aramaic-Ammonite inscription on the plastered wall of a sanctuary.

The inscription opens with the words, 'The account of Balaam, son of Beor, who was a seer [*'ašhaze(h)*] of the gods. The gods came to him in the night, and he saw a vision like an oracle of El' (Hackett, 1984, 29). Balaam weeps at what he has seen, and explains the vision and its meaning. Similarly, Numbers 24:3–4, 15–17, give

> The oracle of Balaam the son of Beor,
> the oracle of the man whose eye is opened,
> the oracle of him who hears the words of God,
> who sees the vision of the Almighty.

Balaam is called a 'seer', and he sees visions. The same title, *hōzeh*, is used of the tenth-century BC prophet Gad (2 Sam. 24:11) and of the eighth-century BC prophet Amos (Amos 7:12; cf. also Mic. 3:5–8; Isa. 29:10; 2 Kings 17:13). Seeing visions seems to have played an important part in a prophet's activity, as is shown by the many visions described (e.g., that of Micaiah ben Imlah in 1 Kings 22:19–23; cf. Amos 7:1–9; 8:1–3; 9:1; Isa. 6:1–13; Ezek. 1:4–28; Zech. 1:7 – 6:8). The comment of 1 Samuel 9:9, that 'he who is now called a prophet was formerly called a seer' indicates that this aspect of prophecy was important from the beginning.

Prophetic activity of the early eighth century BC is described in the Aramaic inscription of Zakir, king of Hamath in Syria. When attacked by a coalition of kings led by Barhadad, son of Hazael, Zakir prayed to his god:

> 'I lifted up my hand to Be'elshamayn, and Be'elshamayn heard me. Be'elshamayn spoke to me through seers and through diviners. Be'elshamayn said to me: Do not fear, for I have made you king, and I shall stand by you and deliver you from all these kings who set up a siege against you.' (ANET 501–2)

An earlier picture of prophetic behaviour appears in the story of Wen-Amun (written in Egypt in the eleventh century BC), which tells of an Egyptian official sent to Phoenicia to claim tribute. He met opposition from the king of Byblos until a young man was seized by the god and in a state of ecstatic inspiration informed the king that the god approved of the official Wen-Amun. There are a number of biblical stories which show prophets behaving in an abnormal and ecstatic fashion under the compulsion of the spirit of Yahweh (1 Sam. 10:5–6, 9–13; 19:23–24) and seen as madmen (2 Kings 9:11; Hos. 9:7). The spirit of God (*ruah Yahweh*) which inspired these prophets was the same spirit of God which had roused the pre-monarchic war-leaders, the 'judges', to action (e.g., Jephthah, Jud. 11:29), and we find the spirit of God moving Saul to prophecy (1 Sam. 10:9–13) or to battle (1 Sam. 11:6). Judges could be prophets (e.g., Deborah, Jud. 4:4), and prophets could be involved in war or military coups (cf. Elisha, 2 Kings 3:13–19; 9:1–3). The Nazirites (Amos 2:11–12; cf Samson, Jud. 13:5) and the Rechabites (2 Kings 10:15–16; Jer. 35:2–19) may have been in origin early enthusiasts and zealots for Yahweh, with a lifestyle not unlike that of the prophets.

Two early prophets, Nathan and Gad, are associated in particular with the court of king David. Nathan delivers to David an oracle promising a dynasty, rebukes David for his affair with Bathsheba, and actively plots with Zadok the priest and Benaiah the commander of the mercenary troops for the succession of David's son Solomon to the throne. Gad advises David on his campaign strategy (1 Sam 22:3–5) and the location of the future temple (2 Sam: 24:18). Both in fact play the role of political counsellor as well as prophet. They have often been described as 'court seers', and whether such a recognisable class of seers existed or not, certainly many of the early seers or prophets are presented as active in and around the royal court – for example, Samuel, Nathan, Gad, Ahijah of Shiloh, and an unnamed prophet (1 Kings 13:1), Jehu the son of Hanani (1 Kings 16:1–4), Micaiah the son of Imlah (1 Kings 22:5–28), Elijah and Elisha. This may reflect the particular concerns and themes of the Deuteronomistic Historian and so give an unbalanced picture of prophetic priorities; but it is clear that later Amos takes it upon himself to prophesy at a royal sanctuary (Amos 7:13), that Isaiah and Jeremiah address kings, and that after the exile Haggai and Zechariah are much concerned with the possibility of the restoration of monarchy. The court and sanctuary are obvious targets for any anti-establishment prophets.

## Amos

The earliest prophets whose words reached book form were Amos and Hosea. The editor of Amos notes that Amos prophesied in the days of Jeroboam the son of Joash, king of Israel (788–748 BC), two years before the earthquake (perhaps that which damaged Hazor stratum VI and Samaria in the first half of the eighth century BC; cf. also Zech. 14:5). Perhaps Amos' activity belongs to the decade following 760 BC, towards the end of Jeroboam's reign. Recent research has suggested that this was a period when Judah was a vassal to Israel (Jehoash of Israel had defeated Amaziah of Judah earlier in the century, cf. 2 Kings 14: 8–12), and Israel had regained some Transjordanian territory from Syria (2 Kings 14:25). The earlier part of Jeroboam's reign was one of comparative prosperity and security; in the later years, however, Assyria's weakness allowed Syria, Phoenicia and Philistia to put external pressure on Israel, resulting in internal pressures as well. In his final years, it is possible that Jeroboam II had to contend with a rival to the throne, the Syrian-backed Pekah, whose allotted twenty years' reign (2 Kings 15:27) does not square easily with the other synchronisms in 2 Kings unless we suppose that he was a rival for sixteen years against Jeroboam II and his successors Zechariah, Shallum, Menahem and Pekahiah before becoming sole king 734–731 BC. However, the pro-Syrian, anti-Assyrian policies of Pekah were ended by the reappearance of Assyria in the west under Tiglath-pileser III, who captured Damascus in 734 BC (2 Kings 16:9).

Amos was active when Israel's major enemy was Damascus, before Assyria had become an urgent threat. The prosperity of Israel under Jeroboam and of Judah under Uzziah was beginning to show signs of decline. Though a Judean, from Tekoa south of Jerusalem, Amos prophesied mainly in the northern kingdom, in particular at the sanctuary of Bethel (7:1–10), against the king and aristocracy of Samaria, for this was where the power lay. Analysis of the book of Amos shows that it was compiled from several major complexes of oracles. The first is the sequence of oracles against Damascus, Gaza, Tyre, Edom, the Ammonites, Moab, Judah and Israel in chs. 1–2. (The oracles against Tyre and Edom have unnecessarily been regarded as inauthentic; the oracle against Judah (2:4–5), however, does seem to suggest later interests, and without it we have a list of seven nations ending with Israel.) In these oracles, the foreign nations are attacked for various acts of cruelty in or after war against their neighbours, for which they will in turn suffer appropriately, while Israel is castigated for crimes against her own people, the righteous and the poor, the Nazirites and the prophets, for which Israel will suffer what appears to be some kind of inescapable military disaster (2:13–16).

Amos 3–6 is a collection of several 'words' against Israel (3:1; 4:1; 5:1), threatening the encirclement, destruction and plundering of the land and its strongholds (2:11), the destruction of the altar of Bethel and the royal palaces (3:14–15), the exile of the wealthy women of Samaria (4:1–3), the decimation of Israel's population (5:3), the destruction of the sanctuaries of Gilgal and Bethel (5:4–5), and exile for the confidently secure leaders of Jerusalem and Samaria (6:1–8), who at present rejoice in certain minor victories (6:13) but will be oppressed by a foreign nation (6:14). The sins of Israel's leaders are robbery and violence (3:10), oppression of the poor and irresponsible pleasure-seeking (4:1; 5:11; 6:4–6; 8:4–6), failure to establish justice (5:12,15,24; 6:12), and insincere worship (4:4–5; 5:21–24). For these sins, Israel must prepare to meet its God (4:12), or, better,

> Seek the LORD and live,
>    lest he break out like fire in the house of Joseph,
> and it devour, with none to quench it . . .

> Seek good, and not evil,
>    that you may live;
> and so the LORD, the God of hosts, will be with you,
>    as you have said.
> Hate evil, and love good,
>    and establish justice in the gate;
> it may be that the LORD, the God of hosts,
>    will be gracious to the remnant of Joseph.

(Amos 5:6, 14–15)

It seems that Amos did envisage the possibility that Israel might avoid disaster. Those, however, who expected the Day of the Lord, when it came, to bring redemption to Israel would get a shock:

> Woe to you who desire the day of the LORD!
>    Why would you have the day of the LORD?

It is darkness, and not light;
  as if a man fled from a lion,
  and a bear met him;
or went into the house and leaned with his hand against the wall,
  and a serpent bit him.
Is not the day of the LORD darkness, and not light,
  and gloom with no brightness in it?

(5:18–20)

Chapters 7–9 include a set of visions, in which Amos sees first locusts, and secondly, fire devouring the land. He intercedes with God, and God relents. Thirdly, he sees the Lord standing by a wall, holding a plumbline (or, in another interpretation of the Hebrew, standing by a wall of tin, holding tin). In either case, the message is one of threat against the sanctuaries of Israel and the dynasty of Jeroboam (cf. 7:10–17; Hos. 1:4–5). (To this threat has been appended the story of the priest Amaziah's accusation that Amos prophesied the death of Jeroboam in Amos 7:10–17). In the fourth vision, Amos sees a basket of summer fruit (figs?; Hebrew *qayiṣ* ), which is interpreted by means of a word play to mean that 'the end' (or perhaps, 'the last month'; Hebrew, *qeṣ* ) 'has come upon my people Israel', and there would be corpses and mourning within the palace (or temple). In a final vision (9:1–4), Amos sees the Lord standing by the altar (probably at Bethel), commanding the destruction of the sanctuary, apparently by earthquake. No one will be left alive. These visions predict disaster for Jeroboam's dynasty, and the physical destruction of the sanctuary of Bethel and perhaps the palace of Samaria. Chapter 8:9–14 also appears to threaten mourning and a period of confusion, particularly for the young men and women who swear by the gods worshipped in Samaria, Dan and Beersheba.

Amos' words and visions seem aimed particularly at the monarchy and aristocracy of Israel. The book, as it stands, however, does not envisage an apocalyptic end of everything. 'It may be that the LORD . . . will be gracious to the remnant of Joseph' (5:15); 'I will not utterly destroy the house of Jacob' (9:8). If 9:11–12, 13–15 are authentic words of Amos (Wellhausen rejected them, describing their message as 'roses and lavender instead of blood and iron'), Amos predicted the restoration of the Davidic dynasty, the reconstruction of the cities of Israel, and the return of paradisal conditions. The difficulty is that Israel's cities were not ruined and the Davidic dynasty did not fall until 722 BC and 587 BC respectively, and the idea of the 'remnant' of Joseph or Israel is one that is more familiar from the exilic or post-exilic period. There is a strong case for the view that these expressions of future restoration belong to a later editor of Amos.

An editorial hand is visible in the arrangement of the book (which begins with threats and ends with promises), in the introduction (1:1–2), perhaps in the oracle against Judah (2:4–6), in the introduction to the collected sayings (3:1–2), and in the intrusive verse 3:7 (with its Deuteronomistic phrase 'his servants the prophets') and the biographical section 7:10–17. These passages suggest that the book was edited by a Deuteronomistic hand from Jerusalem in the late seventh – early sixth century BC. Chapter 7:10–17 contains Amaziah's perhaps inaccurate accusation that Amos predicted Jeroboam's death by the sword, and Amos' much debated denial of his prophetic status (7:14). Amos appears to be saying in this verse that though he was not by profession a *nabhi'* of the kind to be found in royal courts acting as the king's yes-men (e.g., 1 Kings 22:6) but a herdsman and dresser of sycomore trees, God had commanded him to prophesy (cf. 3:8). His prophecy is directed firmly against the royal house of Israel, the successors of Jeroboam II and the priest of Bethel (whose sanctuary the Deuteronomistic Historian regarded as the sin of Jeroboam I) and predicts the exile of Israel (seen by the Deuteronomistic Historian as punishment for Israel's cultic sins, 2 Kings 17:7-18). Amos 7:10-17 seems strongly influenced by the Deuteronomistic picture of the kings and sanctuaries of Israel and of the prophetic attitude towards them. That is to say, our present book Amos may derive from the exilic period, with Amos' oracles edited and arranged so as to provide a message appropriate to that period. The final oracle of the book would be particularly appropriate:

> 'Behold, the days are coming,' says
> the LORD,
> 'when the ploughman shall over-
> take the reaper
> and the treader of grapes him who
> sows the seed;
> the mountains shall drip sweet wine,
> and all the hills shall flow with it.
> I will restore the fortunes of my
> people Israel,
> and they shall rebuild the ruined
> cities and inhabit them;
> they shall plant vineyards and drink
> their wine,
> and they shall make gardens and
> eat their fruit.
> I will plant them upon their land,
> and they shall never again be
> plucked up
> out of the land which I have given
> them,'
> says the LORD your God.

(Amos 9:13-15)

## Hosea

The Deuteronomic superscription to the book of Hosea states that Hosea was active in the reigns of Uzziah, Jotham, Ahaz and Hezekiah, kings of Judah, but in the case of Israel mentions only Jeroboam. Internal evidence, however, shows that Hosea knew of the end of the dynasty of Jehu (1:4; cf. 2 Kings 15:10) at the hand of Shallum the son of Jabesh, the Syro-Ephraimite war of 735–734 BC (Hos. 5:8 – 6:6), the alliance with Egypt in Hoshea's reign (Hos. 7:11; 9:3; 11:5; 12:1), the submission of Menahem and Hoshea to Assyria (2 Kings 15:19–20; 17:3), the rapid succession of kings – Zechariah, Shallum, Menahem, Pekahiah, Pekah, Hoshea – in the final years of Israel's existence (7:7; 8:4), and the capture of Hoshea by the king of Assyria (13:20; 2 Kings 17:1-5). Samaria is expected to fall (13:16) but the event itself is not mentioned. Hosea therefore was probably active *c.* 750–725 BC. His oracles are directed against the northern kingdom (often called 'Ephraim' after its largest constituent tribe) and its cities or sanctuaries, Samaria, Shechem, Bethel and Gilgal. A later editor has made some of the threats against Ephraim apply to Judah also (e.g., 5:5; 6:4,11; 10:11). In chs. 1–3, however, the original material has been expanded in a different way, the Lord's unforgiving attitude to Israel being contrasted with his pity for Judah (1:7). Another addition looks for the future unity of Israel and Judah (1:11). These are probably signs of different stages of the editing of the collection after the fall of the northern kingdom in 722 BC.

The book consists of two, or three, main sections. Chapters 1–3 form a recognisable unit, focusing on and interpreting Hosea's much debated marriage with a harlot (1:2-3) and/or an adulteress (3:1-3). These accounts have been explained as parallel versions of the same story, as referring to two stages of Hoshea's marriage with Gomer, or as referring to two different marriages. It is probably impossible to use such theologically loaded narratives as a secure basis for reconstructing Hosea's biography. Hosea's act in taking a wife who was or became promiscuous is symbolic of God's love for Israel. The symbolism is developed by the account of the birth and naming of the three children (compare the message conveyed by the names of Isaiah's children in Isa.7–8): Jezreel, punning on 'Israel' and referring to the murders by which Jehu established his dynasty (2 Kings 9:37); Lo-ruhamah, 'not pitied', and Lo-ammi, 'Not my people', indicating that the Lord's special covenant relationship with Israel was about to come to an end. In ch.2, Israel's promiscuity is identified as her disloyalty to Yahweh in giving her allegiance to her lovers, the Canaanite gods, the Baals. Hosea 1–3 seems to act as a preface to the book as a whole.

Chapters 4–14 are a collection of mainly critical pieces. It is not easy to discern any very clear arrangement, but comparatively easy to list the main themes. First, Hosea condemns 'harlotry' (i.e., disloyalty to Yahweh) in worshipping other gods (3:1) – the fertility gods of Canaan, El and Asherah, Baal and Anath, and others – sacrificing at hilltop sanctuaries and under sacred trees, visiting cult prostitutes to ensure fertility at home and on the land, worshipping metal idols ('the calf of Samaria') (cf. 2:2-13; 4:13-14; 8:4b-6,11; 9:1-4,10; 10:1-2; 11:1-2; 13:1-3). Hosea is attacking the association, particularly tempting in an agricultural society, of Israel's God Yahweh (who brought Israel out of Egypt) with the Canaanite Baal (who provided corn, wine, oil, wool and water). Israel must rediscover that it is the Lord who provides these things for her (2:5-8), and return to him; he must allure her, as once he did in the wilderness (2:14-15).

Secondly, Hosea attacks the harlotry of Ephraim's political errors in seeking help from Assyria (5:13; 7:11; 8:4–10), committing political murder (6:8–10) and intrigue (7:1–7), setting up kings not approved by God (8:4) and trusting in human forces (10:13–15). Thirdly, Hosea castigates the failings of priests and prophets (4:4–6; 5:1–2; 6:9; 9:7–9) and kings (5:10; 7:7; 9:15; 10:3,7). And fourthly, Hosea portrays God's feelings for Israel, which include both anger and compassion (e.g., 5:16–6:6; 9:10–14; 11:1–9; 13:4–14; 14:1–8):

> Ephraim is like a dove,
> > silly and without sense,
> > calling to Egypt, going to Assyria.
> As they go, I will spread over them a net;
> > I will bring them down like birds of the air;
> > I will chastise them for their wicked deeds.
> Woe to them, for they have strayed from me!
> > Destruction to them, for they have rebelled against me!
> I would redeem them,
> > but they speak lies against me.

(Hos.7:11–13)

As Abraham Heschel commented, 'Hosea's emotional solidarity with God is apparent throughout the book' (this is the point of Hosea's marriage in chs. 1–3). Hosea knows Gomer as the Lord once knew Israel (13:5); the ideal is that Israel in turn should know the Lord (8:2; 13:4), but, as Hosea complains, there is 'no knowledge of God in the land' (4:1), the people are destroyed for lack of knowledge because the priests have rejected knowledge (4:6), and God 'desires steadfast love and not sacrifice, the knowledge of God rather than burnt offerings' (6:6). Knowledge of God would mean the absence of swearing, lying, killing, stealing, adultery, and murder (4:2), now rampant in the land.

It is clear that Hosea is especially opposed to the cultic practices of eighth-century Israel, and in particular to the association of Yahweh with the sexual rites of the Canaanite cult. Evidence for such syncretism in the mid-monarchic period is perhaps demonstrated by archaeological discoveries at a site called Kuntillet 'Ajrūd, 50 km south of Kadesh Barnea. In a building thought to be a wayside shrine were found various graffiti on plaster as well as inscriptions on pottery jars (the jars were manufactured near Jerusalem). One inscription includes the words, 'I bless you by Yahweh . . . and by his Asherah', which thus appears to associate Yahweh with a female deity, perhaps as a consort (Kenyon, rev. Moorey, 1987, 121–24). A ` similar eighth-century inscription from Khirbet el-Qōm near Lachish includes the words 'May Uriah be blessed by Yahweh and by his Asherah'. It is not clear whether the word Asherah here refers to the goddess or to a cult object, the wooden pole symbolising the goddess, but in either case Yahweh is, at the very least, associated with the Canaanite goddess. This may well illustrate the religious beliefs and practices to which Hosea was opposed.

Hosea counters such popular syncretistic religion by reminding Israel of her own traditions. He knows of the destruction of the cities of the plain

(Gen.19:24–25; Hos.11:8), of Jacob's rivalry with Esau (Gen.27–28) and wrestling with the angel at Penuel (Gen.32:24–30); Hos.12:3–4), of God's appearance to Jacob at Bethel (Gen.28:10–22; Hos.12:4), of Jacob's flight to Aram and his marriages there (Gen.29–30; Hos.12:12), of God's appearance to Moses (Exod.3:14; Hos.1:9), of the exodus from Egypt and Israel's wanderings and murmurings in the wilderness (Hos.2:14; 11:1; 12:13; 13:4–6), Israel's apostasy at Baal Peor (Num.25; Hos.9:10), and the disgraceful event at Gibeah (Jud.19:22–30; Hos.9:9; 10:9). In particular, Hosea emphasises that it was Yahweh who knew Israel in the wilderness (13:5), called Israel out of Egypt (11:1), taught Ephraim (11:2), gave Israel the law and covenant (8:1), and provided the grain, wine, oil, and the silver and gold used for images of Baal (2:8). Chapter 4:2 perhaps reflects Hosea's knowledge of the Ten Commandments (Exod.20; Deut.5). Hosea mentions most of these things to underline Israel's subsequent rebellion:

> When Israel was a child, I loved him,
>   and out of Egypt I called my son.
> The more I called them,
>   the more they went from me;
> they kept sacrificing to the Baals,
>   and burning incense to idols.
> Yet it was I who taught Ephraim to walk,
>   I took them up in my arms;
>   but they did not know that I had healed them.

> (Hos.11:1–3)

and to point to coming punishment:

> Ephraim's glory shall fly away like a bird –
>   no birth, no pregnancy, no conception!
> Even if they bring up children,
>   I will bereave them till none is left.
> Woe to them
>   when I depart from them.
> Ephraim's sons, as I have seen, are destined for a prey;
>   Ephraim must lead forth his sons to slaughter.
> Give them, O LORD –
>   what wilt thou give?
> Give them a miscarrying womb
>   and dry breasts.

> (Hos.9:11–14)

But the threat of punishment (cf. 11:5–6; 13:16) is followed by the promise of compassion:

> How can I give you up, O Ephraim!
>   How can I hand you over, O Israel!
> How can I make you like Admah!

How can I treat you like Zeboiim!
My heart recoils within me,
   my compassion grows warm and tender.
I will not execute my fierce anger,
   I will not again destroy Ephraim;
For I am God and not man,
   the Holy One in your midst,
   and I will not come to destroy.

(Hos.11:8–9)

It is hard to dissociate this element of compassion (cf. also 2:14–15, 16–29; 14:4–8) from the work of the original Hosea and see it as a later glossing of the prophet's original criticisms. Anger and love can be two sides of the same coin. In the opening chapters, Hosea is commanded, first, to have children by a prostitute and give them names indicating God's rejection of Israel, and then to 'love a woman who is beloved of a paramour and is an adulteress; even as the LORD loves the people of Israel, though they turn to other gods', and here, as the editor perceived, lies the paradox of the book. Not surprisingly, the editor closes the book with the comment,

Whoever is wise, let him understand these things;
   whoever is discerning, let him know them;
for the ways of the LORD are right,
   and the upright walk in them,
   but transgressors stumble in them.

(Hos.14:9)

## Isaiah

The book of the prophet Isaiah is, after Genesis, perhaps the best-known of the Hebrew Bible or the Old Testament. It is a large book, and from it come many memorable and much quoted passages. Best known of all, at least among Christians, is Isaiah 7:14, usually quoted in the translation from King James' Bible, 'Behold, a virgin shall conceive, and bear a son, and shall call his name Immanuel', a verse applied in St Matthew's Gospel to the birth of Jesus of Nazareth (Mt.1:23). From the book of Isaiah comes also the famous portrait of the 'Suffering Servant' in ch.53:

He was despised and rejected by men;
   a man of sorrows, and acquainted with grief . . .
Surely he has borne our griefs
   and carried our sorrows . . .
All we like sheep have gone astray;
   we have turned every one to his own way;
and the LORD has laid on him
   the iniquity of us all.

From Isaiah 65:17–25 comes the famous vision of the new world:

'For behold, I create new heavens and a new earth;
  and the former things shall not be remembered
  or come into mind.
But be glad and rejoice for ever
  in that which I create;
for behold, I create Jerusalem a rejoicing,
  and her people a joy . . .
The wolf and the lamb shall feed together,
  the lion shall eat straw like the ox;
  and dust shall be the serpent's food.
They shall not hurt or destroy
  in all my holy mountain,

says the LORD.'

The modern reader, however, is not always aware that the first of these three oracles was uttered by Isaiah of Jerusalem *c.* 735 BC, the second by 'Second Isaiah' *c.* 550–540 BC, and the third by perhaps another prophet active in Jerusalem towards 500 BC. The book of Isaiah comprises the work of at least three major figures and probably several lesser ones, its unity being one of theology rather than authorship. The different major sections of the book are easily distinguished on grounds of content and style. Chapters 56–66 refer to the situation in Jerusalem in the late sixth century BC, after the exile; chs. 40–55 to the situation of the exiles in Babylon towards the end of their exile; and chs. 1–39 to the situation in Jerusalem in the last four decades of the eighth century BC, when the Assyrian empire was in its most dangerously expansive mood.

Our present concern is with chs. 1–39. Even a casual reading shows that this work is made up of separate sections, distinguished in part by their editorial headings. Isaiah 1–39 as a whole is introduced by the superscription of Isa.1:1. Chapters 2–12 are introduced by the heading, 'The word which Isaiah the son of Amoz saw concerning Judah and Jerusalem', and are rounded off by thanksgiving psalms. Chapter 13 begins a series of oracles about different places and peoples, usually headed 'The oracle concerning...' (chs. 13–14, Babylon; chs. 15–16, Moab; ch. 17, Damascus; ch. 18, Ethiopia; ch. 19, Egypt; ch.21, 'the wilderness of the sea' and Arabia; ch. 22, 'the valley of vision', ch. 23, Tyre). Chapters 24–27 have often been described as 'the Isaian apocalypse'. Chapters 28–33 are a collection of oracles containing both threat and promise, opposing rebellion against Assyria in reliance on Egyptian help. Chapters 34–35 probably belong with chs. 40–55; chs. 36–39, much of which appear also in 2 Kings 18–20, are a collection of biographical material about Isaiah's activity at the court of king Hezekiah of Judah in Sennacherib's reign, *c.* 701 BC (chs. 36–37), and at the time of a Babylonian embassy to Jerusalem, perhaps *c.* 713 BC (chs. 38–39).

A recent commentary has argued that chs. 1–27, at least, present Isaiah's work in correct chronological order. Chapters 1–5 start with reference to the famous earthquake of Uzziah's reign (1:5–9; 2:12–17, cf. Amos 1:1), and focus on the social problems of Jerusalem in the reigns of Uzziah and Jotham, and on coming judgment. Chapter 6 reflects the coronation ritual of the new king Ahaz, and 'marked a shift in Isaiah's ministry rather than an inaugural call' (Hayes and Irvine, 1987, 109). Chapters 7–12 contain a variety of materials referring to the political crisis of 735–734 BC, when Rezin of Syria and his ally Pekah of Samaria tried to force Ahaz of Judah into an anti-Assyrian alliance. The oracles mainly against foreign nations in chs. 13–23 relate to a series of political events: ch. 13 to Assyria's suppression of Babylon's rebellion in 731–729 BC; 14:1–27 prophesies the death of Tiglath-pileser III (he became king of Babylon in 729 BC and died in 727 BC); 14:28–32, dated to the year of Ahaz's death (727 BC), warns the Philistines not to rejoice at Tiglath-pileser's death. Chapters 15–17 are taken to reflect an Assyrian response to rebellion on the part of Moab, Syria and Israel early in the reign of Shalmaneser V (727–722 BC); ch. 18 refers to negotiations in 727 BC between Assyria and Egypt, then ruled by an Ethiopian dynasty (cf. 20:3,5), and ch. 19 refers to Sargon V's new anti-Ethiopian policy in Egypt (720 BC). Chapter 20 dates itself to Ashdod's rebellion against Assyria in 713–711 BC; Isaiah opposes Judah's participation. Chapter 21:1–10 refers to Sargon's attack on lower Mesopotamia after the suppression of Ashdod, and 21:11–17 to Assyrian attacks on the Arabs. Chapter 22:1–14 perhaps refers to Jerusalem's ignominious defeat in battle after Judah's participation in Ashdod's rebellion, but also to Jerusalem's relief when the Assyrian forces departed without inflicting serious punishment on the city itself. Chapter 23 celebrates Tyre's diminishing power in Mediterranean trade as a result of new political alignments after 709 BC, while chs. 24–27 are seen as a liturgical composition celebrating Judah's declaration of independence from Assyria on the death of Sargon in 705 BC. Chapters 28–33, however, are taken to refer to the last years of Israel's freedom (728–725 BC) before the Assyrian attack on Samaria and its destruction in 722 BC. Chapters 36–39 refer to events of 701 BC and an earlier occasion in Jerusalem.

This reconstruction interprets the oracles of Isaiah 1–33, 36–39 against an historical background reconstructed mainly from biblical and Assyrian sources. It has the merit of simplicity, and rejects the more sophisticated critical approaches which reduce Isaiah 1–39 to a collection of virtually unrelated fragments, many of indeterminate date. The literary problem will not entirely go away, however. Chapters 28–33 do not fit very neatly into the scheme, and the links between chs. 34, 35 and 40–55 show that chs. 36–39 are an intrusion at this point, based on the Deuteronomistic History, designed to prepare the way for the message of ch. 40. The precise historical background and reference of Isaiah 24–27 remains speculative, and it must be admitted that chs. 24–39 remain a complex compilation of material. If chs. 34–35 (to set aside chs. 36–39 for a moment) have any clear unifying theme, it is that of Israel's future salvation. It is noticeable that these chapters do not have editorial superscriptions such as are found in chs. 1–23, the editor who added these chapters to the previous corpus perhaps not having any information to offer.

The composition of chs. 1–12 seems also to have been a complex process. It is not certain that 1:5–9 is an early Isaianic oracle referring to Judah's experience of the earthquake in Uzziah's reign. Many scholars have referred it to Sennacherib's devastation of the land in 701 BC, and certainly 1:7–8 might indicate human rather than natural activity. Chapter 1 as a whole has been understood as a selection of Isaiah's sayings put together to provide a preface to, or programmatic summary of, Isaiah's teaching; similarly, the superscription introduces the whole collection of chs. 1–39. The superscription of ch. 2 may relate to chs. 2–4, or perhaps to chs. 2–12; ch. 12, consisting of two short psalms of thanksgiving, makes an appropriate endpiece to these chapters.

Within chs. 2–12, several blocks of material are clearly distinguishable: 2:1 – 4:6 (itself clearly composed of several separate pieces; thus 2:2–5 reappears in Mic. 4:2–6); 5:8–30 with 8:21 – 10:4; 10:5 – 11:6; and 6:1 – 8:20, which seem to have separated 5:30 from 8:21. Chapters 6:1 – 8:20 present a careful composition, ch. 6 (in the first person) acting as a preface to the prophetic biography in ch. 7 and autobiography in ch. 8:1–20. The core of these three chapters lies in the names of the three children (cf. 8:18): Shear-jashub ('a remnant will return'), Immanuel ('God with us'), and Maher-shalal-hash-baz ('the spoil speeds, the prey hastens'). These symbolically named children (probably the prophet's children) convey the message that Jerusalem will not be destroyed by the alliance between Israel and Syria in 735–734 BC; only a remnant of Syria and Israel will return to their land; God will be with Judah; the wealth of Damascus and the spoil of Samaria will be carried away. The reinterpretation of the Immanuel oracle, originally one of hope and comfort to Ahaz, to a message of coming disaster, is clear at the end of 7:17b, and in the appended oracles beginning 'in that day' in 7:18–25. In short, there are abundant signs of composition and compilation in chs. 2–12, at the heart of which lie chs. 6:1 – 8:20, themselves probably compiled long after the prophet's activity (cf. the explanatory reference of 7:8b), and though their compiler may have understood the contents of chs. 2–5 to belong to the reigns of Uzziah and Jotham, and chs. 6–12 to belong to the reign of Ahaz, there is no guarantee that all the contents can be so easily dated (particularly if 5:8–30 belong with 8:21 – 10:4). Much doubt has been expressed in particular about the oracles 2:2–5, 4:2–6, 9:2–7 and 11:1–9, largely on the grounds that they convey promises rather than the threats which scholars have expected of eighth-century prophets; but the assumption that Isaiah was limited to threats is unfounded, as the naming of his children shows.

This raises the major question of the message of the eighth-century prophet Isaiah. Isaiah was active over four decades, and his message at different periods reflected the changing social and political circumstances. Accurate exegesis of Isaiah's oracles depends on our being able to assess their authenticity and date them correctly, aware that the present arrangement of the material is the work of an editor who has already had to make similar assessments. Chapters 1–5 certainly reveal that Isaiah, like Amos, was concerned for social justice (1:17, 21–23; 5:8–23, cf. 9:8 – 10:4), that the leaders and aristocracy were particularly at fault (1:23; 3:1 – 4:1), and that judgment has come (1:7–9) or is coming (1:19–20; 2:1–22; 3:13 – 4:1), whether by way of exile (5:13), earthquake (5:25) or invasion (5:26–30). In ch. 6, God instructs his prophet that the people are to be kept uncomprehending 'until cities lie waste, without inhabitant, and houses without men, and the land is utterly desolate, and the LORD removes men far away' (6:11–12), which indicates a devastating destruction. Chapters 7:1 – 8:20, however, promise in the circumstances of the Syro-Ephraimite invasion of 735–734 BC that Ahaz and Jerusalem need not fear; it is Damascus and Samaria which will not survive. Chapters 9:8 – 10:4 continue to threaten Israel: God's anger is not turned away. In 10:5–11, 13–19 Isaiah presents Assyria as the rod of God's anger against Israel (a 'godless nation', 10:6) but also as threatening Jerusalem (10:11), and as a result being threatened herself with God's punishment for her sin of pride (10:13–19). These oracles against Israel and Damascus are in effect political promises for Judah, and make it hard to argue that Isaiah was nothing more than a prophet of doom. Chapter 12 also makes it clear that Isaiah is conveying, or was understood by the editor to convey, news of salvation to Zion. Isaiah's very name means 'Yahweh saves', and we need not simply assume that the promissory oracles of 2:1–4, 4:2–6, 9:2–7, 11:1–9 are necessarily later, inauthentic additions to the book, even if their precise historical reference remains obscure (9:2–7 and 11:1–9 seem to refer in glowing terms to the accession of a new king, perhaps Hezekiah in 727 BC).

The oracles of chs. 13–23, as we have seen, threaten Babylon (or the Assyrian ruler of Babylon), Moab, Damascus, the Ethiopians and Egyptians, Arabians, and people of Tyre and Sidon. Chapter 17:4–11 threatens Israel; the somewhat enigmatic ch. 22 tells Jerusalem that the recent defeat should prompt penitence rather than rejoicing. (A separate narrative in 22:15–25 prophesies personal disgrace for a royal official and also for his successor.) These chapters, then, are altogether threatening, to Israel and Judah as to other nations. By contrast, chs. 24–27 offer a more hopeful message, at least to Jerusalem. In ch. 24 the earth is to be laid waste and creation to be uncreated (24:18–20) and the rulers of the earth punished, after which the Lord will reign on Mount Zion (24:23). Chapter 25 praises God for wonderful things done 'on this mountain' (i.e., Jerusalem); 26:1–4 is a song of thanksgiving for Jerusalem; 26:7–19 is a prayer of trust in God and 26:20 – 27:13 in various ways expresses confidence in the future of Israel. Because there is no clear, explicit reference to the political background, these chapters are enigmatic. Many scholars have seen this somewhat eschatological picture as a post-exilic addition to the book; more recently there has been a tendency to assign it to the eighth-century prophet. If so, it shows an eighth-century confidence in Yahweh as the God of Jerusalem's salvation, and probably reflects the liturgy of the Jerusalem temple.

Chapters 28–33 are confusing because threats of destruction, and promises of salvation, as elsewhere in Isaiah, are proclaimed side by side. Ephraim and Judah will be punished, but God's threshing does not last for ever (ch. 28). The nations' attack on Jerusalem will turn out to be as a dream (29:1–8); present conditions will be reversed (29:17–24). Israel will be punished for reliance on Egypt and for her rebelliousness (30:1–14), but 'the LORD waits to be gracious' (30:18), and the Assyrians, once the rod of God's anger, will themselves be smitten with the rod (30:31). Chapter 31 has a similar message, ch. 32 pictures a new paradisal kingdom and ch. 33 looks ahead to the future prosperity of Jerusalem:

Your eyes will see the king in his beauty;
　they will behold a land that stretches afar . . .
Look upon Zion, the city of our appointed feasts!
　Your eyes will see Jerusalem,
　　a quiet habitation, an immovable tent,
whose stakes will never be plucked up,
　nor will any of its cords be broken.

(Isa.33:17,20)

Isaiah 1–33 expresses the rebelliousness and disobedience of Israel and Judah, their coming punishment and the need to repent, as well as the expectation of salvation from Yahweh. Isaiah's preaching was not limited to doom; on the other hand, he did not preach that Jerusalem was inviolable, whatever the behaviour of her people. He demanded repentance and trust in Yahweh (7:9; 8:17; 28:16; 30:15). In Isaiah, Yahweh is the King, the Lord of Hosts 1:9; 6:3,5; 10:16; titles used in the temple liturgy, cf. Ps.24), the Holy One of Israel (1:4,24; 10:17; 12:5). Isaiah's concern is both for Israel and Judah (5:7), but for Judah, Jerusalem (Zion) and the Davidic dynasty above all. For him, God dwells in Zion: 'Behold, I and the children whom the LORD has given me are signs and portents in Israel from the LORD of hosts, who dwells on Mount Zion' (8:18) cf. Ps 132:13–14). Isaiah's concern for Jerusalem, its present faithlessness, its coming redemption, and future centrality as the source of God's teaching for the nations are seen clearly in 1:1 – 2:5. If the famous oracles of 2:1-4, 4:2-6, 9:2-7, 11:1-9 and 32:1-8 come from Isaiah's pen, Isaiah had a vision of a paradisal, holy Jerusalem in which a Davidic king would rule with justice and righteousness. Whoever wrote these passages, however, the vision they express has remained powerful through two and a half millennia.

The final section of Isaiah 1–39 (chs. 36–39; cf. 2 Kings 18–20) is concerned with Sennacherib's attack on Judah and Jerusalem in 701 BC. After the death of Sargon in 701 BC, Hezekiah joined Egypt, Ashkelon and Ekron in rebellion against Assyria. In 702 BC Sennacherib campaigned in the west. He defeated the Egyptians at Eltekeh, took forty-six Judean cities, built a siege wall round Jerusalem and shut up Hezekiah in there 'like a bird in a cage'. Hezekiah capitulated and sent tribute (2 Kings 18:13-16). Jerusalem was thus spared the horrors of being sacked but was humiliated and forced to pay heavily. So much is clear from Sennacherib's own annals, preserved on the Taylor Prism in the British Museum, and from 2 Kings 18:13-16. However, there follow in 2 Kings 18:17 – 19:7, 36-37 and 19:8-35 two parallel narratives (given also in Isaiah 36:2 – 37:8; 37-38, and 37:9-36) describing how (1) the Assyrian king's officer makes two speeches to the officers of king Hezekiah on the wall of Jerusalem, urging Jerusalem's submission. Hezekiah, hearing them, sends to the prophet Isaiah, who replies that Hezekiah is not to fear, for God will cause the Assyrian king to fall by the sword in his own land; (2) the king of Assyria sends messengers to Hezekiah, demanding submission. Hezekiah prays, and Isaiah sends an oracle and a sign to Hezekiah promising that the king of Assyria will not besiege

. Jerusalem. Jerusalem is saved by the intervention of the angel of the Lord, who that night slew 185,000 men in the Assyrian camp. These parallel accounts are designed to underline that Yahweh had miraculously saved Jerusalem, as predicted by Isaiah. In the version given in Isaiah chs. 36–37, however, all reference to the political realities of Hezekiah's submission to Assyria and payment of tribute has been omitted, and emphasis is put on the idea that God would defend Jerusalem to save it 'for my own sake and for the sake of my servant David' (Isa. 37:35). The themes of Yahweh's defence of Jerusalem from attack by foreign nations, and of Yahweh's support for the Davidic dynasty, appear regularly in the Psalms (e.g., Pss. 2, 46, 48, 76) and were clearly part of the theology of the Jerusalem cult. They influenced the prophet Isaiah, and also these narratives about Isaiah. In ch. 39, Isaiah is presented in a different light as a miracle-worker and healer, and also as one who predicts the Babylonian exile centuries before it happened. This prediction prepares the way for the immediately following chapters 40–55, thus linking the first and second parts of this great book.

## Micah

The prophet Micah (Jer. 26:18), according to the superscription of the book which bears his name, was Isaiah's contemporary. He was not a Jerusalemite, however, but a countryman, perhaps one of 'the people of the land', that is, the country landowners, from Moresheth-gath (Mic. 1:1,14), Tell Judeideh, about 10 km southeast of Gath, and 11 km northeast of Lachish, in the Shephelah region of southwest Judah. Chapter 1:10–16 mentions a number of towns and villages of this region. Jeremiah 26:18 reveals an early sixth-century BC memory of Micah as one who prophesied that Jerusalem would become a heap of ruins (quoting Mic. 3:12). The title of the book, however, indicates that Micah spoke against Samaria as well as against Jerusalem, and various references to northern places and traditions in chs. 6 and 7 have suggested to some scholars that these two chapters at least derive from a prophet of the northern kingdom.

The opening oracle (1:2–7) describes the Lord appearing from his temple in Jerusalem and threatening Samaria (so the oracle presumably dates from before 722 BC). Destruction is prophesied also for Judah and Jerusalem (1:8–9), and the prophet laments the trouble about to come upon the cities of the Shephelah (1:10–16). Chapter 2:1–5 denounces covetous land-grabbers, and 2:6–11 the prophet's opponents. In parallel fashion 3:1–4, 5–10 denounces unjust rulers and misleading prophets. They are confident in their own security (3:11), but it is because of them that

> Zion shall be ploughed as a field;
> Jerusalem shall become a heap of riuns,
>     and the mountain of the house a wooded height.

These three chapters have long been seen as the genuine pre-exilic core of the book (apart from 2:12–13, which reflects knowledge of the exile), and they are focused on the disaster about to come upon Jerusalem (to which the destruction of Samaria is the prelude). Chapters 4–5 are very different, and speak of the future of Zion in promising, not threatening, terms. Chapter 4 opens with the oracle found also in Isaiah 2:1–5, presenting the temple of Yahweh in Zion as the place to which in the latter days the nations will come to learn God's law:

> For out of Zion shall go forth the law,
>   and the word of the LORD from Jerusalem.

Chapter 4:6–8 speaks of the return of the exiles to be ruled over by God from Mount Zion; 4:9 – 5:15 contrast the present troubles of Zion ('now', 4:9,10,11; 5:1) with the future in which a ruler from Bethlehem (i.e., of David's dynasty) will feed the flock and bring security (5:2–4). There will be deliverance in Israel (5:5–6) and the remnant of Jacob will prosper among the nations (5:7–9). However, 5:10–14 reads very much like a threat which might belong more properly with chs. 1–3, but which in its present position appears to be understood as a promise, glossed by verse 15 which seems to make the previous verses refer not to Israel but to the nations. In sum, the threats of Micah 1–3 are balanced by the glowing promises of Micah 4–5, a sure mark of editorial compilation and arrangement. A similar arrangement of threats followed by promises is seen in chs. 6 and 7. In 6:1–5 the Lord challenges the people to stand up in court and face his charges, in response to which Israel meditates on what is required (6:6–8):

> 'With what shall I come before the LORD,
> and bow myself before God on high? . . .
> He has showed you, O man, what is good;
>   and what does the LORD require of you
> but to do justice, and to love kindness,
>   and to walk humbly with your God?

In 6:9–16 the Lord proclaims his judgment:

> I have begun to smite you,
>   making you desolate because of your sins.
> You shall eat, but not be satisfied,
>   and there shall be hunger in your inward parts . . .
> You shall sow, but not reap;
>   you shall tread olives, but not anoint yourselves with oil;
>   you shall tread grapes, but not drink wine.

Israel responds with a lament (7:1–11):

> Woe is me! For I have become as when the summer fruit has been gathered,
>   as when the vintage has been gleaned:
> there is no cluster to eat,
>   no first-ripe fig which my soul desires.

The final verses of the book, however, show confidence that God will plead

Israel's cause (7:8–10), that people from Assyria to Egypt will look to the rebuilt Jerusalem (7:11–13), that Israel will once again feed on the fertile Transjordanian plains of Bashan and Gilead (7:14), that God will act as at the exodus (7:15), and the nations will turn in dread to the Lord (7:16–17). The book ends with a picture of God's compassion for Israel, based on God's promises to the patriarchs (7:18–20). This section has long been dated to the exilic period, and this dating is perhaps supported by the description of Israel as 'a remnant of his inheritance' (7:18), by the hope of rebuilding and regaining land (7:11,14), by the allusions to Exodus 34:6 (7:18), and to the patriarchs (7:20).

This book is clearly the result of careful editorial arrangement, in which threat and promise, judgment and salvation alternate (threats: 1:2 – 2:11, 3:1–12; 5:10 – 6:16; with a lament in 7:1–7; promises: 2:12–13; 4:1 – 5:9; 7:8–20). Not all the oracles are original to the eighth-century Micah; 2:12–13 has long been suspect, 4:1–4 appears to have been borrowed, while the rest of chs. 4–5 (apart from 5:10–14) and 7:11–20 are full of themes and allusions relating to the exilic period. Apart, perhaps, from 5:2–4, which promises a Davidic ruler, the promissory sections in Micah seem to belong to later theological editing of Micah's oracles. Brevard Childs has argued convincingly that the Micah tradition 'was transmitted and reshaped by a circle of editors similar to those who treasured the Isaianic corpus' (Childs, 1979, 434–5). Childs points to the similar pattern in each of judgment and salvation, to the common use of the promise made in Micah 4:1–4 and Isaiah 2:1–4, to liturgical influence visible in the editing of each, and to the common use of several otherwise rare expressions. This editing made Micah's work (mainly chs. 1–3, 5:2–4, 10–14; 6:1 – 7:7) relevant to a later age, much as the original work of Isaiah in eighth-century Jerusalem was given extended and developed reference and relevance by being bound up with the later work of Second Isaiah (40–55) and Third Isaiah (56–66).

Much of the promissive material in Micah may in its present state reflect knowledge of Israel's sixth-century BC exile in Babylon (cf. 4:10, for example), but this does not mean that Micah was limited to proclamations of doom. Micah 5:2–4 is a case in point; verses 2 and 4 are the core of this oracle, promising a new ruler of David's line, but verse 3 is an additional, intruded comment, explaining the delay in the fulfilment of the oracle by reference to the miseries of the exile and looking forward to the return of Israel from exile as the preliminary to the reign of the new king. The intrusion itself indicates that the original oracle is earlier, and perhaps belongs in general sentiment with the oracles of Isaiah 9:2–7 and 11:1–9.

The original Micah was concerned with social and political problems – especially with the ways in which wealthy leaders of the community used their position to fleece the people and the official prophets gave false reassurances (2:1–5, 6–11; 3:1–4, 5–8, 9–12). In particular, Micah is sharp about the grasping ways of lawyers, priests, prophets and traders in Jerusalem (3:9–11; 6:10–11). The thousands of temple offerings are of no importance compared with the need to do justice and walk humbly (6:6–8). Reliance on military power (chariots, fortresses) is just as pointless as reliance on sorcerers, soothsayers, and cult images

(5:10–14). Micah's prophecy that Jerusalem would be as a ploughed field made an impression and was still remembered a century later (Jer. 26:18), but the presence of chs. 4–5 does something to counter that impression, while 7:8–20 reflects the view of a more pietistic theologian who sees a merciful and compassionate God who is faithful to the promises made to Israel through the patriarchs. The book illustrates clearly how the preserved words of a prophet can, as time passes, gather theological reinterpretation by the addition of new material and by the adaptation of the original. The prophet's original accusations are made the basis for extended reflection on the future place of Jerusalem among the nations (7:16–17) or on the mercy of the incomparable God to his people (7:18–20) – themes which reappear particularly in the exilic period in the work of Second Isaiah (Isa. 40–55).

## The late seventh-century prophets

The Bible does not contain the work of any prophets who can be dated to the first half of the seventh century BC. Given that the kingdom of Samaria had been destroyed in 722 BC, and Judah seriously damaged in 701 BC, this is hardly surprising. The next prophets we hear of are those who belong to the last quarter of the seventh century BC, to the final years of the Assyrian empire. The books of Nahum, Habakkuk and Zephaniah are less read and known than those of the eighth-century BC prophets, though the writing can be just as dramatic and the vision just as compelling. The title of the book of Nahum describes the book as 'an oracle concerning Nineveh', the capital of Assyria which fell to the Babylonians and their allies in 612 BC. A second title reads 'the book of the vision of Nahum of Elkosh', the vision perhaps being that described in 2:3–12. The book begins with an incomplete acrostic poem describing the appearance of the avenging and wrathful Lord to destroy his enemies (1:2–8). This poem provides a theological preface to the book. Three short oracles follow, threatening pro-Assyrian politicians in Jerusalem (1:9–11), promising Judah's release from Assyria's yoke (1:12–13), and threatening the Assyrian king in person (1:14). The following verse introduces a vivid vision of an army plundering Nineveh (2:3–12), followed by a summarising prose comment in 2:13. Chapter 3 pronounces woe on Assyria, whose fate will be that of Egyptian Thebes, destroyed by Assyria in 663 BC. The author's feelings are made clear in the final verse:

> All who hear the news of you
>   clap their hands over you.
> For upon whom has not come
>   your unceasing evil?

Nahum has often been seen as an example of precisely the sort of salvation prophet condemned so heartily by Jeremiah and other biblical prophets for preaching peace where there was no peace. Such prophets often operated from within the cult, and this may have been the case with Nahum, who uses mythological language drawn from the Jerusalem cult (1:3–5), and nowhere criticises it but encourages Judah to keep the feasts and pay cultic vows (1:15). Some scholars have suggested that the book was actually designed for liturgical use, but this seems less likely. It remains a prophecy of the disaster coming upon Nineveh, and perhaps dates from shortly before 612 BC.

'The oracle of God which Habakkuk the prophet saw' is an enigmatic work. It begins with the prophet's lament at the destruction, violence and perverted justice he experiences (1:1–4), to which God replies that he is rousing the Chaldeans (i.e., the Babylonians), 'that bitter and hasty nation, who march through the breadth of the earth, to seize habitations not their own' (1:5–11). The prophet may mean that the Chaldeans are being sent to punish Judah's wickedness, or perhaps Assyria's violence; but it seems more likely that the opening verses refer to the prophet's experience of Babylonian violence. The prophet responds (1:12–17) by recognising that the Babylonians are sent as judgment; but

> Is he then to keep on emptying his net,
> and mercilessly slaying nations for ever?

The Lord responds by promising a vision (2:1–4), a vision which is not described unless it is to be seen in 3:2–15 (though this is described as a prayer), which describes God's appearance in wrath for the salvation of his people (3:13) in language like that of other theophanies (e.g., Jud. 5, Deut. 33, Ps. 68). Chapter 2:5 seems to be an added comment; 2:6–19 is a series of woes uttered presumably against the various crimes of the Babylonian aggressor. The book ends with a personal note which reveals clearly the prophet's situation – in the midst of trouble he will wait in quiet confidence for God's salvation:

> I hear, and my body trembles,
> my lips quiver at the sound;
>> rottenness enters into my bones,
>> my steps totter beneath me.
> I will quietly wait for the day of trouble
>> to come upon people who invade us.
>
> Though the fig tree do not blossom,
>> nor fruit be on the vines,
> the produce of the olive fail
>> and the fields yield no food,
> the flock be cut off from the fold
>> and there be no herd in the stalls,
> yet I will rejoice in the LORD,
>> I will joy in the God of my salvation.
> GOD, the Lord, is my strength;
>> he makes my feet like hinds' feet,
>> he makes me tread upon my high places.

(Hab. 3:16–19)

Habakkuk's book seems to belong to or derive from the context of worship. The opening and closing words of ch.3 show that it was sung like a psalm, and 1:2–4, 12–17 are also prayers and laments addressed to God. After the woe against the Babylonian idols in 2:18–19, 2:20 comments

> But the LORD is in his holy temple;
>   let all the earth keep silence before him.

This again suggests that the prophet's connections were with the cult. Habakkuk may, therefore, have been a prophet who operated from within the temple. He is called *nabhī'* in the opening superscription, and this title is given also to two post-exilic prophets, Haggai and Zechariah, who were both much concerned with the restoration of the temple. However, though the title *nabhī'* may have suggested a 'temple prophet' or form of central intermediary figure to some, it may rather be that *nabhī'* was the customary title for a prophet in later monarchic times, where formerly the title 'seer' was used (cf. 1 Sam. 9:9). The figure of Habakkuk was evidently popular; he reappears in a tale in the Apocrypha (Bel & Dr. 33–39) in which he is taken by an angel from Judah to Babylon to deliver dinner to Daniel in the lions' den. The book of Habakkuk itself probably dates from the turn of the seventh-sixth centuries BC, when the Babylonians under Nebuchadnezzar were extending their conquests into the Levant and into Judah itself.

The book of Zephaniah is dated by its superscription to the reign of Josiah (640–609 BC). It may belong early in the reign, before Josiah reformed the cult, for Zephaniah threatens those in Judah and Jerusalem who worship Baal, the heavenly host, and Milcom rather than Yahweh (1:2–6). Wealthy officials, royalty, the violent, the fraudulent, and traders are all threatened with the coming day of Yahweh:

> The great day of the LORD is near,
>   near and hastening fast;
> the sound of the day of the LORD is bitter,
>   the mighty man cries aloud there.
> A day of wrath is that day,
>   a day of distress and anguish,
> a day of ruin and devastation,
>   a day of darkness and gloom,
> a day of clouds and thick darkness,
> against the fortified cities
>   and against the lofty battlements.
>
> (Zeph. 1:14–16)

Chapter 2:4–15 threatens the nations: the Philistines, the Moabites and Ammonites will become desolate, plundered and taken over by Israel; the Ethiopians will be slain, Assyria will become a total desolation. Chapter 3 begins with threats against Jerusalem and her officials, judges, prophets and priests (3:1–5), but the tone changes through the chapter. In 3:6–13, God speaks, first noting that Israel has not repented in spite of seeing what God has done to the nations. He promises to punish the nations (3:8), but also to convert them to his worship (3:9–10) and to purge Israel, leaving her 'a people humble and lowly' (3:12):

> they shall do no wrong
>> and utter no lies,
> nor shall there be found in their mouth
>> a deceitful tongue.

In the final verses the prophet invites Zion to rejoice because

> The LORD has taken away the judgments against you,
>> he has cast out your enemies.
> The King of Israel, the LORD, is in your midst;
>> you shall fear evil no more . . .
> On that day it shall be said to Jerusalem:
>> 'Do not fear, O Zion . . .
> Behold, at that time I will deal
>> with all your oppressors.
> And I will save the lame
>> and gather the outcast,
> and I will change their shame into praise
>> and renown in all the earth.
> At that time I will bring you home,
>> at the time when I gather you together;
> yea, I will make you renowned and praised
>> among all the peoples of the earth,
> when I restore your fortunes
>> before your eyes', says the LORD.

(Zeph. 3:15–16, 19–20)

As it stands, the book appears to conform to the well-known arrangement of threats of judgment against Judah, judgment against the nations, and promises of salvation, though 3:1–7 disrupt this pattern a little. Possibly the final oracles, 3:9–20, which refer to disaster, oppression and return from exile, are additions from the exilic period. The expectation that the Gentile nations will be converted to Yahwism (3:9–10) is reminiscent of the post-exilic work of Zechariah 8:20 and Isaiah 61, though the earlier oracles of Isaiah 2:1–4 (Mic. 4:1–4) spoke of nations coming to the temple to learn the law of the Lord. Further signs of the influence of the exilic period are found in the references to 'the remnant of Judah' and 'the remnant of my people' in 2:7,9). Exilic revision of these oracles is hardly surprising; the original message is perhaps summed up in 2:1–3:

> Come together and hold assembly,
>> O shameless nation,
> before you are driven away

like the drifting chaff,
before there comes upon you
  the fierce anger of the LORD,
before there comes upon you
  the day of the wrath of the LORD.
Seek the LORD, all you humble of the land,
  who do his commands;
seek righteousness, seek humility;
  perhaps you may be hidden
  on the day of the wrath of the LORD.

## Jeremiah

Along with Isaiah, Jeremiah is probably Israel's best-known prophet. The noun 'jeremiah' is still used to denote a gloomy pessimist, and a 'jeremiad' is the complaint of such a person. The book of Jeremiah is a long and complex collection of material, and the quest for the historical Jeremiah is nearly as popular and just as frustrating as the quest for the historical Jesus, for Jeremiah's teaching has been subject to much editorial revision. The book is usually seen as dividing into three parts.

Chapters 1–25 are a collection of Jeremiah's oracles, mostly in poetic form, with some prose passages interwoven. This collection opens with the divine commissioning of the prophet (1:4–10) which follows the pattern of other divine commissionings in which the chosen person, confronted by the word of the Lord and his commission, objects that he is inadequate, and is reassured, and given some sign of God's support. This narrative has Jeremiah protesting, like Moses, his lack of eloquence (cf. Exod. 4:10), to which God replies that 'whatever I command you shall speak . . . behold, I have put my words in your mouth', which is very reminiscent of Deuteronomy 18:18. The effect of these allusions is to establish Jeremiah in the reader's mind as a prophet like Moses (cf. Deut. 18:15), appointed in particular to proclaim the destruction and overthrow of nations (Jer. 1:10). Chapters 1–25 close with the promise that God will bring upon the land all the words that Jeremiah has uttered against it, 'everything written in this book, which Jeremiah prophesied against all the nations' (Jer. 25:13). This introduction and conclusion reveal very clearly the hand of an editor, the existence of a book, and a particular understanding of the contents of that book as including oracles against the nations. In fact, however, chs. 1–25 do not include oracles against foreign nations, which appear in the Hebrew bible in chs. 46–51 and in the Greek translation immediately after 25:13, which perhaps suggests that the Greek editors at least realised the need to have some oracles against the nations to hand, and suggests also that the Greek editors started with the basic collection of Jeremiah 1–25 more or less as it appears in the Hebrew Bible.

These chapters show many internal signs of their compilation. Chapters 1–10 are a collection of several lengthy poetic pieces, attacking Israel's apostasy

(2:1 – 4:4), threatening the arrival of disaster by way of judgment (4:6 – 6:30; 8:4 – 9:25), with a prose sermon in Deuteronomistic style attacking the temple (7:1 – 8:3). Chapters 11–20 describe in prose various episodes in Jeremiah's prophetic career, including the episode of the loincloth (13:1–11), his visit to the potter and his symbolic smashing of the pot (18–19) and his imprisonment in the stocks (20), together with a number of poetic oracles including the so-called 'confessions' or lamentations of Jeremiah in which the prophet laments the persecutions which result from his calling (11:18–20; 12:1–13; 15:15–18; 17:14–18; 18:19–23; 20:7–12). Chapters 20–24 include oracles against the monarchy (21:1 – 23:8), prophets (23:9–40), and a famous oracle portraying those exiled in 597 BC by Nebuchadnezzar as good figs, and king Zedekiah and those remaining in Judah as bad figs. Much of this is in prose, but the prose and the poetry are interconnected, as is seen clearly in 20:1–6 where Jeremiah's opponent, the high priest Pashhur, is nicknamed 'Terror on every side', and in 20:7–12 where the phrase is incorporated into Jeremiah's lament, or again in 22:24–27, 28–30 where Coniah's fate is described in prose and poetry.

Though Chapter 25 is seen as completing a major section of the book, it is not altogether easy to dissociate it from what follows in chs. 26–29, 32–45, a prose narrative describing Jeremiah's prophetic conflict with royalty, usually regarded as the second major constituent of the book. These chapters begin by presenting Jeremiah as a prophet who, in the name of the Lord, threatens the city of Jerusalem and its temple because the people of God do not walk in God's law or heed the words of his servants the prophets (26:1–6). This is the Deuteronomistic view of prophets, as found in the Deuteronomistic History (cf. 2 Kings 17:13). Jeremiah is threatened with death by the priests and the prophets, but saved by Ahikar the son of Shaphan. In chs. 27–29 Jeremiah opposes those prophets who are teaching Israel ('prophesying a lie to you in my name') that within two years God will have destroyed the power of Babylon. In ch. 32 Jeremiah, though clear that Nebuchadnezzar would capture Jerusalem, demonstrates his confidence in the future by purchasing land; in ch. 33 he promises God's future restoration of Jerusalem. Chapter 34, apparently dating from the time of Nebuchadnezzar's siege of Jerusalem in Zedekiah's reign (588-87 BC), again threatens destruction for Jerusalem and Judah, while ch. 35 contrasts the obedience of the Rechabite family with the general disobedience of the people of Judah and Jerusalem. A key chapter is 36, in which Jeremiah has his oracles against Jerusalem read publicly in the temple by his scribe Baruch; when the words are read to king Jehoiakim, he systematically destroys the scroll by cutting it into pieces and burning it. The narrative implies a deliberate contrast between the behaviour of Jehoiakim and that of his father Josiah, who treated the scroll found in the temple in his day with much greater respect. Chapters 37–45 tell of Jeremiah's prophecy of the fall of Jerusalem to the Babylonians, his imprisonment on false charges of desertion, his release by the Babylonians after their capture of Jerusalem, the events leading up to the flight to Egypt of Jewish military leaders and others, who took Jeremiah with them, and Jeremiah's oracles in Egypt.

The third major section of the book is a collection of oracles 'concerning the nations' (chs. 46–51), threatening Egypt (to be destroyed by Babylon at the battle of Carchemish in 605 BC: 46:1–25), the coast of Phoenicia and Philistia (47:1–7), the Moabites (48; cf. Isa. 15–16), the Ammonites (49:1–6), Edomites (49:7–22), Damascus (49:23–27), Arabian Kedar (49:28–33), Elam (49:35–39) and Babylon (50:1 – 51:64). In the case of Egypt (46:25–26), Moab (48:47), the Ammonites (49:6), and Elam (49:39) (but not in the case of the other nations) a later editor appears to have added the promise of future restoration. Another editorial addition, probably drawing on Second Isaiah, has added comforting words to Israel (46:27–28; cf. 30:10–11). These chapters appear in the Greek version after ch. 25. Which order is original is hard to say. Some prophetic books (cf. Isa. 13–23; Ezek. 25–32) place oracles against foreign nations between oracles of judgment against Judah and Israel and oracles of final salvation; others (Joel 3; Zech. 14) put such material at the end of the book. In the case of Jeremiah, an editorial hand is visible at 51:64, 'Thus far are the words of Jeremiah', and the editor ends the book with ch. 52, a passage from the Deuteronomistic History describing the end of Jerusalem, appropriate for a book whose prophet had correctly predicted it.

To summarise the contents of the book in this way is only to hint at the problems it has set for scholars. The first twenty-five chapters may relate directly or indirectly to the contents of the scroll containing Jeremiah's oracles which the king destroyed (ch. 36) – probably indirectly, for there are clear signs of Deuteronomistic editing in these chapters. Chapters 26–45 tell a story about Jeremiah whose main aim is to underline Deuteronomistic theology by showing how Jeremiah was a true prophet over against various false prophets, and how the word of God spoken by Jeremiah to the kings of Judah was rejected by them but nevertheless came to pass. The connection of the book of Jeremiah with the Deuteronomistic tradition has long been accepted. Since the work of Mowinckel, it has been generally agreed that we get nearest to the actual words of Jeremiah in the poetic oracles of chs. 1–25, 30–31, and 46–51. Mowinckel then isolated third-person biographical prose material about Jeremiah, and prose discourses or sermons. E. W. Nicholson demonstrated clearly in 1973 that the language and style of these discourses and biographical material was Deuteronomistic and represented a Deuteronomistic picture of Jeremiah's teaching and ministry. At the heart of this presentation lay the Deuteronomistic view of prophecy given in Deuteronomy 18:15–22 and 2 Kings 17:13–14:

> 'I will raise up for them a prophet like you from among their brethren; and I will put my words in his mouth, and he shall speak to them all that I command him. And whoever will not give heed to my words which he shall speak in my name, I myself will require it of him. But the prophet who presumes to speak a word in my name which I have not commanded him to speak, or who speaks in the name of other gods, that same prophet shall die.' And if you say in your heart, 'How may we know the word which the LORD has not spoken?' – when a prophet speaks in the name of the LORD, if the word does not come to pass or come true, that is a word which the LORD has not spoken; the prophet has spoken it presumptuously, you need not be afraid of him.

It was the duty of the king (Deut. 17:18) to write for himself a copy of the Deuteronomic law and read it and learn to fear the Lord. According to 2 Kings 17:13–14,

> The LORD warned Israel and Judah by every prophet and every seer, saying, 'Turn from your evil ways and keep my commandments and my statutes, in accordance with all the law which I commanded your fathers, and which I sent to you by my servants the prophets.' But they would not listen, but were stubborn, as their fathers had been, who did not believe in the LORD their God.

The word of the Lord came to Israel by the prophets; Israel rejected it, and judgment followed (2 Kings 17:18). This is the story-line of 26:4–6, and of 36 also. Jeremiah's scroll is read (36:1–8), is rejected by the officials and the king (36:9–26), and judgment is pronounced (36:27–31). Deuteronomy and the Deuteronomic History are much against false prophets who prophesy lies in the name of God, and this is a recurrent theme in the prose passages of Jeremiah (Jer. 14:13–16; 23:16–17, 23–40; 27–29). The Deuteronomistic Historian explains the reason for the calamity in Israel in the following terms:

> And this house will become a heap of ruins; everyone passing by it will be astonished, and will hiss; and they will say, 'Why has the LORD done thus to this land and to this house?' Then they will say, 'Because they forsook the LORD their God who brought their fathers out of the land of Egypt, and laid hold on other gods, and worshipped them and served them; therefore the LORD has brought all this evil upon them.' (1 Kings 9:8–9; cf. Deut. 29:21–27)

Jer. 5:19 uses almost identical language (cf. also 9:12–16; 16:10–13; 22:8–9):

> And when your people say, 'Why has the LORD our God done all these things to us?' you shall say to them, 'As you have forsaken me and served foreign gods in your land, so you shall serve strangers in a land that is not yours.'

The prose sermons in 7:1 – 8:3, 11:1–17; 17:19–20; 34:8–22 all emphasise in Deuteronomistic language that Judah has disobeyed the law (cf. the reference to the Ten Commandments in 7:9), failed to heed the words of the covenant (11:3; 34:18), failed to keep the sabbath (17:19–27), and so incurred God's judgment. In short, the prose material presents Jeremiah as a Deuteronomistic prophet; the people's rejection of his call to obey the Deuteronomistic law led, as always, to the destruction of Jerusalem. This material aims to explain the disaster of 587 BC by Judah's disobedience; it underlines the centrality of the law, the covenant, the importance of the sabbath, and the dangers of false prophecy.

If we turn at this point to the poetic oracles of Jeremiah, we can see the similarities and the differences. Jeremiah 2:1 – 4:4 presents a vivid picture of Jerusalem as a young bride who once devoted herself to her husband Yahweh but, in spite of being redeemed from Egypt and given land by Yahweh, turned faithless and lusted after foreign gods. Chapters 4:5 – 6:30 repeatedly picture war coming from the north against Jerusalem (4:5–8):

Declare in Judah, and proclaim in Jerusalem, and say,
'Blow the trumpet through the land;
   cry aloud and say,
"Assemble, and let us go
   into the fortified cities!"
Raise a standard toward Zion,
   flee for safety, stay not,
for I bring evil from the north,
   and great destruction.
A lion has gone up from his thicket,
   a destroyer of nations has set out;
   he has gone forth from his place
to make your land a waste;
   your cities will be ruins
   without inhabitant.
For this gird you with sackcloth,
   lament and wail;
for the fierce anger of the LORD
   has not turned back from us.'

This war would bring devastation, the dissolution of creation:

I looked on the earth, and lo, it was waste and void;
   and to the heavens, and they had no light.
I looked on the mountains, and lo, they were quaking,
   and all the hills moved to and fro.
I looked, and lo, there was no man,
   and all the birds of the air had fled.
I looked, and lo, the fruitful land was a desert,
   and all its cities were laid in ruins
   before the LORD, before his fierce anger.

(Jer. 4:23–26)

The reason is that Jerusalem does not know the law, and has been faithless:

Run to and fro through the streets of Jerusalem,
   look and take note!
Search her squares to see
   if you can find a man,
one who does justice
   and seeks truth;
that I may pardon her.

(Jer. 5:1; cf. 5:2–9, 30–31; 6:19–21)

The same picture continues in 8:4 – 9:25 (e.g., 8:18–19):

My grief is beyond healing,
   my heart is sick within me.

> Hark, the cry of the daughter of my people
>    from the length and breadth of the land:
> 'Is the LORD not in Zion?
>    Is her King not in her?'
> 'Why have they provoked me to anger with their graven images,
>    and with their foreign idols?'
> 'The harvest is past, the summer is ended,
>    and we are not saved.'

Jeremiah's own compassion is visible in these verses; his suffering and pain for his people is dramatically presented in 15:15–21, and his desperation as he suffers for his prophetic calling surfaces in 20:7–18:

> O LORD, thou has deceived me,
>    and I was deceived;
> thou art stronger than I,
>    and thou hast prevailed.
> I have become a laughing stock all the day;
>    everyone mocks me . . .
>
> Cursed be the day
>    on which I was born!
> The day when my mother bore me,
>    let it not be blessed!
> Cursed be the man
>    who brought the news to my father,
> 'A son is born to you',
>    making him very glad.

The remarkable thing is that the book of Jeremiah also credits the prophet with a message of hope. In 24:4–10, Jeremiah sees two baskets, one of good figs, representing the exiles, and one of rotten figs, representing those left in Judah in 597 BC. In 29:3–9, 10–14, Jeremiah instructs the exiles by letter to build houses and live in them, plant gardens and eat their produce, take wives and bear children, and seek the welfare of the city to which God has exiled them,

> 'For thus says the LORD: When seventy years are completed for Babylon, I will visit you, and I will fulfil to you my promise and bring you back to this place. For I know the plans I have for you, says the LORD, plans for welfare and not for evil, to give you a future and a hope. Then you will call upon me and come and pray to me, and I will hear you. You will seek me and find me; when you seek me with all your heart, I will be found by you, says the LORD, and I will restore your fortunes and gather you from all the nations and all the places where I have driven you, says the LORD, and I will bring you back to the place from which I sent you into exile.'

In ch. 32, Jeremiah buys property as a sign of his confidence in the future of the land. 3:15–18 looks forward to a time when 'Jerusalem shall be called the throne of the LORD, and all nations shall gather to it'. 23:1–6 promises a return from exile and a new Davidic king; 33:14–16, 17–26 include with this hope the possibility of a new Levitical priesthood.

What the historical Jeremiah expected, however, is not clear, for these prose passages just quoted betray Deuteronomistic theology (cf. Deut. 30:1–6; 1 Kings 8:22–26) and traditional Davidic dynastic hopes already seen in Isaiah and the psalms. The vision of the baskets of figs and the letter to the exiles suggest that Jeremiah looked to the exiles for the future of Israel, but this too may reflect an attempt to use Jeremiah's authority to support the later position of the returned exiles. The real Jeremiah may be indicated by the story of the purchase of land just outside Jerusalem as a symbolic gesture of confidence.

Confidence is the mark of the poetic oracles in the separate collection found in chs. 30–31, 'the book of consolation'. These oracles incorporate passages which read like the authentic Jeremiah of before 587 BC (30:5–7, 12–15, 23–24; 31:15, 21–22), but to these have been added oracles which sometimes sound more like Second Isaiah than Jeremiah (30:1–3, 8–11, 16–17, 18–22; 31:2–6, 7–9, 10–14, 16–20). The editor is determined that the gloom of the pre-587 Jeremiah shall not have the last word, and provides us with a vision of the restored Judah which does not easily square with the picture we have of Jeremiah after 587 in exile in Egypt (cf. chs. 44, 45). These chapters reach a climax with a passage of pure Deuteronomistic theology which has captured the imagination of theologians and believers through the centuries, to such an extent that its central phrase, 'a new covenant', has become the title of the Christian scriptures (usually called 'The New Testament', testament being the Latin word for the Greek *diatheke* and Hebrew *berith*, 'covenant'). It hardly matters whether these words came from Jeremiah or from his later Deuteronomistic editor. They use traditional Deuteronomistic language, and yet transcend Deuteronomistic ideas. They sum up the Deuteronomistic theology for the era ending in 587 BC, and point the way forward to a new era.

> 'Behold, the days are coming, says the LORD, when I will make a new covenant with the house of Israel and the house of Judah, not like the covenant which I made with their fathers when I took them by the hand to bring them out of the land of Egypt, my covenant which they broke, though I was their husband, says the LORD. But this is the covenant which I will make with the house of Israel after those days, says the LORD: I will put my law within them, and I will write it upon their hearts; and I will be their God, and they shall be my people. And no longer shall each man teach his neighbour and each his brother, saying, "Know the LORD", for they shall all know me, from the least of them to the greatest, says the LORD; for, I will forgive their iniquity, and I will remember their sin no more.' (Jer. 31:31–34)

Jeremiah may not have uttered these words, but they provide an answer to his cry, 'remember and do not break thy covenant with us' (14:21), and by these words this most despairing of all the prophets is not inappropriately remembered.

Jeremiah's book in its present form, like other prophetic books, derives from witnesses to the fears and hopes and intellectual activity of the exilic age. It was important for them to keep alive Jewish faith in God, and they did this partly by preserving the words and deeds of each prophet and reinterpreting them for the benefit of their contemporary hearers or readers. The book of Jeremiah may derive from theologians among the exiles, whose return to the land and whose future importance are emphasised (cf. 24:4–7; 29:10–14; 30:2–3; 32:36–41). The Deuteronomistic editor presents Jeremiah as 'a prophet to the nations' (1:5), not because Jeremiah actually prophesied to the nations but because Jeremiah was important to the Jewish exiles among the nations. This book is one of several important works from the exilic period, different in that it expresses more clearly and vividly than most the pain of the prophet at the suffering of the people. To read the poetic oracles of Jeremiah 1–25 is to make direct contact with a mind that feels keenly the tragedy of an unnecessarily destroyed city, and that suffers for speaking a truth which no one wants to hear (cf. Jer. 20:7–12).

## Bibliography

B.W. Anderson, *The eighth-century prophets: Amos, Hosea, Isaiah, Micah* (London: SPCK; Philadelphia: Fortress Press, 1978)

A.G. Auld, *Amos* (Old Testament Guides) (Sheffield: JSOT Press for the Society for Old Testament Study, 1986)

J. Blenkinsopp, *A history of prophecy in Israel* (London: SCM Press; Philadelphia: Westminster Press, 1983

R.P. Carroll, *When prophecy failed: reactions and responses to failure in the Old Testament prophetic traditions* (London: SCM Press, 1979)

R.P. Carroll, *From chaos to covenant: uses of prophecy in the book of Jeremiah* (London: SCM Press, 1981)

R.P. Carroll, *Jeremiah* (Old Testament Guides) (Sheffield: JSOT Press for the Society for Old Testament Study, 1989)

B.S. Childs, *Isaiah and the Assyrian crisis* (London: SCM Press, 1967)

R.E. Clements, *Prophecy and tradition* (Oxford: Blackwell, 1975)

R.E. Clements, *Isaiah and the deliverance of Jerusalem: a study in the interpretation of prophecy in the Old Testament* (Sheffield: JSOT Press, 1980)

R. Coggins, A. Phillips and M.A. Knibb, *Israel's prophetic tradition: essays in honour of Peter Ackroyd* (Cambridge: Cambridge University Press, 1982)

J.A. Hackett, *The Balaam text from Deir 'Alla* (Harvard Semitic Monographs 31; Chico, Cal.: Scholars Press, 1984)

J.H. Hayes and S.A. Irvine, *Isaiah, the eighth-century prophet: his times and his preaching* (Nashville: Abingdon Press, 1987)

A.J. Heschel, *The Prophets: an introduction* (New York: Harper Torchbooks, 1962)

J. Lindblom, *Prophecy in ancient Israel* (Oxford: Blackwell, 1962)

D.L. Petersen, *Prophecy in Israel* (Issues in Religion and Theology 10) (Philadelphia: Fortress Press: London: SPCK, 1987)

J.F.A. Sawyer, *Prophecy and the prophets of the Old Testament* (The Oxford Bible Series) (Oxford: Oxford University Press, 1987)

J.A. Soggin, *The prophet Amos: a translation and commentary* (London: SCM Press, 1987)

C. Westermann, *Basic forms of prophetic speech* (London: Lutterworth Press, 1967)

# 7    Chaos and Creation

The history of ancient Israel has long been divided, by academic convention, into two halves, labelled 'pre-exilic' and 'post-exilic' or, more recently, 'First Temple' and 'Second Temple'. The intervening 'exilic' period is usually treated with the 'post-exilic' period, the real break being seen to come with the fall of Jerusalem to Nebuchadnezzar's Babylonian army in 587 or 586 BC. The fall of Jerusalem did indeed close an era. Judah ceased to be an independent or even a vassal kingdom, and Jerusalem lost her temple, her walls and defences, her palaces and major buildings, and her population. According to 2 Kings 25:11,

> the rest of the people who were left in the city and the deserters who had deserted to the king of Babylon, together with the rest of the multitude, Nebuzaradan the captain of the guard carried into exile. But the captain of the guard left some of the poorest of the land to be vinedressers and ploughmen.

The chief priest, the second priest, the temple doorkeepers, the commander of the professional army and the officer in charge of general conscription, five of the king's privy counsellors, and sixty of the landed aristocracy of Judah were taken to Nebuchadnezzar at Riblah in Syria, where they were executed. King Zedekiah was also taken to Riblah; his life was spared, but he was forced to watch the execution of his sons before having his eyes put out, and being taken into exile in Babylon. Here he presumably joined his predecessor Jehoiachin, who had been exiled in 597 BC. Jehoiachin was more fortunate than Zedekiah; cuneiform tablets found during R. Koldewey's excavations (1899–1917) in an underground building attached to the palace at Babylon record the rations of oil allowed to Jehoiachin, his five sons, and eight other Judeans (Winton Thomas, 1958, 84–86); and we know from 2 Kings 25:27–30 that in 561 BC, on the accession of Evil-Merodach (Amel Marduk), Nebuchadnezzar's son, Jehoiachin was released from prison, and given 'a seat above the seats of the kings who were with him in Babylon', dining regularly at the king's table.

This detail underlines the important point that, though the events of 597 BC and 587 BC mark the end of an era in the history of Judah, nevertheless there was some continuity. The Babylonians did not entirely destroy Judah's royal line, but removed from power those who had led Judah's rebellion against Babylonian rule. In their place they appointed one Gedaliah, from one of the ruling families in Jerusalem (cf. 2 Kings 22:12; Jer. 26:24), as governor, operating from Mizpah, some 5 miles NNW of Jerusalem. Though the Babylonians were careful to appoint Babylonian advisers (cf. 2 Kings 25:25), rule of Judah was thus apparently in the hands of a leading Jewish figure, and it is interesting that he was soon killed by Ishmael, the son of Nethaniah, himself a member of the royal family (2 Kings 25:25). According to the account preserved in Jeremiah 41:1–18, Ishmael killed Gedaliah's staff, both Jewish and Babylonian, and 'took captive all the rest of the people who were in Mizpah, the king's daughters and all the people who were left at Mizpah, whom Nebuzaradan, the captain of the guard, had committed to Gedaliah . . . and set out to cross over to the Ammonites.' An army captain called Johanan the son of Kareah blocked Ishmael's route 'at the great pool which is in Gibeon', and forced Ishmael to hand over his prisoners; Ishmael then escaped to the kingdom of the Ammonites, east of the Jordan. What subsequently became of the king's daughters and Ishmael is unknown, but the royal line of Jehoiachin survived the Babylonian exile. Jehoiachin's son Shenazzar (1 Chron. 3:17) is perhaps to be identified with 'Sheshbazzar the prince of Judah' who brought back temple vessels from Babylon to Judah and laid the foundations of the new temple (Ezra 1:8; 5:14), while Zerubbabel the son of Shealtiel, the governor of Judah in 520 BC (Ezra 3:1; Hagg. 1:1), was probably the son of Shealtiel, son of Jehoiachin (1 Chron. 3:17) (though 1 Chron. 3:19 lists Zerubbabel as the son of Shealtiel's brother Pedaiah). Zerubbabel, grandson of king Jehoiachin, did not become king and restore the monarchy in Judah, but it seems likely from Zechariah 6:9–14 that there were those in Judah who hoped for the restoration of a king to sit and rule on the throne alongside the high priest, who would rule in the temple (Zech. 3:6).

This sketch of the fortunes of Judah's royal house in the exilic period shows that, while there was a major political upheaval in 587 BC, so that things were never quite the same again, nevertheless history did not come to a stop, and the break with the past was not complete. The royal house in fact provided one of the links between the monarchy and the new form of rule which emerged in the Persian period. There were other links too, the most obvious being the fact that even after a gap of two, if not three, generations the returned exiles, urged on by the prophet Haggai and led by Zerubbabel the governor and Joshua the high priest, rebuilt the destroyed temple. With the temple, naturally, went the liturgy, which in the Psalms drew on a long tradition stretching back into the monarchic period.

Mention of Haggai reminds us that the tradition of prophecy had not expired with the exilic break. The books of Ezekiel and Jeremiah bear witness to the editing and interpretation of the oracles and these prophets during the exilic period; thus Jeremiah's oracles were made the basis of 'preaching to the exiles' by the Deuteronomistic school. The Deuteronomists also added to Jeremiah's oracles a number of prose sermons showing how Yahweh had called Israel to obey the law, explaining why Jerusalem had experienced the disasters of 587 BC, and exhorting the survivors to live according to the law (cf. Jer. 11:17). The writings of the anonymous prophet known to us as Deutero-Isaiah, or Second Isaiah (Isa. 40–55), at work among the exiled community in Babylon in the mid-sixth century BC, reveal prophetic genius of a very high order, concerned to demonstrate that Yahweh alone had power in the world, and that Israel still had a vocation and a future. His work was used and added to by a successor, usually known as Trito-Isaiah, or Third Isaiah (Isa. 56–66), who seems to have been active in Jerusalem at the beginning of the fifth century BC. A continuing intellectual link may also be seen in the wisdom tradition, from which, during the post-exilic period, came such works as the book of Job (whose exploration of the problems of theodicy may owe much to the Israelite experiences of the sixth century), the book of Proverbs in its final form, and later the books Ecclesiastes, Ecclesiasticus, and the Wisdom of Solomon.

Thus scholarly minds were clearly at work in the exilic period recording and editing Israel's historical traditions. Presumably the fall of Jerusalem and the destruction of the temple had alerted priests and others to the need to preserve and record memory of Israel's history; the tradition of God's saving activity for Israel in the past became important as the basis for hope in the future. As Second Isaiah saw, the God who had led his people out of Egypt would similarly lead his people out of Babylon. It is not surprising, then, to find that it is precisely in the exilic period, after the trauma of 587 BC, that there was a surge of literary activity which resulted in the two major collections of Israelite tradition which might be described as the Priestly History (Genesis – Numbers) and the Deuteronominstic History (Joshua – 2 Kings, introduced by Deuteronomy). These great collections not only preserved folk legend, archival material, law, liturgical tradition, and other community memories which might otherwise have been lost, but also gave them a focus by using them to show how the people of Israel had become the people of Yahweh, why they had suffered the disasters of 721 BC and 587 BC, and how they should legislate for the future. The very collection and presentation of all this material was itself an important link binding the pre-exilic and post-exilic communities; the tradition of the pre-exilic monarchy was creative of the post-exilic nation (see ch. 3 above).

To the creative effect of the disaster of 587 BC on the self-understanding, faith and theology of Israel we shall return; for the moment it is important to grasp that the fall of Jerusalem was in a very real sense not the end, but the beginning of a development which was to change the local religion of the small kingdom of Judah into the wider-ranging Judaism of later centuries and the parent of Christianity. Those who suffered the experience of 587 BC, however, can be forgiven for not seeing it in that light. There is a good deal of evidence for how they did in fact see it. In the book of Ezekiel, a number of oracles take their starting point from what is said to be a proverb or saying current at the time. Thus in Ezekiel 12:22 the word of the Lord comes to Ezekiel:

> 'Son of man, what is this proverb that you have about the land of Israel, saying,
> "The days grow long, and every vision comes to nought"?'

and in 12:27,

> 'Son of man, behold, they of the house of Israel say, "The vision that he sees is for
> many days hence, and he prophesies of times far off."'

Clearly, the people were disillusioned with the prophets and their visions, and

Ezekiel dismisses his contemporary fellow prophets as 'foolish prophets who follow their own spirit, and have seen nothing' (Ezek. 13:3), 'like foxes among ruins' (13:4), men who 'see delusive visions and who give lying divinations' (13:9), who 'prophesied concerning Jerusalem and saw visions of peace for her, when there was no peace' (13:16).

Of their present situation, the people had another saying (Ezek. 18:1-2; cf. Jer. 31:29):

> The word of the LORD came to me again: 'What do you mean by repeating this proverb concerning the land of Israel, "The fathers have eaten sour grapes, and the children's teeth are set on edge"?'

The complaint that the present predicament is the fault of the previous generation has been heard in many ages, and it rapidly leads to the corollary, 'The way of the LORD is not just' (Ezek. 18:25). Similarly Second Isaiah quotes the complaint of his exiled people:

> Why do you say, O Jacob,
>   and speak, O Israel,
> 'My way is hid from the LORD,
>   and my right is disregarded by my God?'
>
> (Isa. 40:27)

A slightly more penitential, but despairing note appears in Ezekiel 33:10,

> 'And you, son of man, say to the house of Israel, Thus have you said: "Our transgressions and our sins are upon us, and we waste away because of them; how then can we live?"'

and the despair is more dramatically portrayed in the saying quoted in 37:11,

> 'Behold, they say, "Our bones are dried up, and our hope is lost; we are clean cut off."'

It was perhaps this saying which prompted Ezekiel's vision of the valley of bones, in which the spirit of the Lord gives life to the bones (identified as the house of Israel) and they live. There seems little reason to doubt that the book of Ezekiel is quoting precisely the sort of thing that was being commonly said in the final years of the kingdom of Judah, and it is instructive to read how the prophet counters these views.

It is also instructive to consider what effect the disaster of 587 BC had on the people's attitude to their god. It would perhaps not have been surprising had people interpreted the fall of Jerusalem as indicating that Yahweh had been conquered by more powerful gods, who must now be worshipped in his place. When the Assyrians attacked Jerusalem in 701 BC, they tried to undermine the people's morale by arguing that Yahweh was too weak to save Jerusalem:

> 'Beware lest Hezekiah mislead you by saying, "The LORD will deliver us." Has any of the gods of the nations delivered his land out of the hand of the king of Assyria?

> Where are the gods of Hamath and Arpad? Where are the gods of Sepharvaim? Have they delivered Samaria out of my hand? Who among all the gods of these countries have delivered their countries out of my hand, that the LORD should deliver Jerusalem out of my hand?' (Isa. 36:18-20)

At least some of the people of Jerusalem and Judah may have accepted that line of argument in 597 BC and 587 BC, and were worshipping other gods in hope of salvation. Ezekiel in a vision saw elders censing idols and women weeping for Tammuz (i.e., lamenting the annual death of the vegetation god) (Ezek. 8:7-15); Jeremiah (44:2-3) blames Judah's disaster on her people's worship of foreign gods, but they respond that it was their failure to worship the queen of heaven (the Assyrian-Babylonian goddess Ishtar) that had led to disaster (Jer. 44:17-18).

The book of Ezekiel as a whole must be considered a prophetic reaction to the fall of Jerusalem. Ezekiel, himself exiled in 597 BC, began to prophesy in the fifth year of Jehoiachin's captivity (593-92 BC) (Ezek. 1:2). In the sixth year he had a vision of apostasy in the temple (ch.8), and in the seventh responded with a sermon against the elders (ch.20). In the ninth year he prophesied woe to the besieged Jerusalem (ch.24); he records hearing news of its fall in the twelfth year (33:21-22). In the tenth, eleventh and twelfth years he prophesies against Egypt, whose Pharaoh Hophra has made an abortive attempt to assist Judah (29:1-16; 30:20-26; 31:32). In the eleventh year he prophesied against Tyre, besieged by Nebuchadnezzar from 585-573 BC, (ch.26); Nebuchadnezzar's failure, to be compensated for by success against Egypt, is recorded in the twenty-seventh year (29:17-20). Ch.40:1 dates Ezekiel's final vision, of the restoration of the temple, to the twenty-fifth year of the captivity, i.e., 573-72 BC. The book opens with a reference to visions of God seen in the thirtieth year; it may indicate that Ezekiel's final, climactic vision has become set at the beginning of the book.

This sequence of dated oracles locates Ezekiel's prophetic career firmly between 593 and 570 BC. Between these dated oracles, however, much other material has been incorporated, and the sequence, which has been slightly reordered, does not control the present shape and arrangement of the book. The book opens with the commissioning of Ezekiel (chs. 1-3), continues with Ezekiel's teaching against Judah and Jerusalem (chs. 4-24), the oracles against foreign nations (25-32), and ends with promises of restoration (33-48), in this conforming to a general scheme found in other prophetic books. However, another sequence is also visible. The book begins with the vision of the glory of the Lord (ch.1); in ch.8:1-4 Ezekiel is taken in visions of God to Jerusalem, where he sees the glory of the God of Israel (8:4) at the temple threshold (9:3), lifted up by the cherubim (10:19) and carried away from the midst of the city to stand on the Mount of Olives to the east (11:23). In ch.40 Ezekiel is returned in visions of God to Israel and sees the glory of God return from the east to fill the temple (43:1-5). The editor is fully aware of this sequence, and underlines it for the reader (43:3). This sequence frames the book and provides an overall theological context in which Ezekiel's original oracles are to be interpreted.

Ezekiel's original oracles (so far as we can distinguish them with confidence) contain much that is prophetically critical of the people of Judah: for example, their false prophets and their idolatry (12:21–14:11). In ch.16 Ezekiel tells in an allegorical parable how God found Jerusalem as an abandoned child, adopted and cared for her as she grew, gave her wealth and position – yet Jerusalem rewarded God by becoming a harlot, an adulterous wife, and would receive her adulterer's punishment. Three other oracles offer what amount to prophetic sermons on God's justice in the light of the fall of Jerusalem. In Ezek.33:1–20 the message is that God is just:

> When the righteous turns from his righteousness and commits iniquity, he shall die for it. And when the wicked turns from his wickedness, and does what is lawful and right, he shall live by it. Yet you say, 'The way of the Lord is not just'. O house of Israel, I will judge each of you according to his ways.

Ezekiel 18 develops the message: each generation gets its deserts. Jerusalem may not claim that 'the fathers have eaten sour grapes, and the children's teeth are set on edge'; God's response is that 'The soul that sins shall die. The son shall not suffer for the iniquity of the father...' (18:20). In Ezekiel 14:12–20, a further point is made that when God punishes a land for its sin, 'even if these three men, Noah, Daniel and Job, were in it, they would but deliver their own lives by their righteousness'. The presence of a few righteous people would not save Jerusalem.

The book also contains promises of restoration from exile (11:14–21; 28:35–36) and of the renewed Davidic monarchy (37:21–28). These are probably secondary interpretations of Ezekiel's message, but it is hard to deny the hope expressed in the vision of the valley of bones as authentic (37:1–14) or to reject entirely Ezekiel's vision of a restored temple (chs.40–48), though much here may be secondary development of Ezekiel's hopes. These chapters respond to the disaster of Jerusalem's fall by picturing a restored land whose fertility will derive from the central temple, surrounded by priests and levites to guard its holiness.

Further theological responses to the destruction of Jerusalem and the exile can be found in the Psalms and in Second Isaiah. Psalm 44 outlines Israel's traditions and experience of God's past acts of salvation and laments that

> Thou hast made us like sheep for slaughter,
>> and hast scattered us among the nations...
> All this has come upon us,
>> though we have not forgotten thee,
>> or been false to thy covenant...

and ends with the prayer

> Rouse thyself! Why sleepest thou, O Lord?
> Awake! Do not cast us off for ever!

Similar feelings surface in Psalms 74 and 79:

> O God, the heathen have come into thy inheritance;
>> they have defiled thy holy temple;
>> they have laid Jerusalem in ruins...
> Do not remember against us the iniquities of our forefathers;
>> let thy compassion come speedily to meet us,
>> for we are brought very low.

> Help us, O God of our salvation,
> for the glory of thy name;
> deliver us, and forgive our sins,
> for thy name's sake!
> Why should the nations say,
> 'Where is their God?'

Psalm 44 suggests that God has cast his people off unjustly; Psalms 74 and 79 speak of God's anger, and Psalm 79 of the sins of the forefathers and even of the present generation. But in each psalm, the psalmist makes clear that God has a committed and continuing relationship with his people (the covenant, Ps. 44:17; 74:20), and that God has saved Israel in the past (Ps. 44:4–8; cf. Ps. 74:12–17; 79:9) and therefore might be prevailed upon to do so once again. But whereas these psalms do indeed suggest that God allowed these disasters to come upon Judah, Lamentations ch.2 strongly underlines the idea that God has acted deliberately:

> How the Lord in his anger has set the daughter of Zion under a cloud! . . .
>
> The Lord has destroyed without mercy all the habitations of Jacob . . .
>
> He has cut down in fierce anger all the might of Israel . . .
>
> He has bent his bow like an enemy . . .
>
> The Lord has become like an enemy,
> he has destroyed Israel . . .
>
> The Lord determined to lay in ruins
> the wall of the daughter of Zion . . .
>
> The Lord has done what he purposed,
> has carried out his threat . . .

The last verse of this lamentation (Lam. 2:22) describes the destruction of Jerusalem as happening 'on the day of the anger of the LORD', that is, a day on which Israelites traditionally looked for the destruction of their enemies (compare the prophecy of Amos 5:18–20). It was hardly surprising that the disaster could be interpreted as God's punishment of Judah for her sins. In 2 Kings 23:26–27 the Deuteronomistic historian blames the catastrophe on the way king Manasseh (696–642 BC) had provoked the Lord by supporting non-Yahwistic religious cults in Jerusalem (cf. 2 Kings 21:1–18). The Deuteronomic editors of Jeremiah explain Judah's exile in similar terms:

> 'And when your people say, "Why has the LORD our God done all these things to us?" you shall say to them, "As you have forsaken me and served foreign gods in your land, so you shall serve strangers in a land that is not yours,"'
>
> (Jer. 5:19; compare Deut. 29:21–27; 1 Kings 9:8–9)

A similar understanding appears in Ezek. 36:18,

'So I poured out my wrath upon them for the blood which they had shed in the land, for the idols with which they had defiled it. I scattered them among the nations, and they were dispersed through the countries; in accordance with their conduct and their deeds I judged them.'

Towards the end of the exile, Second Isaiah refers to this theme in his opening oracle:

Comfort, comfort my people, says your God.
Speak tenderly to Jerusalem,
    and cry to her
that her warfare is ended,
    that her iniquity is pardoned,
that she has received from the LORD's hand
    double for all her sins.

(Isa. 40:?)

Second Isaiah was psychologically right to begin by proclaiming the end of Judah's punishment. A nation or people which accepts that it is being punished, endlessly, is a nation with no sense of hope. Second Isaiah's oracles are concerned above all with the restoration of hope and confidence in his people. They proclaim the power of God to do something new. All the themes of this incomparable prophet speak of the power of the God of Israel to act in the world on Israel's behalf. In Israel's situation of chaos, Yahweh is creative. From Israel's Babylonian captivity, Yahweh can offer redemption, as once he did from Egypt. For Israel in the wilderness, Yahweh will once again produce water. To Israel among the nations and other gods, Yahweh will demonstrate their weakness and his power. Israel, the offspring of Abraham, is once again called from the farthest corners of the earth to be Yahweh's servant. Israel, once despised and abhorred by the nations, the servant of kings, will now receive the homage of kings. Jerusalem, once devastated and depopulated, will be rebuilt and repeopled, and the ancient covenant with David will be re-enacted in revised form. It is clear, even from this brief list of the prophet's themes, that the prophet is taking Israel's ancient traditions – creation from chaos, the promises to the patriarchs, the exodus, the wilderness, the occupation of Canaan with its pagan gods, the Davidic monarchy, the submission to foreign empires – and making them serve the present situation of the Jewish exile and captivity.

Some scholars see Isaiah 40–55 as a series of independent oracles, like a row of pearls on a thread, but these chapters should rather be compared with a tapestry in which the themes and motifs are interwoven and recurrent, repeated yet varied. Yet the tapestry tells a story, and has a beginning, a middle and an end. It begins with the prophet's commission to proclaim God's message of comfort; it proceeds with the description of God's creative power, his call of Israel, his preparation of a new exodus event (heralded by the appearance of Cyrus the Persian in the east), the fall of Babylon, the return of the exiles, the coming restoration of Zion-Jerusalem; and it ends with the accomplishment of God's prophetic word. This magnificent theological work, rivalled in conception and

131

design only by the book of Job in the Old Testament and by the Fourth Gospel in the New Testament, needs to be read in full, at one sitting. Every paragraph cries aloud for quotation, but the redevelopment of early traditions to proclaim the new hope, the imminence of the kingdom of God, may be seen clearly in the following examples:

> Thus says the LORD,
>   who makes a way in the sea,
>   a path in the mighty waters,
> who brings forth chariot and horse,
>   army and warrior;
> they lie down, they cannot rise,
>   they are extinguished, quenched like a wick:
> 'Remember not the former things,
>   nor consider the things of old.
> Behold, I am doing a new thing;
>   now it springs forth, do you not perceive it?
> I will make a way in the wilderness
>   and rivers in the desert.'
>
> (Isa. 43:16–19)

> How beautiful upon the mountains
>   are the feet of him who brings good tidings,
> who publishes peace, who brings good tidings of good,
>   who publishes salvation,
>   who says to Zion, 'Your God reigns.'
> Hark, your watchmen lift up their voice,
>   together they sing for joy;
> for eye to eye they see
>   the return of the LORD to Zion.
> Break forth together into singing,
>   you waste places of Jerusalem;
> for the LORD has comforted his people,
>   he has redeemed Jerusalem.
> The LORD has bared his holy arm before the eyes of all the nations;
>   and all the ends of the earth shall see the salvation of our God.
>
> (Isa. 52:7–10)

Second Isaiah's theological contribution, however, has not yet been fully stated. These chapters are probably best known for the four poems separated out from the text by B. Duhm in 1892 and named the 'servant songs' (42:1-4; 49:1-6; 50:4-9; 52:13 – 53:12). In the first, God introduces a figure called 'my servant' with a commission to bring God's *mišpat* ('justice') and *tôrāh* ('teaching') to the coastlands and islands (42:1-4). In the second (49:1-6) the servant figure himself speaks, addressing the coastlands and distant peoples, describing his commission, originally to bring back Jacob, or gather Israel, to

God, but now to be 'a light to the nations, that my salvation may reach to the end of the earth.' In the third, the servant again speaks, describing his personal sufferings in the execution of his prophetic task and his trust that God will vindicate him (50:4–9). The most difficult song is the last one (52:13 – 53:12); the Hebrew text itself seems slightly disturbed, and the meaning of the Hebrew words is not always certain. It begins by introducing the servant as one about to prosper and be exalted, to the astonishment of kings, and continues by having some unidentified speakers present the servant as having been despised and rejected, oppressed and afflicted, 'cut off out of the land of the living, stricken for the transgression of my people'. The passage ends with the prospect of the servant's vindication.

These 'servant songs' have challenged exegetes for centuries, from the editor who identified the servant by inserting the word 'Israel' in Isaiah 49:3, to the Ethiopian eunuch who, hearing this passage read, asked, 'About whom, pray, does the prophet say this, about himself, or about someone else?' (Acts 8:34). Bound up with the problem of the identity of the servant are other problems: what was his commission? how did it relate to the situation otherwise described in Isaiah 40–55? how should we interpret the suffering? in what sense (if any) was the suffering to achieve anything for the servant's people? in what way was the servant to be vindicated? who are the speakers in ch. 53? and are these oracles an integral part of Isaiah 40–55, or are they originally independent poems inserted or incorporated into the text?

It has always been clear that the songs do not differ in style or content from their surroundings, and it is increasingly clear that they are far more closely woven into their literary context than was once thought. This might have an important bearing on the problem of the servant's identity; for example, it might make it more likely that the servant is to be identified as Israel (as he is clearly in Isa. 41:8–10, which might well be taken as the first of five servant songs); or it might make it more likely that the servant is to be identified as the prophet himself (which would explain why the servant was first given a mission to restore Israel, 49:5f.). It is not impossible that the servant figure is to be interpreted on two levels: the prophet may be presenting his own experience and commission, and presenting it as a parable of Israel's own vocation. (The early Christian apologists interpreted it as foretelling the vocation of Jesus.) On the first level, the suffering and vindication refers to the prophetic experience of preaching God's message to an unbelieving people (compare the commission and sufferings of Jeremiah, Jer. 1:4, 9f.; 15:15–21); on the second level, the suffering refers to Israel's recent historical experience, and the coming vindication to God's imminent restoration of Israel, which will be a signal of the power of the God of Israel to the nations, who will then perceive something of God's justice and law. (It has been suggested by von Rad that the servant figure owes much to the model of Moses the lawgiver, the servant of God.)

All this makes clear that the anonymous prophet known to us as Second Isaiah was recreating and representing the traditions of his people to convey anew in a time of crisis that as God had acted previously to save his people so he would again. Second Isaiah illustrates superbly how tradition can be recreated, and how this recreation is part of the theological process itself. Thus the idea of God creating out of the waters of chaos (an idea whose background lay in the ancient near-eastern myth of Tiamat divided into two by Marduk) is re-used to describe the saving act of God at the Red Sea, where the waters are divided; and the Red Sea event is in turn used as a type of the new redemptive exodus from Babylon (Isa. 51:9–11):

> Awake, awake, put on strength,
>     O arm of the LORD;
> awake, as in days of old,
>     the generation of long ago.
> Was it not thou that didst cut Rahab in pieces,
>     that didst pierce the dragon?
> Was it not thou that didst dry up the sea,
>     the waters of the great deep;
> that didst make the depths of the sea
>     a way for the redeemed to pass over?

The idea is further developed in the New Testament, where Moses and Elijah speak in the Transfiguration scene of the *exodus* Jesus is to accomplish at Jerusalem (Lk. 9:31).

The re-presentation of tradition to provide a message for exiled Israel is seen also in the Pentateuch, which (see ch. 3 above) certainly reflects some of the major theological concerns of the exilic period. Jewish exiles would, after all, have needed considerable reassurance. Faced with a culture which had its own myth of creation and emphasised the power of Marduk, the god of Babylon, and the importance in daily life of other deities and heavenly bodies, a Jewish theologian would first of all wish to emphasise the creative power of the one God who mattered to Israel, and to deny the right to worship and indeed the very existence of others. Then again, faced for the first time with the realisation of the size and scale of the world of the nations and of Israel's comparative insignificance, he would wish to indicate Israel's relationship to them (for they could not be ignored), and to support Israel's *amour propre*. These last two points are made clearly by the table of nations (Gen. 10), the subsequent scattering of the nations after the incident of the tower of Babel (a name strongly reminiscent of Babylon), and the call of Israel's ancestor Abraham from Ur of the Chaldees and Harran (which also makes the point, in a Mesopotamian context, that Israel could boast of a very respectable historical origin).

Surrounded by the symbols and cultic activities of an alien religion, a Jewish theologian would certainly feel the need to emphasise the major features of his own religion: thus the Sabbath is stressed (Gen. 2:1–4; Exod. 31:12–17; cf. Ezek. 22:8,20; 23:38; Isa. 56:2; 58:13) as being observed from the very beginning. The law that blood shall not be eaten is stressed as having been observed by all since the time of the flood; circumcision is stressed as the particular mark and requirement of the descendants of Abraham (Gen. 17; cf. Isa. 52:1; Ezek. 44:7).

Living in a land considered impure (Ezek. 4:13), a strange land to which the God of Israel was foreign (Ps. 137:4), a Jewish theologian would want to emphasise the need for cultic and ritual purity (cf. Lev. 19:2, 'You shall be holy; because I the LORD your God am holy'). In Ezekiel 22, the prophet castigated Jerusalem for all the sins which had made her unclean; the priests themselves had failed to distinguish between the sacred and the common, the clean and the unclean (Ezek. 22:26), though in the restored Jerusalem they would fulfil this obligation (Ezek. 44:23f.).

The Jewish theologian could thus see the exile as a time of purification for God's people and living in exile among a foreign people, he would remember and repeat the story of God's redemption of Israel from Egypt with new meaning. This was a period when the rite of the Passover would have particular relevance: as Yahweh had once before overcome the gods of Egypt, so now he might overcome the gods of Babylon and allow his people to set out for home, in which case the stories of Israel travelling through the wilderness to the promised land would again have forceful meaning. It may also be relevant to note that, as once it was Joshua the son of Nun who led the Israelites into the promised land, so after the exile the first priestly leader was another Joshua, or Jeshua, the son of Jozadak (Ezra 3:2; Hag. 1:1).

Finally, living and working among a Babylonian community, with its own legal tradition, a Jewish theologian would also naturally wish to underline the Yahwistic origin of Israel's laws, and to present the keeping of them both as Israel's response to God's gift of a covenant with Abraham and equally as a prerequisite for Israel's repossession of the promised land. The Pentateuch ends with the Israelites on the verge of entry to the promised land; for the Pentateuchal editor or author, this was Israel's situation in his own time. The whole sequence had direct relevance.

The presentation of Israel's history in the books of Joshua, Judges, Samuel and Kings, introduced by the book Deuteronomy, (the 'Deuteronomic History') also spoke to the exilic age, as we saw in chapters 4 and 5. This history explained Israel's exile by the readiness of her kings and people to adopt foreign idolatry, against which the prophets had uttered continuous warnings (2 Kings 17:7–18), and Judah's exile by her readiness to follow Israel's example (2 Kings 17:19–20). For the Deuteronomistic Historian, the essential marks of the people of God were the worship of Yahweh before all other gods, obedience to the Deuteronomic law and the word of God as expressed by the prophets, practice of the sacrificial cult at Jerusalem alone, loyalty to the Davidic monarchy (itself subject to the law and the prophetic word), and the possession of the land under the terms of the covenant. It was because Israel and Judah and their kings had failed to keep the covenant or obey the law and the prophets that disaster had happened and the land, the temple, and the Davidic kingdom had been lost. It is precisely when a nation suffers disaster that historical explanations become important.

The exilic age was inevitably, therefore, a time for preserving and recording the traditions of Israel's past. Doubtless such priests and government officials as survived the fall of Jerusalem would be aware of the need in a time of chaos to preserve what could be preserved of their nation's cultic and intellectual inheritance, and the more theologically concerned would perceive that the teaching of Yahweh's past activities on Israel's behalf was important as the basis for hope in the future. This period of chaos must surely be recognised as one of the most creative periods of Israel's history, comparable to the Tannaitic and Mishnaic period which followed the fall of Jerusalem to the Romans and the destruction of the temple in AD 70. The list of written works compiled or edited in the sixth century BC is a long one, probably including not merely the Pentateuch but also the Deuteronomic History, the prophetic words of the eighth-century BC Isaiah, the work of Second Isaiah, the books of Jeremiah and Ezekiel and perhaps also the book of the twelve minor prophets. It was, perhaps, at this stage that the basic concept of 'the law and the prophets' as the overall description of Israel's religious literature arose, with its background in the Deuteronomic idea of the law preached and presented by the prophets (2 Kings 17:13). The classical age of the kings of Israel and Judah had gone; but even as they tried to record and preserve it, the Jewish theologians were creating something new. They were preparing the moulds for what became known as Judaism.

## Bibliography

P.R. Ackroyd, *Exile and restoration: a study of Hebrew thought of the sixth century BC.* (Old Testament Library) (London: SCM Press; Philadelphia: Westminster Press, 1968)

P.R. Ackroyd, *Israel under Babylon and Persia* (Clarendon Bible) (London: Oxford University Press, 1970)

R. Davidson, *The courage to doubt: exploring an Old Testament theme* (London: SCM Press, 1983)

J.H. Eaton, *Job,* (Old Testament Guides) (Sheffield: JSOT Press for the Society for Old Testament Study, 1985)

S. Mowinckel, *The Psalms in Israel's worship,* 1, 2 (Oxford: Blackwell, 1967)

E.W. Nicholson, *Deuteronomy and tradition: literary and historical problems in the book of Deuteronomy* (Oxford: Blackwell; Philadelphia: Fortress Press, 1967)

E.W. Nicholson, *Preaching to the exiles: a study of the prose tradition in the book of Jeremiah* (Oxford: Blackwell, 1970)

L. Sabourin, *The Psalms: their origin and meaning* (New York: Alba House, 1974)

M. Weinfeld, *Deuteronomy and the Deuteronomic School* (Oxford: Clarendon Press, 1972)

C. Westermann, *The structure of the book of Job: a form-critical analysis* (Philadelphia: Fortress Press, 1981)

R.N. Whybray, *The second Isaiah* (Old Testament Guides) (Sheffield: JSOT Press for the Society for Old Testament Study, 1983)

# 8     Temple, Law, and Jerusalem

The fall of Jerusalem in 587 BC ended the monarchy of Judah, and the fall of Babylon in 539 BC ended the empire of Babylon. The first saw the destruction of the Jerusalem temple, and the second brought an imperial decree which allowed for its rebuilding (cf. Ezra 1:2–4; 6:1–5; the 'Cyrus Cylinder'). The gap between the destruction of the first Jerusalem temple in 587 BC and the completion of the second in 515 BC was just over seventy years, but if the foundation stone of the new temple was laid shortly after the fall of Babylon, as the present text of Ezra 3:8–13 suggests, then it is possible that there were present 'old men who had seen the first house' (Ezra 3:12) some fifty years previously. (The suggestion of Hag. 2:3 there were those left in 520 BC who had seen the first temple is barely possible.) The author of Ezra 1–6 stresses the continuity between the two temples by noting that 'Cyrus the king also brought out the vessels of the house of the LORD which Nebuchadnezzar had carried away from Jerusalem and placed in the house of his gods' (Ezra 1:7), giving them to Sheshbazzar to take back to Jerusalem. The rebuilding, whether it began in the second year of the return to Jerusalem of Zerubbabel the son of Shealtiel the governor and Jeshua the son of Jozadak the high priest (Ezra 3:8) or the second year of Darius (Hag. 1:1) – if these dates did not originally refer to the same year – is itself an impressive sign of the sense of continuity felt by the community. It seems likely that the impetus came from returned exiles, though whether the two prophets Haggai and Zechariah, who urged the rebuilding, had been in exile is not stated. The new temple seems to have been built along the lines of the old, details of which came to be preserved in the Deuteronomic history (1 Kings 6:2–10): a similar picture is given by Ezekiel 40:48 – 41:26, and much the same plan was followed by Herod's temple. In spite of Jeremiah's famous attack on the self-deception of those who trusted for Jerusalem's safety in the presence of 'the temple of the LORD' (Jer. 7:2–4), post-exilic Judah began its reconstruction by replacing the temple.

This, at least, is the impression that the opening chapters of the book Ezra wish to give the reader. It is important to realise that our biblical sources tell us very little about the history of Judah throughout the Persian period, from Cyrus' capture of Babylon in 539 BC to the defeat of Darius III by Alexander in 331 BC, and what they do tell is focused on three main topics: the rebuilding of the temple under Zerubbabel and Jeshua, the establishment of the Law under Ezra (together with the prohibition of marriage between Jews and Gentiles), and the rebuilding of the walls of Jerusalem under Nehemiah. Many minor details of Judah's governance and history can be reconstructed from stray references, from the evidence of archaeological excavation and occasional finds, and from such history of the Persian empire as is known from the Greek historian Herodotus and the limited surviving records of the Persian rulers. But the Old Testament writers were not primarily antiquarians, and they used their skills and resources to present events in the perspectives that mattered to them and which reflected their perception of how things ought to have been. From the standpoint of a Jewish historian writing perhaps in the fourth or third century BC, what mattered in post-exilic history was the rebuilding of the temple, the establishment of the law of Moses, and the renewed autonomy of the city of Jerusalem, in that order.

Closer analysis of the biblical sources reveals that the history of Judah in the Persian period was not quite so straightforward. The letter to Darius I in 520 BC from Tattenai, governor of the province of Beyond the River, given in Ezra 5:6–17, quotes the elders of Judah as saying that the foundations of the house of God were laid by one Sheshbazzar when he delivered the temple vessels from Babylon, apparently in the first year of Cyrus (Ezra 5:16; cf. Ezra 1:1–11), and that the temple was in building from then until Darius' time. However, Ezra 3:6 notes that in the seventh month (apparently of the coming of Jeshua and Zerubbabel to Jerusalem from Babylon) 'the foundation of the temple of the LORD was not yet laid', and Ezra 3:8 makes clear that they 'made a beginning' of the work in the second year of their coming, in the second month. Haggai 1:1 states that, in the second year of Darius, the people were saying that the time had not yet come to rebuild the house of the Lord. Then they were told to bring materials, and the work seems to have started on the 24th day of the sixth month of the second year of Darius, under the leadership of Zerubbabel and Jeshua and at the prompting of Haggai. This tallies with Ezra 5:1–2, according to which Zerubbabel and Jeshua 'arose and began to build the house of God' at the instigation of Haggai and Zechariah, in the reign of Darius. All this suggests that according to one major tradition, represented by Ezra 3–6, Haggai 1, and Zechariah 1, the temple rebuilding took place in 520–515 BC, and the return of Zerubbabel and Jeshua a year or two earlier, about the beginning of Darius' reign. Another tradition or reconstruction, however, credits the beginning of the laying of the foundation to Sheshbazzar, perhaps a generation earlier, in the reign of Cyrus. What is quite clear from a reading of Ezra 1–6 is that the editor or compiler wishes to present us with a narrative which suggests at first sight that the rebuilding of the temple followed immediately and successfully on the return of the exiles (listed in chapter 2), while a reading of Haggai suggests that the rebuilding did not happen until Darius I's second year, in or after a period of severe economic depression. Ezra 4:1–5, however, likewise suggests that there were delays in the rebuilding but blames these on opposition from the adversaries of Judah and Benjamin (unidentified) and 'the people of the land' (perhaps the populace in occupation of the land when the exiles returned) who 'discouraged the people of Judah, and made them afraid to build, and hired counsellors against them to frustrate their purpose, all the days of Cyrus king of Persia, even until the reign of Darius king of Persia'. It is more than possible that those who had worked the land of Judah through the exilic period resented returnees who now wished to reclaim their ancestral homes and to use the province's limited resources to rebuild the ruined temple. Clearly the author of Ezra 1–6 is on the side of the returned exiles.

A certain amount of extra light is thrown on the period by the 'night visions' of the prophet Zechariah (Zech. 1:7 – 6:15), incorporated with some additional material into the literary composition of Zechariah 1–8 (chapters 9–11, 12–14 are two separate collections of material added later). Zechariah 'saw in the night' a sequence of visions. The first (1:7–17) portrays horses and their riders sent to patrol the earth, which is now at rest; the second (1:18–21) describes four 'horns' (symbols of military or imperial power) 'which have scattered Judah, Israel and Jerusalem', and four smiths to cast down the horns; the third (2:1–5) portrays an angel measuring Jerusalem with an eye to its coming reinhabitation. The fourth (4:1–5, 10b–14) reveals a lampstand with seven lamps between two olive trees symbolising 'the two anointed who stand by the Lord of the whole earth'. The fifth pictures an enormous flying scroll representing a curse on those who break the commandments, and the sixth continues the theme by picturing a woman (representing iniquity) being thrust into a barrel and taken off to Babylonia to be set up there on a base, like a statue (5:1–4; 5–11). The last vision, like the first, shows the Lord's chariots patrolling the four quarters of the earth: 'those who go towards the north country' (i.e., Babylon) 'have set my Spirit at rest in the north country' (6:1–8). The overall picture presented by these visions (which seem to have a chiastic sequence) is clear: after a period of upheaval and instability, the near east is at peace; Darius has established himself in his empire. The powers that destroyed Israel and Judah are themselves destroyed. Jerusalem is to flourish again, under the leadership of the 'two sons of oil', probably the two anointed persons, one royal, one priestly. The land is to be cleansed of sinners, and sin is to be repatriated to its proper home in Babylon. God's spirit will be at rest in the world, especially in Babylon. Central to all this seem to be the two anointed figures and the lampstand between them (the lampstand, a piece of temple furniture, presumably here represents the temple). God will rule Jerusalem through his temple and his royal and priestly lieutenants.

Interspersed among these visions are additional pieces of interpretative material, some oracles relating to the refounding of the temple (e.g., 4:7–10), and two important passages referring, first, to the investiture of the high priest Joshua (3:1–10), and, second, at least originally, to the crowning of a royal figure, probably Zerubbabel (6:9–14). In the first, the high priest Joshua, representing his people, a brand plucked out of the fire (i.e., of the destruction of Jerusalem and the exile), has his filthy garments replaced with clean ones (symbolising the removal of iniquity) and a turban (cf. Exod. 28:4) set on his head, and it is explained that he shall rule God's house (i.e., the temple) and its courts, and even have access to the heavenly council. In the second, gold and silver are taken from returning exiles and made into a crown, to be placed on the head of Joshua the high priest. But the following words show that the crown was for another figure, whose name is the Branch (cf. 'my servant the Branch, who will be brought to Joshua', 3:8), and who will build the temple, bear royal honours, and rule upon his throne, 'and there shall be a priest by his throne, and peaceful understanding shall be between them both.' These two passages perhaps expand the reference to 'the two sons of oil', who appear side by side, and reflect the hope that a descendant of David will build the temple (as Solomon had built the first temple) and sit on the royal throne, and that a high-priestly figure will preside over the temple and its courts. This last was itself a new feature, for the title 'the high priest' does not appear until after the exile. The second passage, however, in its present form appears to reflect the reality of the post-exilic period, that apart from the Persian-appointed governor of Judah, the leading figure in Judah was the anointed high priest. (De Vaux argues that before the exile the rite of anointing originally applied not to high priests but to kings; after the exile the rite was transferred to high priests as heads of the new community (Exod. 29:7; Lev. 8:12), and then to priests (Exod. 40:12–15).)

Further additions to the first Zechariah collection (Zech. 1–8) indicate the fasting and mourning for the fall of Jerusalem as a thing of the past (Zech. 7:1–7, 8:18–19), and that a paradisal future awaits Jerusalem (Zech. 8:1–8); indeed, Jerusalem will be the focus of the new religious understanding of the nation (Zech. 8:20–22);

> 'Thus says the LORD of hosts: Peoples shall yet come, even the inhabitants of many cities; the inhabitants of one city shall go to another, saying, "Let us go at once to entreat the favour of the LORD, and to seek the LORD of hosts; I am going." Many peoples and strong nations shall come to seek the LORD of hosts in Jerusalem, and to entreat the favour of the LORD. Thus says the LORD of hosts: In those days ten men from the nations of every tongue shall take hold of the robe of a Jew, saying, "Let us go with you, for we have heard that God is with you." '

This idea of Jerusalem's religious centrality was appropriate at a time when Jews had been forced to reconsider their relationship with the nations of the world and had reflected on the power of their God over against the gods of their enemies. There were basically two approaches that Jewish theologians could adopt; they could either say (as many did) that God would in the end destroy Israel's foreign enemies (e.g., Joel 3:9–21), or they could say that Israel's enemies in whole or part would come to recognise Israel's God. Zechariah 8:20–22 takes this course; cf. Isaiah 2:2–4; 60:1–22. (Perhaps the book of Jonah also belongs here, for its author in his ironical way seems to express a much more sympathetic attitude towards the nations: the attitude of the sailors from Joppa and of the king and people of Nineveh towards the word of the Lord compares very favourably with Jonah's attitude.)

Useful evidence for the theological concerns of Jerusalem in the decades after the return from exile and the rebuilding of the temple can be seen in the writings known as Third Isaiah (Isa. 56–66) and Malachi. Third Isaiah is perhaps the most difficult of all biblical writings to evaluate and interpret. Its precise origin and background is uncertain, and there is a great danger of arguing in a circle, using a guess about its background (drawn from its contents) to explain its contents and confirm one's original guess. P.D. Hanson has reconstructed from these chapters a situation in which a prophetic, visionary party, the intellectual descendants of Second Isaiah, with an eschatological ideal of the community and its destiny, is in conflict with a more pragmatic group of returned exiles led by Zadokite priests. That is, Isaiah 56–66 represents the work of something like an apocalyptic sect, which tries to compensate for present miseries by the hope of a coming divine irruption ('O that thou wouldst rend the heavens and come down . . . to make thy name known to thy adversaries, and that the nations might tremble at thy presence!', Isa. 64:1f.). Hanson is here drawing on an earlier analysis of the post-exilic community in Judah as divided between two theological streams: a theocratic stream, based on the importance of the temple, priesthood, cult and torah, represented particularly by the writings of P and the Chronicler, and an eschatological stream which resisted the complacency of the temple party and whose work may be seen in Isaiah 24–27, Zechariah 12–14, Joel and Daniel. Hanson traces these two theological approaches back to Ezekiel and Second Isaiah respectively, and sees the visionary party as the seedbed from which the later apocalyptic writers sprang. The very neatness of this view invites a measure of suspicion, and the major difficulty is that there is no concrete evidence allowing us to identify the supposedly conflicting parties represented in Isaiah 56–66 with prophetically minded Levites opposing establishment-minded Zadokites.

A number of things do stand out in this material, however. The first is that all is not well in the society addressed by the prophet. The leaders are venal and drunken (56:9–12), the righteous and the devout are the losers in the social struggle (57:1–2), cults involving child-sacrifice, sexual practices and idolatry are practised (57:9–13), fasting and sabbath-observance are less than sincere (58:1–14), and justice is perverted (59:1–15). The whole is summed up in 59:12–15:

> For our transgressions are multiplied before thee,
>     and our sins testify against us;
> for our transgressions are with us,
>     and we know our iniquities:
> transgressing, and denying the LORD,
>     and turning away from following our God,
> speaking oppression and revolt,
>     conceiving and uttering from the heart lying words.
> Justice is turned back,
>     and righteousness stands afar off;
> for truth has fallen in the public squares,
>     and uprightness cannot enter.
> Truth is lacking,
>     and he who departs from evil makes himself a prey.

The prophet presents his answer (59:15–19):

The LORD saw it, and it displeased him
    that there was no justice.
He saw that there was no man,
    and wondered that there was no one to intervene;
then his own arm brought him victory,
    and his righteousness upheld him.
He put on righteousness as a breastplate,
    and a helmet of salvation upon his head;
he put on garments of vengeance for clothing,
    and wrapped himself in fury as a mantle.
According to their deeds, so will he repay,
    wrath to his adversaries, requital to his enemies;
to the coastlands he will render requital.

So they shall fear the name of the LORD from the west,
    and his glory from the rising of the sun;
for he will come like a rushing stream,
    which the wind of the LORD drives.

This picture of God's intervention points to the second major feature of these prophetic oracles, the prophet's vision of the glorious future of 'the City of the LORD', 'the Zion of the Holy One of Israel' (60:14). The prophet (in words reminiscent of Isa. 49:22f.) sees the nations and their kings coming to rebuild Jerusalem and beautify its sanctuary (60:1–16); violence and destruction will be a thing of the past, the sun and moon will be replaced by the Lord as an everlasting light. The prophet knows he is to bring good news to the afflicted, to proclaim the year of the Lord's favour (61:1f.), the divine vindication of Jerusalem followed by God's vengeance on her enemies, especially Edom (63:1–6). As ch.62 shows clearly, this prophet is building on the work of his predecessor, Second Isaiah, re-using and reinterpreting his words, and recasting his vision:

Go through, go through the gates,
    prepare the way for the people;
build up, build up the highway,
    clear it of stones,
    lift up an ensign over the peoples.
Behold, the LORD has proclaimed
    to the end of the earth:
Say to the daughter of Zion,
    'Behold, your salvation comes;
behold, his reward is with him,
    and his recompense before him.'
And they shall be called The holy people,
    The redeemed of the LORD;
and you shall be called Sought out,
    a city not forsaken.

(62:10–12; cf. 40:3, 10)

The final chapters of Third Isaiah begin (63:7–14) with an account of the history of God's dealings with Israel; there follows a long, passionate prayer to God for help in time of trouble (the trouble appears to be the destruction of Jerusalem and its temple, perhaps in 587 BC; cf. 63:18; 64:11). God replies that he 'was ready to be sought by those who did not ask for me':

> I said, 'Here am I, here am I,'
>     to a nation that did not call on my name.
> I spread out my hands all the day
>     to a rebellious people,
> who walk in a way that is not good,
>     following their own devices;
> a people who provoke me
>     to my face continually,
> sacrificing in gardens
>     and burning incense upon bricks;
> who sit in tombs,
>     and spend the night in secret places;
> who eat swine's flesh,
>     and broth of abominable things is in their vessels;
> who say, 'Keep to yourself,
>     do not come near me, for I am set apart from you.'
> These are a smoke in my nostrils,
>     a fire that burns all the day.
> Behold, it is written before me:
>     'I will not keep silent, but I will repay,
> yea, I will repay into their bosom
>     their iniquities and their fathers' iniquities together, says the LORD.'
>
> (Isa. 65:1–7)

God promises that nevertheless he will not destroy all, but distinguish between his servants and others, and pictures the new heavens and the new earth and a paradisal Jerusalem:

> 'For behold, I create new heavens
>     and a new earth;
> and the former things shall not be remembered
>     or come into mind.
> But be glad and rejoice for ever
>     in that which I create;
> for behold, I create Jerusalem a rejoicing,
>     and her people a joy.
> I will rejoice in Jerusalem,
>     and be glad in my people;
> no more shall be heard in it the sound of weeping
>     and the cry of distress.

No more shall there be in it
  an infant that lives but a few days,
  or an old man that does not fill out his days,
for the child shall die a hundred years old,
  and the sinner a hundred years old shall be accursed.
They shall build houses and inhabit them;
  they shall plant vineyards and eat their fruit.
They shall not build and another inhabit;
  they shall not plant and another eat;
for like the days of a tree shall the days of my people be,
  and my chosen shall long enjoy the work of their hands.
They shall not labour in vain,
  or bear children for calamity;
for they shall be the offspring of the blessed of the LORD,
  and their children with them.
Before they call I will answer,
  while they are yet speaking I will hear.
The wolf and the lamb shall feed together,
  the lion shall eat straw like the ox;
  and dust shall be the serpent's food.
They shall not hurt or destroy
  in all my holy mountain, says the LORD.'

(Isa. 65:17–25)

These chapters have all been read as indicating that there are deep-rooted differences in Judah, the prayer (63:15 – 64:12) coming from those whom Abraham does not know and Israel does not acknowledge (63:16), who are hated by their brethren (66:5), and who can be called God's servants, distinct from others in the community who will be slain (65:8–16). Strangely, in view of earlier chapters, there are somewhat disparaging references to the temple and its cult (Isa. 66:1–4). These features may perhaps indicate the theological background of the originators of this material, but here as so often speculation is easier than proof, and the theological conflicts that took place in Jerusalem in the late sixth-early fifth centuries BC remain largely concealed from us. But at the least it seems likely that they focused on the temple, the cult and the priesthood, which were also the points at issue in the second century BC when the sectarians of Qumran established their community.

That these were indeed issues can be seen from the short book of Malachi, which in the Protestant Christian tradition closes the Old Testament (probably because its prophecy has been linked with the figure of John the Baptist whose work begins the story of Jesus). The book Malachi takes the form of a collection of disputations between the Lord (or the prophet who represents him) and the people. It is interesting, to begin with, that the prophet addresses the post-exilic people of Judah (2:11; 3:4) as 'Israel' and its people as 'sons of Jacob' (3:6), probably applying to Judah a theological viewpoint which derives from Deuteronomy and the Deuteronomistic writings in which the people of God is named as 'Israel'.

In Malachi, then, the mantle of the Deuteronomic Israel has fallen on the province of Judah.

In Malachi's first disputation, God's love for Israel is contrasted with his anger at the people of Edom; but in spite of this love, God finds much fault with Israel. The priests cheat by presenting blemished sacrifices (though the Gentiles offer pure offerings) (1:6–14); they corrupt 'the covenant of Levi' (cf. Deut. 33:8–11) by giving false instruction (2:1–9). The men of Judah profane the covenant by divorcing their wives (2:10–16); an addition in verses 11f. makes the extra accusation that they have compounded their sin by marrying foreign women; mistaking good for evil, they complain at the absence of the God of justice (who will appear like a refiner's fire to purify the sons of Levi, i.e., the priests, so that offerings can once again be pure) (2:17 – 3:5); they are robbing God by failing to pay their tithes (3:6–12); they have even asked what was the good of serving God, for evil-doers prosper and escape penalty (3:13–18). Clearly, Malachi is unhappy at the failures of the priests in their two duties of teaching and offering sacrifice in the temple, and at the failure of the laity in matters of marriage and tithing; he accuses them of cynicism (2:17; 3:15) and its effects on their behaviour (3:5). It is the failings of the priests, however, which seem paramount to Malachi, and appropriately enough judgment will start with the temple and with the purification of the Levites (3:1–5):

> 'Behold, I send my messenger to prepare the way before me, and the Lord whom you seek will suddenly come to his temple; the messenger of the covenant in whom you delight, behold, he is coming, says the LORD of Hosts. But who can endure the day of his coming, and who can stand when he appears? For he is like a refiner's fire and like fullers' soap; he will sit as a refiner and purifier of silver, and he will purify the sons of Levi and refine them like gold and silver, till they present right offerings to the LORD. Then the offering of Judah and Jerusalem will be pleasing to the LORD as in the days of old and as in former years.'

The judgment will then pass on to the sorcerers, the adulterers, those who swear falsely, those who oppress the hireling, the widow and the orphan. Chapters 3:16 – 4:3 record the different treatment to be given to the righteous and the wicked.

An editor closed the book by urging the readers to 'remember the law of my servant Moses'; another editor added a verse promising the appearance of Elijah the prophet 'before the great and terrible day of the LORD comes'. The significance of these additions is disputed; were the editors closing this book, or were they closing a larger collection of material? The first addition, cast in Deuteronomic language, underlines the importance for the readers of the prophetic book of the *tôrāh* of Moses, the servant of God, the prophet *par excellence* (cf. Deut. 18:15–22); it may suggest that 'the law of Moses' is now something which exists in written form and can be appealed to as an authority. The second addition seems to refer back to Malachi 3:1; the 'messenger' (*mal'ak*) of 3:1 is the prophet Elijah, here presented as exercising a ministry of reconciliation in Israel in the face of the coming day of the Lord. These additions, then, link Malachi's book with two great prophets, Moses and Elijah, and so perhaps with the prophetic canon as a whole, which through the figure of Moses is equally associated with the *tôrāh*, the law. At all events, the book of Malachi witnesses to the continuing importance of temple, priesthood, law and prophets in Judah, and to the continuance of the concept of Israel binding them together.

The book Malachi is usually taken to reflect the situation in Judah in the first half of the fifth century BC, when a Persian governor (1:8) ruled and the first flush of enthusiasm for the restored temple was past, but before the reforms of Ezra and Nehemiah; in fact, however, it is impossible to be sure whether Malachi came from an earlier or later period of Persian rule. Much the same can be said of the book of Joel. Joel the son of Pethuel presented his message in a sequence of dramatic pictures. Locusts have devastated the land:

> The vine withers,
> > the fig tree languishes.
> Pomegranate, palm and apple,
> > all the trees of the field are withered;
> and gladness fails
> > from the sons of men.

> (Joel 1:12)

A fast is proclaimed, the people lament:

> Alas for the day!
> For the day of the LORD is near,
> > and as destruction from the Almighty it comes.
> Is not the food cut off
> > before our eyes,
> joy and gladness
> > from the house of our God?

> (Joel 1:15–16)

The picture changes: with the arrival of the day of the Lord, the army of locusts becomes a 'great and powerful people' (2:2), turning the land into a wilderness, and darkening sun and stars:

> Fire devours before them,
> > and behind them a flame burns.
> The land is like the garden of Eden before them,
> > but after them a desolate wilderness,
> > and nothing escapes them.

> Their appearance is like the appearance of horses,
> > and like war horses they run.
> As with the rumbling of chariots,
> > they leap on the tops of the mountains,
> like the crackling of a flame of fire
> > devouring the stubble,

like a powerful army
   drawn up for battle.
Before them peoples are in anguish,
   all faces grow pale.
Like warriors they charge,
   like soldiers they scale the wall.
They march each on his way,
   they do not swerve from their paths.
They do not jostle one another,
   each marches in his path;
they burst through the weapons
   and are not halted.
They leap upon the city,
   they run upon the walls;
they climb up into the houses,
   they enter through the windows like a thief.

The earth quakes before them,
   the heavens tremble.
The sun and the moon are darkened,
   and the stars withdraw their shining.
The LORD utters his voice
   before his army,
for his host is exceedingly great,
   he that executes his word is powerful.
For the day of the LORD is great and very terrible;
   who can endure it?

(Joel 2:3–11)

God calls for repentance (his graciousness is proclaimed in famous words taken from Exod. 34:6f. and repeated also in Jonah 4:2), a fast is again proclaimed, and the restoration of the land and people pictured in memorable language:

'Fear not, O land;
   be glad and rejoice,
   for the LORD has done great things!
Fear not, you beasts of the field,
   for the pastures of the wilderness are green;
   the tree bears its fruit,
the fig tree and vine give their full yield . . .

The threshing floors shall be full of grain,
   the vats shall overflow with wine and oil . . .

You shall eat in plenty and be satisfied,
   and praise the name of the LORD your God,
   who has dealt wondrously with you . . .

And it shall come to pass afterwards,
  that I will pour out my spirit on all flesh;
your sons and your daughters shall prophesy,
  your old men shall dream dreams,
  and your young men shall see visions.
Even upon the menservants and maidservants
  in those days, I will pour out my spirit.'

(Joel 2:21–29)

God will pour out his spirit, he will judge the nations in the valley of Jehoshaphat (the name means 'God judges') outside Jerusalem, he will once again dwell in Jerusalem, and the land will enjoy paradisal plenty and fertility:

'And in that day
the mountains shall drip sweet wine,
  and the hills shall flow with milk,
and all the stream beds of Judah shall flow with water;
  and a fountain shall come forth from the house of the LORD
and water the valley of Shittim.'

(Joel 3:18)

The occasion of the locust plague of ch.2 is unknown, and the locusts are rapidly transformed in the prophet's description into an even more threatening heavenly army, to which the only possible response is cultic (2:12–16), involving priestly intercession between the vestibule of the temple and the altar (2:17, i.e., at the holiest spot of the temple complex barring only the Holy of Holies into which the High Priest alone could enter, on the Day of Atonement), and the only possible outcome is an eschatological one, the final destruction of the nations and the restoration of paradisal Judah (2:20–29). To this material has been added further more prosaic description of the end (2:30 – 3:3), and specific accusations against the people of Tyre, Sidon and Philistia (3:4–8), who have apparently pillaged Judah and 'sold the people of Judah and Jerusalem to the Greeks', for which they in turn will be sold to the Sabaeans in southern Arabia, well-known slave-traders. As Sidon was destroyed in 343 BC by Persia, this addition probably dates from the first half of the fourth century BC, the later period of Persian rule in Judah.

What is particularly interesting in Joel is the unrelievedly hostile attitude shown towards the nations, whose wickedness is great and is to be punished. Strangers shall never again pass through Jerusalem (3:17) to defile its holiness, for this is where God dwells (3:21). Jerusalem, its temple, and the priestly leadership are central. The Lord is 'jealous for his land, and had pity on his people' (2:18); 'I, the LORD, am your God and there is none else' (2:27), a formula reminiscent of the language of Second Isaiah. (Second Isaiah, however, writing from an exilic context, has a much wider vision.) If Joel belongs to the century between Nehemiah and the fall of Sidon (*CHJ* I. 175), he is working in a period when the now long-established Persian empire is beginning to disintegrate. Cyrus' rebellion in 401 BC, Egyptian rebellion and advance in Palestine at the turn of the fifth-fourth century BC, the 'revolt of the satraps' from 360 BC, and the rebellion of the Phoenicians in the 340s show how much the Persian empire was under pressure – and Judah, on the borders of Egypt, was in a position to note the pressure and hear the tramp of armies along the coast. Judah, as Joel 3:1-8 shows, was aware of the Greek world to her west. Joel's vivid expectation of the end of nations hostile to Judah may have its background in these circumstances.

One other aspect of Joel may be noted. The book contains a number of allusions to, or borrowings from, other biblical writings. For example, Joel 1:15 and 2:10 should be compared with Isaiah 13:6,10,13; Joel 2:14 with Exodus 34:6 and Jonah 3:9; Joel 2:32 with Obadiah 17; Joel 2:11, 31 with Malachi 3:2, 4:5. The phrase 'as the LORD has said' in Joel 2:32 suggests that the author knows that he is quoting (cf. Wolff, 1977 68: 'a conscious proclamation of transmitted material'), and this makes the book a self-conscious piece of literary material. Many commentators have noted that in tone it begins to approximate to the apocalyptic literature of the second and first centuries BC; but in fact, though the young men shall see visions and the old men dream dreams, and though the descriptions of the locust plague and the army of northern peoples are as vivid as any vision, Joel is not cast in the form of an apocalypse, in which other-worldly figures reveal heavenly mysteries to the visionary.

The book of Jonah is also a self-conscious literary piece, carefully crafted. Jonah is remembered by most people only as a man swallowed by a great fish, but, as so often, it is the incidental detail that has been remembered and the main point forgotten. Jonah's name ('dove, son of faithfulness') has been taken from 2 Kings 14:25; ch. 3:8,10 are reminiscent of Jeremiah 18:7-10, and ch. 4:2 of Exodus 34:6; ch. 2 incorporates a thanksgiving psalm used here because of the imagery of the sufferer as a drowning man. The author of Jonah, then, like Joel's author, can draw on a known body of literature; but what he creates is a didactic story in the best Jewish tradition, spiced with ironic humour. The figure of Jonah, who receives the word of the Lord like a prophet, is a caricature of a narrow-minded, self-centred, self-righteous man who thinks that he knows better than God, and who thinks (so far as he thinks at all) that God's power is limited to Palestine, and that foreigners should get their obvious deserts. The story, carefully arranged in two balanced scenes, cuts Jonah down to size. It pays to read this short story with close attention to detail, for the author makes his points with no little subtlety.

Jonah receives a prophetic commission from God, and immediately goes to sea to escape God's presence. God's presence, however, makes itself felt in a storm, and the Gentile seamen pray to their gods and call on Jonah to pray to his. As Gentiles, they comment that Jonah's God will perhaps give thought to them and save them from perishing. Jonah is forced to admit, somewhat inconsistently in view of his attempt to escape by sea, that he worships the Lord, the God of Heaven, who made the sea and the dry land. Jonah suggests that the sailors throw him into the sea to appease God; the Gentile sailors at first try to avoid this, eventually doing so only after praying to the Lord. When the sea stops raging, 'then the men feared the LORD exceedingly, and they offered a sacrifice to the

LORD and made vows.' Jonah is swallowed by a fish, prays to God, and is vomited out – a further humiliating experience for this unheroic prophet. In all this, the Gentile sailors are favourably contrasted with the Jewish Jonah.

The Lord now repeats his instruction to Jonah to go to Nineveh, and this time Jonah obeys. Nineveh's great days as capital of the Assyrian empire were in fact over; the author of Jonah knew of it as a Gentile city of legendary size. Jonah now receives a second shock: on hearing his message, Nineveh responded with sackcloth and ashes, and when God saw this, he 'repented of the evil which he had said he would do to them; and he did not do it.' The Ninevites understand God's grace (3:9) rather better than Jonah does (4:2), and Jonah responds by sulking. Just as in the first scene he was ready to offer himself to death out of pride and stupidity, so now he prays to God for death. Just as in ch. 1 he is humbled by the indignity of being swallowed by a fish, so now he is humbled by the lesson he is made to learn from the plant:

> And the LORD said, 'You pity the plant, for which you did not labour, nor did you make it grow, which came into being in a night, and perished in a night. And should I not pity Nineveh, that great city, in which there are more than a hundred and twenty thousand persons who do not know their right hand from their left, and also much cattle?'
>
> (Jonah 4:10–11)

Clearly, the author of Jonah had much more respect and sympathy for non-Jews than had the author of Joel, and it has often been suggested that he wrote to counter the more usual Jewish exclusivism represented in the books of Ezra and Nehemiah, where marriages between Jews and Gentiles were prohibited, and foreign wives put away. Such exclusivism is perhaps not surprising in a small country which had suffered much from the large empires of Assyria, Babylon and probably also Persia (for the Persians were not always such gentle imperialists as they have sometimes been portrayed). The author of Jonah, however, says that Israel's God pities the people of Nineveh, and the puzzlement of Jonah himself in the story is understandable. John Sawyer may be right to see Jonah as 'a lonely, suffering servant of God, bewildered by the ways of God' (Sawyer, 1987, 114). God is teaching Jonah an important lesson, and this strand in Jewish theology should not be ignored. It is also important to see that here, as so often elsewhere in Jewish tradition, the theological point is made through the medium of a story, and with the help of humour. The authority and value of the Bible does not stand on the acceptance of every detail in Jonah as factually true; the story is to be seen rather as a parable; compare the New Testament parable of the Good Samaritan.

The book of Jonah has taken us away a little from what appear to have been the major concerns of Judah in the Persian period (though even Jonah includes references to the Jerusalem temple, in the psalm incorporated in ch.2). The work which comes nearest to making a systematic theological presentation of Judah's political and religious institutions in the Persian period is 1 and 2 Chronicles. This work, clearly based on the earlier books of Samuel and Kings, gives an account of the history of God's dealings with the people of Israel. It begins with a series of genealogies leading from Adam to the tribes of Israel (of which Judah is the most important), and to the list of returned exiles (1 Chr.9:2–44). The core of the work is given over to the work of David and Solomon (who respectively planned and built the temple). The following chapters (2 Chr.10–28) describe the period of the monarchy, focused on Jerusalem, its temple and its dynasty, until the seventy years' exile of Judah. Many scholars see the books Ezra and Nehemiah as a continuance of this work, in which case the story ends with the restoration of the temple by Joshua and Zerubbabel, the return of the exiles and the restoration of the temple vessels, the rebuilding of Jerusalem's walls by Nehemiah and the proclamation of the law of Moses by Ezra. The last verses of 2 Chronicles refer to the establishment of the kingdom of Persia, and 1 Chronicles 29:7 says that in David's time ten thousand 'darics' were given for the service of the temple. 'Darics' were Persian coins first minted *c.* 515 BC by Darius I (522–485 BC). The genealogies of 1 Chronicles 3:17–24 carry the Judaean royal family two generations beyond Zerubbabel, who was active in Jerusalem as governor *c.* 520 BC. Clearly the Chronicler is writing in the Persian period, no earlier than the mid-fifth century BC; if his work included most of Ezra and Nehemiah, its date must probably be brought down to the fourth century BC. The quotation of Zechariah 4:10b in 2 Chronicles 16:9 again suggests that the Chronicler is working no earlier than the mid-fifth century BC, and perhaps later. Some scholars have found evidence of fourth-century additions to the book.

Given this historical background, what was the Chronicler's purpose in rewriting the history presented in Samuel and Kings? He is apparently concerned to stress that the community of Israel is a unity, focused on Jerusalem, its Davidic monarchy, and the worship of its temple (cf. Abijah's speech before battle with Jeroboam, 2 Chr. 13:4–12). The northern tribes, who had separated themselves politically from Judah at the end of Solomon's reign and had temporarily forsaken God, had been invited to return and share the worship at Jerusalem by King Hezekiah. The Davidic dynasty is obviously very important, being introduced by the early genealogies. The work of David and Solomon takes up the major part and centre of the book, and the subsequent chapters describe the reigns of Solomon's successors in Judah, largely ignoring the non-Davidic, northern kings of Israel. It is on two counts that the Davidic dynasty seems to be especially important: first, it planned, built and provided for the temple and its cult, and secondly, it was responsible before God to the people for the observance and promulgation of the law. Thus, for example, Solomon's successor Rehoboam forsook the law (2 Chr. 12:1), but Asa 'did what was good and right . . . and commanded Judah . . . to keep the law and the commandment' (2 Chr. 14:2–4). Jehoshaphat had peripatetic Levites teach the law from the book of the law of the Lord throughout Judah (2 Chr. 17:8–9). Hezekiah celebrated a passover such as had not been celebrated since Solomon's day, and the priests 'took their accustomed posts according to the law of Moses' (2 Chr. 30:16). In Josiah's time, Hilkiah the priest 'found the book of the law of the LORD given through Moses' (2 Chr. 34:14), and Josiah's good deeds were 'according to what is written in the law of the LORD' (2 Chr. 35:26).

Temple and law are the Chronicler's primary concerns (and these concerns are prominent in the book Ezra, which completes the Chronicler's history by telling of the reconstruction of the temple and the re-establishment of the law). Why these are so firmly linked with the Davidic dynasty is less immediately clear. The royal connection with the temple was both a matter of historical fact and of theological importance, and continued after the return from the exile, as is shown by Zerubbabel's part in its rebuilding. The royal connection with the law of Moses continues a theme already present in the Deuteronomist (cf. Deut. 17:18–20), but there could be little reason to found the law on the monarchy once the monarchy had disappeared, and in fact the book of Ezra founds the law on a priestly figure, Ezra, presented as a descendant of Zadok the priest of Jerusalem and Aaron, Moses' brother (Ezra 7:1–6). In 1 and 2 Chronicles, however, while the priests and the Levites can be interpreters of the law on occasion (2 Chr. 17:7–9), the priests are concerned mainly with ministry at the altar and the Levites with servicing the temple and its cult (cf. Ezek. 44:9–31).

Why, then, did the Chronicler wish to maintain and emphasise these royal links at a time when the monarchy had long since disappeared? The fact that the Chronicler takes care to trace the family of the last surviving king of Judah, Jehoiachin, past Shealtiel and Zerubbabel through six further generations (1 Chr. 3:16–24) perhaps suggests that he still thought the Davidic dynasty important and perhaps even hoped for some kind of restoration. Particularly notable is 'his direct equation of kingship in Israel with the kingdom of God' (Williamson, 1982, 26). Thus in 1 Chronicles 28:5, David is made to say, 'of all my sons . . . he has chosen Solomon my son to sit upon the throne of the kingdom of the LORD over Israel.' Israel is God's kingdom; this is a thought that reappears particularly in later apocalyptic literature (e.g., Dan. 2:44), and it is perhaps surprising to find it in the Chronicler two centuries earlier. But here, as later, it expresses the idea that Israel will not be overcome by the kingdoms of the world; it will be ruled by God, and God's rule is symbolised by the Davidic dynasty. In 2 Chronicles 6:42, at the very end of Solomon's prayer, the king prays that God would remember his steadfast love for David, almost certainly alluding to Isaiah 55:3 and perhaps suggesting that the dynasty should be permanently established (cf. v.16, 'There shall never fail you a man before me to sit upon the throne of Israel, if only your sons take heed to their way, to walk in my law as you have walked before me'). This faith in the continuance of a monarchy that had disappeared in all but historical remembrance and the survival of a few descendants, nonentities in the Persian political world so far as we know, reveals the mind of an academic theologian, remote from the political realities and content to be so, presenting an ideal world-view by which Israel was to live and keep her *amour propre*.

Perhaps of a piece with this is the Chronicler's clearly expressed view that Israel's prosperity and success depend upon her faithfulness to the demands of the law and the prophets, and the readiness of the people or their king to repent when necessary. This retributive theology, which has its background in a similar Deuteronomistic theology, is presented clearly in the Lord's response to Solomon's prayer at the consecration of the temple (2 Chr. 7:11–22); if Solomon walked before God as David had done, keeping God's statutes and ordinances, the royal dynasty would be established; if Solomon forsook these statutes and ordinances, and served other gods, then

> I will pluck you up from the land which I have given you; and this house, which I have consecrated for my name, I will cast out of my sight, and will make it a proverb and a byword among all peoples. (2 Chr. 7:20).

However, in time of trouble

> if my people who are called by my name humble themselves, and pray and seek my face, and turn from their wicked ways, then I will hear from heaven, and will forgive their sin and heal their land. (2 Chr. 7:14)

Such repentance might be the result of a prophetic warning (cf. 2 Chr. 12:15), though such warnings were not always heeded (cf. 2 Chr. 25:15f.), and disaster then followed. The results can be seen in the judgments expressed on the various kings, for example, on Saul:

> So Saul died for his unfaithfulness; he was unfaithful to the LORD in that he did not keep the command of the LORD, and also consulted a medium, seeking guidance, and did not seek guidance from the LORD. Therefore the LORD slew him . . .
>
> (1 Chr. 10:13)

or on Jehoshaphat:

> The LORD was with Jehoshaphat, because he walked in the earlier ways of his father; he did not seek the Baals, but sought the God of his father and walked in his commandments, and not according to the ways of Israel. Therefore the LORD established the kingdom in his hand . . .
>
> (2 Chr. 17:3-4)

For the Chronicler, what mattered about these kings was their attitude to the law, their faithfulness to the Lord, their refusal to worship other gods, and their support for the temple and its cult. In this, the Chronicler was in fact following and expressing the developing tradition of his people.

## Bibliography

P.R. Ackroyd, *Exile and restoration: a study of Hebrew thought of the sixth century B.C.* (Old Testament Library) (London: SCM Press; Philadelphia: Westminster Press, 1968)

E. Bickermann, *Four strange books of the Bible: Jonah, Daniel, Koheleth, Esther* (New York: Schocken Books, 1987)

J. Blenkinsopp, *Wisdom and Law in the Old Testament: the ordering of life in Israel and early Judaism* (The Oxford Bible Series) (Oxford: Oxford University Press, 1983)

J. Boardman, N.G.L. Hammond, D.M. Lewis and M. Ostwald (ed.), *The Cambridge Ancient History*, 2nd ed., IV: *Persia, Greece and the Western Mediterranean, c. 525-479 B.C.* (Cambridge: Cambridge University Press, 1988)

R.J.Coggins, *Haggai, Zechariah, Malachi* (Old Testament Guides) (Sheffield: JSOT Press for the Society for Old Testament Study, 1987)

W.D. Davies and L. Finkelstein (ed.), *The Cambridge History of Judaism* I: *Introduction: The Persian period* (Cambridge: Cambridge University Press, 1984)

P.D. Hanson, *The dawn of apocalyptic* (Philadelphia: Fortress Press, 1975)

M. Noth, *The Chronicler's history* (Sheffield: JSOT Supplement Series 50, 1987)

M. Smith, *Palestinian parties and politics that shaped the Old Testament* (New York: Columbia University Press, 1971)

D. Patrick, *Old Testament law* (London: SCM Press, 1986)

E. Stern, *The material culture of the land of the Bible in the Persian period 538–332 B.C.* (Warminster: Aris and Phillips; Jerusalem: Israel Exploration Society, 1982)

H.G.M. Williamson, *Ezra and Nehemiah* (Old Testament Guides) (Sheffield: JSOT Press for the Society for Old Testament Study, 1987)

# 9     The Challenge of the Hellenistic World

The biblical books examined in the last chapter were written in Judah during the Persian empire. Judah was a small province of the southwestern end of the satrapy called Eber-nahara, 'across the River' (i.e., the River Euphrates). The Jews looked east, as they had for centuries, for their rulers – indeed, further east than usual, for Persia lay east and south of Israel's former masters in Assyria and Babylon. The Persians, however, saw the Jews as lying on the western edge of their empire, where the huge satrapy of Eber-nahara ran out towards the highly desirable and profitable regions of Arabia and Egypt. Next door to the Jews were the Phoenicians, whose ships, based on Tyre, Sidon, and other ancient coastal cities with fine harbours, might control the eastern approaches of the Mediterranean for Persia. Ever since Cyrus the Great had captured Sardis in 546 BC, and the Greek cities of western Anatolia had lost their independence and become part of the Persian empire, the Mediterranean had been of prime importance to the Persians. In 512 BC, Darius had campaigned in Europe, crossing the Danube in pursuit of the Scythians. When the Greek cities of Ionia rebelled in 498 BC with the support of Athens, the Persian attempts under Darius in 490 BC and Xerxes in 480 BC to punish Greece were frustrated by courageous and intelligent Greek defence. However, Persia continued to maintain control and defend her imperial interests along the eastern Aegean seaboard, increasingly employing Greek mercenary soldiers in her armies. Darius had employed a Greek sea-captain, Skylax, to explore the Indus. Artaxerxes I had welcomed Themistocles of Athens, who had done so much to frustrate Xerxes' intentions in 480 BC, as an exile.

Under the Persian empire, many Greeks thus gained firsthand experience of the Persian world and the lands of modern Turkey, Syria, Iraq and Iran. Best-known are the thirteen thousand Greek mercenaries who, in 401 BC, marched from Sardis almost to Babylon in support of Cyrus against his brother Artaxerxes II; after their defeat at Cunaxa, ten thousand of them escaped north through Armenia to Trebizond, the Black Sea, and home. Such contacts alerted the east to the intellectual and military challenge posed by the west, and showed the Greeks the possibilities afforded by the wealth of the east. The result was the conquest of Asia by Alexander the Great, who crossed the Hellespont in 334 BC. The period between his arrival in Asia in 334 BC and the arrival of Pompey the Great in Syria in 63 BC is known to biblical and other historians as the Hellenistic period. During this period, Judah was ruled by the Ptolemaic dynasty of Egypt from 320 to 200 BC, by the Seleucid dynasty of Syria from 200 to 142 BC, and by the Hasmonaean family of Judah from 142 to 63 BC.

Greek influence in the east had begun long before Alexander the Great, even in Palestine, but Alexander's campaigns changed the political map and left a long-abiding social and cultural legacy. Alexander was the son of Philip II, who had taken advantage of the enfeebled state of the once-powerful Greek cities of Athens and Sparta to develop his kingdom of Macedon. 'Philip turned you into city-dwellers, and civilised you by the gift of good laws and customs' was Alexander's reported comment to his Macedonian soldiers. By 338 BC, Philip was master of Greece and planning (on the pretext of avenging the Persian invasions of Greece under Darius and Xerxes, but more realistically in search of wealth and land for his growing population) an invasion of the weakening Persian empire. After his assassination in 336 BC, his twenty-year-old son Alexander took over the project, and in 334 BC crossed to Asia with 37,000 men. He defeated Darius III at Issus near Iskanderun in 333 BC, and marched south towards Egypt, capturing Tyre and Gaza *en route*. Josephus reports that he visited Jerusalem and paid his respects to the high priest, but this is fiction. In Egypt, he founded the city of Alexandria, certainly the most successful of all his foundations, and visited the oracle of Ammon at Siwa, where 'the priest told the king that he, Alexander, was the son of Zeus' (Callisthenes). The assumption of divine honours and the founding of a city became regular features of Alexander's career in the east. From Egypt he marched east to defeat Darius III again at Gaugamela, and took Babylon and its gold reserves, and then Persepolis and Pasargadae at the heart of the Persian empire. In 330 BC he had dedicated arms and bulls' skulls at the sanctuary of Athene at Lindos on the isle of Rhodes, and revealed his ambitions by recording that 'King Alexander, having defeated Darius in battle and become Lord of Asia, sacrificed to Lindian Athene in accordance with a prophecy in the priesthood of Theogenes, son of Pistocrates'. From Persia he went east through what is now Iran to the Indus valley: the influence of his conquests here was proved by the establishment in the mid-third century BC of the Indo-Greek kingdom of Bactria, whose kings bore Greek names – Euthydamus, Demetrius, Eucratides, and Menander. Alexander died in Babylon in 323 BC, leaving a quarter of the northern hemisphere to be ruled by his successors, who divided it between them: Cassander took Greece and Macedonia, Lysimachus Thrace, Antigonus and his son Demetrius Poliorketes (the Besieger) Asia Minor, Seleucus Babylon and Syria, and Ptolemy Egypt (to which he soon added Palestine).

The story of Alexander has often been told, and has been retold briefly here because his conquest of the ancient near east had profound results even for the isolated community of Judah, as the authors of Daniel 7:7, 8:5, 11:4, and 1 Maccabees 1:1–4 realised very well. But what made the difference for the Jews and others was not just the change of ruler from Darius III to Ptolemy or Seleucus. The world around them was changing socially and educationally, to begin with, and, as in our own late twentieth century, it was an age of travel. Mercenaries, architects, engineers, statesmen, doctors, lawyers, administrators, athletes, musicians, teachers, writers, poets, pilgrims and, of course, traders all travelled. The Greek historian Polybius mentions seven different delegations visiting Alexandria simultaneously (Polyb. 28:19.2–5; cf. Walbank, 1981, 68f.). 1 Maccabees 8 describes a Jewish diplomatic mission to Rome in 161 BC while 2 Maccabees 4:18 notes that the hellenising high priest Jason, *c.* 170 BC, sent envoys from the citizens of Jerusalem to take an offering of three hundred silver drachmas for the sacrifice to Hercules at the quadrennial games at Tyre (though Jewish scruples prevailed among the delegates, and the money was in fact given for building triremes). The sheer quantity of Rhodian jar-handles (from jars carrying wine from Rhodes) found in late-third- to early-second-century BC archaeological sites in Palestine, such as Samaria and Jerusalem, is an indication of the trade that came from the Mediterranean.

This trade had been developing for some time, especially along the Palestine coast. Attic red-figured ware of the fourth century BC has been found at Akko and inland at Samaria. Large quantities of Persian and Hellenistic-period storage jars have been dredged up by fishing vessels along the coast near Dor, Caesarea, Ashdod, and Ashkelon; off this last port was found a Greek helmet. Many other finds point the same way; a terracotta figurine of Demeter and Persephone from a third- to second-century BC temple at Beersheba has a parallel in a similar object from Larnaka in Cyprus. The town of Marisa in Idumaea was populated by colonists from Sidon, and their tombs contain Greek inscriptions and wall-paintings of animals described by their Greek names (*elephas, rhinokeros*). Judah's interest in ships in the second and first centuries BC is shown by the report that Simon the Maccabee decorated his family tomb at Modin in 140 BC with ships (1 Macc. 13:29), and by the wall-picture in Jason's tomb in Jerusalem, which shows a Greek monoreme chasing a cargo ship. Exactly how deeply the Jews themselves were influenced by this access to the Mediterranean Hellenistic cultural world remains a matter of debate, but in our own time we might compare the situation of Ireland, on the extreme west of Europe, as it comes to terms with the increasing influence of the European community in its social, economic, political and religious life.

Influence was hardly restricted to trade. Alexander had hoped to control his huge empire by the foundation of cities settled by his mercenary soldiers. Tyre and Gaza were resettled in this way; Samaria and Gerasa received Macedonian colonists. East of the Tigris there were probably some twenty strategically placed city settlements (e.g., Alexandria Arachosia, Alexandria on the Oxus, Alexandria Eschate, i.e., 'Furthest Alexandria'). Many Greeks were settled in Bactria but, nostalgic for the Greek way of life of their original homelands, they rebelled and were massacred. The Seleucid dynasty in particular took good care to colonise and urbanise their conquered territories. Macedonian soldiers were given land as colonists and encouraged to take local wives; new towns were established, named after the towns of their Macedonian homeland (Larissa, Beroea, Europus, Edessa) or members of the Seleucid royal family (Antiocheia, Seleucia, Laodicea, Apamea). The Ptolemies in similar fashion renamed some cities in Palestine and Transjordan; Akko became Ptolemais, Rabbath-Ammon became Philadelphia, Eloth became Berenike. (Under Seleucid rule, Jerusalem itself perhaps for a time became known officially as Antioch at Jerusalem, (cf. 2 Macc.4:9,10) though this is not certain, and the title Antioch in Judaea is perhaps more likely.) Government administration might also be conducted in Greek; in the mid-third century BC the Egyptian official Zenon wrote his official correspondence in Greek, and in 195 BC the Seleucid administration erected an inscription near Bethshan recording various orders given by Antiochus III and his son to the military governor of Coele-Syria and Palestine. The aim in all this was the more efficient control of the subject territories. It is not too difficult to imagine the effect such policies might have on the local population.

Also important to Hellenistic rulers was how they presented themselves to their people. A Hellenistic ruler whose not so distant ancestors had been army officers or minor officials in Macedonia had to appear rather larger than life when ruling the inheritance of the Pharaohs or of the Persian kings. Alexander, taking seriously the oracle from the priest of Zeus Ammon at Siwa, had demanded of his Greek and Macedonian followers that they adopt the Persian custom of obeisance (*proskunesis*) in front of their ruler, and those who opposed him were executed. Ptolemy I set up a cult of Alexander (whose body he had hijacked and given an impressive burial and tomb in Alexandria). Ptolemy II in 283 BC declared his father Ptolemy I to be a god; later, he proclaimed himself and his sister-consort Arsinoe *theoi adelphoi*, brother gods. Subsequently both Ptolemaic and Seleucid rulers adopted titles suggestive of divinity, such as *Soter* (Saviour), *Euergetes* (Benefactor) and *Epiphanes* (Manifest); this last was the title of Antiochus IV whom the Jewish historians came to portray as an arrogant blasphemer (Dan.11:36; 2 Macc.9:1–12).

Alexander himself had wished to make the conquering Macedonians and the conquered Persians joint masters of his new empire. After executing those Macedonians who opposed this ideal, he prayed, at the banquet he held in Susa to celebrate the end of the Persian empire and the beginning of his own, 'for harmony and fellowship in the empire between the Macedonians and the Persians' (Arrian, *Anabasis* vii.11.9). His followers in fact rejected this ideal. In both the Seleucid and Ptolemaic empires, but especially the latter, the native peoples were kept from administrative or political power, which was limited to Greeks and those natives who turned themselves into Greeks. This became one of the major factors behind the Maccabaean rebellion in Judah; citizenship, and high-priestly and priestly power, had become limited to upper class hellenising Jews, whose life and privilege focused on the Hellenistic institutions of the citizen assembly and the council, the gymnasium, and all the attendant cultural and educational institutions (cf. 2 Macc.4:7–17).

It is interesting to note how the Jews, a few years later, under their now successful Maccabaean leaders, went to great trouble to emphasise their fictitious links with Sparta (1 Macc.12:1–23; 14:20–23). They may have chosen Sparta as their Hellenistic twin city because Sparta too was famous for its lawgiver (Lycurgus) and for its military traditions, and also for its opposition to Athenian liberal democracy. The choice was a clever one, and revealed the Jewish mind. The Jews were prepared to be part of the Hellenistic world, but, like the

Spartans, would retain their independence. They were conscious of their call and election as the people of Yahweh, and would not readily subscribe to a *Weltanschauung* that approved of *homonoia*, intermarriage, and equality in rule between two very different peoples. Not that most Greeks were really very different from the Jews in this matter. The Greeks saw themselves as infinitely superior to the Persians, whom they despised, and indeed to any barbarians (i.e., non-Greeks). Plato had said that war between Greeks was civil war; real war was fought against barbarians. Aristotle had said that slaves were slaves by nature and barbarians were naturally slaves. But in the Hellenistic period, new and more liberal and cosmopolitan philosophies had appeared. The famous Cynic Diogenes (*c.* 400–325 BC) had claimed to be a *cosmopolites* as distinct from being merely the citizen of some local town. The Stoics followed Zeno, of Semitic ancestry from Citium in Cyprus, who, according to Tarn, 'dreamt of a world which should no longer be separate states, but one great city under one divine law, where all were citizens and members of one another.' The Stoics asked their followers to live in conformity with nature, and the Epicureans asked theirs to live without fear of the irrational and the divine. The Hellenistic age was one of increasingly liberal and critical education, symbolised by the Museum at Alexandria, 'the birdcage of the Muses', full of philosophers, literary men, inventors. Indeed, when one thinks of the Hellenistic world, one thinks of Alexandria first of all; and Alexandria had great importance for the Jewish people and for the history of their scriptures.

Before turning to that, however, we should take a glance at the Hellenistic city. In the second century BC there were those in Jerusalem who wished to make Jerusalem a city after the Hellenistic ideal, and in New Testament times Herod the Great created Hellenistic cities in Palestine, and Paul visited Hellenistic cities throughout the Mediterranean world. Anyone who has seen the remains of places like Pergamum, or Priene, or Perge, knows that at their best such cities must have been pleasant places in which to live, humanely ordered and functionally elegant. Their predecessors, whether in Greece or the near east, tended to be warrens of housing squashed round an acropolis with its temple, palaces and military defences, and surrounded by a wall. The Greek cities would have an *agora* or public market place surrounded by public buildings such as law courts, temples, a theatre and a gymnasium; the near-eastern cities might have had an open area inside the city gate, serving much the same purpose as the *agora*, where the city elders might meet to dispense justice and the traders to sell their wares, but the theatre and the gymnasium would be missing. So too for the most part was sanitation.

The Hellenistic world brought great improvements. The Hellenistic city was laid out on the gridiron plan commonly attributed to Hippodamus of Miletus (who died *c.* 500 BC). At its centre, or near the water front if the city lay on the sea, would be the *agora*, surrounded by shops on three sides. Next to it would be the main temple of the city, dedicated to its patron god or goddess. Lawcourts, council offices and a council chamber would be nearby; also a gymnasium, and a theatre; outside the walls might be a stadium. The streets were no longer twisting alleys between houses or a road running round inside the walls, but broad, straight thoroughfares at right angles to one another, dividing the city into well-built blocks of houses. The central streets, running across the city from city gate to city gate, might be extra wide to allow room for processions and parades; the Canopic Way at Alexandria was 100 feet wide. Such streets would be lined with colonnades and paved in stone (Herod paid for the paving of a lengthy stretch at Antioch in Syria) for the benefit of shops and pedestrians. A *nymphaeum* (fountain) provided running water for the citizens. Such streets were showpieces, giving a sense of order, perspective and dignity. In this age, public ornaments could be large and impressive; one thinks of the Mausoleum at Halicarnassus, the Colossus at Rhodes, the lighthouse (Pharos) at Alexandria, and the altar of Zeus at Pergamum. Despotic rulers, then as now, needed to provide splendour and work for the people, to keep them content under absolute rule and bureaucratic supervision. Herod the Great thus enhanced Jerusalem with his rebuilding of the temple, and when it was completed in the early 60s of the first century AD the resulting unemployment probably contributed greatly to the malaise which caused the Jewish revolt in AD 66.

Cities such as this made a great difference to the quality of life. The city was now too big to be an open democracy of the Athenian type in which all free citizens could vote on state policy. Not only that, but people were aware that their own city was interlinked with others and that since Alexander's day at least they were part of the larger *oikoumene*, the inhabited world. 'A vast uncertainty had come into men's lives. This was no neat little world in which Zeus or the providence of the gods saw to it that the just man had a reasonable measure of prosperity and the unjust man of punishment. It might be ruled by a blind Fortune, or again by an unchangeable Fate written in the stars or determined by them . . . the effective answer was to make the gods lords of the stars' (A.D. Nock, 1933, 100). Some sought salvation by renouncing the earthly city and looking for illumination from the heavenly mysteries, becoming initiates of one of the mystery cults. Others accepted foreign deities such as Egyptian Isis, or Syrian Atargatis; others again solved the religious problems of the *oikoumene* by syncretism. In Egypt Ptolemy I translated the cult of the dead Apic calf Osarapis of Memphis into a Greek cult of Sarapis at Alexandria, worshipped in his temple the Sarapeum. The later slogan was 'There is one Zeus Sarapis.' Others accepted fate and resigned themselves to it, arguing the pointlessness of prayer. Men and women needed and looked for *soteria*, salvation, from their human predicament. If the old Homeric gods were not powerful enough to save them (as with their all-too-human behaviour they were seen not to be), men and women had to resort to their own self-sufficiency (*autarkeia*). The Stoics taught people to live in accord with nature (cf. the Roman emperor, Marcus Aurelius; see Barrett, 1958, 70); the Epicureans taught them to be free of supersitition, fear of the gods and of death, and to live untroubled in *ataraxia*. The Cynics stressed the advantages of living free of earthly cares and interests.

In the various cities of this world – Alexandria, Antioch, Pergamum, Sparta, Delos, Halicarnassus, Rhodes, Phaselis, Side and others: cf. 1 Maccabees 15:22f. – lived many Jews. In due course their synagogues would be found alongside the meeting places of other religions (as at Corinth, Delos and elsewhere), but synagogues did not become common until the first century AD. In this environment Christianity also flourished. But the Jewish involvement in the Hellenistic world of Syria and Egypt, at least, is reflected in a certain amount of Jewish literature preserved from this period, some of which has found its way into the pages of the Old Testament and the Apocrypha.

Much of this literature comes from Egypt, where the Hellenistic age saw the rise of a large Jewish population. Egypt had always been a refuge for Jews escaping from famine (Gen.12:10; 42:1f.), or political oppression (1 Kings 11:26–40), or conquest (Jer.42:1 – 43:7). We hear of a Jewish military garrison which had settled on the island of Elephantine in the sixth century BC and whose temple was destroyed by the local Egyptians at the end of the fifth century; we hear of Jewish captives taken from Jerusalem in 312 BC by Ptolemy I, some of whom (according to the Letter of Aristeas) were repatriated in the reign of Ptolemy II Philadelphus; we hear of Jewish synagogues at Alexandria, Crocodilopolis, Arsinoe, Athribis and elsewhere in the reign of Ptolemy III, and Jews in the Egyptian countryside (*chora*) as farmers, artisans, soldiers, policemen, tax-collectors, bank managers and administrators. In the second century BC Onias IV, son of the assassinated high priest Onias III, fled to Egypt and founded a temple at Leontopolis (Tell el-Yehudiya), perhaps for a local Jewish garrison or even as a religious centre for the Jews settled in the Delta region. By the first century AD so many Jews lived in Egypt (Philo said there were over a million) that there was racial tension, disputes about citizenship, rioting, and delegations from Jews and Alexandrian authorities to the emperor Caligula. This, in due course, led to the important decision from the emperor Claudius that the Alexandrians should allow the Jews to live in peace in accordance with their own legal tradition, and that the Jews should not seek membership of the gymnasia and the privileges of citizenship but should enjoy property 'in a city not their own'.

The Ptolemies were Macedonian by origin, and they ruled Egypt from the newly founded city of Alexandria. The administration of the country was conducted by Greek officials, and the records were kept in Greek. In order to prosper under the Ptolemies, the Jews settled in Egypt would need to know Greek, and it is not surprising that the first known Greek translation of the Hebrew scriptures was produced, according to the second-century BC Letter of Aristeas, in Alexandria in the reign of Ptolemy II Philadelphus. The 'Letter' or discourse of 'Aristeas' tells how the Jewish law was translated into Greek in Alexandria by learned translators sent from the high priest in Jerusalem at the request of Ptolemy II, whose librarian Demetrius needed a copy for his library. The author's purpose was apologetic, to demonstrate to the Alexandrian Jews that their Greek scriptures were legitimate and needed no revision, being based on an officially approved Hebrew text from Jerusalem, and translated with the full support and encouragement of the Ptolemaic ruler. The author is also concerned to show that, while the law is 'divine, full of wisdom, faultless' (31), 'made for righteousness' sake, to promote holy meditation and perfecting of character' (144), and designed to distinguish Jews from Gentiles (139), nevertheless

Jewish monotheism is seen as not inconsistent with Greek philosophy (15, 132). The author is clear that Jews can hold their own at an intellectually sophisticated Gentile court, before a benevolent philosopher king, and he describes the translators sent from Jerusalem as men 'of the best character and the highest culture', proficient in both Jewish and Greek literature. The Jewish scriptures, translated into Greek, can now witness to the one God of heaven in the language of educated people. This 'Letter' is largely directed at the Alexandrian Jews, encouraging them to be both Jews and good Alexandrians, and to accept that the two callings are not incompatible.

It is not so clear, however, that the Letter correctly explains the origins of the Greek translation, which are usually thought more likely to lie in the practical needs of the Alexandrian Jewish community than in the wants-list of the king's librarian. Some scholars have thought that behind Aristeas' account lies an attempt to replace an earlier third-century BC Greek translation by a later, more accurate second-century one, or the replacement of an earlier Alexandrian version with one more firmly based on the Jerusalem tradition. Other scholars believe that Aristeas is defending the original Greek translation against an attempted revision. The origins of the Septuagint (so called from the tradition that seventy (*septuaginta*) translators were involved) remain obscure. What has become clear is that what we now know and print as 'the Septuagint', based on such fourth- and fifth-century AD manuscripts as Codex Sinaiticus and Codex Vaticanus, is far from being a single translation datable to one particular year or even decade. Different books and sections of books seem to have been translated at different times and by translators of varying ability and interests. The translators do not always seem to have worked from the Hebrew text now known as the Masoretic Text (MT); the Greek translation of Samuel and Kings, for example, may derive from an earlier, superior Hebrew text, while for whatever reason the Greek translations of Job and Jeremiah are shorter than our Hebrew version. In some books, for example, Esther and Daniel, the Greek translators have added material not found in the Hebrew text. Further, more than one Greek translation of the Hebrew scriptures appeared; in the second century AD there were Jewish revisions of the Greek translation by Rabbi Aquila (*c*. AD 130), who produced a very literal translation; by Theodotion (a Greek convert to Judaism), who corrected the Septuagint by reference to the Hebrew text known to him, and whose version of Daniel replaced the earlier Greek version in nearly all Greek manuscripts; and by Symmachus, who tried to produce an accurate translation in good idiomatic Greek. These Jewish scholars were probably reacting to what had amounted to a Christian take-over of the Jewish Greek scriptures. From the start, New Testament writers like St Paul, writing in Greek to their converts in Rome, Corinth, Bithynia and elsewhere, found it convenient to use the Greek version of the Jewish scriptures, for reasons both practical and theological. Jewish teachers probably needed to distance themselves from a version popular among Christians, and therefore produced versions which conformed more closely to the content of their Hebrew text and translated it more accurately (they might with reason, for example, reject the translation *parthenos*, 'virgin', for the Hebrew '*almah*, 'young woman', at Isa.7:14, because this text had become a proof text for Christian theologians).

The subsequent history of the Septuagint need not concern us, but its earlier history still remains obscure. Kahle (1915) argued that there was no one original, single, official translation of the Hebrew scriptures into Greek, but rather several unofficial versions from different communities side by side among Jews of the dispersion. It took several centuries for an official, authoritative text to emerge in the Christian church. Most scholars, however, prefer to think of a single original for each book or major section of the Septuagint, from which variants developed or to which alternatives were written. But the really important point is that, while the Septuagint may be used (with some care) as evidence for the underlying third- to second-century BC Hebrew text – for the most part otherwise no longer accessible to us – the Greek translation above all reveals how the Hebrew scriptures were interpreted in the Greek-speaking Jewish community of Alexandria in the last three centuries BC. To take a point made long ago by A. Deissmann, 'the Bible whose God is Yahweh is a national Bible; the Bible whose god is *kurios* [Lord] is a universal Bible'. 'The LXX belongs to the history of Old Testament interpretation rather than to the history of the Old Testament text. It can be used as a textual witness only after its own understanding of the OT text has been made clear' (Bertram, *BZAW* 66 (1936), 109). Sebastian Brock makes the interesting point that the Septuagint is the only long oriental religious text to have been translated into Greek. It was not a translation made by Greeks for Greeks; Greeks writing to expound others' religion wrote potted histories (as did Manetho and Berossus), not translations. The Septuagint was translated by Jews and was in effect the Jewish answer to the Greeks' Homer; it indicated (as Aristeas and other Jewish apologists suggest) that the Jews had their ancient learning just as much as the Greeks had theirs. It was translated for educational rather than liturgical purposes; the liturgy would have remained in Hebrew. But as M. Hengel points out, 'The striking thing in the Septuagint was that fundamentally the translators were very little influenced by the Greek spirit. Anyone who was interested in the holy scriptures was no advocate of assimilation' (Hengel, 1974 I.114).

Jewish apologetic concerns are further revealed by other Hellenistic Jewish writings from Alexandria. A Hellenistic Jewish historian called Demetrius, writing in the reign of Ptolemy IV Philopator (221–204 BC) attempted to reconcile historical and chronological difficulties in the biblical texts. Aristobulus (perhaps mentioned in 2 Macc.1:10), living under Ptolemy VI Philometor (181–145 BC) met Greek criticisms of the anthropomorphisms used of God in the Hebrew scriptures, and tried to suggest by his interpretation of the *tôrāh* that Greek philosophy was indebted to Moses and Jewish philosophy. Similarly, Artapanus (third-second century BC) presented Abraham as an astrologer, Joseph as the founder of the Egyptian system of land allotment, and Moses as a polymathic inventor, educator, administrator, philosopher, general and miracle worker; Moses even introduced to the Egyptians their native gods! Moses is presented as the archetypal educated Hellenistic man, and the Egyptians were indebted to him.

The *Sibylline Oracles* take their name from an ancient Greek prophetess called the Sibyl, who in ecstasy uttered oracles to those who sought her advice. Jews of second-century BC Hellenistic Egypt adopted her and turned her into a Jewish prophetess, building her into biblical history as the daughter-in-law of Noah. In time she was adopted by Christian writers, who added many books of Christian oracles to the earlier Jewish collection. For these oracles they used the traditional form of the Greek hexameter verse made famous by Homer and read throughout the Greek world. The second-century BC playwright Ezekiel presented the biblical Exodus story in the form of a Greek tragedy, this being one obvious way to represent the national saga to hellenised Jews (and perhaps to Gentiles as well).

None of these works reached biblical or even apocryphal status, however; they are merely tantalising fragments suggestive of Jewish intellectual effort in Alexandria in the third and second centuries BC. We know that the work of Jesus ben Sira from Jerusalem, written *c.* 180 BC in Hebrew, commonly entitled Ecclesiasticus, was brought to Egypt by the author's grandson in the thirty-eighth year of Ptolemy VIII Euergetes II, i.e., 132 BC, most probably to Alexandria, and translated there 'for those living abroad who wish to gain learning, being prepared in character to live according to the law' (Prologue). In 78/77 BC a Jerusalem priest called Dositheus brought to Alexandria a Greek translation of Esther, an anti-Hellenistic work. Similarly 2 Maccabees, an abridgement of the five-volume work of Jason of Cyrene, may have been sent to Alexandria at some stage from Jerusalem, for it is prefaced by two letters addressed from Jerusalem to Jews in Egypt. The only apocryphal book certainly deriving from Alexandria is the Wisdom of Solomon, from the late first century BC. This book combines biblical history, biblical ideas of rewards and punishment, and the biblical figure of Wisdom with Hellenistic ideas of *philanthropia* and universalism and the contemporary Stoic doctrine of *pneuma*, spirit.

Also from Egypt in the late first century BC were the romance of *Joseph and Aseneth*, which dealt with the problem that arises when a Jewish boy falls in love with a Gentile girl (who solves the problem by embracing Judaism), and the tale of 3 Maccabees, whose theme is racial tension in Alexandria and the threat of persecution: Ptolemy IV Philopator tried to massacre the Jews he had packed into the hippodrome by loosing on them intoxicated elephants. They turned on the Egyptians instead, and the king changed his mind. Serious rioting against the Jews in fact took place in Alexandria in AD 38–39; the Alexandrian Jews rebelled in AD 66 and AD 115–117, and suffered terrible consequences.

Such writings reflect varying attitudes within the Jewish community of Alexandria. On the whole, to judge from this literature, the Alexandrian Jews seem to have been as ready to share in the cultural life of the city as they were anxious to share its political life (a privilege denied them by the Greek community of Alexandria and their Roman rulers). Jews might also be anxious to boast of their contribution to the society in which they lived, and to demonstrate their loyalty to it. However, Jewish writers were also anxious to demonstrate to their fellow Jews, and doubtless to their Gentile neighbours, that the Jewish traditions, laws, history, literature, piety and mores were by no means inferior to those of the Gentiles, and indeed were often superior and of greater antiquity. Jewish monotheism was better than Greek polytheism or native Egyptian idolatry, which the Jew must avoid at all costs. The translator of Ecclesiasticus pointedly notes that he is concerned for those living abroad who wish to keep the law.

Some of the Jewish literature of this Hellenistic period seems to have its background or origin among the Jews of the eastern diaspora, as in the case of the stories of Daniel and his companions (Dan.1-6, the Prayer of Nabonidus, Susanna, Bel and the Dragon), the story of Tobit, and perhaps the Epistle of Jeremiah (Baruch 6), which is a strong polemic against idolatry from the third or second century BC. Whereas Jewish literature originating in Egypt, with its pro-Hellenistic attitudes, does not appear to have been accepted into the canon of scripture, that from Babylon, which emphasises Jewish tradition, appears in both the Hebrew bible and the Apocrypha. These writings are for the most part to be classed as didactic stories, illustrating how a diaspora Jew ought to behave, and how their trust in the law will be vindicated. Daniel 1 shows how the Jewish young men at the Babylonian court can compete favourably in wisdom and understanding with the Babylonian court magicians, in spite of being limited to a diet approved by the Jewish law. Daniel 3 and 6 demonstrate how God will preserve, against terrible persecution, faithful Jews who refuse to bow down to idols or give up prayer to God. Daniel 2, 4 and 5 tell how God

> changes times and seasons;
>> he removes kings and sets up kings;
> he gives wisdom to the wise
>> and knowledge to those who have understanding;
> he reveals deep and mysterious things.

> (Dan.2:21-22)

Gentile kings cannot rule independently of God, and it is the Jewish Daniel who reveals God's purposes to Nebuchadnezzar and Belshazzar. (The story of Nebuchadnezzar's illness in Dan.4 shows similarities with the earlier tradition preserved in the Aramaic Prayer of Nabonidus, fragmentarily preserved at Qumran, according to which a Jewish exorcist, perhaps Daniel, healed Nabonidus after a seven-year illness and ordered him to publicise the matter, giving credit to the Most High God.) The story of Susanna demonstrates how God, by means of the wisdom of Daniel, preserves an innocent woman falsely accused. The stories of Bel and the Dragon mock idolatry, while that of Tobit shows how all things finally work out for good for those who love God – the righteous Tobit recovers his money and his sight, the innocent Sarah, who had lost seven husbands, becomes Tobit's daughter-in-law, and all ends happily ever after. In this short novel, the ideals of Jewish piety are clearly presented, in the words of advice given by Tobit to his son Tobias (Tob.4:5-19).

All these stories reflect the life of a Jew living abroad in reasonable peace and prosperity, though sometimes under threat of persecution and reflect the possibility that Jews might reach positions of importance at a foreign court under a Gentile ruler (who is not always unsympathetically portrayed). They indicate high regard for learning, loyalty to the God of Heaven and avoidance of idolatry, prayer, sabbath observance, keeping the food laws, and practising charity to Jewish brethren. The Jerusalem temple hardly features, though Daniel prays towards Jerusalem, and Tobit recalls how he used to go to Jerusalem for the feasts. Perhaps strangely, circumcision is not mentioned in this literature, though the Babylonians and Persians were uncircumcised, and one might have expected the difference to have been emphasised somewhere in this literature from the eastern diaspora. Otherwise, however, these writings were very much concerned to stress those traditional practices which distinguished Jews from their non-Jewish neighbours, and the teaching is done by reference to the example of such wise and righteous people as Daniel, Susanna, Tobit, or to the arrogance of kings and the folly of idol-worshippers.

This leaves a large amount of literature from this period which was probably written in Jerusalem or Judah, though it is sometimes impossible to be certain: Ecclesiastes (third century BC), Ecclesiasticus (early second century BC), Judith (mid-second century BC?), 1 Enoch (third-second century BC), 1 Maccabees and 2 Maccabees (?) (late second-early first century BC), 1 Esdras 3–4 (probably a Judaised folk-tale from the late Persian or early Hellenistic period added to the second-century BC book 1 Esdras, which is a Greek translation of parts of Ezra-Nehemiah). Similarly, the Prayer of Azariah and the Song of the Three Young Men may also be third-century BC pieces, later added to Daniel 3. Daniel 7–12 certainly belong to the mid-second century BC, as do probably the non-biblical Book of Jubilees (a rewriting of the patriarchal stories from Gen.1 – Exod.14) and the history of Eupolemus, of which only fragments exist. Some of this material will be considered in the context of the Maccabaean revolt in the next chapter; here we will focus on Ecclesiastes, Ecclesiasticus and 1 Enoch as literature deriving from Judah or Jerusalem before the Maccabaean revolt.

From the third century BC comes the book Ecclesiastes, and probably, though not certainly, the very different 1 Enoch 1–36, 72–82. Ecclesiastes is dated to third-century BC Ptolemaic Judah partly because its vocabulary includes Persian words which have passed into the language (e.g. *pardes*, 'garden', 2:5; *pithgam*, 'edict', 8:11) and Aramaisms and later Hebrew expressions, but also because the descriptions of society in 5:8, 10:5, and 10:20 fit the Ptolemaic period well:

> If you see in a province the poor oppressed and justice and right violently taken away, do not be amazed at the matter; for the high official is watched by a higher, and there are yet higher ones over them. But in all, a king is an advantage to a land with cultivated fields.

> There is an evil which I have seen under the sun, as it were an error proceeding from the ruler: folly is set in many high places, and the rich sit in a low place. I have seen slaves on horses, and princes walking on foot like slaves.

> Even in your thought, do not curse the king,
>   nor in your bedchamber curse the rich;

for a bird of the air will carry your voice,
 or some winged creature tell the matter.

It is clear that Ecclesiastes is known to the early second-century BC Ben Sira (cf. Eccles.3:1; Ecclus.4:20). The author is individualistic, fatalistic, resigned, and critical. It is not easy to summarise his wide-ranging message, but the gist of it might run as follows: God is creator (12:1), universal and real, but remote, sovereign but concealed, arbitrary (2:26; 9:1) and impossible to understand (3:11; 7:14). Man should say little and fear him (5:2,3,7). Life is brief, purposeless, and ends in oblivion; 'the fate of the sons of men and the fate of beasts is the same; as one dies, so dies the other. They all have the same breath, and man has no advantage over the beasts' (3:19). One should not expect to find justice or reason in things. Even wisdom has its limitations; it is better than strength or weapons (9:16; 9:18), and better than folly (10:12) – or is it? 'How the wise man dies just like the fool!' (2:12–17). 'In much wisdom is much vexation, and he who increases knowledge increases sorrow' (1:18). Wisdom is a good, God-given thing, but it is still subject to time and chance. It does not always win bread, but Ecclesiastes values it highly, for it is his tradition (12:9). More positively, Ecclesiastes urges his readers to avoid self-deception, and find enjoyment in the experience of living (5:19). He does not counsel hedonism, but temperate behaviour; it is folly to be wicked, and wickedness is man's fault, not God's.

Ecclesiastes, like the modern humanist, appeals to an educated, upper-class audience which could enjoy the luxuries of wealth and had leisure for contemplation. His environment was a wealthy one, and his virtues the aristocratic ones of prudence, restraint and loyalty. His resigned pessimism is of a piece with this; as G.F. Moore observed, 'It is not those people whose life seems to us most intolerable that are most discontented with life: despair is a child of the imagination and pessimism has always been a disease of the well-to-do, or at least the comfortably well off.' Ecclesiastes is concerned with the individual and the problems of human existence before God, with the questions of fate, time and chance; he is hardly concerned at all with the nation and its religious tradition. It has often been suggested that he drew indirectly on Greek writers such as Hesiod and Theognis, or that he had something in common with the Stoic fatalism or Epicurean tranquillity of mind (*ataraxia*) and reflected something of the *Zeitgeist* of the Hellenistic age, with its emphasis on fate (*tyche*), but though there are parallels, dependency on Greek thought, however indirect, is less likely than that the Hebrew and the Greek authors were expressing in their own ways a common human experience.

Ecclesiastes is one of a number of writings that adopted King Solomon as its honorary author. Proverbs, the Song of Songs, the first-century BC Psalms of Solomon and the Wisdom of Solomon, and the first- or second-century AD Odes of Solomon also witness to this tradition. In Jewish Hellenistic writers such as Aristobulus and Josephus (*Ant*.8.44) Solomon could be presented as a philosopher, and as skilled in medicine and other arts; the aim was to show that the Jewish record in philosophy and medicine was no less distinguished than the Greek. Within the Palestinian Jewish tradition, however, Solomon was popularly known for his wisdom, his wealth, his love of women (as well as for his temple-building), and Ecclesiastes perhaps chose Solomon as the fictive author 'because the figure of the wisest and richest king formed an effective foil for his basic thesis of the vanity of human existence' (M. Hengel 1974, 130); perhaps also in Solomon could be seen a figure like that presented in the intellectually minded Ptolemy II Philadelphus of the Letter of Aristeas.

One of the most interesting figures of this period is a writer whose name and background (almost uniquely in the Hebrew scriptures) is known to us: Jesus, son of Sira, son of Eliezer, of Jerusalem (Ecclus.50:27) (or possibly, 'son of Eliezer, son of Sira'). In a preface, his grandson tells us he came to Egypt in the thirty-eighth year of Ptolemy Euergetes (Ptolemy VIII, 170–116 BC), that is, 132 BC, and published a Greek translation of the book 'for those living abroad who wished to gain learning, being prepared in character to live according to the law'. The grandfather therefore may have flourished about the beginning of the second century BC, and his description of the high priest Simon, son of Onias (ch.50), probably refers to Josephus' Simon II, whose son Onias III was killed in the reign of Antiochus IV (Jos.*Ant.*XII.4.10 (224); XII.5.1 (239); 2 Macc.4:33–38). Jesus ben Sira, then, perhaps wrote *c.* 180 BC. He describes himself as an experienced scribe and counsellor, a student of wisdom, and a teacher with his school (51:13–30), who will pour out teaching like prophecy for the benefit of future generations. He has a high regard for the law, which fills men with wisdom (24:25), and can even be identified with the figure of Wisdom (24:1–29). He is proud of the famous men of Israel's history, whose roll-call (chs.44–49) he follows with a magnificent word picture of Simon, the high priest, officiating at the temple, blessing his people (ch.50). Here is a writer who stands in the tradition of the wise, the prophets, and the priests of Israel, and can weave this threefold cord into one. It is almost impossible to summarise his teachings, which range widely over practical conduct in public and private affairs and theological speculation and instruction on such matters as the freedom of human will (15:11–20) (Josephus later distinguished the Pharisees, Sadducees and Essenes by their attitude to this problem) and the problems of theodicy (40:1 – 41:4), man's position before God (16:24 – 18:14), and God's relationship to creation (42:15 – 43:33). Ben Sira understands very well the ambivalence in life and its decisions: there are two sides to most things, including lending (29:1–13), the medical profession (38:1–15), and death (42:1–4); indeed, there is a general uncertainty in all things (11:2–6).

Basically, however, Ben Sira is concerned with wisdom. He begins with wisdom as created before all things and given by God to those who love him, and he ends with a statement of his own quest for wisdom and his readiness to teach it. His instruction is interspersed with poems in praise of wisdom (e.g., 4:11–19; 6:18–37; 14:20 – 15:8), culminating in the description of the scribe as wise man *par excellence* (38:24 – 39:11). Wisdom is the fear of the Lord and it brings gladness, joy and satisfaction, much as the study of the law does in Psalm 119. What is new in Ben Sira is that wisdom now includes the *tôrāh*. The very heart of the book is chapter 24, in which the Jewish figure of Lady Wisdom (cf.

Prov.8:22–31) introduces herself, describes her career, her establishment in Jerusalem and its temple, and her beauty, and issues her invitation:

> 'I came forth from the mouth of the Most High,
>    and covered the earth like a mist.
> I dwelt in high places,
>    and my throne was in a pillar of cloud . . .
>
> Then the Creator of all things gave me a commandment,
>    and the one who created me assigned a place for my tent.
> And he said, "Make your dwelling in Jacob,
>    and in Israel receive your inheritance."
> From eternity, in the beginning, he created me,
>    and for eternity I shall not cease to exist.
> In the holy tabernacle I ministered before him,
>    and so I was established in Zion . . .
>
> I grew tall like a cedar in Lebanon,
>    and like a cypress on the heights of Hermon . . .
> Like a vine I caused loveliness to bud,
>    and my blossom became glorious and abundant fruit.
>
> Come to me, you who desire me,
>    and eat your fill of my produce.
> For the remembrance of me is sweeter than honey,
>    and my inheritance sweeter than the honeycomb.
> Those who eat me will hunger for more,
>    and those who drink me will thirst for more.
> Whoever obeys me will not be put to shame,
>    and those who work with my help will not sin.'

Ben Sira goes on to identify the Wisdom figure with 'the book of the covenant of the Most High God, the law which Moses commanded us as an inheritance for the congregations of Jacob'. Ben Sira thus locates the *tôrāh* in the wider concept of wisdom; *tôrāh* is part of the development of God's wisdom. This is a remarkable theological synthesis. Ben Sira has neatly married two major strands of Israelite theology, *tôrāh* and wisdom, following the lead of the Deuteronomist in the sixth century BC, who also understood the connection:

> 'Behold, I have taught you statutes and ordinances, as the LORD my God commanded me, that you should do them in the land which you are entering to take possession of it. Keep them and do them; for that will be your wisdom and your understanding in the sight of the peoples, who, when they hear all these statutes, will say, "Surely this great nation is a wise and understanding people."'

> (Deut.4:5–6)

It has sometimes been suggested that Ben Sira was a religious conservative reacting against the hellenising tendencies of his days and presenting a 'controversy with Hellenic liberalism' (Hengel). Scholars have seen Ecclesiasticus 3:21–24 as polemic against Hellenistic philosophical speculation, and 41:8–9 as polemic against hellenising apostasy; but the speculation may have been apocalyptic, and apostasy was nothing new in Israel. Hengel believes that Ben Sira's view of creation has points in common with the Stoic view – cf. 43:26f.:

> ... by his word all things hold together.
> Though we speak much we cannot reach the end,
>   and the sum of our words is: 'He is the all.'

– and that he shared with the Stoics the idea that 'the whole world is a single cosmos permeated and shaped by an eternal power, deity'. But in fact there is little to compel the idea either that Ben Sira shares some Hellenistic ideas or that he opposes others. He seems totally traditional in his prayer for Jerusalem (36:1–17), his praise of Israel's heroes (chs.44–49), his encomium of the high priest Simon (ch.50), and his emphasis on wisdom and law (ch.24). The Greek world is nowhere expressly mentioned; Ben Sira seems virtually unconscious of it. The problems of the Maccabaean period had not yet arrived.

The book known as 1 Enoch does not appear in the Hebrew scriptures, but the figure of Enoch does (Gen.5:18–24), and it is particularly interesting that this otherwise barely known figure is picked out for mention in Ecclesiasticus 44:16 and 49:14, which suggests that for some reason he had become important. The Book of Jubilees, a mid-second-century BC retelling of the stories of Genesis 10 – Exodus 14, says of Enoch that

> he was the first among men born on earth to learn to write and to acquire knowledge and wisdom; and he wrote down in a book details about the signs of heaven, according to the order of their several months... and he bore witness to the Watchers, who had sinned with the daughters of men ...

This sounds like a reference to two sections of the book 1 Enoch, namely the 'Astronomical book' (1 Enoch 72–82), and 'The book of the Watchers' (1 Enoch 1–36), of which fragmentary Aramaic texts, datable on palaeographic grounds to the early second century BC, were found in Cave 4 at Qumran. In short, it seems possible that these sections of 1 Enoch existed as early as the end of the third century BC. If so, new light is thrown on the extent of astronomical knowledge and calendric practice and on the intellectual interests and concerns of third-century BC Judah. As in the Book of Jubilees, the author describes a 364-day solar calendar – of 12 months of 30 days with 4 intercalated days – in contrast to the lunar calendar; this lies behind a calendrical dispute of later times between the Qumran community and the Jerusalem community. The 'Book of the Watchers' uses the story of Genesis 6:1–4 to tell how evil entered the world; the angels pleaded with God for mankind (1 Enoch 8). God arranged to save Noah, but to bind and punish the wicked angels and destroy the giants which resulted from the angels' intercourse with the daughters of men, and so to renew the earth. The figure of Enoch now appears in the narrative, and when he announces the coming punishment, the guilty angels (i.e., the 'Watchers') ask for his intercession on their behalf. Enoch went away to Galilee and saw a vision that he should reprove the Watchers; he returns to them and recounts his ascent to the heavenly temple of ice and fire, and reports God's decision: 'You will not have peace'. There follow two descriptions of Enoch's tour of the universe (17–19; 20–36) to see the place of punishment: the reference to 'the river of fire whose fire flows like water and pours out into the great sea which is towards the west' (17:5) has reminded scholars of the Greek Puriphlegethon in western Greece, near the traditional entrance to the underworld. The second journey, however, takes Enoch east to Paradise, and reveals considerable knowledge of the geography of the near east as well as of the topography and environs of Jerusalem.

What this material reveals is a third-century BC Jewish writer with a remarkably wide range of knowledge and interests, and perhaps a deep knowledge of Jewish tradition now otherwise lost to us. That the writer should be concerned with the origins of evil, and should develop a biblical myth to explain it, or that he should describe a visionary ascent to heaven clearly owing much to Ezekiel 1, is not surprising. We see here how the earlier biblical literature and traditions were being re-used and reinterpreted, as happens also in Ecclesiasticus 44–49, Daniel 9 and elsewhere. But the extent of the author's interests in astronomy, the calendar, meteorology, technology, geography and other subjects perhaps shows the effect of the opening up of the east by Alexander's campaigns and the results of the development of science by the Hellenistic savants – and possibly also the beginnings of Jewish awareness of Greek literature. Such speculative material suggests an origin among educated people; if the author or authors belonged to the priestly and scribal circles of men like Ben Sira, his (or their) mental horizons were clearly not limited to the traditional concerns of such groups.

## Bibliography

M. Barker, *The lost prophet: the book of Enoch and its influence on Christianity* (London: SPCK, 1988)

J.R. Bartlett, *Jews in the Hellenistic world: Josephus, Aristeas, The Sibylline Oracles, Eupolemus* (Cambridge Commentaries on writings of the Jewish and Christian world 200 BC to AD 200, Ii) Cambridge: Cambridge University Press, 1985)

E. Bickerman, *From Ezra to the last of the Maccabees* (New York: Schocken Books, 1962)

E.J. Bickerman, *The Jews in the Greek age* (Cambridge, Mass.: Harvard University Press, 1988)

L.H. Brockington, *A critical introduction to the Apocrypha* (London: Duckworth, 1961)

J. Crenshaw, *Old Testament wisdom: an introduction* (London: SCM Press 1982)

R. Gordis, *Koheleth: the man and his world* (New York: Schocken Books, 1968)

M. Hadas, *Hellenistic culture: fusion and diffusion* (New York: W.W. Norton, 1959)

P.D. Hanson (ed.), *Visionaries and their apocalypses* (Issues of Religion and Theology 2) (London: SPCK; Philadelphia: Fortress Press, 1983)

M. Hengel, *Judaism and Hellenism* I, II (London: SCM Press, 1974)

M. Hengel, *Jews, Greeks and barbarians*, (London: SCM Press, 1980)

H. Jagersma, *A history of Israel from Alexander the Great to Bar Kochba* (London: SCM Press, 1985)

S. Jellicoe, *The Septuagint and modern study* (Oxford: Clarendon Press, 1968)

B.M. Metzger, *An introduction to the Apocrypha* (New York: Oxford University Press, 1957)

A. Momigliano, *Alien wisdom: the limits of hellenization* (Cambridge: Cambridge University Press, 1975)

G.W.E. Nickelsburg, *Jewish literature between the Bible and the Mishnah* (London: SCM Press, 1981)

R.E. Murphy, *Wisdom literature: Job, Proverbs, Ruth, Canticles, Ecclesiastes, Esther* (The Forms of Old Testament Literature 13) (Grand Rapids: Eerdmans, 1981)

G. von Rad, *Wisdom in Israel* (London: SCM Press, 1972)

M.E. Stone, *Scriptures, sects and visions: a profile of Judaism from Ezra to the Jewish revolts* (Oxford: Blackwell, 1982)

F.W. Walbank, *The Hellenistic world* (London: Fontana, 1981)

# 10 A Kingdom once again

As we have seen in the previous chapter, it is not easy to assess the extent of Hellenistic influence upon the intellectual life of the Jewish people. It seems likely that it was greatest in the Alexandrian community, and least evident in the Babylonian diaspora. How influential Hellenism was in Judah is a moot point. There is certainly evidence that Greek trade and artefacts had been known in Palestine well before Alexander the Great, but how far the life-style of cities like Marisa or Scythopolis influenced Jews in Jerusalem is less clear, at least before the *akme* – the peak – of Hellenism which 2 Maccabees 4:13 dates to the time of the high priest Jason in about 175 BC. The evidence of Ecclesiasticus, *c.* 180 BC, does not suggest that a liberalising Hellenism had had any great effect upon Jerusalem, nor does the evidence of Josephus, who records that in 197 BC Antiochus III decreed that the Jews could govern themselves in accordance with their traditional laws, giving them an allowance for various sacrifices and for temple repairs, and reinforcing the Jewish prohibition of the entry of foreigners to the temple enclosure (*Ant.* XII.3.3 (138–46) ).

However, there is no denying that Judah was affected politically by the new Hellenistic empire of Alexander and his successors. From 320 to 200 BC Judah was under the control of the Ptolemaic dynasty in Alexandria; from 200 to 142 BC it was under the progressively weakening control of the Seleucid dynasty in Antioch and from 142 to 63 BC it developed its own short-lived Hasmonaean dynasty, which, though utterly nationalistic in outlook, nevertheless showed many signs of imitating the habits of the other Hellenistic kingdoms. It is not surprising that much of the surviving Palestinian-Jewish literature of this period either focuses on the political turmoil or comes from those who opted out of the politics of Jerusalem and withdrew to the wilderness to practise an ascetic life of prayer, study and physical labour in their new community.

Politically, the Ptolemaic and Seleucid periods really belong together as the background to the Maccabaean rebellion of the mid-second century BC and the rise of the Hasmonaean kingdom. Historically, the land of the ancient kingdoms of Judah and Israel has had political independence only when both Syria and Egypt have been weak. At other times, the land between these two powers has been subject to whichever was dominant or has suffered as the pawn in the middle. At the end of the Late Bronze Age, the land of Canaan was subject to declining Egyptian control. The monarchies of Judah and Israel survived pressure from Syria because Syria was threatened by the more powerful Assyrian and then

Babylonian empires, but Israel herself fell to Assyria in 722 BC, and Judah to Babylon in 597 BC. The Persians took over Samaria and Judah from Babylon in 539 BC, and immediately went on to capture Egypt, but their hold on Egypt was never very secure, and the fifth century showed Egypt's determination to be free. When Alexander's empire was divided among his successors, Ptolemy I took Egypt and moved swiftly to annex Palestine and southern Syria, while his fellow generals Seleucus and Lysimachus were struggling to defeat Antigonus Monophthalmus in Turkey. A century later, Antiochus III 'the Great' defeated Ptolemy V Epiphanes at Paneion and replaced Ptolemy as ruler of Coele-Syria and Phoenicia, together with Samaria and Judah. The days of the Seleucid empire, however, were already numbered. Seleucus I had ruled an empire stretching from the Indus valley and Bactria in the east to Cilicia in the west; in 250 BC Bactria seceded to become an autonomous kingdom, followed by Parthia in 247 BC, and though Antiochus III regained Parthia his successors were not able to hold it. Under pressure in the east, the Seleucids looked west to the Aegean and beyond, but their prospects there were limited by the creation of the kingdom of Pergamum, the growing maritime power of Rhodes, the arrival of the Galatians in central Anatolia, and at the beginning of the second century the arrival in Greece of the Romans, who expelled Antiochus III from Greece and the Aegean and imposed upon him the crushing terms of the Peace of Apamea in 188 BC. The Seleucids were thus effectively limited to Syria, Cilicia, and Mesopotamia; Antiochus IV's attempt to expand into Egypt in 169–168 BC was firmly prevented by the Romans.

The Seleucid take-over of Judah after the battle of Paneion in 200 BC was probably welcomed by many in Jerusalem, especially as Antiochus made tax concessions to the clergy and promised that the Jews could live in accordance with their ancestral laws. What changed the situation was the Seleucid need for money, following the Roman fine of 15,000 talents imposed by the Treaty of Apamea, and the demand by one section of the Jewish population for the hellenising of Jerusalem. In 175 BC Seleucus IV's minister Heliodorus attempted to seize the deposits held in the Jerusalem temple; by 171 BC rivals for the Jerusalem high priesthood, Jason and Menelaus, were outbidding one another to obtain the high-priestly office for themselves and the privilege of a Hellenistic constitution for Jerusalem. Jerusalem would thus acquire a new status, perhaps a new name, a new citizen body, and a gymnasium where the young citizens might train. In future Jerusalem could send its representatives to the games at Tyre (2 Macc. 4:18–20), and the Seleucid king could be received with the pomp and ceremony due to a Hellenistic monarch (2 Macc. 4:21–22). The king would benefit both by the increased tribute and by the formal loyalty of an important city on the borders of his empire.

Antiochus probably saw the internal opposition to his appointment of Menelaus (not of high-priestly descent) to the high priesthood as rebellion against his authority, and his resultant firm measures and raid on the temple on his return from his Egyptian campaign in 169 or 168 BC caused resentment and escalation of the opposition. His attempt to enforce hellenisation in religious matters led to an outbreak of violence led by the Maccabaean family, and an increasing Seleucid presence in Judah. In 164 BC the Maccabees forcibly seized the temple area in the face of a Seleucid garrison in Jerusalem, and in the same month Antiochus died. Negotiations, and the restoration of the Jews' right to live under Jewish (not Greek) law, however, did not halt the violence, which was becoming a struggle for total political independence. The first rebel leader, Judas, was killed in 160 BC, the hellenising high priest Alcimus died one year later, and the Seleucid general Bacchides, having effectively garrisoned Judah, departed, leaving Judas' brother Jonathan exercising some informal rule. The arrival of the Seleucid pretender Alexander Balas in 152 BC opened a new phase of activity. Balas gained Jonathan's support by offering him the high priesthood (which Jonathan accepted, though he had no hereditary right to it). On the death of Balas (and also of Ptolemy VI of Egypt) in 145 BC, Jonathan switched to supporting the rightful Seleucid heir, Demetrius II, but soon changed allegiance to the young Antiochus VI and his regent Tryphon. Tryphon, however, seeing Jonathan as a danger, captured and killed him, whereupon Jonathan's older brother Simon took over, established a new constitution for an independent Judah, and so paved the way for his son, John Hyrcanus (134–104 BC), and his successors – the Hasmonaean dynasty – who ruled Judah until Pompey took Syria and Palestine for Rome in 63 BC.

The Hasmonaean period saw the final emancipation of Judah from Seleucid rule, the expansion of Judah's territory at the expense of her neighbours, the development of the Maccabaean military leadership into a monarchy, and the growing divisions in Judah between those who accepted the combination in one figure of high-priesthood and monarchy and those who did not. Freedom from Seleucid control came when Antiochus VII was killed campaigning against the Parthians in 129 BC. This allowed John Hyrcanus to continue the expansion of Judah already begun under Jonathan (161–142 BC), who had added one town (Akkaron) from the coastal eparchy (Paralia) to the west, and three towns (Lydda, Aphaerema, and Ramathaim; 1 Macc. 11:34) from the borders of Samaria to the north. Simon had annexed Gazara and the port of Joppa, thus giving the Jews access to the coast. From Joppa, under Hyrcanus (134–104 BC) and Jannaeus (103–76 BC), Jewish control expanded along the coast, reaching Dor in the north (though not Ptolemais), and Gaza, Raphia, and Rhinocorura to the south. Inland, Hyrcanus took Samaria, and his successor Aristobulus (104–103 BC) took Galilee, and Ituraea beyond. In the south, Hyrcanus invaded and Judaised, by enforced circumcision, Idumaea, and threatened to cut off Nabataean access to the sea at Gaza, which was subsequently taken by Jannaeus. In Transjordan, Hyrcanus and Jannaeus extended Judah's control to Galaaditis and Gaulanitis in the north, and Moabitis in the south, though east of the Jordan from Petra to Damascus the Nabataeans remained a serious threat. Jannaeus built forts at Alexandrium, Hyrcania, Masada and Machaerus, partly to protect his eastern and southern borders, but partly also to provide secure retreats for himself and his family in time of trouble.

Simon had been appointed in 142 BC as high priest, military commander (*strategos*) and civil ruler (ethnarch), and his son John Hyrcanus succeeded him in these offices in 134 BC. Josephus says that Hyrcanus' son Aristobulus I (104–103 BC) was the first to call himself king, but the evidence of coins and of Strabo suggests that Jannaeus was the first to take the title. Some of Jannaeus' coins bear a bilingual inscription, 'Jonathan the king' (Hebrew), and 'King Alexander' (Greek). His wife Salome succeeded him; Josephus calls her queen, but as a woman she could not be high priest, and she appointed her son Hyrcanus to that office. When she died, in 67 BC, Hyrcanus resigned the royal and high-priestly offices to his younger brother Aristobulus, but in 63 BC Pompey the Great removed Aristobulus and left Hyrcanus as high priest, but not as king.

The Hasmonaean attempt to combine the two offices in one person had not been popular. Judas Maccabaeus' brother Jonathan had no hereditary right to the office, which he accepted at the hands of Alexander Balas, a pretender to the Seleucid throne, in 152 BC (his acceptance may have caused the withdrawal of some of his opponents to Qumran, to found a community in opposition to the now unlawful regime at Jerusalem). John Hyrcanus was advised by the Pharisees to give up the high priesthood, and Jannaeus, officiating as high priest at the feast of Tabernacles, was pelted by his people with citrons. He responded with a massacre, which led to civil war and the crucifixion of eight hundred of his opponents. Hyrcanus II failed as a king and was left as high priest, but his ambitious nephew Antigonus later incapacitated Hyrcanus for this office by having his ears cut off.

The Hasmonaean monarchy came to an end when Pompey the Great took Syria for Rome in 63 BC, and moved into Judah to settle the power struggle between Hyrcanus (supported by Aretas of Nabataea and Antipater of Idumaea) and his brother Aristobulus. The Hasmonaean monarchy was weak for a number of reasons: the conquered territories of Samaria, Idumaea, Ituraea, and the Greek towns of the coast and of Transjordan, could not be easily held in spite of mercenary troops, and Rome was waiting in the wings; there were rivalries within the ruling family; and its assumption of the high-priestly office was unpopular (especially with the Pharisees and Qumran community). John Hyrcanus was at first supported by the Pharisees, a movement which may have originated among the group called the Hasidim (Hasidaeans, 1 Macc. 2:42; 7:13; 2 Macc. 14:16), 'the loyal ones', who emerged at the time of the Maccabaean rebellion, probably from among the scribal class. The Hasidim began as political activists, ready to do battle for the law (1 Macc. 2:42), and concerned that the high priest should belong to the house of Aaron (1 Macc. 7:13). It was probably this that was the root of the Pharisees' opposition to the Hasmonaean unlawful assumption of high-priestly office. The Pharisees ('separatists') became a pietist party, separating themselves from all uncleanness, and from the uneducated 'people of the land' who might be less than strict about keeping the laws of ritual purity relating to food and personal behaviour. They were, however, highly influential with the people, and on his deathbed Hyrcanus advised his wife Salome to begin her rule by making peace with the Pharisees, which she did so successfully that they became, according to Josephus, the real rulers of the state (*BJ* I. 111). Another group was that of the Sadducees ('Zadokites'?), who were probably the priestly aristocrats of

Jerusalem, more willing to compromise with the Hellenistic way of life and with foreign rulers such as the Romans than were the Pharisees. They do not appear to have bequeathed any writings to posterity.

A further party which became important in the Hasmonaean period was the sect Josephus called the Essenes. His description of them is so strongly reminiscent of the sectarians from Qumran known to us from their own writings and from the reference to them in the elder Pliny's *Historia Naturalis* V.17 that some link between the people of Qumran and the wider sect of the Essenes seems certain. The Qumran community seems to have settled at Qumran in the mid-second century, and to have lived there until an earthquake in 31 BC disrupted their life and caused a hiatus in occupation. They returned and rebuilt the site early in the first century AD and occupied it until the community was attacked and destroyed by the Romans in AD 68. Apart from Qumran, the Essenes are not well known; Josephus says that 'many of them dwell in every city' (*BJ* II. 8.4 (124) ). The name 'Essene' may derive from an Aramaic word meaning 'holy', and, like the Pharisees, the Essenes probably aimed at holy lives lived at some remove from those of ordinary people; they seem to have had a strong sense of community, separating themselves into close-knit groups in the towns (these Essenes are perhaps those who, according to Josephus, practised marriage) and into something more like a monastic order at Qumran. However, they do appear to have been totally secluded from the political world, for Josephus credits them with an aptitude for prophecy, and refers to an Essene called Judas who prophesied the death of Antigonus at Strato's Tower (*BJ* I.3.5 (78–80)), an Essene called Menahem who prophesied the length and nature of Herod's reign (*Ant.*XV.10.5 (373)), and another called Simon who prophesied the length of Archelaus' reign (*BJ* II.7.3 (113)).

It is not surprising that this Hasmonaean period, with its nationalistic politics and religious enthusiasms, should have produced a great deal of literature. Not all of this literature is well known, because much of it does not appear in the Hebrew scriptures or the Apocrypha. The best-known work from the Maccabaean-Hasmonaean period is probably the book of Daniel. Daniel 7–12 clearly refers to the events of the third-second centuries BC, culminating in the years 167–164 BC. These chapters are in fact our earliest and most important historical source for the background to and the beginnings of the Maccabaean struggle. They are presented as prophecy of what is to come, by which the author is saying that these events are part of God's ordained plan of what must happen before the expected final vindication of Israel and the coming rule of God. The end will arise directly out of the appalling events of the reign of Antiochus IV. Daniel 7–12 consists of four vision accounts, all sharing the same format. A date is given (the first and third years of Belshazzar, the first year of Darius the Mede, the third year of Cyrus the Persian); Daniel sees a vision, which he describes (though in the third account, the vision is replaced by reference to a text from the prophet Jeremiah); an angelic figure explains the vision; Daniel's reaction of alarm or dismay (7:28; 8:27) or a further query (12:6) closes the account. The visions all focus on the events of the reign of Antiochus IV. In the first, Daniel sees four terrible animals representing world empires (the Babylonians, the Medes, the Persians, and the empire of Alexander the Great). The worst is the last one, its rulers being represented by horns, of which the worst is again the last: 'in this horn were eyes like the eyes of a man, and a mouth speaking proud things' (7:8). The last beast is slain and destroyed, and 'one like a son of man' comes before the Ancient of Days and is given everlasting dominion over all peoples, nations and languages. After further details about the fourth beast and the final horn, it is explained that after the destruction of the eleventh horn, dominion shall be given to 'the people of the saints of the Most High' (7:27), that is, to the people of Israel.

In the second vision, Daniel sees a two-horned ram (the Medes and the Persians) trampled down by a he-goat with four conspicuous horns (Alexander and his successors), out of which came a little horn which 'grew exceedingly great toward the south, toward the east, and toward the glorious land. It grew great, even to the host heaven . . . it magnified itself, even up to the Prince of the host; and the continual burnt offering was taken away from him, and the place of his sanctuary was overthrown' (8:10f.). An angel announces that it will be 2,300 evenings and mornings (i.e., 1,150 days) before the sanctuary is restored.

The third account provides an exegesis of the 70 years of Babylonian exile described in Jeremiah 25:11f. and 29:10. Daniel 9:24–37 turns these 70 years into 70 weeks of years (i.e., 490 years); from the announcement of the restoration of Jerusalem to the coming of an anointed one, a prince (Cyrus? cf. Isa. 45:1), would be 7 weeks (49 years); the next 62 weeks (434 years) would see Jerusalem rebuilt with squares and a moat, but not at peace; and the last week (7 years) would see the cutting off of the anointed one (the death of Onias the high priest, 2 Macc. 4:34?) and the destruction of the city and its sanctuary, with the cessation of sacrifice and offering for 3½ years (167–164 BC).

The fourth and last account is the longest and most complex. Daniel sees a dramatic angelic figure, who reveals to Daniel in considerable detail the history of Palestine under the Ptolemies and Seleucids (Dan. 11:2–21), and in even greater detail the career of Antiochus IV (Dan. 11:21–39), up to the profanation of the temple, the setting up of the 'abomination that makes desolate' (probably a pagan altar on the Jewish altar of burnt offering), and the beginning of the Macabbaean resistance. So far the author gives an accurate and detailed account of the course of events. From this point on, however, he tries to forecast the nature of the end of Antiochus IV, and does not seem to know that Antiochus IV died on campaign in Persia in December 164 BC. The angel ends his words with the prediction of an unprecedented time of trouble, and the promise of the deliverance of the people; many, including the wise (among whom the author of Daniel might have counted himself), would be raised from death to everlasting life, others to shame and everlasting contempt. The vision ends, and Daniel asks 'How long shall it be till the end of these wonders?', and is told, 'a time, two times, and half a time'. A further addition says that there shall be 1290 days from the time that the abomination of desolation is set up (i.e., 15 Kislev 167 BC, 1 Macc. 2:54), which is just over the 3½ years indicated by a 'a time, two times, and half a time'. A further note suggests that a span of 1335 days is expected, adding another 45 days to the previous total. The earlier reference (8:13) gave 1150 days, i.e., almost exactly 3 years, for the period of desolation, which was accurate. This might suggest that the author saw the restoration of the sanctuary by the Maccabaeans in December 164 BC, but that the expected end had not yet come and the date therefore had to be revised.

These chapters in Daniel seem to be a contemporary record of events in Judah and Jerusalem under Antiochus IV, but it is important to note that here, as ever, events are seen in a particular light. The author had his own interpretation of events (or at least the interpretation of the group to which he belonged) to put upon them. He believes that the kingdoms and empires of the world will be ultimately swept away before the everlasting dominion which shall not pass away, the kingdom which shall not be destroyed, which will be given to the one like a son of man, a figure which is the heavenly representative of Israel. The present war is being fought out in heaven as well as on earth; Persia, Greece and Israel all have their angelic princes doing battle on their behalf (10:13, 20). Antiochus IV is above all 'a contemptible person to whom royal majesty has not been given' (11:21), whose mouth speaks 'great things' (7:13,20), who 'shall speak words against the Most High' (7:25), who grew great 'even to the host of heaven, and some of the host of the stars it cast down to the ground, and trampled upon them. It magnified itself, even up to the Prince of the host' (8:10f.); 'he shall exalt himself and magnify himself above every god, and shall speak astonishing things against the God of gods' (11:36). Antiochus' sin is pride and arrogance (cf. 2 Macc. 9:4, 8, 12), but the blame for Israel's troubles was not entirely his; Daniel knows that within Israel there were differing attitudes. 'He shall seduce with flattery those who violate the covenant' (Daniel may be referring to the hellenising party of Jason and Menelaus) 'but the people who know their God shall stand firm and take action. And those among the people who are wise (cf. 12:3) shall make many understand, though they shall fall by sword and flame, by captivity and plunder, for some days. When they fall, they shall receive a little help' (Daniel may be referring to the Maccabees by this phrase) (Dan 11:32–34). The author of Daniel seems to align himself with 'the wise', the *maskilim*, who at the resurrection 'shall shine like the brightness of the firmament', but exactly who these are is a difficult question. The author may be ranging himself with people like Jesus ben Sira, whose book of wisdom was probably already in circulation, and with people like the Hasidaeans and scribes of 1 Maccabees 7:12, who trusted in the Aaronite priesthood and sought peace. He does not, at all events, speak directly of a hellenising party or appear to blame them for everything, or to give full support to the nationalist Maccabees; he does not share the emphasis of the author of 1 Maccabees, who blamed lawless men from Israel who covenanted with the Gentiles, and supported the ancestors of the Hasmonaeans, the Maccabees, to the hilt. The author of Daniel thinks of the righteous as the core of Israel, fighting a spiritual battle against the wickedness of a world ruler like Antiochus IV. The outcome is in the hands of God and his angels, and is revealed by God to the wise. Daniel's approach may be seen further developed in the literature from Qumran, for example, The War of the Sons of Light against the Sons of Darkness. Daniel does not find the answer to the persecution of Antiochus to lie with the politicians or freedom fighters of his day, who are but 'a little help'.

The story of Judith perhaps also reflects the events of Antiochus' reign. Judith is a somewhat inaccurate historical novel whose aim is to demonstrate in time of trouble that God is 'God of the lowly, helper of the oppressed, upholder of the weak, protector of the forlorn, saviour of those without hope', and that 'there is no other who protects the people of Israel but thou alone' (9:11,14). But God saves Israel through the wisdom and decisive action of Judith, a model of piety and devotion (8:6–8). The story-teller recounts how Nebuchadnezzar, king of the Assyrians, sends his general Holofernes to punish those of his subjects who had disobeyed the summons to campaign with the king. All his disobedient subjects yielded, except 'the people of Israel living in Judea'. When Holofernes approached, the Ammonite Achior advised him that Israel would be defended by God (unless they sinned), and was sent bound to Israel for his pains, to suffer with Israel in the event of Holofernes' victory. Holofernes besieged the town of Bethulia and the widow Judith devised a plan to gain access to him, befuddle him with wine, and behead him. When his head was displayed on the walls of Bethulia, his troops fled, and Achior the Ammonite was promptly converted to Judaism, and circumcised.

Names like Holofernes and Bagoas, as well as other details, suggest that the story originated in the Persian period, but the themes (the religious arrogance of Nebuchadnezzar, who challenges God's power, and the combination of faithfulness and loyalty to the Jewish tradition and the readiness to fight for it) strongly suggest the Maccabaean period. Judith is a heroine cast in the mould of earlier heroines such as Miriam (Exod. 15), Deborah (Jud. 5), Jael (Jud. 5), and the women of Thebez and Abel-beth-maacah (Jud. 9:53f.; 2 Sam. 20:14–22), and is almost the feminine counterpart of Judas Maccabaeus himself; as Judas dedicated the temple, so Judith comes to Jerusalem and dedicates all the vessels of Holofernes, and they feast in the sanctuary for three months (16:18–20).

The books 1 and 2 Maccabees are two independent works, both dating from the period of the Hasmonaean monarchy and recording in different ways and from different angles the events of the Maccabaean rebellion. 1 Maccabees records the history from the beginning of Antiochus IV's reign to the death of Simon in 134 BC, while 2 Maccabees ends with the death of Judas in 161 BC. 1 Maccabees, written in Hebrew in the reign of John Hyrcanus or shortly after, strongly supports the Hasmonaean dynasty and its political achievements; 2 Maccabees, written in Greek perhaps early in the first century BC, is more concerned with the theological lessons to be learned from the war. There are differences of chronology and detail between the two books, and reconstructing the course of events and the original political motivation behind them from 1 and 2 Maccabees (and Daniel) is not easy.

1 Maccabees, however, presents a well-organised and coherent account. It begins by outlining the background to the struggle against Antiochus; the author blames in particular the 'lawless ones' (the hellenising party of Jason and then

Menelaus) who 'came forth from Israel, and misled many, saying, "Let us go and make a covenant with the Gentiles round about us, for since we separated from them many evils have come upon us".' (1 Macc. 1:11f.). In ch. 2, we are introduced to the priest Mattathias and his sons, whose faithfulness to the law and covenant and whose military and political skills will bring Israel's restoration. Chapters 3:1 – 9:22 describe how Judas set about restoring Israel. He defeats a series of increasingly professional forces sent against him, captures and rededicates the temple in Jerusalem, forces the Seleucids to repeal the infamous decree, and negotiates a treaty with Rome, before being killed in battle. 1 Maccabees presents him as a new Saul fighting the Philistines, and at his death Israel laments him in familiar words,

> 'How is the mighty fallen,
>    the saviour of Israel!'

(1 Macc. 9:21; cf. 2 Sam. 1:19)

In 9:23 – 12:53, the struggle continues under Judas' youngest brother, Jonathan, who is made 'ruler and leader, to fight our battles' (1 Macc. 9:30). Jonathan concludes the war with Bacchides, the Seleucid general, and begins to 'judge' Israel (1 Macc. 9:73); soon he accepts the high-priestly office as well. Here we see a foreshadowing of the combination of royal and priestly roles in the Hasmonaean monarchy. The author brings his work to a climax with the rule of Simon (13:1 – 16:17), under whom the state was given a new constitution and 'the yoke of the Gentiles was removed from Israel' (1 Macc. 13:41). 1 Maccabees sees this as the establishment of a new era, and describes it in paradisal terms (1 Macc. 14:11f.):

> He established peace in the land,
>    and Israel rejoiced with great joy.
> Each man sat under his vine and his fig tree,
>    and there was none to make them afraid.

Simon's position as 'high priest, commander and ethnarch of the Jews' is emphasised (1 Macc. 13:41; 14:17, 35, 38, 41, 47; 15:2), as is Hyrcanus' position as his heir (1 Macc. 13:53; 14:49; 16:1–3, 23f.). 1 Maccabees is thus in effect an apologia for the Hasmonaean monarchy. When two subordinate commanders, Joseph and Azariah, tried to copy Judas' success, they failed disastrously, because 'they did not belong to the family of those men through whom deliverance was given to Israel' (1 Macc. 5:62). Simon and his brothers, however,

> exposed themselves to danger and resisted the enemies of their nation, in order that their sanctuary and the law might be preserved; and they brought great glory to their nation. (1 Macc. 14:29)

2 Maccabees is a carefully crafted literary work, as is clear from the prologue (2:19-30) and epilogue (15:37-39). (The two letters prefacing the work, 1:1-9, from 124 BC, and 1:10 – 2:18, perhaps from 163 BC, urge Egyptian Jews to celebrate the feast of temple rededication, and perhaps suggest that 2 Macc. might

have been read at such a festival.) The author intends to tell

> The story of Judas Maccabaeus and his brothers, and the purification of the great temple, and the dedication of the altar, and further the wars against Antiochus Epiphanes and his son Eupator, and the appearances which came from heaven to those who strove zealously on behalf of Judaism, so that though few in number they seized the whole land and pursued the barbarian hordes, and recovered the temple famous throughout the world and freed the city and restored the laws that were about to be abolished. (2 Macc. 2:19–22)

He is apparently summarising the five-volume work of an otherwise unknown Jason of Cyrene, and it is just possible that these volumes corresponded to the five sections into which 2 Maccabees (apart from the prologue and epilogue) can be divided: (1) 3:1 – 6:11, the attack on the Jewish temple and religion by Seleucus, Antiochus IV, and the Jewish Hellenists; (2) 6:18 – 7:42, the martyrdom of Eleazar, the seven brothers and their mother; (3) 8:1 – 10:9, the defeat of the Seleucid general Nicanor, the death of Antiochus and the celebration of the purification of the temple; (4) 10:10 – 13:26, events under Antiochus V Eupator, leading to (5) 14:1 – 15:37, the defeat and death of Nicanor, and the decree for the future celebration of this day of victory. Sections 3 and 5 seem to correspond, the former celebrating the defeat of Nicanor and the purification of the sanctuary, and the latter the death of Nicanor and the celebration of the day. This schematisation has resulted in a difference of chronology between 1 and 2 Maccabees; thus, most obviously, 2 Maccabees places the death of Antiochus IV before the purification of the temple, while 1 Maccabees places it after (in fact, the two events both belonged to December 164 BC).

2 Maccabees is less concerned with historical details than with the theological message that they can convey. The author sees the Maccabaean rebellion as a struggle between Judaism and Hellenism (he is the first writer to use these words in contrast); the saintly high priest Onias is opposed by the wicked high priests Jason and Menelaus. At the centre of the author's Judaism is 'the most holy temple in all the world' (5:15), but the author knows that 'the Lord did not choose the nation for the sake of the holy place, but the place for the sake of the nation' (5:19). The struggle is therefore one for the salvation of God's people. The nation's sufferings under Antiochus are seen as punishment for the nation's apostasy (4:16f.) and as a corrective discipline (6:12); the suffering of Israel's apostates or enemies (e.g., Antiochus IV) is made to fit the crime (cf. 5:9; 9:5–28). The nation is saved by the faith and prayers of Judas and his men (8:1–5; 15:7–11), which is what brings victory in battle (15:20–27), and by the faith and endurance of the martyrs and heroes (Eleazar, the seven brothers and their mother, and Razis, 6:18 – 7:42; 14:37–46), who can expect the reward of resurrection (7:9, 11, 14, 23, 29; cf. Dan. 12:2f.).

2 Maccabees thus uses the story of Antiochus and the Maccabaean rebellion to underline the basic tenets of Judaism: the temple, the laws (especially the sabbath), loyalty under persecution, faith in God's mercy and power to act on behalf of his people. This author's standpoint is similar to that of the author of

Daniel; perhaps both came from the ranks of the descendants of the Hasidaeans (cf. 1 Macc. 2:42; 7:13), to which group Judas is said to have belonged (2 Macc. 14:6). The author is more concerned with Judaism and its belief than with the monarchic nationalism of the Hasmonaeans; he ignores the Hasmonaean successors of Judas totally. Yet though his concern is for a strongly orthodox Judaism, he writes in Greek, not Hebrew, in a Hellenistic rather than Hebraic genre, and his work, like that of his master Jason of Cyrene, may have been directed at diaspora Jews, to focus their minds on the true loyalty of a Jew in the Hellenistic world.

A number of other, non-biblical, works derive from this Maccabaean-Hasmonaean period, and need brief mention here. One of the most interesting writers known to us is Eupolemus. His work survives only in fragments quoted by the fourth-century AD church historian Eusebius from the excerpts of Eupolemus preserved by a first-century BC historian Alexander Polyhistor. The title of Eupolemus' work is not certain (possibly 'On the Jews'), but Eupolemus himself is generally identified as the diplomat sent by Judas Maccabaeus to Rome in 161 BC (1 Macc. 8:17); his father had served as a diplomat a generation earlier (2 Macc. 4:11; cf. Jos. *Ant.* XII.3.3 (138–44)). Eupolemus was probably a Jerusalem priest; his Greek name ('good at war') is noteworthy (cf. 2 Macc. 4:13–15). The extant fragments of his writings show his central concern for the temple and its glory, and the wealth and power of David and Solomon (in particular, Eupolemus underlines that they in their day controlled the countries ruled in his day by the Ptolemies and the Seleucids). He presents Moses as the first wise man, the mediator of the alphabet to the Jews, and so through the Jews to others, and the first to write down laws for the Jews. Coming soon after Antiochus IV's attempt to suppress the Jewish law and turn the Jewish temple into a temple to Zeus, Eupolemus' work, stressing the supremacy of the law, the lawgiver and the temple, may have extra point. Eupolemus wrote in Greek, presumably for a Greek readership, and it would be interesting to know exactly who were his first readers.

Another non-biblical work from the mid-second century BC is the Book of Jubilees. In this, the biblical Genesis and Exodus 1–12 are re-presented as an angel's address to Moses on Mount Sinai (compare the story in 2 Esdras 14), and the work witnesses to the importance of the scriptures in the mid-second century BC, and to the way in which they could be used. The patriarchal stories are retold to emphasise the correct way the patriarchs kept the feasts, according to the solar calendar of 364 days, and the book counsels against intermarriage or eating with foreigners, idolatry, nakedness, and other breaches of the *tôrāh*. Abraham in particular is presented as a man who rejects astrology and idolatry, but studies the *tôrāh* and teaches the Gentiles certain agricultural practices, and is a model of faithfulness and endurance when tested by God. All this would be highly appropriate in the Maccabaean period, and the apocalyptic passage of Book of Jubilees 23:16–32 may refer to the events of the 160s BC:

> And they will quarrel with one another, the young with the old, and the old with the young, the poor with the rich, the lowly with the great, and the beggar with the

> prince, because of the law and the covenant; for they will forget commandment, and covenant, and feasts, and new moons, and sabbaths, and jubilees, and all the customary observances. And some among them will take their stand with bows and swords and other weapons of war to restore their kinsmen to the accustomed path; but they will not return until much blood has been shed on the earth on either side. And those who have escaped will not return from their wickedness to the path of righteousness; but they will all attempt to enrich themselves by dishonest means and filch all they can from their neighbours, and they will call themselves by the great name, but not in truth and not in righteousness, and they will defile the holy of holies with their uncleanness and the corruption of their pollution.

> (Jub. 23:19–21)

Manuscripts of this work were found at Qumran, where the same solar calendar was used, and where the study and interpretation of the scriptures was a major activity. Possibly the Book of Jubilees derives from the sort of people, the Hasidim, from whose ranks the Qumran community was founded in the mid-second century BC. Another work known to have existed at Qumran and perhaps to be dated to the late second century BC was the so-called 'Epistle of Jeremiah' (=Baruch 6), which is a piece of Jewish satire on idolatry.

From much the same time comes the epic poem of Theodotus 'On the Jews', written in Greek hexameters, of which fragments were preserved by Alexander Polyhistor and Eusebius. Because it talks of Shechem, it has often been assigned to Samaritan authorship, but it may rather be Jewish nationalistic propaganda glorifying John Hyrcanus' conquest of Shechem in 129 BC. A Samaritan origin is also argued for the work of Pseudo-Eupolemus, a work of Hellenistic historiography which describes how Abraham discovered astrology, conveyed 'Chaldaean science' to the Phoenicians and Egyptians, and was entertained on Mount Gerizim, the site of the Samaritan sanctuary destroyed by Hyrcanus in 129 BC. From Jerusalem, however, came the early first-century BC Greek translation of the text of Esther. This translation incorporated a number of additions to the original Hebrew text, underlining Gentile hostility to the Jews, the loyalty of the Jews to their Gentile rulers, the problems of intermarriage between Jew and Gentile, the importance of prayer, and the belief that God would vindicate his people. The translation is especially interesting for the colophon, which states that

> In the fourth year of the reign of Ptolemy and Cleopatra, Dositheus, who said that he was a priest and a Levite, and Ptolemy his son brought to Egypt the preceding Letter of Purim, which they said was genuine and had been translated by Lysimachus the son of Ptolemy, one of the residents of Jerusalem.

The date is either 114 BC (if Ptolemy VIII is meant) or 77BC (if Ptolemy XII). The translator was a Jewish resident with a Greek name, and the men who took the translation to Egypt were a priest and his son, both also bearing Greek names. If Alexander Jannaeus could be known by both Greek and Hebrew names, and put both Greek and Hebrew titles on his coins, it is not surprising to find a Greek translator and a priest with Greek names, working in Jerusalem and having contact with Egypt. As the letters prefixed to 2 Maccabees and the Letter of Aristeas show, such Jerusalem-Alexandria contacts had a long history.

Lastly, we should mention the Psalms of Solomon, composed in Hebrew in the mid-first century BC. These seem to oppose the Hasmonaean dynasty, which 'took away our place with violence' (17:6), and to deplore Pompey's conquest of Jerusalem in 63 BC (Pss. 1, 2, 8, 17), and to rejoice over his death in Egypt (2:3). They support those 'that loved the assemblies of the saints', who fled to the desert (17:18–20), by whom may be meant the sectarians of Qumran, or similar people. The author perhaps came from the ranks of the Pharisees, who suffered so much under Jannaeus.

## Bibliography

J.R. Bartlett, *Jews in the Hellenistic world: Josephus, Aristeas, the Sibylline Oracles, Eupolemus* (Cambridge Commentaries on writings of the Jewish and Christian world 200 BC to AD 200, Ii) Cambridge: Cambridge University Press, 1985)

E. Bevan, *Jerusalem under the high priests* (London: E. Arnold, 1918)

J.H. Charlesworth (ed.), *The Old Testament Pseudepigrapha*, I, II (London: Darton, Longman and Todd, 1983, 1985)

J.J. Collins, *Daniel, with an introduction to apocalyptic literature* (The Forms of Old Testament Literature 20) (Grand Rapids: Eerdmans, 1984)

J.J. Collins, *Daniel, 1 and 2 Maccabees* (Old Testament Message 15) (Wilmington, Delaware: M. Glazier, 1981)

P.R. Davies, *Daniel* (Old Testament Guides) (Sheffield: JSOT Press, for the Society for Old Testament Study, 1985)

R. Doran, *Temple propaganda: the purpose and character of 2 Maccabees* (CBQ Monograph Series 12) (Washington DC: Catholic Biblical Association of America, 1981)

A. Lacocque, *The book of Daniel* (London: SPCK, 1979)

D.S. Russell, *The method and message of Jewish apocalyptic, 200 BC-AD 100* (Old Testament Library) (London: SCM Press, 1964)

D.S. Russell, *Apocalyptic ancient and modern* (London: SCM Press, 1978)

V. Tcherikover, *Hellenistic civilisation and the Jews* (Philadelphia: Jewish Publication Society of America, 1966; Jerusalem: Magnes Press, The Hebrew University, 5727)

# 11    'The Kingdom of God is at hand'

*Jesus and the New Testament*

Jesus of Nazareth in Galilee was born at the end of the reign of Herod the Great, the king of Judaea, and in the middle of the reign of Augustus Caesar, the first emperor of the Roman empire. Both these rulers are famous in history, but it is by the year of the Lord Jesus (*Anno Domini*), not by the year of the Lord Augustus or King Herod, that our era is commonly dated, at least in the western world.

It took several centuries, however, for Jesus to win such recognition, first throughout the Roman empire and then through Europe and beyond, and it is too easy to forget that in his lifetime Jesus was a relatively obscure Jew from the northern province of Galilee, bound up in and limited by the political, social and religious world of his time and place. Consequently, this part of our study begins in Chapter 11, by presenting that political, social and religious world, and by showing what particular contribution Jesus made to it. In his teaching and preaching, Jesus was responding to the needs of his society, alongside others who, with different emphases, were also trying to meet those needs.

The work of Jesus resulted in the development of the society we now know as the church. It was in Antioch, the former capital of the Seleucid kingdom in northern Syria, that the followers of Jesus were first called 'Christians' (Acts 11:26), and our earliest evidence of Jesus and Christianity comes from churches in the Hellenistic, Mediterranean world, not from Galilee or Judaea. The leading propagator of the new gospel of Jesus was one Paul of Tarsus in Cilicia, who, after his conversion near Damascus in the early 30s, preached Jesus throughout the Roman empire from Jerusalem to Rome, where he was martyred in the early 60s. Chapter 12, therefore, traces the progress of the developing sect from Jerusalem to Rome, with the help of Paul's own letters and of Luke's Acts of the Apostles, and shows how this new Christian sect met a particular need among the Hellenistic cities of the Mediterranean world. Here again, Christianity was only one movement among many others responding to the contemporary spiritual and social needs.

It was not until some time after the death of Jesus that Christian writings began to appear. Jesus himself left nothing in writing (though in the third century he was credited with a letter to king Abgar of Edessa), and the earliest extant Christian writings are not about Jesus but are letters from Paul to his converts in various churches around the Mediterranean and in central Turkey. These, then, are examined next in Chapter 13; from them we get a remarkable picture of the developing Christian communities in the mid-first century.

It was probably for some of these Mediterranean communities – for Rome and Antioch in particular – that the books we now call the gospels were written in the last three decades of the first century. The gospels were produced to meet the teaching and preaching needs of the churches, not to mention the natural curiosity of Christian converts about their saviour, and they were based on traditions of Jesus as handed down and proclaimed in the churches by missionaries, teachers, and others (Chapter 14). It comes as a surprise to many people to realise that the gospels were not the first New Testament documents to appear but actually among the last. They are not the starting point of first-century Christian literature but its climax, and they cannot be properly understood or interpreted without some understanding of what preceded them and without further examination of how they relate to each other. There is a strong case, then, for urging the student of early Christianity to read the epistles before reading the gospels, and that is the plan followed in this book. It is not surprising, however, that when the corpus of accepted Christian writings was finally brought together – in the second and third centuries AD – into the canon of the New Testament the four gospels were naturally given pride of place, or indeed that the Gospel according to Matthew, with its opening genealogy tracing Christ's ancestry back to Abraham, should come at their head to open the New Testament.

The New Testament as we have it ends with the Revelation to John (the Apocalypse). Of the New Testament books, this was not necessarily the last to have been written and is certainly not the easiest book for a modern reader unused to Old Testament imagery to interpret. The argument of this early Christian prophetic work is explained in Chapter 15. This vision of how God would bring the Roman persecutor of the church to a richly deserved end, with its apocalyptic reminder that the empires of this world are not the final consideration, provides the New Testament with a dramatic ending.

## Expectations of the Kingdom of God

The kingdom of the Hasmonaeans lasted barely two generations before the Roman general Pompey ended it in 63 BC. It might not have ended then but for several inherent faults. It had arisen from a weak economic position, after Ptolemaic exploitation and Seleucid oppression. The conquest of Samaria, Galilee, Ituraea, Transjordan and Idumaea only added to Judah's problems, for in the end these regions could not be held. In particular, there was pressure from the Nabataeans in the Transjordan and the Negeb. The Maccabees had usurped the high priesthood, which had become the prerogative of the family claiming descent from David's priest, Zadok, and this caused trouble for the Hasmonaeans with the Pharisees. Jannaeus had become so unpopular that the people had called in the Seleucid Demetrius III to remove him; when Jannaeus finally won, he crucified his internal opponents. On his deathbed he urged his wife to make her peace with the Pharisees. There were dynastic difficulties: Aristobulus I murdered his brother

Antigonus; his brother and successor Jannaeus murdered another brother. On Jannaeus' death, his widow Salome took the throne herself, but had to appoint one of her sons, Hyrcanus, to be high priest. The result was that Hyrcanus and his brother Aristobulus vied for power, Hyrcanus being supported by the ambitious Antipater of Idumaea and Aretas of Nabataea. Though Pompey imposed a political settlement, the Hasmonaean rivalry did not stop at this point.

Pompey's arrival ended the Hasmonaean kingdom and began a long era of Roman rule in Palestine. (Even Herod the Great owed his throne to Rome, for all his apparent independence of action.) Pompey (104–48 BC) was a Roman general who had learned his trade under the Roman dictator Sulla. He had successfully cleared the Mediterranean of piracy in 67 BC and defeated Mithridates, king of Pontus (in northern Asia Minor) in 66 BC; in 65 BC he annexed Syria for Rome, and sent M. Aemilius Scaurus to deal with the Jews. Scaurus supported Aristobulus against Hyrcanus, but when Pompey arrived in person, and Aristobulus took and fortified Jerusalem, Pompey responded by capturing him, occupying the temple area in Jerusalem after a seven-month siege, and horrifying the Jews by entering the Holy of Holies. Aristobulus he took back to Rome in triumph; Hyrcanus he restored to the high priesthood. Judah was stripped of her conquests apart from Galilee, Peraea (in Transjordan), and four minor southern districts of Samaria, and was virtually reduced to being a religious community under Hyrcanus, subject to the military rule of Rome. Aristobulus tried but failed to regain his kingdom, and when Caesar carried his war against his rival Pompey into the east, Pompey had Aristobulus murdered. After Pompey's death in 48 BC, Hyrcanus and his Idumaean supporter Antipater lobbied Caesar, who confirmed Hyrcanus' position as high priest and ethnarch, and made Antipater the Roman procurator of Judah. Antipater's son Phasael became the military governor of Judaea and Peraea, while his other son Herod became military governor of Galilee, where he began a successful political career by putting down bandits and fighting off an attempt by Aristobulus' son Antigonus to re-establish the Hasmonaean dynasty. Herod was ready to use the Hasmonaean dynasty to establish his own position, however, and he married Hyrcanus' granddaughter Mariamme. In 40 BC the Roman Senate appointed him king of Judah; by 37 BC he was in control of Galilee and Jerusalem. Judaea was a kingdom once again, though a client kingdom of the Roman empire.

Herod is remembered today for the massacre of the infants, told in Matthew 2 as a preface to the life of Jesus, and to judge from Josephus' account of his reign, he was certainly capable of ruthlessness. He is summed up by one modern scholar as follows:

Among the Roman client kings of the transition period he is the outstanding personality; able, cruel, and utterly unscrupulous – the nature of the man is shown in the recipe for success, as correct as abominable, which he gave to Antony: 'Kill Cleopatra' – he succeeded where the far greater Antiochus Epiphanes had failed, and forcibly made of Judaea a very passable imitation of a Hellenistic kingdom. He was not a Hellenistic king, but an Idumaean barbarian moderately well varnished;

but Hellenism was the only system he could apply to his mixed realm, stretching from the Lebanon to Egypt' (Tarn and Griffith, (3rd ed. 1952) 237).

Herod began by having to establish his position. At home, he progressively disposed of the remaining members of the Hasmonaean dynasty. Antigonus, son of Aristobulus II, was killed by the Romans at Herod's behest in 37 BC; Aristobulus III, grandson of Hyrcanus and his obvious successor as high priest, was drowned in Herod's swimming pool at Jericho in 35 BC; Hyrcanus himself was executed in 31 BC, and Mariamme in 29 BC; Hyrcanus' daughter Alexandra, long a sworn opponent of Herod, was killed in 28 BC. To the south, meanwhile, Herod had to face the expansionist aims of Cleopatra of Egypt, who persuaded the Roman triumvir Antony to grant her land which included Herod's balsam groves at Jericho. Herod was also pressured into campaigning against Nabataea on Cleopatra's behalf. He was released from this embarrassing obligation by Octavian's defeat of Antony at the battle of Actium in 31 BC, and lost no time in transferring his allegiance and winning Octavian's friendship and support.

Herod's reign now entered a new phase. He developed Jerusalem by building a new theatre, an amphitheatre and a palace, and began building a new temple. He rebuilt Samaria, naming it Sebaste, and rebuilt the port of Straton's Tower, calling it Caesarea, both in honour of Augustus Caesar. He built other cities and fortresses in his kingdom and contributed generously to public buildings (including temples) abroad, at Rhodes, Antioch, Tyre, Beirut, Athens and elsewhere. He employed hellenised scholars and bureaucrats at his court; he supported Rome and received favours, including territory, in return. But his lack of sensitivity to Jewish religious tradition and his control of the high priesthood incurred the enmity of the Pharisees, and his dictatorial rule alienated his subjects of all classes. His final years were taken up with trying to organise the succession to his kingdom and its continuing independence. In this he failed. He began by nominating his sons by Mariamme, Alexander and Aristobulus, but their rival Antipater, the son of Herod's first wife Doris, finally succeeded in engineering their execution in 7 BC at the hands of a suspicious Herod. Antipater, however, four days before Herod's own death in 4 BC, went the same way. (The emperor Augustus made the famous punning remark that he would rather be Herod's pig (Greek *hus*) than his son (Greek *huios*).) Herod's will nominated his son by Malthace, Archelaus, as king, with his brother Antipas as tetrarch of Galilee, and Philip, Herod's son by Cleopatra of Jerusalem, as tetrarch of Gaulanitis and other Transjordanian regions.

For all his faults, Herod had succeeded both in developing and expanding the kingdom created by the Hasmonaeans and in holding it in the face of the powerful Roman empire. His failure, however, to leave the kingdom in the hands of a competent successor prepared the way for the final disaster of the war with Rome in AD 66 and the destruction of Jerusalem in AD 70 by Titus. It was the success of Herod's kingdom and the prestige of his new temple, rebuilt on a grand scale from 20 BC onwards that created the political situation in which Jesus of Nazareth, born at the end of Herod's reign, lived and worked. When Herod died, Augustus ratified Herod's succession proposals. This worked well for Galilee and

Peraea, where Antipas ruled, and for Gaulanitis, where Philip ruled, but not for Judaea, where Archelaus was deposed from his tyrannical rule in AD 6 and exiled to Vienne in Gaul.

From AD 4 to 41, then, Judah was ruled by Roman prefects, the best known of whom was Pontius Pilate (c. 26–36), under whom Jesus was executed. Between 41 and 44, after the death of Philip and the disgrace of Antipas (AD 39), the emperor put Herod's former kingdom into the hands of Herod Agrippa I (Herod's grandson, the son of Aristobulus; he appears in Acts 12:1–23). Agrippa was popular with his subjects, paying due care and respect to the Jewish law at home and playing the Hellenistic benefactor abroad. After his death, the emperor Claudius returned Judaea to the rule of Roman procurators – Crispus Fadus (44–46), Tiberius Julius Alexander, a lapsed Jew from Alexandria (46–48), Ventidius Cumanus, under whom there were several serious disturbances exacerbated by Roman insensitivity (48–52), and Felix, the brother of Nero's favourite freedman Pallas (52–59). The Roman historian Tacitus said of Felix that with every kind of cruelty and lust he exercised royal power with the mind of a slave (*Hist.* V.9). Felix's vicious misrule stirred an already simmering pot in Judaea. He was succeeded by Festus (Acts 24:17) (59–61), and Festus, after a short but violent gap, by the totally unscrupulous Albinus (62–64).

The climax came with Gessius Florus (64–66), whose villainies made Albinus, according to Josephus (*BJ* II.14.2 (277)) look positively virtuous. Florus' anti-Jewish bias, and his requisitioning of seventeen talents from the temple treasury, set in motion a series of actions and reactions which led to the Jewish revolt, in spite of the attempts of Agrippa II and other Jewish leaders to calm the people and prevent the revolt. In summer AD 66 the temple priests ceased to offer the sacrifices offered daily on behalf of the Roman emperor, and the revolt began. It was a complicated affair, involving civil war as well as rebellion against Rome, and though Jerusalem was captured and destroyed in AD 70, final resistance was not broken until the capture of the stronghold of Masada in AD 74. 'The failure of the revolt led to the destruction of the last independent Jewish state in Palestine until the establishment of Israel in 1948. For Christians, the background to the revolt formed also the background to Jesus' teaching and the growth of the early church in Jerusalem.' (Goodman, 1988, 4).

The causes of the revolt have been much debated. It is easy to point to things which provoked Jewish resentment – for example, Pompey's inspection of the Holy of Holies in 63 BC, Pilate's introduction of Roman military standards into Jerusalem and his use of the temple treasury to finance an aqueduct, and Caligula's expressed intention of placing a statue of himself in the Jerusalem temple. Roman governors could be tactless and insensitive or even deliberately provocative; men like Pilate felt insecure, fearing that adverse reports might get back to the emperor, and insecurity could easily lead to misjudgment of a situation and over-reaction. Not surprisingly, Roman rule and taxation were bitterly resented; the Jewish view was that the land was God's gift to Israel and that the Romans had no right to be there at all. But the Jews, like others in similar situations before and after them, were themselves bitterly divided between those who were intensely nationalist and ready to fight for immediate political freedom, and those who preferred to live quietly under the *Pax Romana* until God brought in a new world in which the Jews reigned over the Gentiles.

Relationships between Jew and Gentile were also part of the social tension of the time. They did not always find it easy to live side by side; at both Alexandria in the 30s and at Caesarea in the 60s, Jews petitioned Rome for equal citizen rights, but were refused. In AD 66 a provocative act by some Caesarean Gentiles caused a riot which Josephus saw as contributing, via Florus' cynical treatment of the Jewish petitioners, directly to the beginnings of the revolt. It has also been suggested that a major cause of the revolt lay in the economic troubles of the land; typically, after a bad year the small farmers would get into increasing debt and if things did not improve, would be forced to sell up, become labourers or beggars, or even in desperation take to robbery. The evidence for such socially motivated banditry is less than was thought, however, at least in Galilee.

A recent study blames the revolt largely on the Roman failure after AD 6 to appoint in Judaea rulers acceptable to the people. This was perhaps not entirely Rome's fault. The Hasmonaeans had been eliminated and the high priesthood seriously weakened by Herod. The landed aristocracy, however, through whom the Romans ruled elsewhere on the grounds that they had vested interests in peace and prosperity, was unacceptable to the Jews (who looked for piety and learning rather than wealth in their leaders), and the popular assembly was anathema to the Romans (who looked for obedience rather than democracy in their subjects). The resultant rule by puppet high priests with their advisory Sanhedrin depended for its stability on holding an uneasy balance; if it lost Roman confidence in its ability to control the Jews, or Jewish confidence in its ability to restrain the excesses of the Roman governor, it was doomed. Thus it is argued that the catalyst for disaster in Jerusalem was the development of the internal struggle within the ruling class.

Different groups and individuals were certainly competing for power under Roman rule in first-century AD Judaea, and this is the context in which Jesus of Nazareth in Galilee began his mission, proclaimed the imminence of God's kingdom, and was executed. Given this background of the Hasmonaean and Herodian kingdoms, it is perhaps not surprising that the religious preachers and writers of this period should be found using the term 'kingdom of God', which is not very common in the earlier, pre-Hasmonaean period. We are told that Jesus preached that 'the kingdom of God is at hand' (Mk.1:15; cf. Lk.16:26), and that he taught his disciples to pray 'Thy kingdom come'. Jesus is drawing on a concept which goes back to the ancient liturgy of the Psalms, in which God's kingly rule (Pss.93, 95–99) and his kingdom (Pss.103:19; 145:11–13) are praised. The concept is more common, however, in the Jewish literature of the second-first centuries BC, whether from the Jewish diaspora (Sib.Or. 3.47, 767; Wisd. Sol. 6:4; 10:10) or from Palestine (1QM 6.6; 12.7; Ps. Sol. 5:21; 17:41, 46), and is illustrated by the prayer, 'May he establish his kingdom in your lifetime and during your days, and within the life of the entire house of Israel, speedily and soon.' In the days of the Hasmonaean and Herodian kingdoms and Roman rule, prayers for

191

the coming of God's kingdom perhaps seemed natural.

The group focused on Jesus and his teaching was not the only recognisable group responding to the needs of the times. The Herodians of Mark 3:6, 12:13 were probably supporters of Herod Antipas who preferred home rule to Rome rule, looking to the Herodian kingdom for political salvation. The Sadducees are first mentioned in Hyrcanus' time (134–104 BC) by Josephus, and frequently in Jesus' time by the gospels. They seem to have been a small social group, drawn from the ranks of the wealthy, the lay nobility, and the chief priestly families; in the all-important matter of how the scriptures were to be interpreted they apparently took a conservative and literalistic stance. They excluded from their belief the idea of resurrection, not finding it demonstrable from the *tôrāh*, and they saw no reason to extend rules of cleanliness meant for the priesthood to the daily lives of the general populace, as the Pharisees did. Their penal code was severe, and their political sympathies hostile to Herod the Great (who was definitely not one of them), but less hostile than others to the subsequent Roman rule. They would see the sacrifice of a Galilaean workman as a small price to pay for continuing peace (as Caiaphas remarks in the Fourth Gospel, 'It is expedient for you that one man should die for the people, and that the whole nation should not perish' (John 11:50) ).

The Pharisees were religious proselytisers (Mt. 23:15), concerned for the holiness of the nation. Their ideal was that everybody in the land should be holy before God. They sought 'to replicate the cult in the home, and thus to effect the Temple's purity laws at the table of the ordinary Jew, and thus quite literally to turn Israel into "a kingdom of priests and a holy nation" ' (Neusner, *ANRW* II.19.2; 23). Jews therefore had to obey the *tôrāh*'s rules on cleanliness and separation from what was unclean, and this meant that the *tôrāh* had to be interpreted, taught, and observed. Interpretation was important, and the 'oral *tôrāh*' as important as the written *tôrāh*. The Pharisees distinguished themselves from 'the people of the land' who did not observe the details of the law; their name meant 'separated' or 'separatists', and they met in associations or assemblies (Mt.22:13) in order to eat together. Pharisees murmured at Jesus and his disciples for eating with tax-collectors and sinners (Lk.5:30), and the problem of table fellowship between Jewish and Gentile Christians, with its background in Pharisaic observance, soon arose in the emergent church (Gal.2:12); Pharisaic converts wanted Gentile Christians to be circumcised and to obey the Jewish Torah (Acts 15:5). The Pharisaic movement was a lay movement (Greek, *hairesis*, Acts 15:5; 26:5), involving some priests. With them were often associated the scribes, who were lawyers and theologians concerned with interpreting the law. The Pharisees were not a ruling political party, but politically they could not be ignored. Jannaeus warned his wife Salome to come to terms with them; Herod had to face their open opposition and refusal to take an oath of allegiance to him (*Ant.* 15:370; 17:42). They expected their rulers to observe the Torah and respect the temple and priesthood. But among the ranks of the Pharisees could be found on the one hand those who would urge the people to accept Herod's rule (*Ant.* XIV. 14.1 (370); XV.1.1(3), 10. 4 (370) ) or Roman rule (*BJ* IV.3.9. (159) ), and on the other hand those who could refuse to take the oath of allegiance to Herod or support a revolutionary party (*Ant.* XVIII.1.1 (4) ). The Pharisees were influential interpreters of Judaism during the period from the first century BC to the first century AD and their teaching lived on in the rabbinic tradition after the fall of Jerusalem. A much-discussed question is how Jesus related to the Pharisees. The gospels present the Pharisees in opposition, but the picture is suspect as reflecting the relationship between the church and the Jews in the second half of the first century AD, and Jesus himself seems to have shared some Pharisaic attitudes, for example, in his approach to the sabbath, or in his attitude to divorce (where he appears to take the line of the stricter school of Shammai), and in his concern for the intention rather than the legality of a person's action.

Far more separatist than the Pharisees, but sharing their concern for holiness and for interpretation of the *tôrāh*, were the Essenes, and in particular that sub-group of the Essenes whose ruined buildings and writings have been found at and near Qumran. Surprisingly the Essenes do not get mentioned in the gospels, perhaps because Jesus and his disciples had little contact with them, and because by the time the gospels were written the Essenes had ceased to be important at all. A number of attempts have been made to link Jesus with them, particularly through the person of John the Baptist, largely on the grounds of his ascetic life-style in the desert; but John was clearly not an active member of an exclusive and withdrawn community. Not that all Essenes lived at Qumran; according to Josephus many Essene families practised their communal discipline while living in villages and towns throughout the country. Their way of life is described in Josephus, and perhaps in the 'Damascus Document', which some scholars see as describing the life of the non-Qumran Essenes, while taking the 'Community Rule' (IQS) to describe the life of the particular community established at Qumran. The Essenes may have begun as a protest movement against the assumption of the high priesthood by Jonathan, brother of Judas Maccabaeus, in 152 BC, though some scholars see them as being originally Babylonian exiles who returned to Palestine in the Maccabaean period. At all events, they were separatists who rejected the Jerusalem temple's non-Zadokite priesthood and lunar calendar for their own Zadokite priesthood and solar calendar (this may be the background of Josephus' otherwise strange comment that they appeared to worship the sun). They had strict rules of probation before entry and of conduct after entry. They held possessions in common, observed an exact hierarchical precedence among themselves, and practised ritual worship and communal meals. The documents found near Qumran show that regular reading and interpretation of the scriptures were central to their way of life; they followed the interpretations of their early leader, the Teacher of Righteousness, to whose pen some scholars have ascribed the *Hodayot* (Hymns). They saw themselves not as a splinter group but as the true Israel, the members of the covenant, the community of God. In short, they reacted to the Hasmonaean kingdom and its political successors by withdrawing, seeing themselves as the true heirs to the tradition and teaching of the scriptures, and awaiting the day when judgment would come, a new temple would replace the polluted Jerusalem temple and the community would be revealed as the true Israel.

This simplified picture glosses over many problems of interpreting highly allusive texts, but it shows that some Jews responded to the times by finding group support in the towns and villages or by withdrawing into a totally separate, ascetic, apocalyptic community in the Dead Sea region. There were others in Palestine who responded more violently. There had been plenty of violence in Judah in the two centuries before the time of Jesus, during the Maccabaean revolt, the development and establishment of the Hasmonaean kingdom, the establishment of the Herodian kingdom (when Herod was opposed by Hezekiah in Galilee), and in the years following Herod's death (when Hezekiah's son Judas saw his chance and Varus had to suppress rebellion in Galilee and Judaea). In AD 6, when Archelaus was removed and Quirinius held a census for taxation purposes (cf. Lk.2:1), Judas from Galilee, with a Pharisee called Zadok, incited rebellion against Rome. Under Tiberius, says Tacitus, all was quiet, though Mark 15:7 refers to rebels 'who had committed murder in the insurrection'; of this insurrection we know nothing. In the 40s, Fadus put down a prophetic demonstration led by one Theudas, and Tiberius Julius Alexander had the sons of Judas the Galilaean crucified. Ventidius Cumanus' failure to punish some Samaritans for the murder of Jews provoked Jewish riots. Felix firmly executed bandits and *sicarii* ('dagger-men') and put down an Egyptian Jew (Acts 21:38) who tried to lead a people's army against the Roman garrison in Jerusalem; his successor Festus put down another similar rising. In AD 66 a new group emerged in Jerusalem from among country refugees fleeing the Roman advance from Galilee (BJ IV.3.1-4 (421-442)); this group became known as 'the Zealots', though the name has often loosely been applied to earlier opponents of Rome in Palestine. The Zealots were opposed to the Jerusalem high priests and leaders, and helped destroy the traditional Jewish leadership in Jerusalem before fighting to the last to defend Jerusalem from Roman capture, while the *sicarii* withdrew to Masada and defended that to the end. The bandits or brigands have been seen as the product of a disaffected peasant society, motivated more by the need to survive than by nationalism, but in Galilee at least those mentioned by Josephus are not so much peasant 'social' bandits as hired thugs. Attempts have been made to locate Jesus in the context of the Zealots or other anti-Roman freedom fighters with the help of the reference to a 'zealot' among his disciples (Lk.6:15), the reference to the disciples' swords (Lk.22:38), the descriptions of Jesus' dramatic entry to Jerusalem and violence in the temple (Mk.11:1-19 and parallels), the charges laid against Jesus (Lk.23:2), his association with Barabbas the brigand (John 18:40; Mk.15:7), and his crucifixion by the Romans (which suggests a political charge). The difficulty with this case is that it squares so badly with the Jesus known to us from the rest of the gospels. 'Lootings, burnings, assassinations, kidnappings, robbery and the framing of persons on their "blacklist"' – the standard zealotic activities – 'do not seem to recall the figure of Jesus or his teaching' (M. Wilcox, *ANRW* II.*25.1 (172)*).

## Jesus and the Kingdom of God

The world of Romans, Herodians, Pharisees, Sadducees, Essenes, bandits, anti-Roman and anti-establishment pietists, dagger-men and Zealots provide the background for the person and mission of Jesus. Though he had contact with such groups and points of similarity with some of them, clearly he belonged essentially to none of them. His career, his death, and the rise of the Christian community that followed require historical explanation. How was it that a career of teaching and healing in Galilee led to the creation of a new sect which soon changed its base from Jerusalem to Antioch, and then from Antioch to Ephesus, and from Ephesus to Rome, leaving behind it for later generations of believers a collection of writings which it came to describe as 'the new covenant'? The short answer is that Jesus gathered round him a small group of followers whose experience of him both before and after his death led them to continue and expand his mission with such success that within one generation small Christian communities were beginning to appear in the cities of the Mediterranean world. These communities produced the literature for their own practical needs of communication and instruction. Within a generation or two, accounts of the life of Jesus were produced for the benefit of believers, and even a history of the early development of the church. These, together with several occasional letters from early Christian missionaries and church leaders, preserved in the first place by the communities to which they were sent, are our main evidence for a reconstruction of the career of Jesus and the development of the church.

Jesus exercised an itinerant ministry of teaching and healing in Lower Galilee. He seems to have worked in villages such as Cana and Capernaum rather than in the larger towns like Sepphoris (the regional capital) and Tiberias (founded on the shore of the Sea of Galilee in AD 19). The political authorities – Herod Antipas and Rome – on the whole seem to have ignored him. As they were perfectly capable of good intelligence gathering, this suggests that they did not find him particularly dangerous. The Jewish religious leaders, however, took an interest, and engaged him in controversy. His career ended in Jerusalem, where he was executed by the Romans, apparently on a charge of claiming kingship for himself. The authors of the gospels, and Paul in his first letter to the Corinthian church (probably AD 55) recount how after his death Jesus was raised and was seen by various disciples and others. What was the real nature of the appearances of Jesus to the disciples after his death? What did the early Christians mean when they spoke or wrote of Jesus being raised? When did the tomb become empty, and by what agency? Why was Jesus put to death, and at whose instigation? What did Jesus teach that led to his execution? What did he teach that was sufficiently controversial? The execution of Jesus *sub Pontio Pilato*, as the ancient Latin creeds have it, is the historical event at the root of Christianity, but the execution alone is not enough to start a religion. And lastly, what was the purpose of Jesus' mission in Galilee?

The presentation of Jesus' career in Galilee in the gospels shows Jesus initially as a disciple of John the Baptist, who preached the coming visitation of God to punish unrepentant Jews coupled with an exhortation to a more honest life-style.

Jesus, in not dissimilar fashion, preached the imminent coming of the kingdom of God, whose arrival was in some way associated with or present in his own activities of healing, exorcising and teaching (cf. Jesus' reply to the questions sent by John the Baptist through his followers, Mt.11:4–6). Jesus' healing and exorcising activities were hardly unparalleled, as is shown by his answer to the Pharisees (Mt.12:27; Lk.11:19), and would not of themselves lead to his execution, though the popularity they brought him could be seen as dangerous in a society whose leaders feared uprisings. That Jesus collected a small group of adherents might also arouse the suspicion of the authorities, especially as the Twelve might be seen to symbolise the twelve tribes of ancient Israel and might suggest to the authorities that Jesus' kingdom was very much of this world. Whether Jesus' teaching alone was sufficiently radical or disturbing to lead to his execution is a moot point. Jesus does not after all seem to have proposed the abolition of the law of Moses, though on some issues, such as divorce, cleanliness and the sabbath, he debated their interpretation, as did many Pharisaic contemporaries. However, he did insist that the kingdom of God was open to prostitutes, tax-gatherers and sinners, by which latter group are meant not those Jews who through some minor transgressions, duly repented of, have failed to keep the *tôrāh*, but those 'who sinned in such a way as to have forfeited their membership in the covenant' (Sanders, *ANRW* II. 25.1, 422). Jesus' particular offence, according to Sanders, was that he proclaimed by his teaching and by the company he kept that God's mercy and his promised kingdom were for those normally considered beyond the bounds of decent Jewish society. The righteous, as Jesus said, had their reward. Equally, Jesus' attitude towards possessions, in particular towards the possession of land (i.e., that one should live free of dependence upon them), would not have been acceptable either to the wealthy landowners or to the Galilaean farmers who knew from experience that the worst thing that could happen to them was that they might lose their land and be reduced to peasantry, servitude or beggary.

What probably caused the greatest offence, however, was Jesus' attitude towards the temple as revealed by one reported saying and one dramatic action. He seems to have prophesied that the temple would be destroyed (Mk.13:2); some said that he had threatened to destroy it himself and to rebuild it after three days (Mk.14:58; Mt.26:61; Mk.15:29; Mt.27:40; Acts 6:14; John 2:18–22). What Jesus actually said is beyond recovery; according to the gospels, even the witnesses at his trial could not agree. But the memory that he had made some such prediction and had perhaps even spoken of his own part in the destruction stuck in the tradition (though Mark's gospel replaces the destroyed temple made with hands by one not made with hands, and John's gospel explains the saying by reference to the temple of Jesus' body and its resurrection – clearly attempts to play down the offence of the saying). Probably even more offensive than this was Jesus' physical action in 'cleansing' the temple. This was surely a symbolic gesture (it changed nothing for more than a few minutes, but left a lasting impression), and either indicated Jesus' opposition to the whole sacrificial system based on the temple or, perhaps, was a symbolic act, in the manner of an Ezekiel, prophesying the divine overturning of the temple when God visited his people.

The problem is that neither Jesus' words nor his acts qualified him for execution under Jewish law, let alone Roman law. Not even the claim to be Messiah or Son of God, if Jesus actually claimed that, was a capital offence. Yet clearly Jesus was offensive and inconvenient to the religious leaders (who were also inevitably political leaders), and he might easily be seen by the Roman authorities as liable to excite opposition or rebellion. The gospels are probably right to present Jesus' death as the result of some interaction and collusion between the Jewish and Roman authorities. It has been clear ever since Paul Winter published his classic monograph, *The trial of Jesus* (1961), that, though the Romans were directly responsible for the crucifixion of Jesus, the gospel texts show a progressive readiness, from apologetic motives, to implicate the Jewish authorities (this is particularly clear in the Fourth Gospel); but even so, the offence Jesus gave to the Jewish authorities cannot be ruled out as an important factor contributory to his death.

Jesus preached the imminent coming of the kingdom of God, which the outcast and poor would inherit, and of which he and his inner circle, the Twelve, would be the nucleus. Jesus was executed, but the mission continued, and the impetus for that mission came, first, from the disciples' experience that in some sense Jesus, after his death, had been raised to life and had been seen, and, secondly, according to the Acts of the Apostles, from the disciples' experience of the gift of the Holy Spirit at the first Pentecost several weeks after Jesus' death. This is not the place to attempt to justify any modern belief in the resurrection, but it is important to point to what Paul in his epistles and the gospel authors said about the resurrection and to examine what they thought it was.

That people might rise again after death into the new kingdom of Israel which God would bring to his suffering people was an idea familiar to the Pharisees and other Jews in the time of Jesus. Nearly two hundred years before Jesus, Jewish martyrs hoped for resurrection (cf. 2 Macc.7). Paul, a Pharisee, believed in resurrection and knew that it was a presupposition for belief in Jesus' resurrection: 'if there is no resurrection of the dead, then Christ has not been raised' (1 Cor.15:13). He is not unsubtle about it; he recognises that it involves change: 'We shall all be changed ... this perishable nature must put on the imperishable, and this mortal nature must put on immortality' (1 Cor.15:53). Paul and the early Christians took over a Jewish belief. What was new, and distinctively Christian, was the belief that Jesus had *already* been raised – not that he would be raised at the end, but that he had already been raised on the third day after his death.

In the first century AD, a Jew put to death unjustly for the sake of his devotion to God might hope to receive (at the last day) the reward of resurrection to life in the kingdom. The Christian disciples, however, proclaimed that Jesus had already been raised, and what made this belief real to them was their personal experience of Jesus' appearances. In 1 Corinthians 15:3–8 Paul quotes what he had received in the tradition he had been taught:

For I delivered to you as of first importance what I also received, that Christ died for our sins in accordance with the scriptures, that he was buried, that he was raised on the third day in accordance with the scriptures, and that he appeared to Cephas, then to the twelve. Then he appeared to more than five hundred brethren at one time, most of whom are still alive, though some have fallen asleep. Then he appeared to James, then to all the apostles. Last of all, as to one untimely born, he appeared also to me.

Similarly in the gospels, all the weight of the resurrection stories goes onto the disciples' meetings with their Lord and his commands to them for the future. (The resurrection is never described.) The earliest gospel, Mark, closes with the angelic message that Jesus is going before Peter and the disciples to Galilee; there they will see him (Mk.16:1–8; verses 9–20 are an additional, non-Markan ending). Matthew enhances the story with added legendary features (e.g., other tombs being opened and their occupants going into Jerusalem to greet their friends), but his main story adapts Mark's: the disciples meet Jesus on a mountain in Galilee, where he instructs them to make disciples and baptise them in the name of the Father, the Son and the Holy Spirit. The risen Jesus is presented as authoritative, as issuing commandments like Moses of old, as eternally present with his disciples. Matthew is spelling out the meaning of the resurrected Jesus for his own and subsequent ages. Luke's resurrection account tells the story of the meeting with Jesus on the Emmaus road, when 'they recognised him in the breaking of the bread'. Luke is telling his readers that they will not meet Jesus in the flesh again, but in the Eucharist. In John's gospel, the resurrection stories are entirely focused on seeing and believing; Mary sees the stone is gone, and fears the worst; Peter saw the linen clothes lying but it was his companion who saw and believed; Mary saw Jesus standing in the garden but did not at first recognise him, and then went to tell the rest, 'I have seen the Lord'. Thomas said that unless he saw, he would not believe; after he has seen and believed, Jesus comments 'Blessed are those who have not seen and yet believe'. The Fourth Gospel shows us the empty tomb and the ravaged body of Jesus and says, firmly, that the essential truths of the resurrection are not to be found there.

The gospels do not describe the resurrection; they describe the disciples' experiences of meeting the resurrected Jesus, and theologise about them. Such theologising derived from the church's experience of the continued presence of Jesus. The church preached the resurrection not in terms of the revival of a corpse – that would have been irrelevant and profitless – but in terms of God's raising Jesus to the heavens to be the church's Lord; and the church was to live accordingly. That is where Paul in his understanding of the resurrection showed himself the most creative theologian of the early church: 'If then you have been raised with Christ, seek the things that are above' (Col.3:1); 'We were buried therefore with him by baptism into death, so that as Christ was raised from the dead by the glory of the Father, we too might walk in newness of life' (Rom.6:4). To talk of resurrection is to talk theology, not history. The actual event, whatever it was, cannot be reached; we know it only through the theological language in which it has been wrapped.

## Bibliography

M. Avi-Yonah, *The Holy Land from the Persian to the Arab conquest (586 BC – AD 640): a historical geography*, revised ed. (Grand Rapids: Baker Book House, 1977)

C.K. Barrett, *The New Testament: selected background documents*, 2nd ed. (London: SPCK, 1987)

R.J. Coggins, *Samaritans and Jews: the origins of Samaritanism reconsidered* (Oxford: Blackwell; Atlanta: John Knox Press, 1975)

S.J.D. Cohen, *From the Maccabees to the Mishnah* (Library of Early Christianity 7) (Philadelphia: Westminster Press, 1987)

P.R. Davies, *Qumran* (Cities of the Biblical World) (Guildford: Lutterworth Press, 1982)

S.V. Freyne, *The world of the New Testament* (New Testament Message 2) (Dublin: Veritas Publications; Wilmington, Delaware: M. Glazier, 1980)

S.V. Freyne, *Galilee from Alexander the Great to Hadrian: a study of Second Temple Judaism* (Wilmington, Delaware: M. Glazier; University of Notre Dame Press, 1980)

R. Grant, *A historical introduction to the New Testament* (London: Fontana, 1963)

M.A. Knibb, *The Qumran Community* (Cambridge Commentaries on the Writings of the Jewish and Christian World 200 BC to AD 200 II) (Cambridge: Cambridge University Press, 1987)

R.A. Kraft and G.W.E. Nickelsburg, *Early Judaism and its modern interpreters* (Atlanta: Scholars Press, 1986)

E. Lohse, *The New Testament environment* (New Testament Library) (London: SCM Press, 1976)

M. McNamara, *Palestinian Judaism and the New Testament* (Good News Studies 4) (Wilmington, Delaware: M. Glazier, 1983)

M. McNamara, *Intertestamental literature* (Old Testament Message 23) (Wilmington, Delaware: M. Glazier, 1983)

J. Neusner, *Judaism in the beginning of Christianity* (London: SPCK, 1984)

N. Perrin and D.C. Duling, *The New Testament: an introduction*, 2nd ed. (New York: Harcourt Brace Jovanovich, 1984)

C. Rowland, *The open heaven: a study of apocalyptic in Judaism and early Christianity* (London: SPCK, 1982)

D.S. Russell, *The Old Testament pseudepigrapha: patriarchs and prophets in early Judaism* (London: SCM Press, 1987)

A.J. Saldarini, *Pharisees, Scribes and Sadducees in Palestine society* (Edinburgh: T. and T. Clark, 1989)

E. Schürer, *The history of the Jewish people in the age of Jesus Christ*, revised edition, I-III, ed. by G. Vermes and F. Miller (I), G. Vermes, F. Miller and M. Black (II), G. Vermes, F. Miller and M. Goodman (III) (Edinburgh: T. and T. Clark, I, 1973; II, 1979; III.1, 1986; III.2, 1987)

H.F.D. Sparks, *The apocryphal Old Testament* (Oxford: Clarendon Press, 1984)

M.E. Stone (ed.), *Jewish writings of the Second Temple period: Apocrypha, Pseudepigrapha, Qumran, sectarian writings, Philo, Josephus* (Compendia Rerum Iudaicarum ad

Novum Testamentum, Section 2: The literature of the Jewish people in the period of the Second Temple and the Talmud) (Assen: Van Gorcum; Philadelphia: Fortress Press, 1984)

W. Tarn and G.T. Griffith, *Hellenistic civilisation*, 3rd ed. (London: Arnold, 1952)

G. Vermes, *The Dead Sea Scrolls in English*, 3rd ed. (Harmondsworth: Penguin, 1987)

G. Vermes, *The Dead Sea Scrolls: Qumran in perspective* (London: Collins, 1977)

# 12 From Jerusalem to Rome

The evidence for the spread of the Christian message from Jerusalem, where Jesus ended his life, to Rome, where Paul and Peter ended theirs, comes from the Acts of the Apostles, a sequel to the Gospel according to St Luke, and from the various epistles preserved by the church in the New Testament, especially the epistles of St Paul. To this must be added a certain amount of evidence from non-Christian sources from the early Roman empire, and our general knowledge of the contemporary Graeco-Roman world of the Mediterranean. In this chapter we shall focus mainly, though not exclusively, on the career of Paul, and the world in which he worked. This is almost inevitable, because it was Paul's work which caught the imagination of the church in general from a fairly early period, and of Luke in particular. Outside the gospels the bulk of the New Testament is taken up by the Acts and the epistles attributed to Paul. We know very little indeed of the churches associated with the Epistle to the Hebrews, the Epistle of James, the Epistles of 1 and 2 Peter and Jude, 1, 2, and 3 John, or the Book of the Revelation of St John the Divine. When and how the gospel reached Alexandria and Egypt, or large parts of modern Syria and Turkey, we can only guess. What has been preserved for us is evidence from Paul himself of his activities or relationships with the cities of Thessalonica, Philippi, Corinth, Rome, and the people of Galatia, and the city of Colossae (if Colossians is authentic) and one of its citizens (Philemon). To supplement that firsthand evidence, and thereby cause some confusion, we have Luke's composition, Acts, in which he presents us with his reconstruction of Paul's journeyings.

Luke begins the story of Acts in Jerusalem, emphasising by the repeated account of the ascension (Acts 1:1–11; cf. Luke 24:50–52) that Jesus' life on earth is over, and announcing the theme of his book in words of commission from Jesus to his disciples: 'you shall receive power when the Holy Spirit has come upon you; and you shall be my witnesses in Jerusalem and in all Judaea and Samaria and to the end of the earth' (Acts 1:8). The Holy Spirit comes at Pentecost, seven weeks after Jesus' death, and a mixed crowd of pilgrims in Jerusalem hear the apostolic message preached by Peter:

> Parthians and Medes and Elamites and residents of Mesopotamia, Judaea (*variant reading*: Armenia) and Cappadocia, Pontus and Asia, Phrygia and Pamphylia, Egypt and the parts of Libya belonging to Cyrene, and visitors from Rome, both Jews and proselytes, Cretans and Arabians. (Acts 2:9–11)

With one or two exceptions, this is a list of places which Paul did not visit, and we hear no more about them. Luke, whose Latin name suggests he was a man of the Mediterranean world, probably knew very little about most of these places. In Acts 2:43 – 5:42, Luke gives us his famous, and probably idealised, picture of the early community of the followers of Jesus in Jerusalem. The apostles attempt to set up a community to which all contribute, not entirely successfully. They perform healings, they preach that Jesus is the Christ, and meet opposition from the Jerusalem authorities. But Luke has little hard evidence about this period. He gives no dates, no indication of the passage of time, and the story is coloured by legend. It is not until chapter 6 that we begin to meet something different.

In theory, the spread of Christianity began with Pentecost. In practice, Luke indicates that it began with a dispute at Jerusalem between converts from Palestinian Judaism ('the Hebrews') and converts from Hellenised Jews ('the Hellenists'), whether from within Palestine or from the diaspora. A convert called Stephen (whose Greek name suggests he may have been one of the Hellenists) got into dispute with Jews from the diaspora in Jerusalem (Acts 6:9) and was accused of attacking the temple and the law, and was stoned. Persecution of the Jerusalem church followed, and Christians were scattered through Judaea and Samaria (8:1); Philip travelled to the coastal towns of Azotus and Caesarea (8:40), while others (including men of Cyprus and Cyrene) reached Phoenicia, Cyprus and Antioch (11:19), 'speaking the word to none except Jews'. The 'persecution that arose over Stephen' began the mission to Jews outside Judaea, and this event saw also the beginning of the involvement of Paul of Tarsus and his mission to the Gentiles, for Luke notes that, as they stoned Stephen, 'the witnesses laid down their garments at the feet of a young man named Saul', who was 'consenting to his death'.

Luke arranged his narrative with considerable skill, as these juxtapositions show. He prepares us by a careful sequence of stories for the coming mission to the Gentiles led by Paul. The gospel is preached to Jews from all over the world (ch.2). Converts are made in Jerusalem from the diaspora (e.g., Nicolaus of Antioch, 6:5). The gospel is preached to Samaritans and to a eunuch (neither being normally admitted to the Jewish community) (8:1–40). At Joppa, Simon stays with a tanner, a man of unclean trade (9:43), and converts and baptises a Gentile centurion at Caesarea, which, along with news from Antioch that the gospel had been preached to Gentiles there (11:20), causes debate at Jerusalem (11:1–18). Meanwhile, Paul has been converted on the Damascus road, and his future mission to the Gentiles is announced to the disciple Ananias and to the reader of Acts (9:15), but not yet to Paul himself. In contradiction to Paul's own account (Gal.1:11 – 2:10), Luke makes Paul begin his preaching career to Jews (ironically, Hellenist Jews who opposed him) at Jerusalem (Acts 9:26–30); it is not until his first missionary journey that Paul declares that he must turn to the Gentiles (Acts 13:46). This passage illustrates another feature of Luke's narrative; Luke takes care to demonstrate that Gentile acceptance of the gospel goes *pari passu* with Jewish rejection of it (cf. Acts 28:17–28). In fact the book as a whole is carefully ordered. It begins with the coming of the Spirit on the apostles, and with a sermon; it goes on to the early ministry of the church in Jerusalem, and then via Samaria to the wider mission of the church and Paul's great journeyings which end in Rome. This arrangement, it has been suggested, follows that of the Gospel according to St Luke, which begins with the coming of the Spirit on Jesus and his sermon at Nazareth; continues with his ministry in Galilee, and then moves via Samaria to Jerusalem, where the gospel ends. The Jews reject Jesus at Jerusalem; so too they reject Paul at Rome.

Acts gives a clear and vivid picture of Paul's career. After his conversion near Damascus (undated, but apparently before the reign of Herod Agrippa I (AD 37–44); cf. 11:28, 12:1), Paul visited Jerusalem, and was sent to Tarsus for a period, perhaps visiting Jerusalem again with famine relief (Acts 11:30; 12:25). He was brought to Antioch, commissioned for mission and travelled through Cyprus, Pamphylia, Lycaonia and Pisidia before returning to Antioch. After visiting Jerusalem for an apostolic conference concerning the terms on which Gentiles should be admitted to the church, Paul travelled from Antioch through Syria and Cilicia to the previously visited Derbe and Lystra; thence to Phrygia and Galatia, Macedonia, Athens and Corinth (during the proconsulship of Gallio), returning by sea via Ephesus to Caesarea, perhaps to Jerusalem (Acts 18:22), and so to Antioch. This was his second major journey. A third journey took him through Galatia and Phrygia to Ephesus, where he stayed two years, and on to Macedonia and Greece; then back through Macedonia and along the west coast of modern Turkey past Rhodes and Cyprus to Tyre, Caesarea, and Jerusalem. Here Paul was arrested in the temple courtyard; after imprisonment in Jerusalem and Caesarea, and hearings before the Sanhedrin, the Roman governors Felix and Festus, and the king Agrippa II, he appealed to the emperor and was sent as a prisoner to Rome, where he lived for two years. After this, according to some later sources (not Luke), he was executed in the reign of Nero.

This picture is not always easy to fit to the evidence of Paul's own writings (which Luke nowhere mentions). The New Testament credits thirteen epistles to Paul, arranging them in order of length: first, those addressed to churches (Romans, 1 and 2 Corinthians, Galatians, Ephesians, Philippians, Colossians, 1 and 2 Thessalonians), and then those addressed to individuals (1 and 2 Timothy, Titus, Philemon). Not all these are certainly authentic; on various grounds Ephesians, Colossians, 2 Thessalonians, and the pastoral epistles (1 and 2 Timothy, Titus) have been attributed to Pauline disciples. If we limit ourselves to the certainly authentic, and try to fix their place of origin and date on the basis of internal evidence, the most likely result is as follows:

| | | |
|---|---|---|
| 1 Thessalonians | Corinth? | AD 50 |
| Galatians | Ephesus? | AD 53? |
| 1 Corinthians | Ephesus | AD 55 (before Pentecost) |
| 2 Corinthians | Macedonia | AD 56 (summer) |
| Romans | Corinth | AD 56–57 (winter) |
| Philippians | Caesarea?/Rome? | AD 57–59/60–61 |
| Philemon | Caesarea?/Rome? | AD 57–59/60–61 |

Ultimately, however, these dates are not based on internal evidence but on the references in Acts to Paul's being brought before Gallio in Corinth (18:12) and to his imprisonment in Caesarea under first Felix and then Festus (24:27). Gallio was proconsul in Corinth from May 51 to May 52. Festus probably succeeded Felix as procurator of Judaea in summer 59, though this is not certain. Another important piece of evidence is 2 Corinthians 11:32–33, which reveals that Paul escaped from Damascus while Damascus was under the rule of Aretas (IV) of Nabataea, that is, between AD 37 and 39.

At this point, we turn to the evidence of Galatians 1–2, where Paul, angrily and on oath, outlines his career to the time of writing in order to demonstrate to the Galatians how rarely he had visited Jerusalem and how little he was subject to the Jerusalem church leaders. He describes his conversion and call (Gal.1:11–16), which was immediately followed by a visit to Arabia (probably Nabataea) before he returned to Damascus; 'after three years' he went up to Jerusalem for fifteen days to see Peter, meeting James, the Lord's brother, also. Then he went to the regions of Syria and Cilicia; 'after fourteen years' he went up again to Jerusalem, with Barnabas and Titus. Here he met James, Peter and John, and it was agreed that he should go to the uncircumcised Gentiles, and they to the circumcised Jews. He describes a subsequent, unhappy meeting with Peter in Antioch. Sometime after this he visited the Galatians, to whom he is now writing, astonished 'that you are so quickly deserting him who called you'.

This summary covers the first part of Paul's missionary career. Unfortunately, it cannot be assumed that it covers all Paul's travels, but only that it covers all those relevant to the points he is making or denying. It is surely trustworthy evidence for Paul's visits to Jerusalem. If we put Paul's return from Arabia to Damascus (assuming a link with 2 Cor.11:32–33) and his first visit to Jerusalem in AD 37, his conversion would then be in AD 34 or 35 (on an inclusive reckoning of 'three years'), and his second visit to Jerusalem 'after fourteen years' might be in AD 50; according to Acts 18:11 Paul stayed for eighteen months before coming before Gallio (between May 51 and May 52). This combination of the evidence of Acts and Galatians is plausible, though it creates problems for Luke's presentation of Paul's travels in Acts, which does not really give Paul enough activity to fill the fourteen years between the Jerusalem visits (whichever of the three Acts visits we identify with the two Galatians visits). If, as is likely, the visit in Acts 15 is to be identified with that described in Galatians 2:1–10 (though there are important differences in the way Luke and Paul describe the occasion), then perhaps the 'famine relief' visit of Acts 11:30 could be identified with that of Galatians 1:18, though the famine is usually dated *c*. AD 44, too late for a visit three years after Paul's conversion. The visit of Gal.1:18 might then be that mentioned in Acts 9:26, but this is unlikely, for Paul swears that he did not visit Jerusalem immediately after his conversion and Acts 9:26 says that he did; and in this case Luke has intruded into Paul's career a 'famine relief' visit which Paul, on oath, does not mention. Possibly the reference to Paul's immediately post-conversion visit to Jerusalem (Acts 9:26–30) is mistaken; the visit to Jerusalem described in Acts 11:30 and 12:25 could then be identified with that in Galatians 1:18, but its association with famine relief would be wrong. In short, to judge from the evidence of Galatians 1–2, the Acts account of Paul's travels between his conversion and the Jerusalem council of Acts 15 is inaccurate or inadequate.

It is a little easier to relate the evidence of the other undoubtedly authentic Pauline letters to the evidence of Acts. 1 Thessalonians shows that Paul has visited Philippi, Thessalonica, and Athens (1 Thess.2:1–2; 3:1; cf. Acts 16:11 – 17:34), and 1 and 2 Corinthians reveal a complex sequence of visits to and correspondence with Corinth. 1 Corinthians 16:1 suggests that Paul has already visited and perhaps written to the Galatians; the visit could be that mentioned in Acts 16:6 between the Jerusalem council and the arrival in Macedonia in AD 50. 1 and 2 Corinthians make clear that Paul had laid foundations in Corinth, had left Corinth (cf. Acts 18:1–18), had written a letter which preceded 1 Corinthians (1 Cor.5:9), had heard from Corinth (1 Cor.1:11; 7:1; 16:17), had 'fought with beasts at Ephesus' (1 Cor.15:32), where he was staying until Pentecost (probably AD 55) (1 Cor.16:8), after which he hoped to visit Corinth via Macedonia (1 Cor.16:5), to winter there before going to Jerusalem with the money he had collected for the poor of Jerusalem. Paul made a second visit to Corinth, but it was a painful one (2 Cor.2:1; 13:1), and he subsequently wrote a tearful letter which he sent to Corinth by the hand of Titus (2 Cor.2:3). He then travelled via Troas to meet Titus in Macedonia (2 Cor.2:12–13; 7:5–6). Titus reassured him about the state of affairs at Corinth, and Paul wrote 2 Corinthians 1–9. (The Corinthian correspondence will be discussed in greater detail in the next chapter.) All this fits fairly well with the sequence recorded in Acts 18–20, in which Paul makes his first visit to Corinth (Acts 18:1–18), returns to Antioch, and then travels to Ephesus (Acts 19:1) – at a time when Apollos was in Corinth (cf. 1 Cor.1:12; 3:5–6,22) – spending two years there before travelling through Macedonia to Greece. (Perhaps this was the occasion of Paul's second, tearful, visit to Corinth (Acts 20:2–3); or perhaps this journey is the one referred to in 2 Corinthians 2:12–13; 7:5–6, in which case Luke has omitted any reference to Paul's tearful visit to Corinth, which presumably took place sometime during the Ephesian ministry.) Acts then describes Paul's journey to Jerusalem, most likely the journey Paul was planning in 1 Corinthians 16:3 and whose purpose was the delivery of the collection to Jerusalem (cf. Acts 24:17). This probably belongs to summer AD 57.

The letter to the Romans also fits in here. It shows that Paul has been at Corinth and Cenchreae (one of Corinth's two ports) (cf. Rom.16:1), and is about to go to Jerusalem 'with aid for the saints' (Rom.15:25) from the churches of Macedonia and Achaia. After visiting Jerusalem, Paul hopes to travel west to Rome and even to Spain (Rom.15:24). He claims to have preached Christ 'from Jerusalem as far round as Illyricum' (Rom.15:19) on the Adriatic. Just when he reached Illyricum is not clear, but he must have taken the opportunity on one of his visits to Macedonia to follow the Via Egnatia westwards across central Greece from Thessalonica instead of turning south to Athens. This is another indication that Acts does not tell us everything.

Philippians and Philemon are both written from prison, probably from Rome, though a case can be made for Caesarea, where Paul was imprisoned for perhaps two years (if Acts 24:27 refers to the length of Paul's stay in prison rather than to the length of Felix's term of office). A case can also be make for imprisonment in Ephesus as the origin of these letters. At all events, the tone of Philippians suggests in several places that Paul half expects his end to come soon (Phil.1:20, 21–24; 2:16,23; 4:11–13). Many scholars have argued that, even if the Pastoral epistles as they stand are not authentically Pauline, certain passages, notably 2 Tim.4:6–18, are authentic and belong to the final stages of Paul's life in prison at Rome.

It is clearly not easy to date and order Paul's travels by a simple correlation of the evidence of Acts and the epistles of Paul, especially for the earlier part of Paul's career. Another problem for the historian is that neither Luke nor Paul reveal much of the missionary work of other apostles or disciples, apart from occasional references to the work of Barnabas and Mark, and Paul's sometimes angry references to rival evangelists preaching what Paul regards as a different gospel which is no gospel. Paul's letter to the Romans reveals that the gospel was taken there by others, long before Paul reached Rome, and the letter to the Colossians shows that it was Epaphras rather than Paul who preached the gospel there (Col.1:3–8; 4:13). It seems that while Paul preached in much of what is now Turkey (Cilicia, Pamphylia, Pisidia, Phrygia, Galatia, and at Ephesus in Asia), there were parts he did not reach, as Luke notes in Acts – Mysia, Bithynia and Pontus to the northwest and north, and Lydia and Lycia to the southwest. The epistle 1 Peter is addressed to 'exiles of the Dispersion in Pontus, Galatia, Cappadocia, Asia, and Bithynia', which seems to cover the areas which Paul did not, perhaps with some overlap in Galatia and Asia, though these two provinces were very large, and the Galatians and Asians of this list may not have known Paul at all. The first three chapters of the Revelation of St John the Divine contain letters addressed to the seven churches in Asia (Ephesus, Smyrna, Pergamum, Thyatira, Sardis, Philadelphia, and Laodicea); there is no evidence that Paul was connected with any of these except Ephesus and Laodicea.

It seems unlikely that the gospel was not preached in Alexandria; perhaps it was taken there by someone from the synagogue of the Alexandrians in Jerusalem (cf. Acts 6:9). We hear in Acts 18:24 of the arrival at Ephesus of a Jew named Apollos, a native of Alexandria, who had been instructed in the way of the Lord but was in need of more accurate teaching, which Priscilla and Aquila gave him; but it is not clear that he came to Ephesus directly from Alexandria. The 30s and 40s were perhaps not propitious decades in which to preach at Alexandria, for in AD 38 there were anti-Jewish riots there which were resolved only by an edict from the emperor Claudius himself commanding the Jews to enjoy prosperity in a city not their own and the Alexandrians to let the Jews live in accordance with their traditions. Later in the century the epistle to the Hebrews may have been sent from, or indeed to, Alexandria; in either case, it suggests that the Christian community there consisted basically of Jewish converts. There is no reference to Christianity elsewhere in north Africa in the New Testament, unless we find it in Mark's reference to Alexander and Rufus, the sons of Simon of Cyrene (Mk.15:21; cf. Rom.16:13, if this is the same Rufus), and in the reference to Libya in Acts 2:10.

Evidence for the growth of Christianity in Syria, outside Damascus and Antioch, is also sparse; possibly the gospels of Luke and Matthew were written for different Syrian churches but this is far from certain. There is no New Testament reference to the large Syrian city of Apamea, nor to the city of Edessa in the Euphrates valley northeast of Syria, where in the second century a church was established which later traced its ancestry back to the missionary work of a disciple sent by Jesus in response to a letter from king Abgar. In the first century, however, Edessa was beyond the boundary of the Roman empire, and Acts may not be entirely wrong in presenting the story of the spread of Christianity as one almost inevitably focused from the start on reaching the hub of empire, Rome. There must have been early preaching in the east – Paul, for example, visited Arabia (Gal.1:17), by which is almost certainly meant Nabataea – but virtually no record of it has survived.

It was to the west, in the Graeco-Roman cities of the Mediterranean, that Christianity was successful. The Mediterranean, its shores and hinterland, now belonged to Rome. Paul's travels took place almost entirely through provinces of the Roman empire, at a time when the empire was well established and at the zenith of its peace and security, after the work of Augustus, Tiberius and Claudius. The first five years of Nero's reign (AD 54–59), in which Paul was at the height of his mission activity, were years of good government, the *quinquennium Neronis*. In his travels Paul met various Roman officials, from army centurions to provincial governors. He ended his career with an epic journey to Rome, where he was eventually executed, in spite of the Roman citizenship claimed for him in Acts.

The Roman empire was well organised for the traveller. The provinces and major cities were linked by paved roads, such as the Via Egnatia which connected the Adriatic and the Aegean seas, from Illyricum to Macedonia. Travellers might rest overnight at the regularly spaced inns (*mansiones*), or take hospitality from relatives, friends, or new acquaintances (as Paul did with Jason at Thessalonica, Acts 17:7), in towns along the way. It was often faster (if riskier) by sea, especially over long distances; an important route across the Mediterranean was that of the imperial grain ships from Alexandria to Rome, used by Paul on his final journey (Acts 27). Acts 20:5,6,13–16; 21:1–8 gives a detailed account, stage by stage, of Paul's journey from Philippi to Caesarea, *en route* for Jerusalem, in AD 57.

The more settled provinces of the empire (including Cyprus, Macedonia and Greece) were governed by proconsuls appointed by the Senate, and the more critical provinces (such as the Rhine and Danube regions, Syria, and Egypt) by legates appointed by and responsible to the emperor in person. (The less important Judaea was governed by imperially appointed prefects – for example, Pontius Pilate, who owed his position to Tiberius' right-hand-man, Sejanus – or, later, by procurators.) In addition to the provinces, there were client kingdoms, often on the edge of the empire, such as Nabataea, and a number of semi-independent cities or city-states, sometimes regulated by a treaty with Rome, and a number of Roman *coloniae*, which were settlements founded by Roman citizens, usually ex-soldiers (e.g., Philippi). According to Acts, Paul met proconsular governors in Achaia (Gallio) and Cyprus (Sergius Paulus), procurators in Judaea (Felix, Festus), the praetors in charge of the colony at Philippi, and local officers such as the Asiarchs at Ephesus and the politarchs at Thessalonica. A Christian called Erastus was *oikonomos* – a city treasurer – at Corinth; he may have been the Erastus who later became an aedile (city magistrate). Paul, born at Tarsus in Cilicia (Acts 21:39), was above all a city man. Jesus had proclaimed the kingdom of God to the country villages of Galilee; Paul proclaimed the Lord Jesus to the cities of the Graeco-Roman world. It is instructive to read Luke's account of Paul's journeys, map in hand, and list the cities mentioned: on the first journey, Antioch, Seleucia, Salamis, Paphos, Perge, Antioch in Pisidia, Iconium, Lystra, Derbe, Attalia, and Antioch; on the second, Derbe, Lystra, and through Phrygia and Galatia to Troas, Samothrace, Neapolis, Philippi, Amphipolis, Apollonia, Thessalonica, Beroea, Athens, Corinth, Cenchreae, Ephesus, Caesarea, Antioch; on the third journey, through Turkey to Ephesus, into Macedonia and Greece returning via Troas, Assos, Mytilene, Chios, Samos, Miletus, Cos, Rhodes, Patara, Tyre, Ptolemais, Caesarea, Jerusalem; and on the last journey to Rome, Antipatris, Caesarea, Sidon, Myra, Fair Havens, Malta, Syracuse, Rhegium, Puteoli, and Rome. To this can be added many cities which Luke does not bother to mention. Titus 3:12, for example, speaks of Paul wintering at Nicopolis, on the Adriatic coast.

A native of Tarsus would have felt very much at home throughout the eastern Mediterranean, for the many cities shared common features. Tarsus itself had a large Roman temple and a gymnasium where the young were educated, and it probably had most of the other features of a Hellenistic city. Many of these cities had begun life as Greek colonies and followed the pattern attributed to Hippodamus of Miletus, by which the area to be settled was divided up into equally sized blocks laid out on a grid system across the terrain, and surrounded by walls. At the centre of the grid, or near the waterfront in the case of a coastal city, two blocks were given over to the *agora* – the market and public meeting place – which might have a colonnade or *stoa* on one or more sides giving shelter for both business and leisure activities. Nearby would be the main temple of the city, and various public offices such as the council chamber (*bouleuterion*); not far away would be the *gymnasion* and *ephebeion* where the young citizens were educated and trained. Public baths, fountains, city gates, a theatre built into a convenient hillside or built up on vaults, a covered *odeion* and a stadium were all regular features of the Hellenistic city. Roman cities followed the orderly grid system, though modifying it by adapting it to the pattern of the Roman military camp with its two main thoroughfares crossing one another (the *via principalis* and the *via decumana*); the *agora* became a *forum;* the *basilica* was the lawcourt, an amphitheatre housed the games and gladiatorial combats, and aqueducts provided water supplies, sometimes over long distances and across hilly countryside. Houses might be built in high blocks of apartments (*insulae*); the unfortunate Eutychus at Troas fell from the third story (Acts 20:9). The wealthy, however, lived in more spacious villas outside the cities.

The Graeco-Roman world was as class-conscious as the modern world. The rich lived off the revenues of their inherited lands and gave their time to various public services, in law, politics, or soldiering. They were expected to contribute generously to public works, and they were careful to leave inscriptional evidence of their munificence. At the top of the Roman social hierarchy (after the emperor and his family) were the six hundred Roman senators (some from ancient families, others new imperial appointees). Below them came the *equites*, originally those who could afford to fight on horseback but now the upper administrative class. These two groups made up a very small but powerful élite. Paul would probably have met such men – Gallio, Sergius Paulus – when brought before their courts, or in unusual circumstances such as those which brought him to Publius, the chief man of the island, in Malta. He certainly met members of the local aristocracy, and moneyed classes, of the cities he visited – men like Dionysus the Areopagite at Athens, Erastus at Corinth, and women like Lydia the seller of purple at Philippi. At Corinth, Achaicus and Fortunatus (1 Cor. 16:17), Lucius and Quartus (Rom. 16:21, 23), who bore Latin names, were perhaps descendants of Roman colonists there. Gaius (Rom. 16:23) had a house large enough to be the meeting place for the local Christian community. Crispus was previously the *archisynagogos* (head of the synagogue) in Corinth. Tertius (Rom. 16:22) was a scribe, Luke (Lucius) a doctor (possibly a former slave). Prisca (or Priscilla) and Aquila, from Rome, with Latin names, were well-travelled tentmakers, Jewish in origin, and apparently with considerable means. Philemon at Colossae was presumably also fairly wealthy, for he owned slaves and the local church met in his house. Paul's companion Barnabas had been a man of means (Acts 4:36), and Mark's mother possessed a house in Jerusalem where many gathered to pray and the maid Rhoda could answer the door (Acts 12:13). At Thessalonica 'not a few of the leading women' joined Paul (Acts 17:4). At the lower end of the social scale, however, Paul's converts included slaves like Onesimus and perhaps 'Chloe's people' (1 Cor. 1:11). He instructs his converts at Thessalonica to live quietly, mind their own business, and work with their own hands so as to command local respect and retain their independence. He can expect that his converts will contribute money on a weekly basis for his collection for the poor in Jerusalem (1 Cor. 16:1–2; 2 Cor. 8:1–24), and he can accept financial support from his friends at Philippi (Phil. 4:14–19). It has recently been strongly argued that the divisions which appear when the Corinthians assemble as a church (1 Cor. 11:17–24), and the divisions between those who are 'strong' and do not object to eating meat formerly offered to idols before being sold in the market place, and the 'weak' who do object, are not unrelated to the social divisions between the haves and the have-nots at Corinth.

In short, as Wayne Meeks has demonstrated by his analysis of the names appearing in Paul's epistles, in the Pauline churches 'people of several social levels are brought together. The extreme top and bottom of the Greco-Roman social scale are missing from the picture' (1983) (72–73). There are no landed aristocrats, and no destitute menials. Meeks suggests that 'the most active and prominent members of Paul's circle (including Paul himself) are ... upwardly mobile; their achieved status is higher than their attributed status' (ibid.) He asks whether Christianity attracted such people, or whether such people, being more noticeable, inevitably got their names into the record.

Christianity was far from being the only movement or religion that attracted people of varied walks of life in the Graeco-Roman cities. The average citizen of Paul's time would have been very aware of the city temple, dedicated to one of the Olympian gods and dominating the *agora* or *forum*, and would attend it for public festivals and for private offerings and prayers. In the Greek temples, the gods were the old gods of Homeric mythology, associated with the mysteries of creation, fertility and the agricultural world (Zeus, Demeter, Aphrodite, Artemis), with the world of politics and war, arts and crafts (Athene, Ares, Hephaestus), and with human life in all its variety. With these were eventually identified the old Roman country gods – Jupiter with Zeus, Juno with Hera, Minerva with Athena, Mars with Ares, Diana with Artemis, and so on. In the Greek world each city had its patron god or goddess with its temple; at Rome, with the development of empire, increasing emphasis was laid on religion as an expression of the unity of the state. In the Roman provinces, beginning with Asia, there developed the cult of the worship of the emperor. This began with the recognition of the dead Julius Caesar as divine, and developed into homage paid to the divine *genius* or spirit of the living emperor Augustus, and then to the recognition of Vespasian as *soter* ('saviour') and Domitian as 'Dominus et deus' ('Lord and god'). The background to this was the earlier Hellenistic ruler cult, popular since Alexander's time, and illustrated by the story of Herod Agrippa I in Acts 12:20–23. The emperor Caligula unwisely went so far as to demand that his statue be set up in the Jerusalem temple; Jewish rebellion was prevented by the delaying tactics of Caligula's legate in Syria, and by Caligula's timely death. However, this was probably not a major issue in the cities Paul visited, where typically people would offer their vows, promises and sacrifices to the ancient gods on public and private occasions in hope of divine favour at the various crises of life.

Increasingly popular in the Graeco-Roman world were the mystery cults. The mysteries of Eleusis (a village outside Athens) were the most famous. The initiate, after appropriate purificatory rites and a solemn procession from Athens to Eleusis, experienced the revelation of a spiritual mystery relating to the annual cycle of life, based on the myth of the rape of Persephone by the god of the underworld. Other mystery cults were those of Dionysus (Bacchus, the god of wine), of the Egyptian Isis (described in the *Golden Ass* of Apuleius), of Artemis of Ephesus (the trade based on her cult at Ephesus is described in Acts 19:23–27), and of Mithras, which spread across the Roman world from Iran. This latter was based on the story of Mithras slaying the heavenly bull and thus releasing the power of life on the earth, and was especially popular in the Roman army. The cult of Cybele from Phrygia was served by ecstatic eunuch priests whose self-castration followed the example of Attis, the former consort of the divine mother Cybele.

Equally demanding, but in a different way, were the various philosophical schools of the Graeco-Roman world, in particular, the Pythagorean and Epicurean schools. The Pythagoreans took their name from a sage who taught at Croton in southern Italy, *c.* 500 BC and founded a religious society, apparently organised on monastic lines. The original school, which was concerned to understand the nature of the cosmos through the study of arithmetic, died in the fourth century BC. The revived first-century AD Neopythagorean school was also interested in the symbolism of numbers, but otherwise not much is known of it, apart from the colourful figure of Apollonius of Tyana, a charismatic, itinerant preacher and miracle-worker. We know more of the Epicureans (cf. Acts 17:18), who organised themselves into household communities without hierarchies of command, emphasising and enjoying mutual affection, respect and friendship. Their philosophy was that of Epicurus of Athens (*c.* 342–270 BC), later latinised by the poet Lucretius in his *De rerum natura* ('On the nature of things'). Its main aim was the cultivation of *ataraxia*, the state of being undisturbed, especially by superstitious fear of divine intervention in the world. (The Stoics, on the other hand, believed that the world was ruled by the providence of the gods.) In this group should also be classed the Cynics, who preached a simple life-style; their model was the third-century BC Diogenes of Sinope, who lived in a barrel. The movement had a late flowering in the first-century AD.

Christian teachers might well have been compared with Neopythagorean, Epicurean or Cynic teachers, partly because in the Hellenistic world the Jews were sometimes seen as philosophers, and partly because Paul (and perhaps other Christian teachers) used in his preaching and writing the rhetorical forms common to such teachers, and partly because the early Christian communities met in small household groups much as the Epicureans and perhaps the Pythagoreans did. The early Christian groups may have looked to some people like voluntary associations such as clubs based on membership of a trade or profession, or burial societies whose members, often from the lowlier ranks of society, clubbed together to provide for their proper burial when the time came. Such groups would meet to regulate their affairs, appoint their officers, and celebrate the more important occasions by dining, much as such associations do to this day. But the early Christian groups were not quite like these; they used a different terminology, demanded a greater and more exclusive loyalty, drew their membership from a wider social spectrum, and saw their local group as part of a greater whole stretching from Jerusalem to Rome – and they focused in worship on one God, whose origin was Jewish.

The place of the Jews in the Graeco-Roman world is also of importance for our understanding of the place of the Christian sect. Formal Jewish relationships with Rome had been initiated by Judas Maccabaeus in 161 BC, and badly damaged by Pompey in 63 BC. It was not surprising that the Jews assisted Pompey's rival, Julius Caesar; in return Caesar supported them at Alexandria and elsewhere, and exempted the synagogue at Rome from his ban on private clubs. Through the reigns of Augustus and Tiberius Jews in the empire (often to the irritation of the cities in which they lived) were allowed exemption from military service, exemption from civic duties on the sabbath, and the freedom to live according to their ancestral laws and send their annual tribute to the Jerusalem temple, where the Jews offered sacrifice on behalf of the emperor but not to him. Thus when the Jews at Corinth brought Paul before Gallio, Gallio dismissed them on the grounds that charges concerning matters of Jewish law had no place in his court. There were Jewish communities in many cities of the Graeco-Roman world, and had been for a long time; the list in 1 Maccabees 15:22-23 shows where Jewish communities were known to exist some two centuries before Paul's time, and Acts records the presence of Jews at Damascus, Salamis, Antioch in Pisidia, Iconium, Thessalonica, Athens, Corinth, Ephesus and elsewhere. In Rome there was a Jewish quarter on the right bank of the Tiber. In the reign of Claudius, however, this *modus vivendi* seems to have run into trouble. At Alexandria, Claudius was forced to adjudicate between the Jews (who were demanding citizen rights) and the Alexandrians (who were denying them); at Rome, according to Acts 18:2, Claudius took the drastic step (reversed under Nero) of expelling the Jewish population. According to the Roman historian Suetonius, the Jews were rioting at the instigation of Chrestus. The name may be Suetonius' mistake for Christus, and the reference may mean that there was trouble in the 40s between Jews and Christians at Rome. Among those expelled were Priscilla and Aquila, who met Paul at Corinth, and became Christian evangelists in Ephesus.

It is clear that the diaspora Jews did not always receive the Christian evangelists kindly. Acts presents diaspora Jews as hostile to Paul, and Paul himself in his writings opposes those who preach the need of circumcision for Gentile converts, or who refuse to eat with Gentiles out of deference to Jewish food laws. Probably diaspora Jews, living among Gentiles, and very conscious of their Jewish tradition, were not at all happy to receive into their community men and women who claimed to be Jews but were ready to dispense with the marks of Judaism that differentiated Jews from Gentiles. Paul saw himself as 'a Hebrew born of Hebrews' (Phil.3:6), a Jew by birth from the tribe of Benjamin, whose most famous member was Saul. Paul emphasises his Judaism at Corinth (2 Cor.11:22), and presents himself as 'extremely zealous for the traditions of my fathers' (Gal.1:14). He believed that circumcised Jews had to keep the *whole* Law (Gal.5:3); that was the logic of their position, if salvation was by the Law. However, he also saw that the resurrected Jesus had to be Lord not only of Jews but also of Gentiles, and the relationship of Jews and Gentiles in the church is one of the major themes of his epistles. Acts 9:15 and Galatians 1:16 both connect Paul's call with the mission to the Gentiles. Paul concluded that 'neither circumcision counts for anything nor uncircumcision, but a new creation' (Gal.6:15), and in Romans 9–11, the climax of the epistle, Paul works out how Jew and Gentile relate in God's plan of salvation (cf. Eph.2:11–22, where the author, whether Paul or a successor of Paul, shows how 'now in Christ Jesus you [Gentiles] who once were far off have been brought near in the blood of Christ. For he is our peace, who has made us both one, and has broken down the dividing wall of hostility.'). This approach arises essentially out of Paul's dilemma of being a Hebrew of the Hebrews and a Roman citizen of Tarsus, no mean city of the Hellenistic world.

The development of this new sect through households like those of Stephanas (1 Cor.1:16), Aristobulus and Narcissus (Rom.16:10,11), and Chloe (1 Cor.1:11) at Corinth, and of Nympha at Colossae (Col.4:15), and doubtless similar households in other cities, is not easy to follow. Acts presents a version which emphasises the development of the Gentile mission as a consequence of the Jewish rejection of Paul's preaching. Paul himself seems to indicate (Gal.1:16) that he had preached to the Gentiles from the start, and that he is concerned to link the Jewish Christian and the Gentile converts into one body by various means. It must also be remembered that, in any case, there was more to the development of the early Church than the Pauline mission; we have said nothing of the work of the other apostles such as James, Peter and John, for nothing much for certain is known of them. Galatians shows Peter visiting Antioch, where Paul objects to his traditional Jewish stance towards the Gentiles. 1 Peter seems to connect Peter with the churches in northern and central Turkey and with 'Babylon' (5:13), which probably refers to Rome. Later tradition connected John with Ephesus. The author of Revelation writes to the seven churches in Asia, and the author of Hebrews writes to a Jewish-Christian community of uncertain address. Paul was not the only evangelist in the early church, and his theology was not the only theology.

Exactly why Christianity took off in the Graeco-Roman world needs some consideration. The message that did take off was not the preaching of Jesus to the villages of Galilee; it was the message as presented by Paul and others in the cities of the Mediterranean world. It appealed to some Jews, such as Priscilla and Aquila, to well-placed women like Lydia at Philippi, to established Roman citizens at the colony of Corinth, to slaves and freedmen, to wealthy heads of households, and to poorer artisans. It appealed over against the loyalties of the Jewish community, against the philosophies of the Epicureans and Stoics, against the particular excitements of the mystery religions, against the deep-rooted appeal of the city temples and their ancient gods. It appealed, perhaps, because it proclaimed one God over against many, one resurrected human leader to whom there were credible witnesses, a high morality which treated individuals from different races and classes as members of one body. It had the religious attractiveness of Jewish monotheism without its disadvantages of circumcision and food taboos; it had the moral attractiveness of the humanist philosophies without their pessimism; it had the initiatory and bonding rituals of baptism and the Lord's supper without the messiness and expense of temple sacrifices; and it offered the social advantages of the voluntary societies but to a less restricted body of people whose contacts spanned the Mediterranean from Jerusalem to Rome. It was as these communities developed throughout the eastern Mediterranean that the different writings appeared which were later collected to become the New Testament.

## Bibliography

C.K. Barrett, *Luke the historian in recent study* (London: Epworth Press, 1961)

E. Best, *Paul and his converts* (Edinburgh: T. and T. Clark, 1988)

F.F. Bruce, *The Acts of the Apostles,* 2nd edition (London: Tyndale Press, 1952)

H.J. Cadbury, *The Book of Acts in history* (London: A. and C. Black, 1955)

H.J. Cadbury, *The making of Luke-Acts* (New York: Macmillan, 1927; London: SPCK, 1958)

F.G. Downing, *The Christ and the Cynics* (Sheffield: Sheffield Academic Press, 1988)

J. Ferguson, *The religions of the Roman Empire* (London: Thames and Hudson, 1970)

M. Goodman, *The ruling class of Judaea: the origins of the Jewish revolt against Rome AD 66–70* (Cambridge: Cambridge University Press, 1987)

M. Grant, *The Jews in the Roman world* (London: Weidenfeld and Nicolson, 1973)

M. Hengel, *Acts and the history of earliest Christianity* (London: SCM Press, 1979)

S.E. Johnson, *Paul the Apostle and his cities* (Good News Studies 21) (Wilmington, Delaware; M. Glazier, 1987)

L.E. Keck and J.L. Martyn, *Studies in Luke-Acts* (London: SPCK, 1968)

H.C. Kee, *Christian origins in sociological perspective* (London: SPCK, 1980)

H. Maccoby, *Judaism in the first century* (London: Sheldon Press, 1989)

W.A. Meeks, *The first urban Christians: the social world of the apostle Paul* (New Haven and London: Yale University Press, 1983)

G.F. Moore, *Judaism in the first centuries of the Christian era,* I–III (Cambridge, Mass.: Harvard University Press, 1927; New York, Shocken Books, 1971)

J. Murphy-O'Connor, *St Paul's Corinth: texts and archaeology* (Good News Studies 6) (Wilmington, Delaware: M. Glazier, 1983)

A.D. Nock, *Conversion: the old and new in religion from Alexander the Great to Augustine of Hippo* (London: Oxford University Press, 1933)

T. Rajak, *Josephus: the historian and his society* (London: Duckworth, 1985)

S. Sandmel, *The first Christian century in Judaism and Christianity: certainties and uncertainties* (New York: Oxford University Press, 1969)

J. Stambough and D. Balch, *The social world of the first Christians* (London: SPCK, 1986)

G. Theissen, *The social setting of Pauline Christianity* (Edinburgh: T. and T. Clark, 1982)

G.A. Williamson, revised by E.M. Smallwood, *Josephus: The Jewish War* (Harmondsworth: Penguin, 1981)

# 13     Letters in the Early Church

The earliest Christian writings preserved for us are letters written by Paul to Christian communities in Thessalonica, Corinth, Rome, Philippi – important cities of the Mediterranean world – and in Galatia, in the centre of what is now Turkey. To these must be added the letter to Philemon at Colossae in the Lycus valley, a hundred miles up country from Ephesus, and perhaps the letter to the Colossians, though many scholars prefer to attribute this to a Pauline disciple. These early letters are private and personal, written by Paul to specific church congregations (and to one individual) to answer certain pressing local needs. Later we find more open letters written for a more general audience: e.g., 'From Jude, to those whom God has called' (no particular place is mentioned); 'James . . . To the twelve tribes in the Dispersion'; 'Peter . . . To the exiles of the Dispersion in Pontus, Galatia, Cappadocia, Asia and Bithynia' (an area which includes rather more than half of modern Turkey); and the Epistle to the Ephesians, whose opening words read, 'Paul . . . To the saints who are also faithful in Christ Jesus' (only some manuscripts include reference to Ephesus in the address, and most scholars believe this epistle was not written by Paul).

Letters are difficult to follow unless we know the writer, the place and date of writing, and the person and situation addressed. It is the mark of a genuine letter, as distinct from a general essay or a homily or some other form of writing, that it has a date and an address. Letters are also difficult to follow unless we have the other half of the correspondence. In 1 and 2 Corinthians, for example, Paul refers to his own previous letter and to what was probably the Corinthian reply to it, but we have only his responses to the Corinthians. It must also be remembered that letters do not always give a balanced picture of the situation addressed, but tend to magnify the issues; and in a real letter, the issue may be clouded by the writer's failure to spell out important information which he and his original reader took for granted.

When Paul and his friends wrote letters they used the Greek of the Mediterranean world to which they belonged (the *koine* or 'common' Greek), and they used the regular Hellenistic letter form: A to B, greeting; a thanksgiving; the particular subject of the letter; salutations from family and friends; a formal ending. The form is illustrated by a letter from Egypt (B.G.U., no. 1897):

> Ammonous to her sweetest father, Greeting.
> When I received your letter, and recognised that by the will of the gods you were preserved, I rejoiced greatly. And as at the same time an opportunity has presented

itself, I am writing you this letter, being very anxious to pay my respects to you.

Attend as quickly as possible to the matters that are pressing. Whatever the little one asks shall be done. If the bearer of this letter hands over a small basket to you it is I who send it. All your friends greet you by name. Celer greets you and all who are with him.

I pray for your health.

Paul was a Jew as well as a man of the Hellenistic world, and his letters reflect both influences. The Jewish greeting was 'A to B, peace', which Paul combines with the Hellenistic greeting and with reference to his own apostleship to produce the following formula (1 Cor.1:1):

> Paul, called by the will of God to be an apostle of Christ Jesus, and our brother Sosthenes, To the church of God which is at Corinth. . .: Grace to you and peace from God our Father and the Lord Jesus Christ.

Paul was writing as an apostle with a commission. His letters are part of his ministry which is at God's call. In his letters he emphasises his commission against opponents (e.g., 2 Cor.10–11), he stresses the tradition of the church against false teaching (1 Cor.11:23–26; 15:3–11), and he carefully distinguishes the Lord's teaching on important issues from his own (cf. 1 Cor.7:10,12). He adapts Hellenistic catalogues of vices and virtues for Christian use (Phil.4:8; 1 Cor.5:11; 6:9–10; 2 Cor.12:20; Gal.5:19), and incorporates early Christian confessions and hymns (Rom.1:3; 10:9; 1 Cor.12:3; Phil.2:6–11). The later, probably non-Pauline, epistles attributed to Paul quote lists of household duties for fathers, wives, children and slaves (Eph.5:22 – 6:9; Col.3:18 – 4:1; cf. 1 Peter 2:18; 3:1–7) – not basically Christian material but taken over as useful and given Christian motivation. As a Jew, Paul quotes the Jewish scriptures, in the Greek translation known as the Septuagint.

The first extant letter of Paul is 1 Thessalonians, written probably from Corinth in AD 50. It is therefore particularly interesting to read it carefully for what it tells us of the nature of the early Christian community twenty years or less after the crucifixion of Jesus and to see what is already taken for granted as being part of the Christian gospel. Paul writes with his colleagues Silvanus and Timothy to a community that is already called a church, an *ekklesia* (1:1), and regarded as part of a larger whole (1:7; 2:14). Paul, though absent, seems authoritative (4:1; 5:12), though he has to labour the point that he and his colleagues are not charlatans using flattery as a cloak for greed (2:1–8). He urges the Thessalonians to respect 'those who labour among you and are over you in the Lord' (5:12), which suggests some sort of ministry but perhaps not a very formalised one as yet. The Thessalonians are addressed as 'brethren' (*adelphoi*: a term used in every New Testament book except 2 John and Jude). Paul speaks of 'our gospel', 'the gospel of Christ', 'the gospel of God', and of giving instructions on behaviour (4:2). He assumes knowledge of God the Father, the Lord Jesus, the Holy Spirit, the death of Christ 'for us' (5:10), the resurrection of Jesus (1:9; 4:14) and of Christians (4:16; 5:10), and the future coming of the Lord (3:13). He deals with three major problems at Thessalonica, first, urging Christians to have a high ideal for sex and marriage (4:3–8); secondly, encouraging the Thessalonians to live quietly, mind their own affairs, and work with their own hands (4:11–12); and thirdly, explaining that Christians who died before the coming of the Lord are still 'in Christ' and will share his expected coming, for which the Thessalonians must remain alert.

2 Thessalonians appears to develop two of the issues raised in the first letter. The author is writing to counter teaching 'to the effect that the day of the Lord has come' (2:2). Where this teaching came from is not clear; possibly from a misunderstanding of Paul's own words. 2 Thessalonians 2 argues that before the arrival of the day of the Lord must come 'the rebellion', with 'the man of lawlessness', who will take his seat in the temple of God 'proclaiming himself to be God' (2:3–4). This enigmatic figure, however, is being delayed by a restraining figure (2:7). Traditional Jewish apocalyptic imagery is being used here; the 'rebellion' probably refers to the Jewish expectation of a final period of wholesale apostasy, and the man of lawlessness may owe something to the figure of Antiochus and the more recent Roman emperor Caligula (who wanted to put his statue in the Jerusalem temple), but the identity of the 'restrainer' or 'restraining thing' is very unclear: the Roman empire? an angelic power? the demonic power currently occupying the world? The second issue raised in 2 Thessalonians is that of work (3:6–13). Some Thessalonians, perhaps because they thought the end was near, or had actually come, and that they were therefore liberated from what free Greeks regarded as appropriate only to slaves, were living in idleness, which was alien to Paul's Jewish work ethic. 'If any one will not work, let him not eat', says the writer grimly. Some scholars, on the grounds that it seems strange that the Thessalonians should suddenly have changed from one belief about the end to another, and that Paul should protest the genuineness of his handwriting so strongly, believe that this epistle is not in fact from Paul's hand.

The next extant letter to have been written was probably Galatians, from Ephesus, *c.* AD 53. Some of the difficulties that this letter raises for Pauline chronology have been mentioned. A more immediate difficulty is that of address; was Paul writing to those properly called Galatians, from the region of north-central Turkey settled in the third century BC by immigrant Celtic tribes from Gaul (hence the name, Galatia), or was he writing to his converts in Pisidia and Lycaonia whose cities Derbe and Lystra had become part of the Roman province of Galatia in 25 BC? If the former, when did Paul evangelise in this region? German scholars tend to adopt the north Galatian address, British scholars (following William Ramsay) the southern. Galatians also stands out from other Pauline letters in that it lacks the usual thanksgiving section at the beginning and the salutations at the end. Paul is writing in obvious anger and perplexity to justify his apostolic standing in the face of rival Christian evangelists and to deplore the Galatians' readiness to accept the demands of these preachers that they be circumcised ('I wish those who unsettle you would mutilate themselves!', says Paul fiercely (Gal.5:12)). Who these people were is uncertain. They want the Galatians circumcised, so they sound like Jewish Christians of a conservative type; but, presumably as a result of their teaching, the Galatians are turning back to what Paul thinks of as enslavement 'to the weak and beggarly elemental spirits' and the observance of 'days, and months, and seasons and years' (Gal.4:9–10). Paul discusses this as if the Galatians were reverting to the observance of the Jewish law, which would be surprising in the case of pagan converts from the highlands of central Turkey. Similar beliefs appear at Colossae in the Lycus valley, west of the Galatians, and some have suggested that the Galatians (and Colossians) were being misled by proponents of a syncretistic cult to see themselves as liberated spiritual beings (*pneumatikoi*, 6:1), able freely to gratify the desires of the flesh (cf. 5:16–21). Whatever the precise teaching of Paul's opponents in Galatia, however, it led him to attack the whole idea of 'justification by works of the law' (2:16) (a theme more fully expounded later in Romans), and this is perhaps the point at which to consider Paul's teaching on this. The overall context is Paul's conviction that the gospel of the Lord Jesus is destined for Gentiles as well as for Jews.

Paul complains that the Galatians are turning to a different gospel, a human gospel contrary to the one Paul preaches. Paul's gospel was not dependent on human authority or tradition, nor on the Jerusalem apostles; Paul received it by direct revelation of Jesus Christ. God revealed his son to Paul that Paul might preach him among the Gentiles, and Paul affirms that the Jerusalem apostles, recognising this, gave him the right hand of fellowship to preach to the uncircumcised Gentiles while they preached to the circumcised Jews. Paul insists, moreover, that circumcision was not compulsory for Gentile converts like Titus. This was in effect to say that the Jewish law was not applicable to Gentile converts. When Peter came to Antioch, he at first accepted that the Gentiles need not obey the Jewish food laws and that he, a Jew, could eat in their company, but later, 'when certain men came from James', he changed his mind out of deference to 'the circumcision party' (Gal.2:12). Paul attacked him sharply for hypocrisy: '"If you, though a Jew, live like a Gentile and not like a Jew, how can you compel the Gentiles to live like Jews?" We ourselves, who are Jews by birth and not Gentile sinners... know that a man is not justified by works of the law but through faith in Jesus Christ' (Gal.2:14–15).

Paul was in fact proud of his Jewish origins and practices (2 Cor.11:21; Phil.3:5; Gal.1:13–14), recognised the privileged position of Israel (Rom.3:1; 9:4), and desired the salvation of the Jews (Rom.10–11). Like other Jews, he recognised that the Law, the Torah, was God's gracious gift to Israel, that Israel should respond by obeying it, and that the Law was good. The problem was that the Law demanded total obedience from the Jews, laid those who failed under a curse, and was not applicable to Gentiles. As it was human experience that no one could observe all the Law's commands, and as the church was to be open to Gentiles as well as to Jews, it was clear to Paul that the Jewish Law had to play a less than leading role in the scheme of salvation. It could at best have a temporary purpose (Rom.3:20; Gal.3:19); it might be seen as a *paidagogos*, the custodian under whose guidance we were confined until Christ came (Gal.3:24). For Paul, scripture had already predicted the salvation of the Gentiles when it said of the Jewish ancestor

Abraham, 'In you shall all the nations be blessed' (Gal.3:8). For Paul, scripture also indicated that it was through Jesus that the promise to Abraham was applicable to the Gentiles. 'If you are Christ's, then you are Abraham's offspring, heirs according to promise' (Gal.3:29). Paul's argument is tortuous, but it is designed to diminish the importance of obedience to the Jewish Law as a route to salvation. The Law had been what had prevented the Gentiles from being members of the family of God, and Paul wants the power of the Law removed so that Gentiles and Jews can enter the kingdom on equal terms. He accuses the Galatians and their new Judaising teachers of being in danger of accepting bondage to the Law when they can be sons of Abraham by faith, without having to accept the Law's demand of circumcision as a requirement of entry. It was the Law which kept Jews and Gentiles apart; in the Christian community there was to be neither Jew nor Gentile, and therefore the barrier of the Law must go to make way for the salvation of the Gentiles.

'Justification by faith, not by works of the Law' is the phrase which sums up Paul's answer to the problem of the salvation of the Gentiles; both Gentile and Jewish converts were to be justified, that is, put into a right relationship with God, not by fulfilment of the demands of the Jewish Law on such matters as circumcision and dietary laws, but by their faith in God's grace towards them. To be more precise, it was a case of justification by God's grace, received through faith; it was God's grace, operating through faith in Jesus and incorporation into the Christian community, the body of Christ, which saved – not human obedience to the Jewish *tôrāh*. E.P. Sanders has recently demonstrated that Paul's theology was deeply rooted in Jewish 'covenantal nomism'; the understanding was that God offered Israel a covenant, which made Israel God's people, and Israel responded by obeying the given law; failure to obey would mean God's rejection of Israel, as having broken the covenant. Good deeds, then, 'works of the law', did not earn the salvation already promised, but were a condition of staying within the covenant. For Paul, the Jewish covenant itself was past and abrogated; what mattered were the earlier promises to Abraham effective for Jews and Gentiles through Christ. Entry to this body of the saved was by justification, being put into a right relationship with God. Once one belonged, however, there were of course behavioural demands, the fruits of the Spirit, love, joy, peace, and their outworkings in practice. The way into this relationship was not by works of the Law, for the Christian any more than it had been for the Jew; but once justified through faith in Christ, one could be judged by one's works (Rom.2:2–6; 1 Cor.3:10–15; 2 Cor.5:8–10), which were to be the fruits of the Spirit rather than the demands of the Jewish Torah.

'Justification by faith' was for Paul only one way of expressing the process by which a person became a Christian. Paul could speak also of sharing in the death of Christ, by which one died to the power of sin and transferred to a new lordship (Rom.6:3–11), being liberated from the bondage of the Law (Gal.4:1–9; 5:1), being transformed into a new creation (2 Cor.4:6; 5:17; Gal.6:15), or being reconciled (Rom.5:10; 11:15; 2 Cor.5:17–21). It is noticeable that Paul uses the language of justification mainly in the context of the discussion of the relationship of Jews and Gentiles within the church, and this point is of importance for an understanding of Paul's most famous work, the epistle to the Romans.

Romans provides a number of puzzles: in particular, why was this letter, perhaps in some ways more a treatise than a letter, sent to the Romans, who were not Paul's converts and were not known personally to him? The last chapter is thought by some to salute Christians in Ephesus, not Rome. However, Paul wrote this letter from Corinth in AD 56–7 as he prepared to travel to Jerusalem (Rom.15:25) to deliver the money he had collected from his converts for the poor of the Jerusalem church (perhaps in fulfilment of his promise to 'remember the poor', Gal.2:10). Paul prays that 'I may be delivered from the unbelievers in Judaea, and that my service for Jerusalem may be acceptable to the saints.' Paul is afraid of the Jews at Jerusalem, who may want to lynch him, and of Jewish Christians who may not be willing to accept his offering from the Gentile churches, and who probably object to his views on the freedom of the Gentile converts from obligations to the Jewish Law. But Paul is also looking ahead to visiting Rome, where again this may be a problem. Claudius had expelled Jews from Rome (AD 49? Acts 18:1–2) but Nero had allowed them back. Possibly there were disputes among Christians at Rome, between the Jewish and non-Jewish members. Paul writes for both sides, telling them firmly that all have sinned, that both Jews and Gentiles can be saved, and that they should be loyal to the emperor and the state (and so avoid another edict of banishment). Thus ch.1 describes Gentile sinfulness, ch.2 Jewish sinfulness, chs.3–8 God's way of saving both, chs.9–11 the way in which Gentiles have been grafted onto Jewish stock, Jewish branches having been cut out to make way for them while the Jews thus excluded, seeing the Gentiles' new status, will out of jealousy turn and repent, and eventually 'all Israel will be saved'. This is the climax of the epistle. Paul's aim, immediately before travelling to Jerusalem and then to Rome, was that of dealing theologically with the problem of the incorporation of Jews and Gentiles on equal terms into the church. (In western Protestant theology since Luther, however, this epistle has been interpreted mainly in terms of the individual Christian's private relationship with God, with the result that commentators have found it difficult to explain the point of chapters 9–11, which have often been seen as an appendix rather than as the focal point of the book. This underlines again how important it is to interpret Paul's letters – or any other ancient documents, for that matter – against their historical context before we reinterpret their message for our own times.)

The epistles to the Galatians and to the Romans were perhaps written in AD 53 and AD 56–7 respectively, or perhaps even closer together in view of the similarity of part of their contents. Between them, probably in AD 55–6, belongs Paul's Corinthian correspondence. The New Testament includes two letters to Corinth, but internal evidence from 1 and 2 Corinthians suggests that there were several letters, 2 Corinthians probably consisting of more than one letter. A fairly clear sequence of events can be reconstructed from 1 Corinthians:

1. Paul has preached, baptised, and laid church foundations in Corinth, with

Silvanus and Timothy (2 Cor.1:19), the first to do so ('I planted', 1 Cor.3:6).

2. Paul has written an earlier letter (1 Cor.5:9), warning the Corinthians against immoral people.

3. Paul has heard from Corinth, via Chloe's household (1:11, cf. 11:18), of their divisions. His mind has been relieved by a visit from Stephanas and others (16:17-18). He has had a letter from the Corinthians raising several important topics (7:1).

4. Paul is now writing to deal with what he has heard and read. With his letter he is sending Timothy, who is to be well received, and sent back to Paul (16:10).

5. Paul is at Ephesus, where in spite of opposition (he has, in an enigmatic phrase, 'fought with beasts', 15:32) he will stay until next Pentecost (16:8), after which he plans to travel through Macedon to Corinth, to winter there before going to Jerusalem with the collection (16:4), about which he has already sent instructions to Galatia (16:1).

6. There are various hints that though Paul is a father to his converts, relationships are strained (4:1-21; 16:10-11). Paul calls the Corinthians childish (3:1-3; 14:20) and defends himself against attack (9:3).

The first four chapters of 1 Corinthians deal with the divisions in the Corinthian church, which seem to focus in particular round Corinthian loyalties to Apollos (whose eloquence and wisdom pleased some; cf. Acts 18:24 – 19:1) and to Paul (whose lack of eloquence and presence at Corinth Paul confesses; cf. 2 Cor.10:10; 11:6). There may have been differences between Apollos and Paul in the understanding and practice of baptism and the understanding of 'wisdom'; Paul explains for some reason that he did not baptise at Corinth except on one occasion, and he rejects eloquent wisdom (1 Cor.1:17, cf. 2:4,13). 1 Corinthians 5:1 – 6:11 deals with a particular problem of immorality at Corinth. The offender (who has taken his father's wife) is to be excommunicated, and recourse to secular courts is to be avoided. Immorality and prostitution are inconsistent with membership of the body of Christ (6:12-19); even if the Corinthians can claim that to enlightened people like themselves all things are lawful, Paul can reply that not all things are helpful (6:12).

In chs.7-16, Paul answers a series of questions put to him in a letter from Corinth, questions which probably arose out of Paul's earlier letter and its instructions. This earlier letter may have urged the Corinthians (1) to avoid immorality and immoral persons; (2) to avoid idolatry and meat sacrificed to idols; (3) at worship, to keep women decently veiled, and to keep the Spirit under control; (4) not to mourn those Christians who had died before the final resurrection; and (5) to contribute to the collection for the poor of Jerusalem. The Corinthians seem to have replied in somewhat critical vein, as we can see from Paul's replies in 1 Corinthians. In ch.7, Paul gives a very balanced answer to a Corinthian plea for sexual abstinence in marriage, and discusses other matters of marriage and divorce. 1 Corinthians 8:1 – 11:1 discusses whether the Corinthians might eat meat which had in the usual way been slaughtered for sacrifice to pagan gods before the remainder was marketed as food. Many Corinthians saw no harm in this, on the grounds that 'all of us possess knowledge' (8:1), 'an idol has no real existence' (8:4), 'food will not commend us to God' (8:8), and 'all things are lawful' (10:23). Paul responds to this strong-minded approach by ruling that such meat could indeed be eaten with a clear conscience, but that those whose conscience allowed them to eat ('the strong') must not give offence to those whose conscience did not ('the weak'). '"All things are lawful", but not all things build up' (10:23). 'Whether you eat or drink . . . do all to the glory of God. Give no offence to Jews or to Greeks or to the church of God' (10:31–32).

Next in 11:2–33, Paul discusses Corinthian practice in the conduct of worship; women may pray or prophesy at worship as men do, but with veiled heads (Paul tries to justify this by theological exegesis, but in the end simply refers to custom), and at the eucharist the haves should not humiliate the have-nots by conspicuous consumption of their own meals; the bread and the cup must not be received in an unworthy manner. 1 Corinthians 12–14 then respond to Corinthian questions about the place of speaking with tongues and prophecy in worship. In a long discussion, Paul insists that these are only two of a number of gifts necessary to the church, and asserts in a famous passage (1 Cor.13) the primacy of love. He argues that 'he who speaks in a tongue edifies himself, but he who prophesies edifies the church. Now I want you all to speak in tongues, but even more to prophesy. He who prophesies is greater than he who speaks in tongues, unless someone interprets, so that the church may be edified' (1 Cor.14:4–5). Paul feels strongly about this, and ends by asserting his authority:

> If anyone thinks that he is a prophet, or spiritual, he should acknowledge that what I am writing to you is a command of the Lord. If anyone does not recognise this, he is not recognised. So, my brethren, earnestly desire to prophesy, and do not forbid speaking in tongues; but all things should be done decently and in order.
>
> (1 Cor.14:37–39).

Chapter 15 responds to the Corinthian disbelief in the very idea of resurrection (1 Cor.15:12), an idea also derided in Athens (Acts 17:32). Paul meets this by referring to the Christian tradition of the appearances of the risen Christ to the apostles and others, including Paul himself, and by explaining that the resurrection is not such a crude idea as the Corinthians suppose. The final chapter (1 Cor.16) gives Paul's instructions about the collection of money for the Jerusalem poor, announces Paul's travel plans, and conveys final instructions and greeting, the greeting written in Paul's own hand and not that of an ammanuensis.

1 Corinthians has been treated at some length because more than any other letter of Paul it gives a superb if allusive picture of the concerns and problems of an urban church in the mid-fifties of the first century. There are divisions based on style and preaching, problems of sex and morality, a major issue of practice, problems of conduct of worship, the theological question of belief in the resurrection, and the practical question of how the collection of money should be handled. Paul's promise that he will send Corinthian representatives with it to Jerusalem may be designed to allay Corinthian suspicions of his probity.

It seems that Paul's Jewish views on morality, worship, belief, and respect for

Jerusalem did not win complete acceptance at Corinth, and that Paul had to argue his case and even modify his stance on some issues. Some time after writing this letter, Paul revisited Corinth, as he had planned (probably AD 55). To judge from 2 Corinthians 2:1, this was a painful visit, perhaps not too surprisingly in view of his recent correspondence. On this visit, someone seriously upset Paul (2 Cor.2:7; 7:12). Paul wrote a tearful letter (2 Cor.2:4,9), perhaps demanding punishment of the offender and saying that he did not want to return to Corinth to be made miserable again. He sent this letter by the hand of Titus to Corinth, and went from Ephesus to Troas expecting to meet the returning Titus there, but eventually met him, bringing reassuring news from Corinth, in Macedonia. It is at this point that Paul now writes 2 Corinthians 1-9, which includes a lengthy apologia for his apostolate (2:14 - 7:4). In chs. 8 and 9, Paul returns to the matter of the collection, notes that it was begun a year previously, and promises that Titus and another brother 'famous among all the churches for his preaching of the gospel' (8:18) could return to Corinth to complete the work. (Paul is clearly taking every precaution to avoid incurring any criticism in this delicate matter; cf. 1 Cor.16; 2 Cor.8:20.) In 2 Corinthians 9:3 Paul reveals that he hopes to come to Corinth, perhaps with some Macedonian brethren (and he hopes that the collection will be ready, so that he and the Corinthians will not be shamed by the already generous Macedonians). After this evidence of restored relationships, chs.10-13 come as a surprise, for here Paul's tact becomes truculence as he returns to emotional self-justification and prepares to visit Corinth for the third time. He is clearly expecting trouble: 'any charge', he says, 'must be sustained by the evidence of two or three witnesses' (13:1). It is often suggested that these chapters were originally from the 'tearful letter' mentioned in 2 Corintians 2:4,9, written before chs.1-9. In this case, the visit of Titus mentioned in 12:18 ('I urged Titus to go, and sent the brother with him. Did Titus take advantage of you?') presumably refers to Titus' first visit to arrange the collection (2 Cor.8:10); it can hardly be the one promised in 8:16-17. But the reference to sending the brother with Titus does fit the circumstances of the visit of 8:16-17, and perhaps therefore chs.10-13 were written *after* that visit, which would seem therefore to have gone disastrously wrong. Paul now writes again in frustration and anger to prepare for a difficult third visit (winter AD 56-7; Acts 20:2?). The outcome of this visit we do not know.

If Paul's dealings with Corinth were fraught and unhappy, his relationship with the church at Philippi in Macedonia was good. The letter to the Philippians was written from prison, perhaps from Ephesus in AD 54, or Caesarea in 58, or Rome *c*. 60. Paul is not sure whether he will be released or executed (1:19-26; 2:17), but expresses some confidence. He has sent Epaphroditus and hopes to send Timothy (2:19-25), warns the Philippians of opponents and suffering (1:28-29), and in a famous passage urges the Philippians to act unselfishly in the interests of others, as Jesus did (2:5-11). At the end he thanks the Philippians for their earlier generosity to him (4:14-19). But this letter also shows signs of being a compilation; 3:2 - 4:9 breathe a different atmosphere, sharply warning the readers against a group demanding circumcision ('dogs', 'evil workers', 'those who mutilate the flesh'), and may belong to a separate letter; a similar suggestion has been made for 4:10–20. If these suggestions are right, Philippians is composite, and evidence for someone's concern to bind together and preserve two or three of Paul's letters addressed to the same place. This could perhaps be the beginning of the collecting of Paul's writings, possibly from sometime in the 60s.

One other letter can be attributed to Paul without question, that addressed to Philemon. In this Paul writes personally to 'Philemon, our beloved fellow worker and Apphia our sister and Archippus our fellow soldier, and the church in your house'. Paul, a prisoner, appeals to Philemon to take back his slave Onesimus, who had probably run away from Philemon and had helped Paul in prison. 'If he has wronged you at all, or owes you anything, charge that to my account. I, Paul, write this with my own hand, I will repay it – to say nothing of your owing me even your own self. Yes, brother, I want some benefit from you in the Lord.' This letter shows Paul at his best. In asking Philemon to receive Onesimus back, not just as a slave to be punished, 'but more than a slave, as a beloved brother', Paul was asking a lot, and one can only suppose that his plea was heard or the letter would hardly have been preserved. Onesimus, according to Col.4:9, came from Colossae, as did Epaphras (Col.4:12); Epaphras, with Mark, Aristarchus, Demas and Luke, sends greetings to Philemon, as they do to the Colossians in Colossians 4:10–17. Archippus (Phl.2) also comes from Colossae, or perhaps from the neighbouring Laodicea (Col.4:17). These connections may help authenticate the epistle to the Colossians, whose Pauline authorship is suspect to many scholars.

Colossians is at least a genuine letter, with an address, thanksgiving, special subject-matter, greetings and ending. It was written to warn the Colossians against false teachers whose 'philosophy and empty deceit' is based on human tradition, the elemental spirits of the universe, and not Christ (2:8). They emphasise ascetic diets and special holy days (2:16, 21–22), self-mortification, worship of angels, and visions (2:18,23). This gives the teachers an appearance of wisdom, but such practices 'are of no value in checking the indulgence of the flesh' (2:23). These teachings sound not unlike those condemned in the epistle to the Galatians, containing a large element of Judaism of some sort. The writer reminds the Colossians that in Christ they have died to such things, and uses language in this connection reminiscent of Romans 6:1–11. But the language and ideas of this letter are not quite those of the Pauline letters discussed so far. There are 35 words in this epistle that appear nowhere else in the New Testament, and 25 that appear only once elsewhere; if the letter is by Paul, he is suddenly using a wider vocabulary. In Colossians, Christ is called 'the head' of the church (1:18); normally Paul refers to the church as 'the body of Christ' and uses the word 'church' (*ekklesia*) of local congregations only, not of the whole. For these and other reasons, Paul's authorship of Colossians has been doubted; but new Christology and new vocabulary might be explained by new circumstances, and the matter remains open.

Ephesians is not so much an epistle (its address to Ephesus is in some doubt) as a comprehensive statement of Paul's teaching. It is closely related to Colossians, incorporating about a quarter of its content. But whereas Colossians is controversialist in tone, Ephesians is meditative; Colossians is a cascade of language, Ephesians is a glacier, slow and smooth, with phrase piled on phrase, full of appositional phrases and dependent genitives (cf. Eph.1:1–14). Its vocabulary contains 90 words not found in the clearly authentic Pauline epistles. Like Colossians, it has a developed idea of the church, built on the foundation of the apostles and prophets; it looks on the conflict of Jews and Gentiles over church membership as a settled thing of the past; and it proclaims Christ ascended and glorified as the church's supreme head rather than Christ crucified. Here the writer is looking back on Paul's conversion and writings (cf. 3:2). The author's problem is, 'How can the church remain apostolic in a period when the apostles are dead?', and he meets it by expounding the ideas of the great apostle Paul. Whether by Paul or not (and probably it is not), this is a masterpiece.

The 'pastoral epistles' claim to be written by Paul to Timothy and Titus as pastors. Both men were important lieutenants of Paul. Timothy (from Lystra, Acts 16:1–2) visited Thessalonica, Philippi and Corinth, and is named as a joint sender of letters to those places. Titus went to Jerusalem with Paul and Barnabas (Gal.2:1), and visited Corinth at least twice as Paul's trusted agent. In the pastoral epistles, these two trusted and experienced men are treated as young and inexperienced, given elementary instruction and told to turn from the wayward impulses of youth (2 Tim.2:22). This might suggest that these letters, if authentic, were written early in the career of Timothy and Titus and relatively early in Paul's, but the various references to Paul's career and travels in 2 Timothy 1:15–18; 3:10–11; 4:6–21 and Titus 3:12–15 suggest that Paul is near the end of his life. Further, many characteristic Pauline words are missing, and there are 131 words not found in the main Pauline epistles. Many scholars have therefore argued that these letters were not written by Paul, but that they incorporate some genuine fragments from Paul's hand, namely the autobiographical references to his career and travels mentioned above.

The letters to Timothy and Titus were written to counter the false teaching of those who peddled 'myths and endless genealogies' (1 Tim.1:4; cf. 4:7), 'godless chatter and contradictions of what is falsely called knowledge' (1 Tim.6:20). These people have 'swerved from the truth by holding that the resurrection is past already' (2 Tim.2:18), and the result of their theology is either ascetic rigour (1 Tim.4:3) or various forms of ungodliness including the love of money and of argument (1 Tim.6:3–10; 2 Tim.3:1–7; Titus 3:9–10). There is much insistence in these letters on the need to guard the deposit of sound teaching which has been learned from Paul (1 Tim.6:20; 2 Tim.1:12–13), who is himself a preacher, apostle and teacher by Christ's appointment (2 Tim.1:11), as well as emphasis on the continuity of office in the church by the laying on of hands (cf. 1 Tim.2:6), and on the careful choice of good teaching clergy (1 Tim.3; 2 Tim.2.2; Titus 1:5–9). The ministry seems fairly well developed; it is already seen as a career (1 Tim.3:1). Provision has to be made for various groups of people in the church, especially the widows. These letters belong to the second or even the third generation of the church, and derive perhaps from Ephesus about the end of the first century AD.

'To the Hebrews' is a title which formed no part of the original letter and is perhaps a later guess based on the very Jewish contents of the work. Hebrews does not claim to be by Paul; it is anonymous. But it is a genuine letter, addressed to a definite community which has suffered persecution in the past. Morale is low, and the author fears it will shortly suffer again, and apostatise (Heb.10:32–39; 12:1–29). The identity of this community and of the writer is not certain. The work was known to Clement of Rome in the 90s, and the author writes that 'those who come from Italy send you greetings' (13:24), but this ambiguous remark may mean that the letter was written to Rome or from it, or from some place which had a resident Italian community. Possibly Hebrews 13:7 looks back to and hints at the deaths of Peter and Paul at Rome, and if so, the reference to 'your leaders' suggests that the letter was addressed to Christians at Rome. The author used the Greek Old Testament and was a man of Hellenistic training and rhetorical skill, perhaps an Alexandrian. Scholars ancient and modern have suggested Apollos (Acts 18:24) as author – a native of Alexandria, an eloquent man, well versed in the scriptures.

If the author is writing to Rome, he is presumably addressing Christians of both Gentile and Jewish origin, and one wonders what the Gentile Christians would have made of an argument based entirely on exegesis of the Jewish scriptures. Perhaps the author, of Jewish origins himself, simply assumed that by his time all Christians would know enough of the Jewish scriptures, or perhaps he was writing for what was basically a Jewish Christian community. (Recently, Jerusalem has been suggested as the destination.) His message is that Christianity transcends Judaism, which was but a shadow of what was to come (10:1). The argument proceeds through a series of comparisons designed to show the superiority of Jesus to the prophets, to the angels, to Moses, and to Aaron (1:1–2):

> In many and various ways God spoke of old to our fathers by the prophets; but in these last days he has spoken to us by a Son, whom he appointed the heir of all things, through whom also he created the world.

The revelation made through the Son was of a higher order than that made through the angels (i.e., the Mosaic law). Moses was but a servant, faithful in God's household; Jesus was a son, set over the household. The Jewish high priest was Aaron of the tribe of Levi; the Christian high priest is Jesus, high priest 'after the order of Melchizedek', and therefore superior to Aaron, because Melchizedek took tithes from Levi's ancestor Abraham. And so Jesus as high priest is correspondingly more effective than Aaron (9:24–26):

> For Christ has entered, not into a sanctuary made with hands, a copy of the true one, but into heaven itself, now to appear in the presence of God on our behalf. Nor was it to offer himself repeatedly, as the high priest enters the Holy Place yearly with blood not his own; for then he would have had to suffer repeatedly since the foundation of the world. But as it is, he has appeared once for all at the end of the age to put away sin by the sacrifice of himself.

Hebrews is a difficult book for the modern reader, but nevertheless a great book, the work of a learned man writing to inspire in his readers, who live with the prospect of persecution before them, confidence in the superiority of salvation through Jesus.

The so-called 'church epistles' attributed to Peter, James and John (traditionally the three closest associates of Jesus) and Jude (James' brother) can be mentioned only briefly. James is a piece of instruction – 54 imperatives in 104 verses – in letter form. There is very little specifically Christian about it. It echoes Greek and Jewish didactic tradition, and mentions the Lord Jesus Christ just twice (1:1; 2:1), though it borrows from the gospels, especially Matthew, and perhaps knows (without understanding) the Pauline debate over faith and works (2:18–26). 1 Peter is more of an exhortatory address than a genuine letter. Up to 4:11 suffering for the faith is only a possibility, but after 4:12 the 'fiery ordeal' is actually 'upon you', and this section seems to be a later expansion of the original work. The earlier section seems appropriate to the context of baptism, and could be a baptismal homily. Christians are encouraged to stand firm in their trials by being reminded of their baptism. It was apparently written from Rome (if that is the reference of 'Babylon', 5:13) to Christian communities across northern and eastern Turkey. The date and authenticity of this letter have been endlessly discussed. The implication of 4:16 that Christians are being persecuted specifically for their Christianity has led many scholars to believe that 4:12ff. reflects the later persecutions of Trajan's time, evidenced in the letters of the younger Pliny (Pliny, *Epistles* X 96).

Jude is polemic against 'ungodly persons who pervert the grace of our God into licentiousness' (4), 'defile the flesh, reject authority' (8), and 'revile whatever they do not understand' (10). They are grumblers, malcontents and boasters (16). Jude describes them and their end in language drawn both from the Old Testament and from books like 1 Enoch. The substance of Jude is incorporated into 2 Peter, which attacks false teachers for their exploitative greed (2:3) and their ability at twisting Paul's letters (and 'the other scriptures') to their own destruction (3:16) ('no prophecy of scripture is a matter of one's own interpretation', 2 Peter 1:20 warns). 2 Peter warns his readers against scoffers who will come in the last days saying 'Where is the promise of his coming? For ever since the fathers fell asleep, all things have continued as they were from the beginning of creation' (2 Peter 3:4). This is one of the latest New Testament writings, dating from well after Paul's letters have been collected and become familiar to Christians.

1 John has no formal letter greeting or ending. It is not a letter so much as a homily. The readers are threatened by former members of their community (2:19) who deny the real incarnation of Christ (2:22; 4:2). They are false prophets, antichrists (4:1–6), and almost, if not quite, past praying for (5:16–17). There is much more to this epistle than is apparent at first sight; it is really concerned with the splitting apart of a Christian community. The author is reassuring those – perhaps the remnant of the community – with whom he identifies himself. The author and his epistle are clearly related in some way to the Fourth Gospel and its author; some think 1 John was an earlier work of the Fourth Evangelist, others that it is later than the Fourth Gospel, perhaps written by a member of the

'Johannine school'. To the same author, whoever he was, can probably be attributed 2 John, a letter written by 'the elder' to 'the elect lady and her children' (probably a local congregation), urging its members to abide in the doctrine of Christ and not to admit the deceivers and antichrists who have parted from the community. 3 John is another real letter, addressed to a difficult situation. The elder writes to one Gaius, pleased to hear good reports of Gaius from some visiting members of his church. He praises Gaius for his support of visiting Christian travellers; he censures one Diotrephes 'who likes to put himself first' and 'does not acknowledge my authority' for refusing 'to welcome the brethren'. He commends a certain Demetrius to Gaius. This brief letter invites all sorts of speculations; we do not know the place of origin, the identity of the author, the place of destination, the date of writing, or the situation to which it is addressed. This letter is an excellent illustration of the difficulties of interpreting letters, as outlined at the beginning of this chapter.

The letters reviewed here are the few that by accident or design were preserved in the early church and survived to be selected for inclusion in the canon, sometime in the late second and early third centuries AD. By this time knowledge of the circumstances that prompted them was already lost, yet they were given a permanent place in the church's canon of scripture, probably because they were penned by, or believed to be penned by, major figures of the early church, but also because they treated matters that were still relevant to the church's continuing life in the cities of the Roman empire. They spoke in a personal way of vital things. By comparison, the gospels, with their story of Jesus of Galilee, must have seemed to many Christians to belong to rather a different world.

# Bibliography

D.E. Aune, *The New Testament in its literary environment* (Cambridge: James Clarke: Philadelphia: Westminster Press, 1987)

F. W. Beare, *The First Epistle of Peter* (Oxford: Blackwell, 1958)

G. Bornkamm, *Paul* (London: Hodder and Stoughton, 1971)

F.F. Bruce, *The Epistle to the Hebrews* (London: Marshall, Morgan and Scott, 1965)

F.F. Bruce, *Paul, apostle of the free spirit* (Exeter: Paternoster, 1977)

R. Bultmann, *Theology of the New Testament*, I, II (London: SCM Press, 1952)

F.L. Cross (ed.), *Studies in Ephesians* (Oxford: Mowbrays, 1956)

W.H. Davies, *Jewish and Pauline studies* (London: SPCK, 1984)

C.H. Dodd, *The Johannine epistles* (Moffatt New Testament Commentary) (London: Hodder and Stoughton, 1946)

W.G. Doty, *Letters in primitive Christianity* (Philadelphia: Fortress Press, 1973)

J.D.G. Dunn, *Unity and diversity in the New Testament* (London: SCM Press, 1977)

B.S. Easton, *The pastoral epistles* (London: SCM Press, 1948)

P.N. Harrison, *The problem of the Pastoral epistles* (London: Oxford University Press, 1921)

J.C. Hurd, Jr., *The origin of I Corinthians* (London: SPCK, 1965)

J. Knox, *Philemon among the letters of Paul* (London: Collins, 1960)

J. Munck, *Paul and the salvation of mankind* (London: SCM Press, 1959)

J.A.T. Robinson, *Redating the New Testament* (London: SCM Press, 1976)

J.A.T. Robinson, *Wrestling with Romans* (London: SCM Press, 1979)

E.P. Sanders, *Paul, the Law and the Jewish people* (London: SCM Press, 1985)

A. Schweitzer, *The mysticism of Paul the apostle* (London: A. and C. Black, 1931)

E.G. Selwyn, *The First Epistle of Peter* (London: Macmillan, 1946)

J. Ziesler, *Pauline Christianity* (The Oxford Bible Series) (Oxford: Oxford University Press, 1983)

# 14    The Four Gospels

The gospels were not the first writings to appear in the developing church. The reason for their emergence in the second half of the first century AD is basically very simple. Paul and other evangelists had been preaching about Jesus throughout the Mediterranean, and in doing so had inevitably drawn upon various traditions about Jesus' life and teaching, his death and resurrection. Paul refers to tradition about the Last Supper (1 Cor. 11:23–25), about the resurrection appearances (1 Cor. 15:3–8), and to Jesus' teaching on divorce (1 Cor. 7:10) (though it must be admitted that Paul appears to know very little about the life and teaching of Jesus and has apparently little interest in it). 1 Peter refers to the way Christ suffered 'on the tree' (1 Pet. 2:24), though his use of a Deuteronomistic phrase to describe the crucifixion (cf. Deut. 21:22–23) shows that he is concerned not merely with the event *per se* so much as with the event as fulfilling the scriptures. However, from the beginning preachers must have been asked who this Lord Jesus was, what he taught, why he died, and what was the evidence for the resurrection. Such questions, directly asked of a preacher or teacher, would probably have received fairly short answers for, apart from those few with firsthand knowledge, teachers would have to rely on such tradition as had been committed to them. Some teachers had perhaps little more to offer than the short, creed-like statements, probably deriving from Christian worship, such as Romans 1:3, where Paul mentions 'the gospel concerning his Son',

> who was descended from David according to the flesh
> and designated Son of God in power according to the Spirit
>   of holiness by his resurrection from the dead

or Romans 8:34

> Christ Jesus, who died . . . who was raised from the dead,
> who is at the right hand of God, who indeed intercedes for us.

But more detailed summaries may have existed, such as one put into the middle of a speech attributed to Peter in Acts 10:36–43:

> You know the word which he sent to Israel, preaching good news of peace by Jesus Christ (he is Lord of all), the word which was proclaimed throughout all Judaea, beginning from Galilee after the baptism which John preached: how God anointed Jesus of Nazareth with the Holy Spirit and with power; how he went about doing good and healing all that were oppressed by the devil, for God was with him. And we

are witnesses to all that he did both in the country of the Jews and in Jerusalem. They put him to death by hanging him on a tree; but God raised him on the third day and made him manifest; not to all the people but to us who were chosen by God as witnesses, who ate and drank with him after he rose from the dead. And he commanded us to preach to the people, and to testify that he is the one ordained by God to be judge of the living and the dead. To him all the prophets bear witness that every one who believes in him receives forgiveness of sins through his name.

Luke, writing *c.* AD 70–90, is unlikely to be quoting the original words of Peter in the 30s; rather, he is giving what he thought Peter ought to have said, which is probably what Christian preachers of Luke's own day were saying or what Luke thought they ought to be saying. One scholar has argued that this summary gives the early skeletonic outline of Jesus' career on which St Mark's gospel was based, for Mark's gospel appears to follow roughly this sequence (one might note, however, that the sequence is more or less inevitable, John the Baptist coming first and Jesus' death and resurrection last; in between there is only 'doing good and healing . . .'). Other scholars argue that this was a later summary of the gospel story, already well-known to Luke, who after all had written with Mark's gospel before him. But at least this passage shows that Luke thought that the Christian preacher might tell the basic outline of Jesus' life, from his baptism by John via his good deeds and healings (teaching, strangely, is not mentioned) to his death and resurrection. The life of Jesus was something one *preached*, to create faith.

The gospels were written to continue the church's work of preaching and expounding the faith, as well as to gratify understandable human curiosity about Jesus, and they were created by early church theologians (for that is not too grand a name to give the gospel-writers) out of individual pieces of tradition about Jesus, in the first place, and their predecessors' reinterpretation of that tradition, in the second. The gospels were composed by human authors, using pen and ink on papyrus or parchment, at particular places, at particular times, and for particular church communities and their problems. The gospels are still church literature, read and heard for the most part in a liturgical setting, a paragraph or episode at a time, and the result is that for most people they are timeless and placeless, archaic yet contemporary, attributed to authors yet of unknown pedigree. They seem anonymous and divorced from the historical context of their writers, in this differing utterly from the epistles.

The modern New Testament scholar, however, is concerned with matters of authorship and historical context, and tries to discover, by examination of the internal and external evidence, who wrote the gospels, when, why, and for whom. The scholar asks why Matthew, Mark and Luke are so closely related to one another, why the gospel according to John is so different, and where the authors got their material. A major aim is to understand more clearly the historical figure of Jesus of Nazareth. But in the course of investigation over the last two centuries, New Testament scholars have come to understand very clearly that the historical Jesus can be seen only through the gospel writers' several presentations of the church's traditions about Jesus, and that those traditions themselves had a historical development before they became fixed in the gospels. Between the death of Jesus and the composition of the first gospel, there were probably some forty years in which stories and traditions about Jesus were told and retold, and retold to make points which mattered to the tellers and to their hearers. And further, the stories about Jesus were retold in the light of the belief in the resurrection of Jesus. This certainly affected the overall presentation of the story, and all four gospels present Jesus to a lesser or greater extent in the light of the resurrection that is coming. Many of those who heard the story of Jesus and passed it on had never known Jesus in the flesh; they knew only the risen Jesus. None of the four gospel-writers claims to have known Jesus personally, though Luke in his prologue refers to what has been handed on by eyewitnesses, and John 19:34 refers to the testimony of an eyewitness, apparently not the evangelist himself.

The gospels in fact present not a Jesus as seen by eyewitnesses but a Jesus as seen through the eyes of faithful believers. The gospel-writers were believers, reinterpreting the traditions about Jesus that they had received from other believers. A strong attempt has been made to show that Jesus, like the later rabbis, taught his disciples to memorise his words and so transmit them accurately to their disciples in turn, but even if this should turn out to be the case, it is clear from comparison of the gospels that the words could be and were adapted for different occasions and purposes, as we shall see, and in any case when we meet them in the gospels they have been through a process of translation from the original Aramaic into Greek. But though the first disciples may or may not have been trained in a rabbinic manner, they and the gospel-writers were Jews and from a Jewish or a diaspora Jewish background. This meant that they saw Jesus, inevitably, in terms drawn from the Jewish scriptures, and they described and interpreted him in those terms. This means that the New Testament scholar has to learn to understand what a first-century Jew meant when he spoke of a son of God, or a son of man, or a Christ, to take only the obvious examples; and similarly we have to ask what such terms meant when transposed into the Gentile Hellenistic world travelled by Paul and Luke.

The obviously difficult word here is the word 'gospel' itself. What was a 'gospel'? The second-century church called the four books about Jesus 'memoirs' (Justin Martyr) or 'gospels' (*euangelia*), taking this name for what was a new literary form altogether from the words with which Mark prefaced his work: 'the beginning of the gospel (*euangelion*) of Jesus Christ, the Son of God.' *Euangelion* meant 'good news', and Mark may have got the word from Paul, who calls down anathemas on anyone – even an angel – who might preach a *euangelion* different from the one he preaches (Gal. 1:6–9). The word was known in a secular, non-Jewish context; in 9 BC the birthday of the emperor Augustus was called on an inscription at Priene 'good news for the world'. When the second-century church used this word of the gospels, it was both classifying the contents and indicating that the gospels were something different; they were not the usual histories or biographies or memoirs, of which the ancient world knew many, but theological compositions, designed for evangelistic or pastoral ends.

The distinctive nature of the gospels has presented a challenge to historians. Many scholars of modern times have tried to get behind the Jesus of faith as presented in the gospels to the 'Jesus of history'. The work of such scholars up to the turn of the nineteenth-twentieth centuries was chronicled by Albert Schweitzer in his famous book *Von Reimarus zu Wrede* (1906), translated into English under the title *The Quest for the historical Jesus* (1910). Schweitzer described their purpose thus:

> They were eager to picture him as truly and purely human, to strip off from him the robes of splendour with which he had been apparelled, and to clothe him once more in the coarse garments in which he had walked in Galilee.

It was the gospel of Mark which appealed above all to scholars seeking the Jesus of history, free from theological, legendary, or mythical overtones. The dynamic figure of Mark's gospel, an itinerant exorcist and preacher, got nearer (it was thought) to the original than Matthew's picture of a new Moses dispensing new laws from the mountain, or Luke's more romantic picture of the friend of women, Gentiles, and sinners, or John's picture of a Jesus whose head, as one commentator put it, was in the clouds and whose feet were six inches off the ground. Mark's Jesus was by comparison recognisable as a down-to-earth Galilaean. But it was soon realised that even Mark's Jesus was not so free from theological interpretation as he seemed at first sight. W. Wrede pointed out in 1901 that Mark's picture of Jesus as trying to conceal his marvellous healings and messiahship did not fit the actual historical situation, which was that healings were expected from an exorcist and could not be concealed, and that Jesus was not thought of as a messiah until after his resurrection. Mark had an apologetic purpose; he was trying to explain why Jesus did not claim to be messiah (*Christos*), though the early church tradition called him that, and why Jesus, though really messiah, came to be killed.

The gospel according to Mark had appealed to those concerned to rediscover the historical Jesus not least because a century of scholarship had demonstrated to most scholars' satisfaction that Mark was the earliest gospel of the four to be written. Matthew, Mark and Luke had long been seen to have a peculiarly close literary relationship. In 1776 J.J. Griesbach argued that the earliest gospel was Matthew, on whom Luke was dependent. Mark was dependent upon both of them, but the ending of Mark was lost, which explained why Mark had so little of the resurrection narratives. J.G. Eichhorn perceived (1804–12) that Matthew and Luke (but not Mark) used a common sayings-source for the teaching of Jesus, and K. Lachmann (1835) that Matthew and Luke both followed the Markan order of events. The case for the priority of Mark was built up from three main considerations: first, nearly everything in Mark's gospel is found somewhere in Matthew and Luke (but the reverse is not true); secondly, where all three gospels tell the same story, Matthew's version and Luke's version contain more than half Mark's vocabulary; and thirdly, wherever either Matthew or Luke appears to diverge from Mark's order of events, the other usually keeps to it, which suggests that Mark's general order of events is basic. The events related, the words used, and the order of events all point to Mark having been used by Matthew and Luke. If that is so, then it becomes clearer why Matthew and Luke were written; part of the answer, at least, must be that they wanted to correct or elaborate the picture that Mark gave. They wished to present a different portrait of Jesus, in order to provide an emphasis appropriate for the particular readers they had in mind.

But though Matthew and Luke apparently used Mark, they had additional sources too. First, they have in common a large amount of material, mostly sayings of Jesus, often given in almost identical wording, which does not appear in Mark. Either, then, Matthew has copied from Luke (or vice versa), or both have copied from another source – the source hypothesised by Eichhorn and, since B. Weiss, known as 'Q' (from German *Quelle*, 'source'). If from Matthew and Luke we set aside the Markan material and the Q material, what is left can be attributed to Matthew and Luke's own special sources or resources, for which the sigla 'M' and 'L' are used. In Matthew's case, M includes a number of sayings and parables of Jesus, and in Luke's case, L includes, for example, the famous stories of the Good Samaritan and the Prodigal Son. Matthew and Luke, then, are composed of three strands: Mark, Q, and M or L.

The earliest gospel, Mark, may itself incorporate material from different sources, but these are hard to identify, and it is not at all clear where Mark obtained his material. The second-century writer Papias, bishop of Hierapolis, quoted the testimony of a man he called 'the Elder', that

> Mark, having become the interpreter of Peter, wrote down accurately all that he remembered of the things said and done by the Lord, but not however in order. (Euseb. *H.E.* III, 39:14)

Links between Peter and Mark may be evidenced by the story of Acts 12:1–17, and the reference to 'my son Mark' in 1 Peter 5:13, but the results of form-critical study of the gospels in the mid-twentieth century made it hard to believe that Mark's gospel was basically a transcription of the memories of Peter.

Form-criticism, pioneered for New Testament study by K.L. Schmidt, M. Dibelius and R. Bultmann immediately after World War I, argued that the various sources of which the gospels were composed were themselves the result of the collection and combination of a number of originally independent units of tradition. These units, varying in form – sayings, parables, miracle-stories, pronouncement-stories such as the story about paying tribute to Caesar, theological narratives about Jesus such as the baptism or transfiguration stories – were in the beginning handed down orally. Each story or saying owed its preservation to a particular teaching need in the early church: should we pay temple tax now we are Christians? should we observe the sabbath now we are Christians? how do we rate John the Baptist? can we eat anything, or must we observe Jewish food laws? (That this last question was a live issue for Mark's readers can be seen in Mark's passing comment in Mark 7:19: 'Thus he declared all foods clean'.) Sometimes independent sayings have been preserved whose original point has been lost; for example, 'where the body is, there the eagles will be gathered together' (Lk. 17:37; Mt. 24:28). Sometimes a saying will be understood and used by the three synoptic gospels in quite different ways. Thus in Mark 4:22 the saying 'There is nothing hid, except to be made manifest' refers to the way the hidden meaning of parables must be made clear. In Matthew 10:26 a similar saying ('nothing is covered that will not be revealed, or hidden that will not be known') seems to refer to the disciples' broadcasting of the truth. In Luke 12:2, however, the same saying refers to the hypocrisy of the Pharisees which, like murder, must out.

If the three evangelists could thus use a saying of Jesus in three totally different ways, clearly we cannot always be sure that we know what Jesus originally meant by a saying or a parable, for we cannot be sure that we have it in its original context. We have the saying only as it was used in the early church, handed down as an independent piece of tradition and used to make a point which may or may not have been the point for which Jesus used it. What Mark and Q did was take these individual parables, sayings, and miracle- and pronouncement-stories and other narratives and group them together, like pearls on a string, to make a necklace of the particular size and arrangement appropriate to the purpose in hand. Sometimes specific groupings of material can be seen in the gospel; thus in Mark 2:1 – 3:6 there is a collection of five stories describing Jesus' controversies with the scribes and Pharisees. They deal in turn with the question of the forgiveness of sins, eating with sinners and tax-gatherers, fasting, plucking grain (i.e., working) on the sabbath, and healing on the sabbath. This collection reveals deliberate arrangement, and the end of this sequence of controversies is that 'The Pharisees went out, and immediately held counsel with the Herodians against him, how to destroy him' (Mk.3:6). The editorial hand of Mark (or perhaps a predecessor) can be seen very clearly. This suggests that the earliest gospel is based on the collection and arrangement of traditional church teaching, and that the order of events is one imposed by Mark, and not necessarily the order in which things happened in Jesus' life.

The work of source-criticism and form-criticism led to a third stage in the scholarly understanding of the gospels and the traditions about Jesus. Mark was not just a stringer of loose pearls, and Matthew and Luke were not just scissors-and-paste men, cutting up and rejoining Mark, Q, and any other materials to hand to make up their own gospels. Each evangelist was a theologian in his own right, presenting Jesus each in his own way and with no little subtlety. Each was writing for a particular community or audience with its own problems and interests.

Many attempts have been made to analyse the structure of Mark's gospel and lay bare its ground plan. It has been suggested that Mark's sequence is dictated by a lectionary scheme, by geography (eastern Galilee, northern Galilee, Judaea, Jerusalem, Galilee), by the outline of Jesus' life preserved in the preaching given in Acts 10:34–43, and by theological considerations. There is, however, some general agreement as to where the major breaks and divisions in the story come, and the author perhaps organised his material into the following major blocks:

| | |
|---|---|
| 1:1–15 | Introductory |
| 1:16 – 3:6 | Initial teaching and challenge |
| 3:7 – 6:13 | Call of the Twelve and continued ministry; rejection in his own country |

| 6:14 – 8:26 | Ministry beyond Galilee |
| 8:27 – 10:52 | Christology and discipleship |
| 11:1 – 13:37 | Final ministry in Jerusalem |
| 14:1 – 15:47 | Passion |
| 16:1–8 | Resurrection |
| (16:9–20 | Non-Markan addition) |

Within these blocks there are several signs of more detailed internal arrangement; for example, it is clear that the narratives of 6:30–7:37 and 8:1–26 follow the same sequence: a feeding and lake-crossing, dispute with the Pharisees, discourse about food and defilement/leaven of the Pharisees, and a healing miracle. The sight-restoring miracle in 8:22–26, at the end of one major section, is closely paralleled by the miracle in 10:46–52, at the end of the next section. Mark's gospel is perhaps not so artlessly composed as has often been suggested. But however it is arranged, the general theme of danger and difficulty is clear throughout. Jesus meets opposition early; even the baptism is understood as something that leads ultimately to death. Jesus three times prophesies his coming death. He is rejected in his home country. He calls his disciples, who never understand him; two of them ask to sit on his right and left hand in glory, but are asked whether they are able to drink the cup that Jesus drinks, or be baptised with his baptism – a clear reference to suffering. On the night before Jesus' death, they do drink the cup, but run away that same night. This is a gospel about the difficulty of discipleship. The Christian's calling is to be a servant, just as the Son of Man came to serve and give his life for many. Not even the resurrection (which is hardly mentioned) brings much light to the gospel; the gospel ends astonishingly when the women run from the tomb in fear and trembling; 'they said nothing to any one, for they were afraid.' Mark's gospel is far from being a simple 'historical' narrative. There is far more here than meets the eye. The theme of the difficulty of discipleship is understandable if Mark is writing at Rome and for the Christians of Rome in the latter part of Nero's reign, when Nero used the Christians as a scapegoat for the fire of Rome, and treated them barbarically.

Matthew's gospel is quite different, though it is clearly built on Mark's. He reproduces nearly all Mark's content, following Mark's language closely though abbreviating many episodes. In general, he follows Mark's outline of the career of Jesus – baptism by John, ministry in Galilee and beyond Galilee, Peter's confession of Jesus as the Christ at Caesarea Philippi, the transfiguration story, the move from Galilee to Judaea, the passion in Jerusalem and the resurrection – but he rearranges much of the teaching and healing stories of Mark, introduces new sayings and parables of Jesus, and most noticeably adds the stories of Jesus' birth, the account of his temptations, and his final great commission to his disciples after the resurrection. As in the case of Mark, there has been much discussion about the gospel's precise structure or plan, but the following major blocks of material seem clear:

| 1:1 – 2:23 | Genealogy, birth and infancy of Christ |
| 3:1 – 4:25 | Preparation and beginning of ministry |

| 5:1 – 7:28 | Sermon on the Mount |
|---|---|
| 8:1 – 9:34 | Ten miracles |
| 9:35 – 11:1 | Instruction of disciples |
| 11:2 – 12:50 | Opposition |
| 13:1–52 | Parables |
| 13:53 – 16:12 | Further instruction, miracles, and disputes |
| 16:13 – 17:27 | Caesarea Philippi, transfiguration, and teaching |
| 18:1–35 | Teaching for the Christian community |
| 19:1 – 20:34 | Teaching in Judaea |
| 21:1 – 25:46 | Teaching in Jerusalem |
| 26:1 – 27:66 | Passion and death |
| 28:1–20 | Resurrection, the final commission |

This is a fairly crude analysis, but it does reveal how in this gospel the material has been systematically organised. This is particularly clear in the case of the miracles, but also in the case of the five major discourses into which the teaching of Jesus is arranged: the Sermon on the Mount (5:1 – 7:27); the mission discourse (10:5–42); the parables (13:1–52); the teaching for the Christian community (18:1–35); the final teaching on judgment (23:1 – 25:46). Each of these sections is clearly marked off by the phrase 'When Jesus had finished these sayings/instructing his twelve disciples/these parables/these sayings/all these sayings'. That there are five discourses has suggested to many scholars that Matthew had in mind the five books of the Jewish law. Certainly the Jewish scriptures were very much in mind; ch.1 begins with a clear reference to Genesis and to the genealogies of the opening chapters of 1 Chronicles, and ch.2, telling how Jesus was taken down to Egypt, is reminiscent of the story of Exodus. In ch.4, Jesus is in the wilderness forty days and forty nights (as the ancient Israelites were in the wilderness forty years), and in ch.5 Jesus dispenses his new law from a mountain. Clear reference is made to the law of Moses and the relationship of Jesus' teaching to it in 5:17:

> Think not that I have come to abolish the law and the prophets; I have come not to abolish them but to fulfil them. For truly, I say to you, till heaven and earth pass away, not an iota, not a dot, will pass from the law until all is accomplished.

That Jesus is the fulfilment of the Law and the prophets is a major theme of this gospel, underlined by a number of quotations from the prophets introduced by the formula 'this was to fulfil what the Lord had spoken by the prophet' or by some variant of this (cf. 1:22; 2:5, 15, 17, 23; 4:14 etc). This theme is naturally connected with the important question of the early church's relationship with the Jews and Judaism. Matthew's gospel seems to be in permanent dialogue with Judaism. Jesus is the fulfilment of the Law, and the church's teaching is a development of the Law; but the Jewish scribes and Pharisees incur bitter criticism (cf. ch.23), and the Jews are made to take total blame for the death of Jesus while Pilate is absolved (27:24–25). And although in Jesus' lifetime the ministry is restricted to Israel (10:5–6, 23, cf. 15:24), after his death the mission is to be universal (28:19), anticipated, it seems, by the story of the coming of the

Gentile Magi to the infant Christ in ch.2. Matthew's gospel seems to be written from a Jewish background, for a community set in a Gentile context and welcoming Gentile converts, but with (as one scholar put it) a Jewish synagogue across the street. Somewhere in the province of Syria seems most likely, towards the end of the first century AD (i.e., after Mark's gospel, and before the reference to Matthew's gospel by Ignatius of Antioch, who died in AD 115). What is particularly clear is that this gospel was written for the instruction of a church community. Of the four gospels, only this one speaks directly of the church (16:18). The disciples are presented as model pupils; their calling is to obedience and righteousness, and they are to be perfect as their heavenly Father is perfect (5:48). The disciple is to hear the words of Jesus and do them (7:24–27), and then to go and make disciples of all nations, 'teaching them to observe all that I have commanded you'. The disciples' mission seems to have a long future; 'I am with you always, to the close of the age' (28:20), though 'you must be ready; for the Son of man is coming at an hour you do not expect' (24:44).

The gospel according to Luke also uses Mark as an important source, and presents the career of Jesus in a now familiar sequence:

| | |
|---|---|
| 1:1 – 2:52 | Prologue; birth and infancy of Jesus |
| 3:1 – 4:13 | Teaching of John the Baptist and baptism of Jesus; genealogy of Jesus; temptation of Jesus |
| 4:14 – 9:50 | Jesus' ministry in Galilee |
| 9:51 – 19:27 | Jesus' journey from Galilee to Jerusalem |
| 19:28 – 21:38 | Jesus' teaching in Jerusalem |
| 22:1 – 23:49 | Passion and death of Jesus |
| 23:50 – 24:53 | Burial, resurrection and ascension of Jesus |

There are some obvious differences, however: to Mark, Luke adds the well-known birth and infancy stories, the teaching of John the Baptist, the genealogy of Jesus and temptation of Jesus, and at the end the stories of the walk to Emmaus and the ascension. Some of this material (e.g., the teaching of John the Baptist and the temptation of Jesus), together with other material recording the teaching of Jesus, is found also in Matthew, and probably derives from their joint source, Q. The non-Markan and non-Q material in Luke is designated by the siglum L, and includes many of the best-known stories in Luke – for example, the infancy narratives, the parables of the Good Samaritan, the Prodigal Son, Dives and Lazarus, the Pharisee and the Publican, and the story of the road to Emmaus. At the original source or sources of L we can only guess; they need not have been written sources, and some at least of this material may be Luke's own composition based upon oral tradition. What is interesting is that Luke has used much less of Mark than Matthew used (omitting altogether, for whatever reason, Mark 6:45 – 8:26), and what he has used appears in separated blocks (4:31–44; 5:12 – 6:11; 8:4 – 9:50; 18:15–43; 19:28–38; 19:45 – 21:4), apart from 21:5 – 24:53 where Markan and L material have been combined. (This led one scholar, B.H. Streeter, to propose that the first edition of Luke's gospel, 'Proto-Luke', consisted of a combination of Q and L material, into which later blocks of

Markan material were fitted, chs. 1–2 being added when Acts was composed as the sequel to the gospel.) It is also interesting that Luke has made a major feature of the journey from Galilee to Jerusalem, incorporating a large amount of material from Mark, Q and L between the start of the journey (9:51) and the final approach to Jerusalem (19:1–27). What is becoming clear is that Luke's gospel, like Matthew's, is the result of the author's considered arrangement and compilation of his material – as indeed the author tells us in his prologue:

> Inasmuch as many have undertaken to compile a narrative of the things which have been accomplished among us, just as they were delivered to us by those who from the beginning were eyewitnesses and ministers of the word, it seemed good to me also, having followed all things closely for some time past, to write an orderly account for you, most excellent Theophilus, that you may know the truth concerning the things of which you have been informed.

That Luke planned the gospel carefully is perhaps also indicated by the fact that his second work, Acts, appears to have a parallel structure. Apart from the fact that each work begins with a preface mentioning Theophilus, each begins with announcements in Jerusalem of what is to come, and continues with the parallel commissioning of Jesus and the apostles with the Holy Spirit. Jesus' opening ministry in Galilee is paralleled by the apostles' opening ministry in Jerusalem; Jesus' lengthy teaching journey from Galilee to Jerusalem is paralleled by Paul's lengthy journey from Jerusalem to Rome. Jesus visits the temple, is arrested and taken before Pilate and Herod; Paul visits the temple, is arrested and taken before Felix and Herod Agrippa. Jesus is executed in Jerusalem; Paul reaches Rome – but continues preaching for two years. This may be a slightly selective way of summarising Luke-Acts, but it is suggestive. If these parallels were in the author's mind, there are implications for our understanding of Luke's evidence for the career of the historical Jesus.

Since H. Conzelmann's study of the theology in Luke in 1960, the gospel of Luke and Acts of the Apostles have been generally seen as presenting a schematised history of salvation, in three periods. The first period is that of the Law and the prophets, culminating in John the Baptist; Luke's gospel, unlike the other gospels, completes the account of John's career and has him imprisoned before turning to Jesus' baptism. 'The law and the prophets were until John; since then the good news of the kingdom of God is preached' (Lk. 16:16). The second period is the time of Jesus, 'the centre of time', in Conzelmann's phrase; his ministry is opened by the descent of the Holy Spirit on him at his baptism (3:21–22) and ended when Jesus commits his spirit to God (23:46). The Jesus of Luke's gospel, and his ministry, are different from the Jesus and the ministry portrayed in the other gospels; Jesus is a spirit-filled divine man, a teacher and healer who is a saviour of royal Davidic ancestry (2:11), with especial concern for the poor and oppressed (4:18), the non-Jew (4:24–27), the leper, the tax-collector, women, Samaritans, the lost sheep, the prodigal son, the people of Jerusalem upon whom disaster is about to come, and the weeping daughters of Jerusalem who meet him on the way to the cross. Luke's Jesus has more sympathy and less dynamism than Mark's, and less concern for the church's perfection than Matthew's. For Luke, however, the church is the subject of the third period, which begins at Pentecost with the gift of the Spirit. The church begins in Jerusalem, the city of David and centre of the Jewish world, and it spreads to Rome, the centre of the Gentile world. Jerusalem was the city which saw the birth of the church and the destruction of the Jewish state; Rome was the city which destroyed the Jews, and was the climax of Paul's mission to the Gentiles. The gospel of Luke and the Acts of the Apostles are much concerned with the Jewish rejection and the Gentile acceptance of the gospel; they are also concerned to show that the gospel stemmed from Judaism and posed no threat to Rome.

Much else could be said of the theological emphases of Luke-Acts – prophecy, the Holy Spirit, the community of the church, for example – but one should note finally that Luke seems to have a longer historical perspective than the other gospels, especially Mark. Between the ascension of Jesus and his final appearance at the Parousia comes the lengthy mission to the Gentiles, which does not end with Paul's teaching in Rome (Acts 28:23–30). Luke presents his history as a history of God's salvation, but he has to a marked degree what we would call a sense of history, and he presents Jesus as an historical person with his feet on the ground, born in the reign of Caesar Augustus. Though Luke shares Mark's and Matthew's concern to present the gospel of Jesus, he was an historian in ways that they were not, and in ways that John was not. But he was an historian, not a mere annalist or chronicler, and his history, like any other history worthy of the title, is an interpretation.

The gospel of John is above all else an interpretation. At first sight this gospel is very different from the other three. The Fourth Gospel focuses Jesus' career on Jerusalem (which he visits five times, not once as in the Synoptics – Matthew, Mark and Luke) rather than on Galilee. Jesus cleanses the temple at the beginning, not at the end, of his preaching career. There is no account of the Last Supper. The crucifixion happens on a different date. Mark's Jesus hides his messiahship; John's Jesus openly claims to be one with the Father, calls himself the resurrection and the life, the bread of life, the light of the world. 'There is no Gethsemane agony, soldiers sent to arrest him fall to the ground; even when crucified his words are not indicative of distress, but "to fulfil the scripture"' (Davidson and Leaney, 1970, 266). The Jesus of the Fourth Gospel is more obviously other-worldly than the Jesus of the first three. But the major and most obvious difference between the Fourth Gospel and the three Synoptics is that of style and presentation. While the Synoptics present the career of Jesus in somewhat disjointed, episodic form, John presents a much more smoothly organised structure, with a theological introduction, a narrative of seven 'signs' developed and explained in the accompanying dialogues and discourses given by Jesus, and a lengthy passion narrative incorporating two long discourses and a prayer of Jesus. Mark's gospel has been called a passion story with an extended introduction; in the Fourth Gospel, the passion narrative (beginning at 13:1) takes up nearly half the book. The structure is as follows:

| 1:1–18; 19–51 | **Prologue; the identity of Jesus** |
|---|---|
| 2:1 – 12:50 | **The book of Signs:** |
| 2:1–11 | changing water into wine at Cana |
| 4:46–54 | healing of the Capernaum official's son at Cana |
| 5:2–15 | sabbath healing of the man in the pool Bethzatha |
| 6:1–14 | feeding of the five thousand in Galilee |
| 6:16–21 | walking on the water |
| 9:1–12 | healing of the blind man |
| 11:1–44 | raising of Lazarus |

Also important to the structure of this section is the sequence of feasts in Jerusalem attended by Jesus:

| 2:13 | Passover |
|---|---|
| 5:1 | 'a feast' |
| 6:4 | Passover (in Galilee) |
| 7:2 | Tabernacles |
| 10:22 | Dedication |
| 11:55 | Passover |

Set amid the signs and feasts are the dialogues between:

| 3:1–15 | Jesus and Nicodemus |
|---|---|
| 4:/–26 | Jesus and the Samaritan woman |
| 5:16–47 | Jesus and the Jews (also 6:25–59; 7:14–44; 8:12–59; 9:13 – 10:39) |

| 13:1 – 17:26 | **Final discourses and prayer of Jesus:** |
|---|---|
| 13:1–20 | footwashing |
| 13:21–30 | departure of Judas |
| 13:31–38 | prediction of Peter's denial |
| 14:1–31 | discourse |
| 15:1– 16:33 | discourse |
| 17:1–26 | prayer of Jesus |
| 18:1 – 20:31 | **Passion and Resurrection** |
| 21:1–15 | **Epilogue: Jesus appears to his disciples in Galilee** |

Chapter 21 and the story of the woman taken in adultery (7:53 – 8:11) are both generally considered to be additions to the original gospel.

Whether the author of the Fourth Gospel actually knew and used the Synoptics has been much debated. The proclamation of the kingdom of God, the exorcisms and the parables are conspicuously absent, and the chronology and the geography are different. The basic plan of a ministry which starts in Galilee and moves to Jerusalem is ignored; Jesus travels regularly between Galilee and Jerusalem for various feasts. However, the narrative begins with John the Baptist; more significantly, the passion narrative has sufficient similarities with the sequence and contents of the Synoptics' passion narrative to show that John knew the tradition and may perhaps have known Mark and Luke; and the sequence of John 6:1–24, in which Jesus crosses the sea, feeds the five thousand,

and walks on the water, is the same as that of Mark 6:30–52. In John 6:25–59 this is followed by discussion on the meaning of the event, as in Mark's second feeding story (Mk. 8:14–21). Other minor verbal similarities have suggested that the author of the Fourth Gospel knew Mark's gospel (e.g., the reference to 200 denarii (Mk. 6:37; John 6:7), or the reference to ointment of pure nard, Mk. 14:3; John 12:3)), and perhaps Luke's gospel (compare John 12:3–8 and Luke 7:36–50). However, while the author of the Fourth Gospel knew and used traditions taken up by Mark and Luke, it cannot be proved that he knew those gospels in their present form. What written sources may have been used by the Fourth Gospel is another disputed question; the only proposal that has found much favour is that John is using and reworking a source different from any known to the Synoptics which told of Jesus' miracles as evoking faith (cf. the references to signs in 2:23; 4:54; 12:37; and 20:30–31).

For many years it was assumed that Mark and the dependent synoptic accounts of Matthew and Luke gave a 'more historical' picture of Jesus than did the Fourth Gospel. This assumption has been challenged; in their own way, the Synoptic Gospels give just as theological a picture of Jesus as the Fourth Gospel does. The possibility that the Fourth Gospel contains reliable historical evidence for the words and works of Jesus cannot be dismissed. The original Aramaic of Jesus and his disciples sometimes seems to lie close to the surface (for example the titles *rabbouni* and *messias* and the names Cephas, Thomas, Gabbatha, Golgotha, Siloam, with a number of more ordinary Semitic expressions or constructions), and a number of the saying of Jesus reported in the Fourth Gospel are similar to saying reported in the Synoptics (e.g., John 1:27, 42, 51; 4:44; 13:21, 38). John may have adapted such sayings to his purposes (as he clearly does with 4:44), but so too do the Synoptics. Indeed, rather surprisingly, the Synoptics contain one famous saying of Jesus whose style sounds much more like that of John's gospel, the so-called 'Johannine thunderbolt' of Mt. 11:25–26, Lk. 10:21 (cf. John 3:35; 10:15). Some of the miracles reported in the Fourth Gospel are not so different from those reported in the Synoptics (e.g., the healings of the official's son (4:46-53), or of the cripple at the pool (5:1-9), or of the man born blind (9:1-12)). Some information given by the Fourth Gospel but not by the Synoptics should probably be taken seriously (e.g., that two of Jesus' disciples were previously John the Baptist's disciples, that Jesus' early ministry overlapped the Baptist's, and that Jesus himself baptised (3:22; though someone found this difficult to accept, as 4:2 shows)). The Fourth Gospel ignores the towns of Galilee and the Decapolis, but mentions a dozen place-names which do not appear in the Synoptics, of which only Cana is in Galilee; Aenon (3:23), Sychar and Jacob's Well (4:4f.) are in Samaria; Siloam (9:7), the Kedron valley (18:1), Solomon's Portico (10:23), the sheep pool called Bethzatha (5:2), and Gabbatha ('the Pavement', 19:13), are all in or around Jerusalem. The Fourth Gospel locates Jesus' activity much more in Judaea and Jerusalem than the Synoptics do, and perhaps these facts too point to sources outside the Synoptics, no less reliable than the Synoptics' own sources.

All four gospels interpret their sources; in the Fourth Gospel the theologian's controlling hand is much more evident than in the other three. The overall picture given of Jesus is quite different from that of the Synoptics. Jesus is a pre-existent being, the Son of God, the word of the Father, who is sent down to a sinful world to reveal the glory and the love of God by means of signs; those who see them, and even those who do not, should have faith and believe; 'he who hears my word and believes him who sent me, has eternal life; he does not come into judgment, but has passed from death to life' (John 5:24). The death of Jesus is the completion of his task and his glorification; after his death, his believers will be supported by the Spirit or 'Paraclete' (which may mean an advocate, or counsellor), who is a kind of successor to Jesus, reminding the believers of what Jesus said and challenging the world that does not believe in Jesus. Those who do believe have made their decision and been judged already; they already have life. This book was written, says the author, 'that you may believe that Jesus is the Christ, the Son of God, and that believing you may have life in his name' (John 20:31).

The intellectual background of this presentation of Jesus has been much discussed. Scholars have endlessly debated whether the background is Hellenistic (in which case the description of the pre-existent Jesus as the *logos* might derive from popular Stoicism, which believed that the universe was pervaded by *logos*, reason, immanent and expressed; and that there were seeds of it in mortal minds which would finally be united as sons of God if men and women lived according to reason), or Jewish (in which case the *logos* idea could be traced to Genesis 1, in which God created by his *word*, cf. Ps. 33:6), or both. If the context were Hellenistic, one might point also to the influence of Platonism, which contrasted the world of sense and experience with a higher, true world of ideas and forms, or to the influence of the mystery religions, which showed in a dramatic revelation how one could pass from this material and evil world to a higher one. Many scholars pointed to Gnosticism, which flourished particularly in second-century Egypt. This taught that from the divine world of light and spirit a particle fell into the demonic world of darkness and matter, which divided up this particle of light into separate sparks. To redeem and restore these lost creatures of the light, the good god of life sent saving knowledge into the world, often in the form of a redeemer figure, who revealed to men and women their true origin (whether they were children of light from above, or children of darkness from below), thus enabling them to return to their true homes after death. The redeemer then re-ascended, making way for the elements of life to follow. The Fourth Gospel, with its descending and ascending redeemer-revealer figure, and the Prince of this world (12:31), may reflect this dualistic background, but if so, it also opposes it with the view that the world is not evil but divinely created and redeemable, that the divine redeemer has become flesh (of all things!) and lived in the world, and that the possibility of redemption of life is open to all in this world. Salvation comes not so much by illuminating knowledge as by the decision of faith.

However, if there are Hellenistic ingredients in the Fourth Gospel, there are certainly Jewish ingredients. Some scholars again look to Egypt and point to Philo (*c.* 20 BC to 50 AD), a Jewish thinker from Alexandria who used an allegorical interpretation of the Jewish scriptures to harmonise Jewish and Greek thought, and who used the Greek idea of *logos*, reason, to describe the creative power ordering the world and the intermediary through whom men knew God. He used 'light' to describe God, thought of the knowledge of God as the true end of existence, and used 'true' in the sense of 'heavenly' or 'divine' (cf. the 'true' bread of the Fourth Gospel). Possibly the author of the Fourth Gospel had a similar end in view – making the Jewish Jesus acceptable to Greek Jews such as the Greeks who wished to see Jesus at the feast (John 12:20). The Fourth Gospel might have its home in Hellenistic Judaism.

Certainly the Fourth Gospel seems far more concerned with Jews than with Gentiles, whom it does not mention (apart from the Greeks of 12:20, Pilate and the Romans). It opposes Judaism; Jesus argues with the Jews, who force a powerless Pilate to crucify him and put out of the synagogue any who confess that Jesus is the Christ (9:22; cf. 12:42; 16:2). The Jewish Nicodemus needed rebirth; the Jewish Joseph of Arimathea was a disciple secretly, for fear of the Jews. Salvation is of the Jews; but the true *shekinah*, the true temple (1:14; 2:21), the true manna (6:32), are to be found henceforth in the person of Jesus, the true king of the Jews (1:49; 19:19f.), the messiah (1:41; 4:25), the shepherd (i.e., the true leader of the flock of Israel, 10:11), and the true vine (15:1; another image for Israel). Moses 1:45; 5:45f., 7:19–24), Abraham (8:39), and Isaiah (12:41) all point to Jesus. The Fourth Gospel is above all thoroughly Jewish, and its essential Jewishness has been in recent years corroborated by the literature from Qumran. Here we find phrases such as 'do the truth' (John 3:21), and 'the sons of light' and 'the sons of error' who 'walk in the ways of darkness' (cf. John 12:36f.). The great Johannine antitheses of light and darkness, truth and error, spirit and flesh, life and death, might have seemed very much at home at Qumran, whose dualism allowed for one God, not two, which made light the symbol of goodness and darkness of moral evil, and which looked to the coming end of evil. The people of Qumran, however, looked for light to their Teacher of Righteousness and his interpretation of the Law; John looked to Jesus and the revelation of God through him.

The relationship of the Fourth Gospel and the Jewish world is complex. As C.K. Barrett has demonstrated, John is both Jewish and anti-Jewish; John combines Gnosis and anti-Gnosticism, apocalyptic and non-apocalyptic material. John writes in Greek, and has in mind Greeks who wish to know more of Christianity. He is concerned with Christian belief and believers, and with the Spirit and its support of Christians, and perhaps with the sacraments of Baptism and Eucharist, but not, apparently, with the institutions of the church, as Matthew's gospel is. All this makes it difficult to place the author, who is probably a former Jew, writing towards the end of the first century AD for a Christian community somewhere in the Hellenistic world, subject to Jewish opposition, and Gnosticising influence.

The internal evidence for authorship is complex. The gospel has two endings (chs.20, 21). In the second ending, we are told (21:24) that the disciple whom Jesus loved wrote 'these things'; but are 'these things' to be identified as ch.21, or chs.1–20, or chs.1–20 with ch.21? The idea that the Beloved Disciple wrote part of the gospel is not easy to accept, for the main part of the gospel (chs. 1–20) mentions that figure only in the third person and makes no claim to be written by an eyewitness. The identification of the Beloved Disciple with John the son of Zebedee first appears in the writings of Irenaeus, Bishop of Lyons towards the end of the second century AD. Irenaeus says that 'John, the disciple of the Lord, who also leaned upon his breast, himself produced his gospel, while he was living at Ephesus in Asia' (*Adversus Haereses*, in Euseb. *H.E.* V.8). Possibly there is some confusion here with another John, John the Elder, also from somewhere in Asia and perhaps from Ephesus, who may be the author of the letters 2 and 3 John. (We have already noted that the language of the Johannine epistles relates closely to that of the Fourth Gospel, but 1 John gives us no other clue as to its authorship or provenance.) The fact that John is also the name of the author of the Revelation, who wrote to the seven churches in Asia, including Ephesus, may have added further confusion to the problem. Speculation abounds; some have identified the author of the Fourth Gospel or its root source with Lazarus (it is said of him, after all, that Jesus loved him), and others with John Mark, writing in later life a new version of the gospel. In fact, the author remains anonymous. His work existed by the early second century, for a papyrus fragment of the gospel was found in Egypt, dated *c.* AD 125; it is housed in the Rylands Library in Manchester. The work probably dates from after *c.* 85 AD, when the rabbis introduced a prayer condemning Christians and heretics, which would have had the effect of forcing their exclusion from the synagogues (cf. John 9:22).

The four gospels thus turn out to be more complex witnesses to the historical Jesus than most people suspect. They were written from within different Christian communities of the first century AD. Mark's Gospel perhaps came from Rome, and Matthew's from Syria. Luke's Gospel might have been written anywhere in the Hellenistic world of the eastern Mediterranean, and the Fourth Gospel is usually credited to Asia and sometimes to Egypt. The authors were not apostles or eye-witnesses (Luke 1:2 and John 19:35 refer to eye-witness tradition), but used written sources and church tradition. What emerges most clearly from critical scrutiny of the gospels is that the twentieth-century enquirer can see the historical Jesus only through the eyes of several late first-century writers whose differing interpretations of Jesus were reconstructions based on the interpretations of their predecessors and on the tradition of the church communities to which they belonged. In this regard, however, Jesus is hardly very different from other historical figures of the ancient world – Socrates of Athens is the example usually quoted – whose words and deeds were preserved in various forms and different interpretations by their disciples and those who followed after. We have to sift the evidence of Plato and Xenophon and others for the historical Socrates, as we have to sift the traditions preserved by John and Mark and others for the historical Jesus. The parallels are not exact, but the historical problems are not dissimilar. In each case the surviving written records are interpretations deriving directly and indirectly from disciples and followers. The problems raised here, however, will be considered in the final chapter.

# Bibliography

J. Ashton (ed.), *The interpretation of John* (Issues in Religion and Theology 9) (London: SPCK; Philadelphia: Fortress Press, 1986)

G. Aulen, *Jesus in contemporary historical research* (London: SPCK, 1976)

C.K. Barrett, *The Gospel according to St John* (London: SPCK, 1967)

C.K. Barrett, *Jesus and the gospel tradition* (London: SPCK, 1967)

C.K. Barrett, *The Gospel of John and Judaism* (London: SPCK, 1975)

G. Bornkamm, *Jesus of Nazareth* (London: Hodder and Stoughton, 1960)

J.S. Bowden, *Jesus, the unanswered questions* (London: SCM Press, 1988)

R.E. Brown, *The community of the Beloved Disciple* (London: G. Chapman, 1979)

J.H. Charlesworth, *Jesus within Judaism: new light from exciting archaeological discoveries* (London: SPCK; Garden City, N.Y.: Doubleday, 1988)

J.M. Creed, *The Gospel according to St Luke* (London: Macmillan, 1942)

R. Davidson and A.R.C. Leaney, *The Penguin guide to modern theology III: Biblical criticism* (Harmondsworth: Penguin, 1970)

C.H. Dodd, *The parables of the Kingdom* (London: Nisbet, 1935)

C.H. Dodd, *Historical tradition in the Fourth Gospel* (Cambridge: Cambridge University Press, 1965)

J. Drury, *The parables in the gospels: history and allegory* (London: SPCK, 1985)

S.V. Freyne, *Galilee, Jesus and the gospels: literary approaches and historical investigations* (Dublin: Gill and Macmillan, 1988)

B. Gerhardsson, *The origins of the gospel traditions* (London: SCM Press; Philadelphia: Fortress Press, 1979)

A.E. Harvey, *Jesus and the constraints of history* (London: Duckworth, 1982)

I. Havener, *Q: the sayings of Jesus* (Good News Studies 19) (Wilmington, Delaware: M. Glazier, 1987)

M. Hengel, *Studies in the Gospel of Mark* (London: SCM Press, 1985)

M. Hengel, *The charismatic leader and his followers* (Edinburgh: T. and T. Clark, 1981)

M. Hilton with G. Marshall, *The gospels and Rabbinic Judaism: a study guide* (London: SCM Press, 1988)

J. Jeremias, *The parables of Jesus* (London: SCM Press, 1963)

H.C. Kee, *Community of the new age: studies in Mark's Gospel* (New Testament) (London: SCM Press, 1977)

R.H. Lightfoot, *The gospel message of St Mark* (London: Oxford University Press, 1950)

J.P. Mackey, *Jesus, the man and the myth: a contemporary Christology* (London: SCM Press, 1979)

I.H. Marshall, *Luke – historian and theologian* (Exeter: Paternoster Press, 1979)

R.P. Martin, *Mark – evangelist and theologian* (Exeter: Paternoster Press, 1979)

N. Perrin, *The Kingdom of God in the teaching of Jesus* (London: SCM Press, 1963)

J. Riches, *Jesus and the transformation of Judaism* (London: Darton, Longman and Todd, 1980)

J.K. Riches, *A century of New Testament study* (Cambridge: Lutterworth Press, 1993)

E. Rivkin, *What crucified Jesus?* (London: SCM Press, 1986)

E.P. Sanders, *Jesus and Judaism* (London: SCM Press, 1985)

E.P. Sanders, *Judaism, practice and belief 63 BCE–66CE* (London: SCM Press, 1992)

E.P. Sanders, *The historical figure of Jesus* (London: Allen Lane, The Penguin Press, 1993)

E. Schillebeeckx, *Jesus, an experiment in Christology* (London: Collins, 1979)

R. Schnackenburg, *The Gospel according to St John*, I–III (London: Burns and Oates, 1980)

A. Schweitzer, *The quest for the historical Jesus* (London: A. and C. Black, 1910)

S. Smalley, *John – evangelist and interpreter* (Exeter: Paternoster Press, 1978)

G.N. Stanton, *The gospels and Jesus* (Oxford Bible Series) (Oxford: Oxford University Press, 1989)

B.H. Streeter, *The Gospel according to St Mark* (London: Macmillan, 1957)

G. Theissen, *The first followers of Jesus* (London: SCM, 1978)

G. Vermes, *Jesus the Jew: a historian's reading of the gospels* (London: Collins, 1973)

G. Vermes, *The gospel of Jesus the Jew* (University of Newcastle upon Tyne, 1981)

G. Vermes, *Jesus and the world of Judaism* (London: SCM Press, 1983)

J. Wilkinson, *Jerusalem as Jesus knew it: archaeology as evidence* (London: Thames and Hudson, 1978)

P. Winter, *On the trial of Jesus* (Berlin and New York: W. de Gruyter, 1961)

# 15    The Revelation to John

The New Testament ends with a work entitled 'The Revelation to John (The Apocalypse)'. The author is clearly not the author of the Fourth Gospel. His book tells of persecution, probably in the late first century AD or the early second, under Domitian or Trajan. He says that he is a prisoner on the island of Patmos 'on account of the word of God and the testimony of Jesus', and he is writing to the seven churches of Asia, which he names as Ephesus, Smyrna, Pergamum, Thyatira, Sardis, Philadelphia and Laodicea. Chapters 1–3 contain his separate letters to these churches, sharply describing their failings (except for the church of Philadelphia), and warning them of what is to come. The book as a whole is a letter, to be read out loud, presumably in the churches addressed. It contains the report of the author's vision, 'the revelation of Jesus Christ, which God gave him to show to his servants what must soon take place' (1:1).

The vision is repetitive, but fairly straightforward in outline. In the opening scene, twenty-four elders and four living creatures worship God on his throne (ch.4). God holds a scroll, sealed with seven seals, which the Lamb takes, amid cries of worship, and opens, seal by seal, revealing conquest, slaughter, famine, death, martyrs, the day of God's wrath against the earth, the sealing of the 144,000 out of the tribes of Israel and the worship of the martyrs in white robes. The Lamb opens the seventh seal, and there is silence in heaven for about half an hour (5:1 – 8:1). There follows a sequence of seven angels; each blows a trumpet heralding disaster for the earth, the sea, the waters, the heavenly lights, and those on the earth (fifth and sixth trumpets) (8:2 – 9:21). Before the seventh trumpet sounds, John is given a scroll, and told to eat it, and a measuring rod, and told to measure the temple. The seventh trumpet blows, and heavenly voices cry, 'The kingdom of the world has become the kingdom of our Lord and of his Christ, and he shall reign for ever and ever', and the elders worship God, and the temple in heaven is opened (11:15–19). The rest of the vision is largely concerned with the heavenly war against the dragon, alias the Devil and Satan, who is the opponent of the woman with child and her offspring, who keep the commandments of God and bear testimony to Jesus (12:1–17). The dragon is thrown out of heaven, and gives his authority to a seven-headed beast who conquers the saints, and to a second beast from the same stable whose number is 666, a coded reference to the Roman emperor Nero (13:1–18). Judgment is announced, the fall of Babylon (Rome) is proclaimed, and the saints are warned to endure, and the angels put in the sickle to start the harvest (14:1–20). Seven angels with seven plagues appear;

disasters end with an earthquake splitting Babylon into three parts; and the woman arrayed in purple and scarlet, drunk with the blood of the saints and martyrs, bearing on her brow the name 'Babylon the great, mother of harlots and of earth's abominations', clearly identified with Rome on her seven hills (17:9), is scheduled for perdition. The end of Babylon/Rome is hymned (as the end of Tyre was hymned in Ezek.27 and Babylon in Isa.47), and heaven resounds with hallelujahs and promise of a marriage feast (chs.18–19). There follows judgment, in several stages (ch.20), and the creation of a new heaven and a new earth, and a new holy city, Jerusalem; it has no temple, for its temple is the Lord God the Almighty and the Lamb (21:22), but through it flows the river of life. Here will be the throne of God and the Lamb. 'And night shall be no more; they need no light of lamp or sun, for the Lord God will be their light, and they shall reign for ever and ever.' The vision ends and John and his readers, are warned that 'I am coming soon'. 'Amen. Come, Lord Jesus!', says John.

The prophecy is clear; those who have suffered persecution or are about to suffer must endure, because Rome is doomed and will shortly receive her deserts. The vision is described, however, in terms of myth and symbolism drawn largely from the Jewish scriptures, especially the books of Ezekiel and Daniel. The numbers 4, 7, and 12 are much in evidence (e.g. four corners of the earth, seven seals, twelve tribes of Israel); the victory over the dragon, the apocalyptic harvest, the new Jerusalem, the heavenly marriage have their background in ancient myths of creation and recreation. The heightened expectation of the coming end draws on the tradition of Jewish apocalyptic, visible also in Mark 13 and its synoptic parallels and in Paul's epistles (e.g. 1 and 2 Thess., 1 Cor.15). The imagery is visual and easily comprehended by anyone brought up in the tradition of the Jewish scriptures and later apocalyptic writings, and probably very satisfying to those who had experienced the persecuting power of Rome firsthand and had despaired. The reason for its inclusion in the New Testament and its final position there is clear. If it does not breathe the spirit of Christian charity, it proclaims loudly the other virtues of faith and hope.

## Bibliography

A. Farrer, *The Revelation of St John the Divine* (Oxford: Clarendon Press, 1964)

W. Barclay, *Letters to the seven churches* (London: SCM Press, 1957)

W.M. Ramsay, *The letters to the seven churches of Asia* (London: Hodder and Stoughton, 1904)

J. Sweet, *Revelation* (SCM Pelican Commentaries) (London: SCM, 1979)

# 16 The Bible: tradition, evidence, faith

These four words summarise a confusion. The Bible is a collection of books containing traditions which are evidence for the faith and belief of the biblical writers and the communities they represented. The modern, historically minded enquirer, however, might well ask how much faith is to be placed in the evidence of the traditions of the Bible? The biblical writers were mainly concerned to describe and support the belief and faith of their communities (and how the beliefs and faith of their ancient communities relate to the belief and faith of modern Jews and Christians is a matter for the theologians); the modern academic historian is mainly concerned to describe and analyse the nature of the ancient society and its beliefs and history. When using the ancient biblical writings as evidence for the quest, the modern historian has to make due allowance for the nature of that evidence.

This book has tried to show the results of the last two centuries' critical enquiry into the contents of the Bible. Biblical criticism has not been destructive of faith as such, but it has challenged and upset naïve views of the nature of the bibilical writings. It has shown, for example, that the purpose of the author of Genesis was not to give a historically accurate picture of the origins of the nation of Israel in the context of Middle or Late Bronze Age Canaan, but to present a picture of God's purpose for the people of Israel symbolised in the figure of the ancestor Abraham and relevant to the needs of sixth-century BC Israelites suffering exile in the land of the Chaldaeans. It has shown that the gospels are not simply biographies, but were written to present a particular interpretation or understanding of Jesus, and were written, as the Fourth Gospel puts it, 'that you may believe that Jesus is the Christ, the Son of God, and that believing you may have life in his name'. The biblical writers, by and large, were not concerned with history or the natural phenomena of this world for their own sake (though intellectual curiosity was certainly present in ancient Israel and the early church, and is visible, for example, in the Deuteronomistic History, or in the book of Daniel, or Proverbs, or the Acts of the Apostles). They were primarily concerned with the community of Israel and its faith, or with the church of Christ and its faith.

This book has shown that the biblical writings grew out of faith, reflect faith, and aim to support faith. They witness to the community or communities that produced them – to their life, their work, their beliefs, their doubts, and their self-understanding. They reveal human beings in a certain historical context reflecting on their situation in hope, or fear, or even despair. They show the inhabitants of Israel and the members of the early church as heirs to a community tradition which has made them what they are. The community is identified by its tradition, it is even created by its tradition, and strengthened and bonded by its tradition. The biblical books were produced out of the community and its tradition, in turn confirmed the community and its tradition, and again in turn became part of that tradition. The Jewish teaching, *tôrâh*, became in time the Torah, and this was further developed by the Mishnah, and then the Gemarah. The Christian good news, or gospel, became enshrined in the books called gospels, and the gospels in turn became part of the Christian tradition and formative of it.

All this does not mean, however, that the biblical writings can be dismissed as purely religious writings and thus ignored by the historian. The biblical books did not drop down ready-made from the top of Sinai or from heaven. They were written on parchment and papyrus in ink by men (and perhaps by women, too) with fingers and human senses and physical organs. To argue that the Bible came directly by dictation from the mouth of God would arouse disbelief in it at once. To demonstrate that these books had a real origin among three-dimensioned human beings who sweated, feared, loved, misbehaved, fought, lusted, observed, recorded, argued, suffered agonies, persecution and even martyrdom, gives these ancient documents credibility as the testimony of humans who wrote what they felt mattered about God, the world, Israel, suffering, wisdom, the teaching of Jesus, the problems of the churches, the rewards of the faithful. All of this was settled over a century ago in *Essays and Reviews*, published in 1860 (just a year after Darwin's *The Origin of Species*). In that book Benjamin Jowett pointed out that 'Educated persons are beginning to ask, not what scripture may be made to mean, but what it does [mean]', and argued that 'scripture is to be interpreted like other books, with attention to the character of its authors, and the prevailing state of civilisation and knowledge, with allowance for the peculiarities of style and language and the modes of thought and figures of speech'. The book caused a furore, as we have seen, but in the long term it was the essayists who won the intellectual battle.

The biblical authors did not write primarily for the benefit of readers two or three thousand years after them. They wrote for their own generations, and they wrote from experience recognisable to their contemporaries of how things were. They may have written to express and create faith; but their faith was built on their experience and expressed their interpretation of what they could see going on around them. Historical events were important to them, for in them, as in natural phenomena, they could see the activity of God. The book of Amos can refer to an earthquake (1:1) (memorable to the author of Zech.14:5), which perhaps inspired Amos' vision of God (9:1). The appearance of Cyrus, the conquering Persian king, was important to Second Isaiah, but the prophet (rightly) was less concerned with the date than with its consequences for the people of Israel. The figure of Darius the Mede is important for the author of Daniel 6, but his importance lies not in the historical existence of a king of this name between Belshazzar and Cyrus the Persian (Daniel is wrong on this point) but in the demonstration that a Jew who keeps the law under persecution will survive and that a persecuting foreign ruler can be brought to see that the Jewish God is the living God. The author of Daniel 11 has given us in verses 1–39 an excellent survey of the Ptolemaic–Seleucid wars of the third–second centuries BC which come to a climax in the appalling wickedness of Antiochus IV; but here history gives way to prophecy of the coming end. The author of Luke–Acts has a strong historical sense and considerable and accurate knowledge of the Roman world, but this does not prevent him from dating the census in Syria under Quirinius some ten years too early, and his chronological error does not invalidate his particular presentation of the person of Jesus any more than the discrepancies between the journeys of Paul as described in Acts and in Galatians devalue Luke's picture of the spread of Christianity from Jerusalem to Rome. These writers have used their historical knowledge in the service of faith, and if they have made mistakes of detail, they are in this no worse than many of their predecessors, contemporaries, or modern successors. The modern historian may be grateful to his predecessors' faith; without it, much historical evidence would have been lost.

As John Barton has recently reminded us, English scholars have tended to ask about the historical truth behind the biblical narratives, and to try to reconstruct what actually happened. (Some have struggled with much urgency to establish the accuracy of all biblical historical statements, as if theological insight or divine revelation depended for its truth on the writer's historical precision, or on the writer's passive transmission of the dictated words of God.) German scholars have preferred to ask what ideas are communicated by the biblical narratives; for example, 'what matters is not the Exodus as it really happened, but the Exodus as the controlling idea in the faith of Israel' (Barton, 1984, 162). That the idea of the exodus is important in the faith of Israel (and in Christianity too) is clear from the biblical pages; the idea remains important into the twentieth century, as Leon Uris' novel *Exodus*, and the events which inspired that novel, show. It is certainly the *idea*, not the original event (whatever it was) that has the power to move people in the present. The original event, in any case, has gone beyond recall; the best we have is the tradition of it as it survived in ancient Israel. Yet each Passover the tradition is re-enacted at the Jewish family table, and the story of the exodus comes alive for the believer. Similarly with the Christian Last Supper. The original event is again beyond recall; we have slightly varied traditions of it, as presented in the Synoptic Gospels and in St Paul's first letter to the Corinthians. Yet each week the tradition is re-enacted at the Christian community's table, and the story, with all its significance, comes alive for the believer. But in each case, the question 'What actually happened?' is impossible to answer. In each case what we have in the biblical narrative or narratives is the community's tradition or traditions of that event, preserved in the community's worship and then in its texts.

The biblical writings are rooted in history and are evidence for history, but for the Jews and Christians whose traditions and wisdom they enshrine, their value and meaning are not limited to that of resource documents for the ancient historian. And yet the historian's place in the interpretation of the tradition may not be denied. The theology does not make sense without the history. And the history is meaningless without the theology.

## Bibliography

J. Barr, *Holy Scripture: canon, authority, criticism* (Oxford: Clarendon Press, 1983)

R.C.P. Hanson and A.T. Hanson, *The Bible without illusions* (London: SCM Press; Philadelphia: Trinity Press International, 1989)

R. Morgan with J. Barton, *Biblical interpretation* (The Oxford Bible Series) (Oxford: Oxford University Press, 1988)

C. Westermann, *Essays on Old Testament interpretation* (London: SCM Press, 1963)

# Chart of Comparative Dates

| DATE | ARCHAEOLOGICAL PERIOD | EGYPT | MESOPOTAMIA AND EAST | ISRAEL PALESTINE JORDAN | LITERATURE RELATED LITERATURE |
|---|---|---|---|---|---|
| 1500BC | LB I | New Kingdom period (Dyn. 18-20) | Kassite period | | |
| 1400 | LB II | 1552–1069 BC | 1600–1150 BC | | |
| 1300 | | | | 'Amarna period' | |
| 1200 | Iron Age I | | | ? Exodus Philistines | |
| 1100 | | Late Period (Dyn. 21-31) | | 'Judges' period | |
| 1000 | | 1069–322 BC | | David Solomon | |
| 900 | Iron Age II | | Neo-Assyrian Empire | divided kingdom | |
| 800 | | | 883–609 BC | Israel c. 930–722 BC | |
| | | | | Judah c. 930–587 BC | Amos Hosea Micah |
| 700 | | | | | Isaiah I Prov. 25–29? Nah., Hab., Zeph. |
| 600 | Iron Age III ('Persian Period') | | Neo-Babylonian Empire 626–539 BC Persian Empire 539–331 BC | Exile 587–539 BC Restoration | Jer., Ezek., Isaiah II Deut. Hist. Pentateuch? Hagg., Zech. 1–8 Malachi |
| 500 | | | | Ezra, 458 BC? Nehemiah (444–432 BC) | Joel? Jonah? Job? Editing of Proverbs, Psalms? Chron., Ezra, Neh. |
| 400 | Hellenistic Period 331–63 BC | Ptolemaic rule 322–30 BC | Alexander the Gt. 336–323 BC Seleucid rule 312–63 BC | Under Ptolemaic rule 320–200 BC | Enoch? |
| 300 | | | | | Ecclesiastes LXX translation of Torah |
| 200 | | | | Seleucid rule 200–142 BC Maccabean revolt 167 BC Hasmonaean rule 142–63 BC | Ecclesiasticus Daniel Judith? Jubilees |
| 100 | Roman period | | Roman rule 63 BC | Qumran founded Roman rule 63 BC Herod the Gt. 38–4 BC | 1 Maccabees 2 Maccabees Psalms of Solomon Wisdom of Solomon |
| 1 BC–AD 1 | | Cleopatra d. 31 BC Roman rule | | Jesus of Nazareth Paul of Tarsus | Epistles Gospels & Acts Revelation |
| AD 100 | | | | | |

# Chronology of the Kings of Judah and Israel

## JUDAH

|  | Bright | Miller & Hayes | Hayes & Hooker |
|---|---|---|---|
| Rehoboam | 922–915 BC | 924–907 BC | 926–910 BC |
| Abijam | 915–913 | 907–906 | 909–907 |
| Asa | 913–873 | 905–874 | 906–878 |
| Jehoshaphat | 873–849 | 874–850 | 877–853 |
| Jehoram | 849–843 | 850–843 | 852–841 |
| Ahaziah | 843/842 | 843 | 840 |
| Athaliah | 842–837 | 843–837 | 839–833 |
| Joash | 837–800 | 837–? | 832–803 |
| Amaziah | 800–783 | ? – ? | 802–786 |
| Uzziah (Azariah) | 783–742 | ? – ? | 785–760 (734) |
| Jotham | 742–735 | ? –742 | 759–744 |
| Jehoahaz I (Ahaz) | 735–715 | 742–727 | 743–728 |
| Hezekiah | 715–687/6 | 727–698 | 727–699 |
| Manasseh | 687/6–642 | 697–642 | 698–644 |
| Amon | 642–640 | 642–640 | 643–642 |
| Josiah | 640–609 | 639–609 | 641–610 |
| Jehoahaz II | 609 | 609 | 609 |
| Jehoiakim | 609–598 | 608–598 | 608–598 |
| Jehoiachin | 598/597 | 598–597 | 598–597 |
| Zedekiah | 597–587 | 597–586 | 596–586 |

## ISRAEL

|  | Bright | Miller & Hayes | Hayes & Hooker |
|---|---|---|---|
| Jeroboam I | 922–901 BC | 924–903 BC | 927–906 BC |
| Nadab | 901–900 | 903–902 | 905–904 |
| Baasha | 900–877 | 902–886 | 903–882 (880) |
| Elah | 877–876 | 886–885 | 881–880 |
| Zimri (7 days) | 876 | 885 | 880 |
| Omri | 876–869 | 885–873 | 879–869 |
| Ahab | 869–850 | 873–851 | 868–854 |
| Ahaziah | 850–849 | 851–849 | 853–852 |
| Jehoram | 849–843/42 | 849–843 | 851–840 |
| Jehu | 843/42–815 | 843–816 | 839–822 |
| Jehoahaz | 815–802 | 816–800 | 821–805 |
| Joash | 802–786 | 800–785 | 804–789 |
| Jeroboam II | 786–746 | 785–745 | 788–748 |
| Zechariah | 746–745 | 745 | 748 |
| Shallum | 745 | 745 | 747 |
| Menahem | 745–737 | 745–736 | 746–737 |
| Pekahiah | 737–736 | 736–735 | 736–735 |
| Pekah | 736–732 | 735–732 | 734–731 |
| Hoshea | 732–724 | 735–723 | 730–722 |

The problem of working out precise dates for the kings of Judah and Israel is discussed in Chapter 5. The figures given above are taken from J. Bright, *A History of Israel*, 3rd ed. (1981), J.M. Miller and J.H. Hayes, *A History of ancient Israel and Judah* (1986), and J.H. Hayes and P.K. Hooker, *A new chronology for the kings of Israel and Judah and its implications for biblical history and literature* (1988).

# Some Landmarks in the Archaeological Exploration of Biblical History

| | |
|---|---|
| 1709 | Publication of *Palestine illustrated by ancient monuments* (A. Reland) |
| 1743–45 | Publication of *Description of the East* (R. Pococke) |
| 1799 | Discovery of the Rosetta Stone, leading to decipherment of Egyptian scripts |
| 1812 | Exploration of Transjordan and rediscovery of Petra by J.L. Burckhardt |
| 1841 | Publication of Edward Robinson and Eli Smith's *Biblical Researches in Palestine, Mount Sinai and Arabia Petraea* (1st ed.) |
| 1845 | Excavation of Nimrud (Calah) and Nineveh by A.H. Layard |
| 1846 | Translation of Persian cuneiform texts of Darius I by H. Rawlinson |
| 1850–63 | Excavation of the Tombs of the Kings in Jerusalem by F.de Saulcy |
| 1865 | Foundation of Palestine Exploration Fund in London |
| 1867 | Exploration and excavation in Jerusalem by Capt. C. Warren |
| 1868 | Discovery of Mesha's inscription by F.A. Klein |
| 1872 | Publication of translation of Babylonian Flood story by George Smith |
| 1880 | Foundation of École Biblique et Archéologique Française in Jerusalem |
| 1882 | Foundation of Egypt Exploration Society by Amelia Edwards |
| 1881, 1889 | Publication of the Survey of Western Palestine (Conder and Kitchener) and the Survey of Eastern Palestine (incomplete) (Conder) |
| 1890 | Excavation of Tell el-Ḥesi by W.M.F. Petrie, with important results for the understanding of stratigraphy and pottery-dating |
| 1891 | Discovery of Merneptah Stele by W.M.F. Petrie |
| 1900 | Establishment of American School of Oriental Research in Jerusalem |
| 1898–1917 | Excavation at Babylon by R. Köldewey |
| 1906–12 | Excavation of Hattusas (Hittite capital) by H. Winckler; 1915, publication of Hittite texts by B. Hrozný |
| 1903–05 | Excavation of Megiddo by C. Schumacher |
| 1907–09 | Excavation of Jericho by E. Sellin and C. Watzinger |
| 1922–34 | Excavation of Ur by L. Woolley |
| 1925–31 | Excavation of Nuzi by ASOR, Harvard and others; publication of Hurrian tablets by E. Chiera, R.H. Pfeiffer and R.F.S. Starr |
| 1929–39 | Excavation of Ras Shamra (Ugarit) by C. Virolleaud, and publication of Ugaritic tablets |
| 1925–34 | Excavation of Megiddo by C. Fisher and others |
| 1926–32 | Excavation of Tell Beit Mirsim by W.F. Albright |
| 1930–36 | Excavation of Jericho by J. Garstang |
| 1932–38 | Excavation of Lachish by J. Starkey, published by O. Tufnell |
| 1931–33 | Excavation of Samaria by J. Crowfoot |
| 1933–38 | Excavation of Tell Ḥariri (Mari) by A. Parrot, and publication of texts |
| 1933–37, 1938–41 | Exploration in Transjordan and excavation of Tell el-Kheleifeh by N. Glueck |
| 1936 | Excavation of Tell Ai by J. Marquet-Krause |
| 1947 | Discovery of Qumran manuscripts, followed by excavation of Qumran by R. de Vaux (1951–58) |
| 1952–58 | Excavation of Jericho by K.M. Kenyon |
| 1955–58 | Excavation of Hazor by Y. Yadin |
| 1961–67 | Excavation in Jerusalem by K.M. Kenyon |
| 1964– | Excavation at Tell Mardikh (Ebla); discovery of 20,000 clay tablets in a hitherto unknown North-west Semitic language 'Eblaite' |
| 1967– | Excavations in Jerusalem by B. Mazar, N. Avigad, Y. Shiloh |
| 1970–90 | Development of techniques of surface surveying in Israel and Jordan, with important results for the interpretation of the history of settlement |

# Bibliography of Biblical Commentaries

Sources relevant to each chapter are listed in separate bibliographies at the end of the chapters. Here are noted some of the best-known modern series of biblical commentaries widely used by biblical scholars and students.

ANCHOR BIBLE (Garden City, New York: Doubleday)
Genesis (1964) E.A. Speiser
Joshua (1982) R.G. Boling and G.E. Wright
Judges (1975) R.G. Boling
Ruth (1975) E.J. Campbell, Jr.
1 Samuel (1980) P.K. McCarter, Jr.
2 Samuel (1984) P.K. McCarter, Jr.
2 Kings (1988) M. Cogan and H. Tadmor
1 & 2 Chronicles (1965) J.M. Myers
Ezra, Nehemiah (1965) J.M. Myers
Esther (1971) C.A. Moore
Job (3rd ed., 1973) M.H. Pope
Psalms I, II, III (1965, 1966) M. Dahood
Proverbs, Ecclesiastes (1965) R.B.Y. Scott
Song of Songs (1977) M.H. Pope
Second Isaiah (1968) J.L. McKenzie
Jeremiah (1965) J. Bright
Lamentations (1972) D. Hillers
Ezekiel 1–20 (1986) M. Greenberg
Daniel (1978) L.F. Hartmann and A.A. di Lella
Hosea (1980) F.L. Anderson and D.N. Freedman
Haggai, Zechariah 1–8 (1987) E. Meyers and C. Meyers
1 & 2 Esdras (1974) J.M. Myers
Judith (1985) C.A. Moore
Wisdom of Solomon (1979) D. Winston
Daniel, Esther and Jeremiah: the additions (1977) C.A. Moore
1 Maccabees (1976) J. Goldstein
2 Maccabees (1985) J. Goldstein
Mark (1986) C.S. Mann
Matthew (1971) W.F. Albright and C.S. Mann
Luke I, II (1981, 1985) J.A. Fitzmyer
John I, II (1971) R.E. Brown
Acts (1967) J. Munck
1 Corinthians (1976) W.F. Orr and J.A. Walther
2 Corinthians (1984) V.J. Furnish
Hebrews (1972) G.W. Buchanan
James, Peter and Jude (1964) B. Reicke
Epistles of John I, II (1982) R.E. Brown
Revelation (1975) J. Massingberd Ford

BLACK'S NEW TESTAMENT COMMENTARIES (London: A. and C. Black)
Matthew (1960) F.V. Filson
Mark (1960) S.E. Johnson
Luke (1958) A.R.C. Leaney
John (1968) J.N. Sanders and B.A. Mastin
Acts (1957) C.S.C. Williams
Romans (1957) C.K. Barrett
1 Corinthians (2nd ed., 1971) C.K. Barrett
2 Corinthians (1973) C.K. Barrett
Philippians (1959) F.W. Beare
1 & 2 Thessalonians (1972, 1977) E. Best
Pastoral Epistles (1973) J.N.D. Kelly

Hebrews (1964) H. Montefiore
James (1980) S. Laws
1 Peter, 2 Peter, Jude (1969) J.N.D. Kelly
Johannine Epistles (1973) J.L. Houlden
Revelation (1966) G.B. Caird

CAMBRIDGE BIBLE COMMENTARY (Cambridge: Cambridge University Press)
Genesis 1–11 (1973) R. Davidson
Genesis 12–50 (1979) R. Davidson
Exodus (1972) R.E. Clements
Leviticus (1976) J.R. Porter
Numbers (1976) J. Sturdy
Deuteronomy (1973) A.C. Phillips
Joshua (1974) J.M. Miller and G. Tucker
Judges (1975) J.D. Martin
1 Samuel (1971) P.R. Ackroyd
2 Samuel (1977) P.R. Ackroyd
1 Kings (1972) J. Robinson
2 Kings (1976) J. Robinson
1 & 2 Chronicles (1976) R.J. Coggins
Ezra, Nehemiah (1976) R.J. Coggins
Job (1975) N.C. Habel
Psalms I, II, III (1977) J. Rogerson, J. McKay
Proverbs (1972) R.N. Whybray
Isaiah 1–39 (1973) A.S. Herbert
Isaiah 40–66 (1975) A.S. Herbert
Jeremiah 1–25 (1973) E.W. Nicholson
Jeremiah 26–52 (1975) E.W. Nicholson
Ezekiel (1974) K.W. Carley
Daniel (1976) R.J. Hammer
Amos, Hosea, Micah (1971) H. McKeating
Joel, Obadiah, Jonah, Nahum, Habakkuk, Zephaniah (1975) J.D.W. Watts
Haggai, Zechariah, Malachi (1977) R. Mason
Ruth, Esther, Ecclesiastes, Song of Songs, Lamentations (1975) W.J. Fuerst
1 & 2 Esdras (1979) R.J. Coggins and M.A. Knibb
The shorter books of the Apocrypha (1972) J.C. Dancy (ed.)
Wisdom of Solomon (1973) E.G. Clarke
Ecclesiasticus (1974) J.G. Snaith
1 & 2 Maccabees (1973) J.R. Bartlett
Matthew (1963) A.W. Argyle
Mark (1965) C.F.D. Moule
Luke (1965) E.J. Tinsley
John (1965) A.M. Hunter
Acts (1966) J.W. Packer
Romans (1967) E. Best
1 & 2 Corinthians (1965) M.E. Thrall
Galatians (1967) W. Neil
Ephesians, Colossians, Philemon (1967) G.H.P. Thompson
Philippians, Thessalonians (1967) K. Grayston
Pastoral Letters (1966) A.T. Hanson

Hebrews (1967) J.H. Davies
Peter and Jude (1967) A.R.C. Leaney
John and James (1965) R.R. Williams
Revelation (1965) T.F. Glasson

NEW CENTURY BIBLE (London: Oliphants)
Exodus (1971) J.P. Hyatt
Leviticus and Numbers (1967) N.H. Snaith
Deuteronomy (1979) A.D.H. Mayes
Joshua, Judges and Ruth (1967, 2nd ed.
1986) J. Gray
1 & 2 Samuel (1971) J. Mauchline
1 & 2 Kings (1984) G.H. Jones
1 & 2 Chronicles (1982) H.G.M. Williamson
Ezra, Nehemiah and Esther (1969)
L.H. Brockington
Ezra, Nehemiah and Esther (1984)
D.J. Clines
Job (1970) H.H. Rowley
Psalms (1972) A.A. Anderson
Isaiah 1-39 (1980) R.E. Clements
Isaiah 40-66 (1975) R.N. Whybray
Ezekiel (1969) J. Wevers
Matthew (1972) D. Hill
Mark (1976) H. Anderson
Luke (1976) E.E. Ellis
John (1972) B. Lindars
Acts (1973) W. Neil
Romans (1973) M. Black
1 & 2 Corinthians (1971) F.F. Bruce
Galatians (1969) D. Guthrie
Ephesians, Philippians, Colossians,
Philemon (1967) G. Johnston
Ephesians (1973) C.L. Mitton
Philippians (1976) R.P. Martin
Colossians & Philemon (1974) R.P. Martin
1 & 2 Thessalonians (1969) A.L. Moore
1 & 2 Thessalonians (1981) I.H. Marshall
Pastoral Epistles (1982) A.T. Hanson
1 Peter (1971) E. Best
James, Jude and 2 Peter (1967)
E.M. Sidebottom

NEW CLARENDON BIBLE (London: Oxford
University Press)
Matthew (1975) H.B. Green
Luke (1972) G.H.P. Thompson
John (1970) J.C. Fenton
Acts (1967) R.P.C. Hanson
Thessalonians (1969) D.E.H. Whiteley
Paul's Letters from Prison (1976)
G.B. Caird
Pastoral Epistles (1963) C.K. Barrett

OLD TESTAMENT LIBRARY (London: SCM Press)
Genesis (1961) G. von Rad
Exodus (1962) M. Noth
Exodus (1974) B.S. Childs
Leviticus (1965) M. Noth
Numbers (1968) M. Noth
Deuteronomy (1966) G. von Rad
Joshua (1972) J.A. Soggin
Judges (1981, 2nd ed. 1987) J.A. Soggin
1 & 2 Samuel (1964) H.W. Hertzberg
1 & 2 Kings (1964, 3rd ed. 1980) J. Gray
Ezra, Nehemiah (1988) J. Blenkinsopp
Job (1985) N.C. Habel
Psalms (1962) A. Weiser
Proverbs (1970) W. McKane

Ecclesiastes (1988) J.L. Crenshaw
Isaiah 1-12(1972) O. Kaiser
Isaiah 13-39 (1974) O. Kaiser
Isaiah 40-66 (1969) C. Westermann
Jeremiah (1986) R.R. Carroll
Ezekiel (1970) W. Eichrodt
Daniel (1965) N. Porteous
Hosea (1969) J.L. Mays
Amos (1969) J.L. Mays
Amos (1987) J.A. Soggin
Micah (1976) J.L. Mays
Haggai, Zechariah 1-8 (1985) D.L. Petersen

PENGUIN NEW TESTAMENT COMMENTARIES
(Harmondsworth: Penguin Books)
Matthew (1963) J.C. Fenton
Mark (1963) D.E. Nineham
Luke (1965) G.B. Caird
John (1968) J. Marsh
Paul's First Letter to Corinth (1971) J. Ruef
Paul's letters from prison (1970) J.L. Houlden
The Pastoral Epistles (1976) J.L. Houlden

WORD BIBLICAL (Waco, Texas: Word Books)
Genesis (1987) G.J. Wenham
Exodus (1987) J.I. Durham
Leviticus, Numbers, Deuteronomy, Joshua,
Judges (in preparation)
1 Samuel (1983) R.W. Klein
2 Samuel (in preparation)
1 Kings (1985) S.J. DeVries
2 Kings (in preparation)
1 Chronicles (1986) R.L. Braun
2 Chronicles (1987) R.B. Dillard
Ezra, Nehemiah (1985) H.G.M. Williamson
Isaiah 1-33 (1985) J.D.W. Watts
Hosea-Jonah (1987) D. Stuart

# Index of Biblical References

262

263

# Index

270